This copy of
ROCK GEAR
belongs to

_____

What To Do When You First Buy This Book

Immediately after buying this book, send off for the eight mail order catalogs listed on page 357 (seven of the catalogs are free, one costs a dollar).

These catalogs will start your rock climbing equipment resource kit. Read them for inspiration, and for comparison-shopping with your local store.

ROCK GEAR

Everybody's Guide to Rock Climbing Equipment

Layne Gerrard

with illustrations by the author

a Bookworks book

TEN SPEED PRESS
Berkeley, California

TEN SPEED PRESS
P.O. Box 7123
Berkeley, California 94707

Cover Design by Fifth Street Design Associates
Typesetting by Meler Type & Graphics, San Diego

First Printing 1990

Library of Congress Cataloging-in-Publication Data

Gerrard, Layne
    Rock gear: everybody's guide to rock climbing equipment/by Layne Gerrard; illustrations by the author.
      p. cm.
    ISBN 0-89815-366-2
    1. Rock climbing — Equipment and supplies.
     I. Title.
GV200.15.G47   1990
796.5'223—dc20   90-30835
                                       CIP

Printed in the United States of America

1 2 3 4 5 — 94 93 92 91 90

Acknowledgements

Many people have contributed to making *Rock Gear* a reality: I thank all of you!

I especially thank my father, Don Gerrard, who has been the midwife in this birth. His patient editing has transformed my writing into readable prose, and his guidance throughout the entire project has been invaluable.

I thank my friends Clark Friedgen, Ron Groth, Hunter Johnson, Erin O'Neil, Anthony Scoggins, and Chris Scoggins for modeling the illustrations and for their support and general help.

I am grateful to Phil Wood at Ten Speed Press for his permission to use the 1860s climber illustrations, which come from his favorite climbing book, *Scrambles Amongst The Alps*.

Also at Ten Speed Press, I thank George Young for sharing our vision for this project from the moment he saw it. I thank Sal Glynn for helping with subsidiary rights, and Sean McCrary for his special sales efforts.

I thank Hal Hershey for efficient production consulting, and for being very patient and understanding.

Brent Beck at Fifth Street Design Associates has designed a wonderful cover, and I thank him for his willingness to hear our ideas, and to integrate them with his own.

I thank my typesetting team at Meler Type and Graphics, including Marta, Ann, Jeff, Kathy, Patsy, Meredith, and Monika, for their excellent work.

Trademarks

The following product names are the trademarks or registered trademarks of their respective companies:

Alien, Aquaseal, Bankle Plate, Barge Cement, Celcon, Cambrelle, Chalk Balls, Copperhead, Cordura, Daisy Chain, Engine Brite, Exacto, Fastrack, Friend, Gemini, Gibbs, Hexentric, Jumar, Kevlar, Krazy Glue, Leeper Z, Lexon, Lost Arrow, Lowe Ball, LPS-1, Lycra, Micro Razor, Nicopress, Nut, Nutter, Offset, Polar Fleece, Polarplus, Quadcam, Rack Belt, Rock, Rock'n'-Roller, RP, RURP, Seilbremse, Shoeper Stik, Shunt, Slider, Soloist, Sorbothane, Spectra, Stealth, Sticht Plate, Stone, Stop Bobbin, Stopper, Synchilla, Teflon, Tri-Cam, Tuber, Versa Climber, Velcro, Wallnut, and Whip End Dip.

Disclaimer

Rock climbing is a potentially dangerous activity. The techniques described in this book are standard rock climbing techniques. However, it is up to you to carry out these techniques properly. Therefore, you are responsible for your own safety when rock climbing.

Likewise, the equipment described in this book is standard rock climbing equipment. Although designed for safety, there is no guarantee that the gear will not fail.

The reader will not hold the author, publisher, distributor, or any other person/organization connected with this book liable for any injury or death that may occur as a result of following the instructions in this book, or those of any gear manufacturer.

General Table of Contents

Appendices

Technique Table Of Contents

Visual Table Of Contents

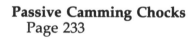

Preface

Two years ago, a friend introduced me to rock climbing. It was part of a deal we had worked out: I took him surfing, he took me climbing. He hasn't surfed since. I, however, have continued climbing; I realized from the first day that climbing was my sport.

We began by bouldering (climbing small boulders) at a local area for several months. During this time we shared his climbing boots. I claimed that I didn't want to invest in something so expensive ($80) until I knew that I was really interested in it. It took him the entire first two months to realize that I was simply a scrooge. He let me know that the game was up and, with a little coercion, I decided to visit my local climbing store to buy my own boots. At the store I was in for a shock: there was so much gear, there were so many boots, that I was overwhelmed and intimidated. I ended up buying the same boots that my partner wore, only because I knew they worked. The other gear was completely beyond my grasp.

Progressing as climbers, we began buying more gear. My partner knew more about climbing than I did, so he made all the buying decisions, while I muttered along behind, questioning what this was, or that, and what were we going to do with all this stuff anyway?

He was reasonably helpful, albeit somewhat impatient with my lack of understanding. However, soon I knew the basics: I could identify a carabiner from a pile of gear, a climbing rope from other ropes, and I even knew what a wedging chock looked like. But I realized that, if I wanted to become a good climber, I had better expand my knowledge of the equipment.

I began by ordering catalogs, reading climbing magazines and books, and talking with the climbers I met about their gear. I was amazed to discover that there was no book devoted to climbing gear, and that the gear sections of most books were woefully inadequate. Incredibly, even though climbers must stake their lives on their gear during almost every climb, information about climbing gear is mostly passed by word of mouth!

My growing fascination with climbing gear, and frustration with the lack of good information about it, led to the writing of this book. I believe *Rock Gear* will provide anyone with the information they need to select, purchase, use, and maintain their climbing gear.

Rock Gear is primarily intended for beginning climbers. Unlike most other climbing books, which are written by "expert" rock climbers, this book is written by someone who still remembers what it's like to be a beginner. Having been introduced to climbing just two years ago, I have retained some sensitivity to the beginner's plight. I am very aware how easy it is to feel confused by this exciting but often overwhelming new world. To help you, the beginner, I have tried to make *Rock Gear* easy to understand, and its information easy to access. The chapter entitled How To Use This Book explains *Rock Gear's* many special features.

Although *Rock Gear* is intended for beginners, it contains information that many intermediate, and perhaps some advanced, climbers are missing. Therefore, you will find *Rock Gear* useful even after you have progressed in ability, and are climbing the harder routes.

How to Use This Book

If you are newcomer to rock climbing, read Starting Out (pg. 5) immediately after you read this short section!

Starting Out contains an overview of the climbing world. It tells you how to get started, what the sport will do for you, and, very importantly, it tells you how much of what gear to buy, and when to buy it. If you are really excited and want to buy some climbing gear immediately so you can try the sport today, the gear lists in Starting Out tell what you will need.

Rock Gear is a reference book. Any good reference book provides easy access to its contents. *Rock Gear* contains several features which will help you quickly find the information you seek. These include:

    3 tables of contents
    alphabetically-ordered gear chapters
    a large combination glossary/index
    key terms printed in bold throughout the text
    frequent cross-referencing
    standard sections in each gear chapter
    text boxes
    additional chapters that cover the basics of rock
        climbing
    multiple appendices.

I will describe each of these features in detail.

General Table of Contents

There are three tables of contents in the book. The first is general, containing the written title and page number of each chapter in this book.

Visual Table of Contents

The second table of contents is a *gear table of contents*. It shows a small illustration of a typical piece of gear from that chapter, and the chapter's page number. For example, the chapter Descenders has an illustration of a Figure-Eight, which is a common descender. This table of contents is useful if you don't know the name of a particular piece of gear, but only what it looks like.

Techniques Table of Contents

The third table of contents lets you quickly access the techniques of rock climbing. It is a techniques table of contents. Because Rock Gear is organized around climbing gear, the technique for using each item of gear will be found in that gear's chapter. If you want to learn how to belay, for instance, look up belaying in the Techniques Table of Contents, then turn to the appropriate page. You will find yourself in the Belay Devices chapter.

Alphabetical Gear Chapters

Note that the gear chapters are organized alphabetically. If you need to quickly find the chapter Pulleys, for example, you can do so without resorting to the table of contents: simply thumb through the book until you reach "P" for pulley.

Glossary/Index

Rock climbers have evolved their own technical language to describe their gear, the specific moves they make to climb over rock, and the important features of rock itself. These terms may seem bewildering at first. To help you understand them, *Rock Gear* has a large combined Glossary/Index. Every word in the Glossary, as I shall refer to it, is followed by a definition and the page numbers on which that term is used throughout the book. However, because some terms are so common, appearing on almost every page of a given chapter, in the Glossary I have listed only the term's first occurrence in each chapter.

Bold Glossary Entries

In addition, the first time a Glossary entry appears in a chapter, I have written it in **bold.** If, when you first read a term, you are uncertain of its meaning, and it is written in bold, you will know that its definition can be found in the Glossary. Cross-referencing throughout the text, you will see frequent page references, such as "see pg. 156." These references occur whenever the term or concept you are reading is elaborated on in other parts of the book.

Standard Sections In Each Gear Chapter

The gear chapters themselves are subdivided into standard sections. Most chapters begin with the heading "What Is A . . . (the name of that piece of gear)?" The next section is usually Types, then comes Specifications, Technique, Materials, General Safety Guidelines, Care, Modifications and Tune-Ups, and finally Accessories.

Text Boxes

Many of the chapters contain small grey shaded blocks, or boxes, of text. These boxes contain information that relates to the subject at hand, but that doesn't quite fit into the text. You may find it interesting to simply thumb through the book, reading each box you see.

The Basics of Climbing

Before and after the gear chapters there are several very important chapters describing other aspects of rock climbing. You should read these chapters, even if you already know how to climb, because they integrate the information in the gear chapters. For example, the chapter "Where To Buy Your Gear" (see pg. 29) describes different buying strategies and the businesses that sell climbing gear. And the chapter "Your Rack" (see pg. 39) suggests various methods of putting your equipment together to form a useful rack.

Multiple Appendices

Finally, the Appendices contain several useful tables of conversion (metric to U.S), a discussion of the various climbing rating systems, and the Glossary, which I have already mentioned. They also contain the addresses of many climbing equipment manufacturers, mail order companies, and climbing magazines, as well as a brief discussion of the UIAA.

I hope you will find *Rock Gear* an exciting, easy-to-read, informative book.

Starting Out

We have all climbed before. As children we spent many hours scrambling up hills and trees, over couches and chairs. Climbing is natural to us. Our Neanderthal ancestors escaped from the hungry mouths of wild predators by climbing trees. You might say that each and every one of us has climbing in our genes.

But why do we climb today? Why do the cliffs attract us like sirens, to face danger and the unknown? It can't be just to reach the summit; there is usually an easier route to the top. We don't climb out of necessity any longer. Instead, I think there are essentially two reasons for climbing: exploring the natural world and exploring the inner self.

Exploring nature from the side of a cliff gives you a very different view of the world! Your perspective is changed considerably. Cliffs look very beautiful and majestic from several thousand feet away. But when you are actually 100 feet up a length of rock, looking through your legs at the ground far below, then you are exploring nature in a way you have never done before!

You may also climb to explore yourself. Climbing is a sport which offers you valuable personal insights. When you are in a potentially dangerous situation you learn a lot about yourself. You may find that you have incredible inner resources. You might not be afraid, although you thought you would be. Or find that you are afraid, but that you can still climb well, and keep your self control. This is the kind of important personal knowledge that you get from climbing. It will give you new confidence in your daily life, as well as insight into who you are.

I think personal insight is what forces me upward. Meeting the challenge of the cliffs successfully gives me new confidence and strength, and new vigor for the pursuit of life. I find that the act of climbing focuses my mind, emotions, and body into one intense purpose. With this focus my life temporarily becomes a meditation, a meditation through movement over rock.

If you are climbing for inner exploration you will find walking in the heights joyful and exciting. The overhangs, **cracks,** and cliffs will become a refuge in the sanity of nature far from the hectic pace of the modern world.

You Can Climb

You do not need to be young and superbly fit to climb rocks. Many people take up climbing when they are in their forties, or even later. And climbing is an excellent sport for children, giving them the chance to explore a new and exciting part of the outdoors.

People seem to have the misconception that climbing takes a great deal of strength. Many big, strong men have found out how wrong this was when they were unable to follow a seemingly frail woman up the rock. Technique, not strength, is what gets you up a climb. Learning climbing technique requires a combination of mental concentration and physical practice. The time it takes to learn climbing technique varies widely; for more information see page 18.

Some General Thoughts About Climbing

A rock's features change very slowly. This is really advantageous to climbers, because it means we can climb the same rock again and again. If you can't climb a cliff today, it will remain unchanged until you can try it again.

Climbing is a smooth, upward-moving sport. As long as you don't fall, you needn't worry about jarring or smashing your body. And if you do fall, your climbing equipment will keep you from injuring yourself on the rock. (Of course, you must place your gear properly for it to do this.) Learning how to place your gear is one of the fascinating aspects of climbing.

Runners are not so lucky. Many ex-runners are painfully aware of the damage done to their knees from hitting the pavement with each step. This kind of jarring impact puts a terrible stress on tender joints. But while climbing, you push off with your limbs instead of landing on them. When I consider all the sports that I have participated in, including soccer, baseball, basketball, karate, biking, swimming, and surfing, I find that, surprisingly, climbing has caused me the least injury. (I say "surprisingly" because my image of climbing is one of danger.)

The element of danger - of the potential to fall - changes rock climbing from a sport into an adventure. I discuss this subject thoroughly in the chapter Falling on page 61. This ever-present threat of falling forces you to use more mental and emotional control than just physical skill. It is this potential danger which provides the challenge that requires you to push yourself to the utmost to succeed.

The Evolution of Climbing Equipment

The element of danger has naturally played a part in the development of climbing equipment. Until fairly recently (after the Second World War) the ropes and other protection equipment that climbers used was not very reliable. Thus, the level of climbing at that time was limited by the psychological barriers of fear and uncertainty.

Imagine yourself tied to a rope (without a **harness**) and wearing **nailed boots** (which are very hard to climb with!). Occasionally you would tie your rope to rock knobs on the cliff. This rope was made of natural fiber; it frayed easily and you were never sure it would hold you if you fell. You had the additional disadvantage of being the first one up the rock; when you don't know what lies ahead you are engaged in a very adventurous game! (These days most climbers have maps to guide them up cliffs that others have already explored.)

Climber in the 1860s

Gradually climbing equipment has improved. As modern climbers we can use our equipment to build a kind of ladder that allows us to climb anywhere we want. We are able to trust that our equipment will catch us if we fall and consequently we are not restricted by the psychological barriers that plagued our predecessors.

But climbing is about adventure. It is about facing dangers and overcoming them with your own resources and skill, without relying on your equipment. To preserve this spirit of adventure, climbers have imposed rules on themselves and their game. (I pursue climbing games and their rules in more detail beginning page 11).

Rock Climbing, Mountaineering, and Caving

The three sports of rock climbing, mountaineering, and caving are intimately connected.

Rock climbing is an offshoot of mountaineering. Mountaineers began rock climbing as a way to train themselves for the tall, technical mountains. It was through rock climbing that prospective mountaineers learned many of their rope-handling skills - they were able to try things out before it really mattered. So rock climbers and mountaineers use similar equipment, and techniques, to achieve their goals.

Cave explorers, or spelunkers, also use gear and techniques similar to those used by rock climbers. To explore some of the more fascinating caves, spelunkers must first rappel into vertical cave entrances. And when they are ready to return to the surface, they must ascend their ropes, just as a big wall climber might.

If you are a skilled rock climber, you will find that you can quickly translate these skills to mountaineering or caving. By learning one sport, you are also learning the basics of two others.

About This Chapter

I am assuming that you are a newcomer to rock climbing. As such, you need an introduction into the climbing world. This chapter will give you that introduction. You will learn everything from how climbers have organized their sport to actual lists of equipment you need to buy to get started. You will see what you can expect to get out of climbing, and how you can go about getting it. This chapter will give you a summary of the world of rock climbing, and will orient you to this new and exciting sport.

The Types of Climbing

Rock has two distinct features, **faces** and cracks. Faces are unbroken slabs of rock. Cracks split these slabs in two. Climbers call these types of climbing face and crack climbing, respectively.

Face climbing is a natural way to climb; it is like climbing a ladder whose rungs vary in distance and shape. These "rungs" are actually called **holds**; they are the rock edges and knobs that you use to make upward progress. But unless you can find some large rock knobs to loop a **runner** (a loop of nylon **webbing**) around, you must drill **bolts** into the rock to keep yourself from falling. So **protecting** a face climb is unnatural; you permanently disfigure the rock.

Crack climbing is the opposite of face climbing: you use unnatural techniques to climb a crack, but you can place your protection in a natural manner. It takes time to learn how to jam your hands and feet, fingers and toes, and arms and legs into a crack. But once you learn how to do it, climbing a crack feels very secure. Placing protection in a crack is fascinating: you insert **chocks** (pieces of machined metal which cam or wedge into the crack). Chocks use the crack's shape to anchor themselves. Because you don't disfigure the rock, protecting a crack is very natural.

Climber on a crack climb

Climber on a face climb

Both face and crack climbing have many different variations. These depend on the type of holds on the face and the size and shape of the crack. To climb each variation you must use a different technique. I will present a brief description of each technique here. Learning all these techniques is a very challenging and interesting part of rock climbing. It is also the subject of several good books. See the Bibliography, page 361.

There are three basic variations of face climbing: **friction, edging,** and **pocket** climbing. The rubber on the soles of your **rock climbing boots smear,** or friction, on smooth slabs of rock. Friction climbing is easiest on grainy, granular rock, such as most types of granite.

Frictioning smooth rock

Edging technique keeps you secure on small edges of rock. Many different types of rock have edges which you can climb on.

Edging the rock

Pocket climbing is available mostly on limestone rock. Often many pockets form together, which means that you can choose from many different holds. But on the harder **routes** you must use them in just the right sequence or you won't make it.

Toeing a pocket

The Types of Rock

There are many types of rock on the earth. Granite, lava, limestone, sandstone, and quartzite are a few of them. They are formed from one of three very basic, but very different, ways.

Igneous rock is melted below the surface of the earth. It then either flies out of the earth's crust as molten lava, or is gradually exposed to the surface by weathering. Most igneous rock is hard, although certain types of lava are soft. The granite domes of the Sierra Nevada are majestic examples of igneous rock.

Sedimentary rock is formed from the decomposed remnants of the other two rock types. Sandstone, limestone, and shale are the three most common types of sedimentary rock. Sandstone is the most commonly observed of the three because it tends to be exposed in cliffs, more so than the others. Some of these cliffs are excellent to climb on; however, many of them are too soft. The sandstone cliffs of Zion National Park in Utah provide some excellent climbing, for example.

Metamorphic rock is either igneous or sedimentary rock that goes through a structural change without melting. Quartzite and marble are two common examples of metamorphic rock. There are not many large outcrops of metamorphic rock, so climbing on metamorphic rock is not as common.

Knowing the type of rock in your area won't always tell you what type of climbing you can expect. Sometimes limestone cliffs are steep, crackless faces, filled with pockets (such as in the

Verdon). Then again, limestone also forms into huge blocks cut both vertically and horizontally by many cracks (the Dolomite Alps are a good example).

Weathering plays a large part in designing a cliff's features. If the rock is cold and icy in the winter, but hot and sunny in the summer, it will split into cracks. In areas where there is often a high wind, the rock may be pitted from sand and gravel. Rivers cut through rock, smoothing and shaping it.

The age of a cliff determines how long it has been weathering. The more rundown and broken up the rock is, the older it is. Old rock eventually crumbles down to dirt and sand, filling the valleys between younger mountains.

Consequently, you must always be ready for falling rock. Rock cliffs are always being changed by weathering; they are in a constant state of decay. You will rarely notice the changes, because the time scale between you and the rocks is so different. But if you are aware that rock is changing, you won't be so surprised when a large boulder rumbles down the cliff!

There are many types of crack climbing, depending on the size of the crack. The largest cracks are **chimneys,** some of which are so large that you must bridge your entire body across them to move upwards.

Offwidths are cracks which are larger than your fist, so you must use your entire arm and foot to hold yourself in them.

Then there are **fist cracks,** which fit your fist very nicely.

Fist jamming a fist crack

Hand cracks require you to jam your open hand in them, while **finger cracks** will only accept your fingers.

Hand jamming a hand crack

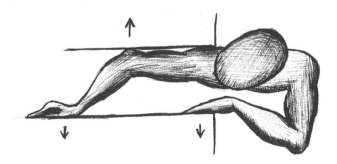

Arm jamming an offwidth

Finger jamming a finger crack

Some of the smallest seam-like cracks (they are called **seams)** may allow in only one digit of each finger, and only at lengthy intervals. You can imagine how difficult it is to climb this kind of crack!

Of course there are many cracks which don't quite fit one description or another. An **off-hand crack,** for instance, is too large to **hand jam** and too small to **fist jam.** Learning how to climb such a crack is very difficult.

Cracks may also be shaped differently. **Parallel cracks** have sides which run evenly next to each other, and are very difficult to climb (there are no irregularities to lock your fingers around).

Flaring cracks widen from the inside out, and can be even harder to climb than parallel ones.

Many cracks are somewhat irregular, though, and offer plenty of opportunities for securely placing your hands and feet.

Both crack and face climbing, with all their variations, may angle from a gradual slope to a flat out, perpendicular overhang.

Each angle adjustment means that you must adjust your body's position to give you the most secure **stance.** Climbing an overhanging crack is very different from climbing a similar crack that is less than vertical. So, besides learning how to climb each different type of crack or face climb, you must also learn how to climb each one at a different angle!

Many climbs offer a combination of crack and face climbing. These climbs make for really interesting excursions, because you can try a wide variety of techniques.

With all of these possible types of climbing to try, you can see why climbing easily becomes a lifetime sport.

The only way you can learn how to climb these different types of rock features is by practicing. Get out there and do it!

Artificial Climbing Surfaces

Besides rock, you can climb on buildings and artificial climbing walls. Climbing on buildings is known as **buildering.** You use whatever is available to make progress, such as window ledges, cracks between bricks, and even cracks between buildings.

Buildering

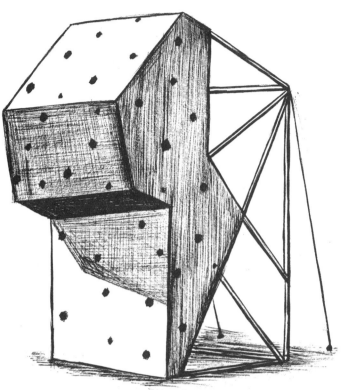

Artificial climbing wall

There are some problems inherent in buildering. You need to be careful where you do it, because it is not legal unless you have permission. (Because of insurance problems, owners aren't likely to give you permission.) You may also be spotted as a cat burglar making an adventurous entry. Despite these problems, buildering can be lots of fun. Always be on the lookout for a good place to climb as you walk around town. A good problem-solving exercise is to try and figure out how to climb a given building in your imagination. Use your creativity, it can be exciting. For more information on mental climbing turn to page xx.

Artificial climbing walls are made to accommodate holds. The walls may be made from a mixture of polyester resin and sand, and look like rock, or they may be plywood boards. The holds are either bolted or screwed on. These holds can be quickly moved or exchanged to alter the difficulty of the climb.

Artificial climbing walls are generally used either for competitions or climbing practice.

A World Cup climbing circuit is sponsored by the Comité Internationale des Competitions d'Escalade (CICE) which is a part of the **UIAA** (Union Internationale des Associations d'Alpinisme). Competitors are sponsored by the climbing manufacturers. Competitors climb as high as they can

without falling (**flash** the route). There are also speed climbing contests.

Climbers practice on artificial walls in climbing-specific gyms as a way to train year round. This is especially nice in the wetter parts of the world! Currently, there aren't many of these gyms in the U.S., although more are opening up. There are quite a few in Europe. To find out if there is a climbing gym near you, ask at your local climbing store, or search the phone book.

Some Climbing Gym Addresses

Here are the addresses of three west coast climbing gyms:

Pacific Nautilus, Inc.
189 W. 8th Ave., Eugene, Oregon, 97401
(503) 485-4475

Portland Rock Gym
2034 S.E. 6th, Portland, OR.,
97214, (503) 232-8310

Art of Climbing
10231-A Topanga Canyon Blvd.,
Chatsworth, Ca., 91311

Climbing on the artificial walls, either in a competition or in a gym, is very safe. Bolts are placed at regular intervals and the walls themselves are never longer than one **pitch** (the distance from one belay station to another, determined by the length of the rope). You can either **toprope** (anchor your rope at the top) or **lead** (place your protection from the bottom) the routes on artificial walls, although you usually do the former when practicing and the latter when competing. The rules for climbing these walls naturally depend on whether you are competing or practicing. Competitions establish their own rules, often requiring the competitors to climb **"on sight"** (climb without previously looking at the route). In the case of a wall in a gym, there are no rules because it is available for training.

The Games

Beyond all the different types of climbing you can do, there are a number of rock climbing games that you can play. These games are differentiated by how much you can rely on your gear.

In addition to dictating the gear you can use, each rock climbing game has certain rules. These rules are very strict in a safe environment, such as your local **bouldering** area, and very lax, sometimes nonexistent, in a dangerous environment, such as the Himalayas.

Although the rules change according to the game you are playing, there is one rule that you must always follow: safety. *You must be a safe climber at all times!* Besides your own life, you must think about the lives of others on the same cliff. Be slow, careful, and deliberate in every move you make. Above all, think about the consequences of your actions. If you carefully think things through, without rushing, you should have no problems.

There are basically six different rock climbing games. They are: bouldering, toproping, **free climbing, aid climbing, multi-day climbing,** and **soloing.**

Most of these games can be either easy or difficult. There are some fairly easy free climbs, for instance, and some very hard bouldering problems. Soloing is never easy, because your safety rests entirely in your mind.

Because you are a beginner, you need to start with the games which are the safest. These are bouldering and toproping. After you learn the basics, you can progress to easy free climbing, then on to aid climbing. Multi-day climbing is much more dangerous because you are exposed to the elements for a long period of time. Try this *only* after you have gained a lot of experience. Soloing is the most dangerous form of climbing. Many climbers never solo; those who do have very good judgement gained from lots of experience.

Bouldering is the least exposed facet of rock climbing. By climbing on small boulders, you have little fear of being overwhelmed by the weather or other potentially hazardous natural events. Most boulders are small enough that if necessary you can comfortably jump down from them.

Bouldering is a fairly safe game. Therefore when you **boulder,** you have to abide by many rules. You cannot use a rope. In fact, you must limit your equipment to your shoes and chalk, and of course your clothes.

Toproping a climb is a more difficult game to play. Because you may be climbing fairly high, perhaps over jumbled and jagged boulders, danger is inherent in your situation. That is why the rules

of toproping are relaxed enough to allow you to use a rope and **anchor** (see page 53).

Bouldering

You set up a toprope by tying the rope into the anchor which is in the rock above where you are going to climb. With the rope above you it is impossible to fall any distance, because your partner will stop the rope. The height of the climb you toprope is limited to the length of your rope, so for most of us it is about 150 feet (using the standard 165 feet rope).

Free climbing up the cliffs is the next step in the game. You are free climbing when one member of your party ties into the rope and proceeds to lead the climb, placing chocks or clipping **carabiners** to bolts for protection. The other member of the

Toproping

A climber leading a route

climbing team **belays** the **leader**, that is, prepares to stop any **leader falls** by using a belay technique to hold the rope.

Leading climbs requires some basic rock climbing knowledge: how to place protection, set up an anchor, tie crucial knots, etc. Leading a climb is the most exciting and challenging aspect of rock climbing. It is also more inherently dangerous than either bouldering or toproping; you need to know what you are doing when you lead a climb.

The increased danger of leading means that the rules are a little more relaxed. You can put in as much protection as you think you need and the cliff provides. Generally your protection takes the form of chocks which you place and your partner, coming behind you, removes. Sometimes you can use bolts that are already in the rock. *Never add bolts to an established route!* Bolts are permanent and scar the rock. Climbers try to preserve the rock as much as possible, and placing unnecessary bolts is unethical.

If the route you are climbing is up a **big wall** (a cliff of at least 1000 feet) the rules become very lax. On a big wall you will be at the mercy of mountain weather. A storm might kick up or some other weather change occur. So you need to move fast.

For instance, you may lead a pitch but your partner, instead of climbing after you, may **jug** up the rope (use **ascenders** to walk up the rope).

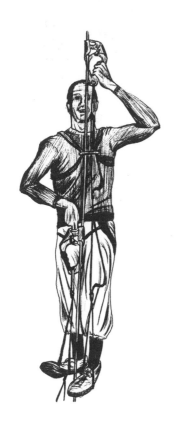

Climber ascending a rope

This saves time and energy. On such an extensive climb, you may have to spend a few nights on the cliff face, which makes you even more vulnerable.

On some climbs, especially big wall routes, you must use aid climbing techniques. Now the game has advanced a long way from free climbing. Aid climbing is essentially building a ladder up the cliff face.

The justification for this is that you are going where it is impossible to free climb, for example, following a seam which is an eighth of an inch wide while putting yourself into a harsh environment. You are climbing a cliff that is impossible without **aid.** That is your justification for relying on your equipment. Although you are supporting yourself with your gear, hard aid climbing requires a lot of previous climbing experience and can be very strenuous.

Soloing (climbing alone, without any protection) is the most dangerous way to climb. As a soloist you have placed a great many rules on your climbing, all of which stem from one big rule: no gear. No gear means no protection and no rests; your safety lies entirely in your judgement, skill, and energy.

Soloing

Many climbers never solo the cliffs; that feat is only for a very few. These are the expert climbers, very experienced and very skilled. They refuse to complete a lot of climbs they begin and only solo climbs that are well within their ability. By doing this they are exercising good judgement. Climbers do not solo to satisfy some ego craving for great-

Aid climbing

ness: to do so would practically guarantee failure and perhaps death. Rather, the soloist's intention is to push back his limits, to explore his mental control.

You do not have to solo to develop yourself, however. You will be able to spend many satisfying years exploring your inner limits through the safer forms of climbing.

Style

Style expresses the way you climb a cliff. Summed up: the harder the climb and the less you rely on your gear, while climbing safely, the more stylish you are. For example, you might decide to free climb an aid route, which, if done without a fall, would be very stylish.

It is not stylish to climb unsafely! Do not allow your ego to control the way you climb. Other climbers will not respect you, or even want to be around you, if you climb unsafely, no matter how stylish you look. It is not hard to climb safely, don't worry. You will make many mistakes at the beginning, everyone does. That is why you climb easy routes at first, allowing yourself time to become acquainted with this sport.

Ethics

Ethics is the term given to important issues which affect the climbing community as a whole. How you treat the rock and another person's route as you climb are ethical issues. For example, bolts cannot be removed once they are placed in the rock. Therefore, they affect everyone who climbs the route in the future, as well as those who just look at it. Bolts must be placed only when they are absolutely necessary, and then carefully. Climbers debate these and other ethical issues very intensely.

As a newcomer you must keep one ethical issue clearly in mind. The way a **first ascent** was accomplished, the style used by the first climbers up that part of the rock, is the minimum style which you must use as well. In other words, *do not attach a bolt if the climb was originally accomplished without any.* If the climb does not have enough protection for you to feel safe, then you should not be climbing it.

Beyond this basic ethical principle, which is followed by most climbers, lies another one. Because climbing equipment can take us virtually anywhere on the rock, we must decide how we are going to use it. This means that the way a first ascent is done becomes both an issue of style and an ethical issue.

There are essentially two schools of thinking on this point. The **"traditionalists"** believe that routes should be climbed from the ground up and that all protection should be put in on the lead. Bolt placements tend to be farther apart (minimizing rock damage) because it is hard to place a bolt from a stance on the cliff. The result is a preservation of the spirit of adventure which many climbers believe to be fundamental to climbing.

A problem with the traditionalist approach is that it is very hard to **put up** a difficult face climb. The only way to protect a face climb is to place bolts, and to place a bolt you must first drill a hole in the rock. This is very hard to accomplish while leading a difficult route. The result is that traditionalists have not been able to put up any routes of the highest level of technical difficulty.

The other school of thinking is known as **"sport" climbing.** Sport climbers place **fixed protection** (bolts) by **rappelling** down from the top of the climb. They have a comfortable stance from their rope and harness, so they are willing to put in more bolts along the route, resulting in more rock damage. Once all the bolts have been placed sport climbers usually practice the climb on toprope. When they feel ready, they try to **redpoint** the climb (lead the entire route without falling, while placing their protection). The spirit of adventure is gone from this type of climbing; it is more like a gymnastic sport. On the other hand, the routes that are possible using this method are very difficult and have raised the limits of climbing to a new level.

Climbers do not have a governing body empowered to decide and enforce these ethical issues. We prefer to govern ourselves, as a true democracy (sometimes an anarchy!). Consequently there is a lot of yelling (back and forth) about what action constitutes proper ethics. But this conflict is valuable since it assures that every new development in our sport comes under close scrutiny.

Both sides of the ethical argument are much more complex than I have just sketched in. But now you have some idea about the central ethical issues. You can choose to get involved or not; as a newcomer you won't be putting up routes so you are not likely to be concerned. However, your local climbers may be biased one way or the other, and you will probably be "trained" in that bias. Being aware of both sides of the issue will more easily allow you to form your own opinion. Keep your eyes and ears open, and make your decisions based on what seems right to you!

Your Potential

As a climber you have unlimited potential. There will always be another level to strive for, a harder climb to complete. And when you get to the place where you are accomplishing first ascents your climbs will be limited only by your imagination. Here you are dealing entirely with the psychological aspects of yourself, with deciding what you want to accomplish. Only a few years ago 5.9[1] (a particular **rating** of a climb, designed to show how hard it is) was the hardest climb available in the world. No one could break this barrier. Climbers have since had the vision to create the technology (by designing more reliable and essentially safer equipment) and increase their skills to try harder and harder climbs. Now we are at 5.14. But you can expect this limit to be pushed back as well: it is just a question of vision, will, and resources. This means that you should allow your imagination to lead you on to new realms, to push back the impossible.

---

[1] For more information on the rating system turn to page 345.

Individuality

Rock climbing is very individualistic. Your ability to get up the rock depends upon your resourcefulness and skill. You must also use your creativity: to get up a length of awkward knobs you may have to become something of a contortionist. And even as you climb you must figure out how to place your protection into the rock as you go. Your creativity gives you the freedom to take advantage of everything that the rock offers.

The Value of Teamwork

Teamwork is surprisingly essential in this most individual of sports. You and your partner trust your lives to each other every time you climb. You must both be competent in basic climbing skills. Success on the cliffs depends on your ability to work as a team, to move smoothly and efficiently together. In case you are wondering how you can find a partner, don't worry, I'll tell you. But there are some other things you need to know first.

Route Information

The **route information** that climbers give each other after a first ascent is important. It provides a map for climbers who later follow the same route. Climbing **guidebooks** supply this information; they show you the location of routes in areas you aren't yet familiar with. Climbing stores sell guidebooks to many local and popular national areas (places such as Yosemite).

While route information takes away much of the psychological aspect of your climb (facing the unknown) it allows you to experience a previous climber's creation. To repeat a first ascent as closely as possible you can sometimes talk to the climber who accomplished it and get the full **"beta"** (information) on the climb.

If you look at climbing as an art form, it may change the way you climb. You will want to make as beautiful a creation of your experience as possible. There is no room for mistakes. You want every move you make to be fluid and precise. Every chock you place in the rock must be perfect, and everything you do must fit into the strategy of the entire climb.

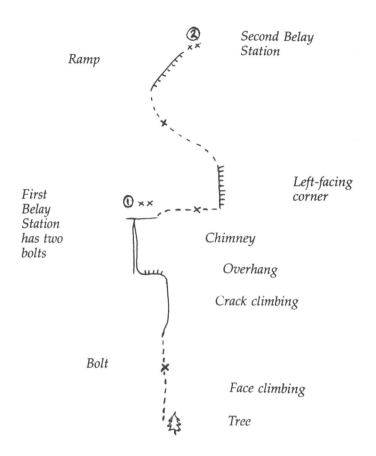

Ramp · Second Belay Station · Left-facing corner · First Belay Station has two bolts · Chimney · Overhang · Crack climbing · Bolt · Face climbing · Tree

Climbing As Art

The climb you accomplish is an art form. You can think of it as a vertical dance. It is ephemeral, it is only in the moment's action, yet it is your creation. Every move you make is a creative expression. The rock is your canvas and your movement the brush you paint with.

The climbs that you have accomplished are for you. You cannot hang them on the wall to show others (although we all try). Names of routes, ratings of difficulty, the protection you used, how many falls, if any, you took to get to the top; all of this information and more is used by climbers to show others their work. But these figures are a poor representation of your creative work. The true climb, or dance, is only for you and your partner to appreciate. Even spectators, witnesses to the climb, are not privy to the thoughts and feelings that accompanied your actions. Thus they must miss the best two-thirds of the dance. Your climb is ultimately yours alone.

It is very difficult to accomplish a climb this way, without mistakes. You must put your entire being into it. By this I mean your mental, emotional, and physical powers must all combine to one purpose.

How do you best use your mental, emotional, and physical selves on a climb? By creating the proper environment in yourself for these three aspects to work together. Try to stay relaxed and focused. Many times I have become frustrated while climbing. Then I become tense and think of my past mistakes. This takes my attention away from the best present move. Invariably I fall, or make more mistakes. These are the direct result of being distracted or tense. It is hard to always maintain the correct environment in yourself, but it is a great challenge to face. You can use the results of this intense personal struggle in other aspects of your life as well.

This combination, this focusing of your entire self, is true for any sport you try. But there is one big difference: the element of danger. I mentioned this once already but now I will elaborate. The danger, your ever-present exposure in high places, helps you stay focused. You cannot afford to let your mind and emotions wander because you might panic. You must concentrate each time you place your protection because it must hold you if you fall. Of course this element of danger also gives you a greater sense of satisfaction after a successful climb - you have met the challenge; you have succeeded. I think that for most climbers meeting danger successfully is psychologically important. It gives us a sense of self-reliance and inner confidence that only comes through facing self-determined hardships.

Develop Good Judgement

But because rock climbing can be dangerous your best safeguard is good judgement. Good judgement is partly common sense and partly knowing, and accepting, your current limits. Both of these are increased with experience and knowledge.

Accepting your limits means climbing within your ability. This does not mean you shouldn't push those limits. On the contrary, by exercising good judgement you can keep yourself within a comfortable **safety margin** even while you are pushing your limits. If I want to attempt a climb that is at the very limits of my current ability I will not lead it. Rather, I will either toprope it or find someone else to lead it, someone who is not pushing his limits by **leading** that climb.

When expert climbers lead really hard climbs they are often pushing their limits. But they have a very sound knowledge of how to protect themselves, so, although they may fall, they are able to make the judgement call on where and how to place equipment. An expert climber using good judgement while soloing (climbing without rope and protection) is safer than you, the **well-protected** beginner. This is because he knows what he is doing. He has a large base of knowledge and experience about rock climbing and his own abilities and limitations. With this information the expert is able to make the correct decisions.

If you use poor judgement, it does not matter how much equipment you employ, it will all become useless. This is why it is important for you to progress naturally and not rush yourself. You will improve your judgement over time as you broaden your knowledge and experience, so be patient and have fun while you are learning!

How Long It Takes

Climbing takes time to learn, and even longer to master. It is a sport which will return to you as much as you give it. To really get the full benefit from this sport you need to explore its possibilities with intensity.

Everyone learns at a different pace, so it is impossible for me to tell you how fast you can progress as a climber. However, I can tell you to expect both fast and slow learning periods. You may take to climbing as if you had climbed for years, but within a few months hit a plateau from which you just can't seem to improve. Everyone goes through these phases; they are a normal part of learning to climb. You can work through a plateau in one of two ways: you can go along with it, or you can fight it. Going along with it is fine, but you must realize that you will not improve very quickly.

Sometimes it is better to learn slowly because you pick up more subtle techniques that someone else might miss. This will help you later, when you are trying harder climbs. If, on the other hand, you want to work through the plateau as quickly as you can, you need to devote more of your life to climbing. You may want to start training and dieting. It helps tremendously to start thinking a lot about climbing, about specific climbs. The most important thing you can do is practice. You must practice climbing to improve quickly. Intensity and commitment are the most important qualities climbers have. With them you will be willing to double your efforts to keep improving.

Your Body

Climbing is an excellent full-body conditioner. It involves your entire body; you are exercising all your major muscle groups. You also use some muscles and tendons that you wouldn't use much in other sports. These include your fingers, forearms, calves, and toes.

Climbing is a symmetrical sport, which means that you use both sides of your body equally. As you climb you will develop a powerful, balanced body, one that is able to work entirely as a unit instead of, as in many sports, being lopsidedly developed. You will also gain strength, agility and flexibility, and increase your coordination. And you will do all of this while having an extraordinary adventure!

Body Weight

Because you are constantly pulling and pushing your body up the rock you might think you want to be as light as possible. This is not necessarily the case, although many of the best climbers are about ten pounds lighter than the average weight for their height.

The most important thing is to be able to move your body effortlessly (or as near to it as possible). Losing weight is a way to achieve this. It means that you won't have to develop as much muscle to move yourself upward. Gaining strength is also a way to achieve easy upward motion. However, if you choose the latter method, you must not become very bulky. It is hard to move over rock with a lot of bulk.

You want a balanced body. While becoming anorexic is not a good solution, neither is becoming Mr. Universe. Somewhere in the middle is ideal. You must find what is right for you. You may be content to maintain the average body weight, or even be a little over that.

Strength and Technique

After your first few days of climbing you will ache in strange places. Most especially, your fingers and forearms will be stiff. This is normal. Finger strength is very important in climbing, especially on the harder routes. In time, you will develop strong fingers, but it does take time because you are strengthening tendons rather than muscles. You cannot rush the development of your tendons without becoming injured. They will strengthen naturally as you climb.

But technique is more important to a climber than strength. You will be able to move across the rocks fluidly and easily when you use the proper technique. Practice is the only way to develop technique, just as swimming is the only way to learn to swim.

Good technique stems from the proper integration of several skills. These include footwork, balance, flexibility, and, of course, skillfully using your hands on various holds and in cracks. Your footwork is always critical. Since your legs are much stronger than your arms, always keep as much of your weight on them as possible. Good body balance is very important as well, as is body flexibility. Learning how to use your hands well is very important, especially for those moments when there is nowhere to place your feet! These things will improve naturally as you climb, but not overnight - it takes time.

As you become more absorbed in climbing you will find that there are three basic ways to practice the sport. You can treat your visits to the crags as you would the monthly family picnic. Relax, be outside, and enjoy your movement upwards is the name of this easy game. Or, you can become more intense, climbing as much as your schedule permits, and between climbs training to improve your ability. Finally, you might move between these two extremes, listening to your inner moods and depth of motivation until you find the commitment to climbing that is right for you. You may be inspired by a story you hear of a great climber or see an exciting video on climbing, and determine to improve your skills. A week later you may decide to slow down and be more relaxed about it. How much you climb is up to you. Any way you use it, climbing offers great personal rewards.

Physical Training

If you decide to climb ever harder routes, you may want to train your body. Remember though that your mind determines the climb and your emotions give you the desire to attain it. So do not become too dependent on body strengthening. Physical training helps a great deal when you are just learning how to climb. However, once you have a strong base and you are climbing harder routes it will take more than physical training to improve your skill.

Training your body increases strength, flexibility, and balance. Exercise your upper body frequently, particularly your fingers and forearms. Remember what I said about strengthening your fingers: go slow because you are building your tendons and you cannot rush their development without risk of injury.

Make sure you develop a strong stomach! After all, your stomach is your center, the connection between your legs and arms. Strong stomach muscles help you bring your feet up and keep your body correctly positioned during awkward moves.

You will also need good leg endurance. Your legs must walk you up the cliff and support most of your body weight the while. You do not want them to become very big, however, because bulky legs will be too heavy to carry along. The best balance is to have endurance-oriented legs, like a runner's. They will be thin and light for the times you need to lift them with your arms, but also strong enough to support most of your weight through a long climb. You can train your legs through running, swimming, biking, or any other distance-oriented and leg-oriented sport.

You can improve your balance by walking on thin boards or by standing on one leg. Once you develop fairly good balance, a tightrope is a great training tool if you have the space to put one up.

Do a lot of body stretching. Becoming more flexible is very important, but it takes time. It's not something you can rush. The secret to flexibility is to stretch lightly but frequently. For example, stretch for five minutes, three times a day. Before you stretch, make sure your body is warm, especially your joints. Cold joints tear easily. Think of your joints as if they were built from lard: they are solid when cold but become liquid when warm. Remember, the point of stretching is to prevent injury, not cause it!

While we're on the subject of warming up: make sure you warm up thoroughly before you climb! The best way to avoid any sort of injury is to climb with a body that is ready for the effort. Injuries do happen. Shoulder, elbow, and finger tendon problems are the most common climbing injuries. You will stress these tendons when you climb. Warm them thoroughly first; that helps prevent injury. Start with a few jumping jacks, just enough to make you breath quickly and maybe sweat. Then slowly stretch your entire body (very important!). Climb a few easy rocks first, until you are feeling really ready to go. Giving yourself the time it takes to warm up is hard to do sometimes, especially when you are really excited that you are out climbing again. But an injury-free climbing career is worth it, don't you think?

Mental Climbing

The mental aspects of learning to survive in the vertical world are very interesting. Before you get on a climb you must study it from below. Try to decide in advance what moves you will need to make as you climb. Mentally work your way up the rock. Try to find your best route to a resting position. When you actually start to climb you can reach this position, rest, and mentally climb from there to the next resting point. As you mentally climb, imagine how your body will respond to a given position: will you be balanced, what holds will be available, can you move into the next position from that location? Considering these things before you get on the rock prepares your body to make the correct motions when you actually need them.

If you are doing a lead, that is, being the first member of your party up the rock, you need to put in "pro" (protection). Before you get started on a climb you should prepare everything you will need. This is where route information becomes valuable: the more you know about a route in advance, the more precisely you can prepare your **rack** (your **gear sling** carrying chocks and carabiners).

As you mentally wend your way upward, imagine placing your protection. Rehearsing this in your mind before the climb allows you to know exactly what you are going to do when you are actually on the rock. Your actual climb will be more precise and efficient, which is essential for success.

When actually climbing, your thinking must stay focused and receptive. Mental focusing keeps you intent on moving upward. You will be able to quickly translate the holds you see into a ladder-like path upward. But to see these holds you must be mentally receptive. Use your eyes, they will give you a precise idea of just how receptive you are. If you have "tunnel vision" you are focusing only on the area directly in front of you. You may be missing a critical hold just one foot away!

"A good climber is one who anticipates possibilities and evaluates the likelihood of their occurrence. He is constantly monitoring his actions and results, maintaining at the same time, a high state of awareness. This to me, is one of the exacting and exciting aspects of the sport." - Bill March[2]

Visualization as a Way to Train

Visualization is an interesting way to train your mind for climbing. Start by attempting to climb a boulder problem, one that you aren't able to do. Work on it until you know all of its holds as well as your body position at each one. Then, whenever you have an idle moment over the next few days, imagine yourself climbing that boulder. Feel your every move as precisely as you can. Since you don't know how to climb the rock, you should mentally try different approaches to it. Use your creativity. Remember, climbing is an art form and as an artist you must be creative. Once you find a way up the boulder in your mind which you think will work, repeat it many times, each time imagining yourself climbing successfully. When you go back to the boulder the next weekend, or whenever you climb there again, you may be surprised to find yourself mastering it very quickly. Sometimes it takes a few weeks, but visualizing a climb beforehand always helps.

Emotional Climbing

I have found my emotional state to be critical to my climbing success. If I am afraid, I climb poorly. If I am calm, I climb well. You will undoubtedly have a similar experience. Just as your mind needs to be relaxed and receptive, but focused, while climbing, so do your emotions need to be positive and balanced.

Every climber becomes frustrated on a climb sooner or later. You may not be able to climb through a **crux** (the hardest point of the climb), and you become frustrated. You try again but can't seem to make any progress. In fact, your climbing is worse! Frustration overcomes you. It becomes

---

[2]Bill March, *Modern Rope Techniques*, 3d ed. (Milnthorpe, England: Cicerone Press, 1973) 75.

impossible to climb well. I have found that the best way to solve this dilemma is to rest, take a few deep breaths, and think about a successful climb. This will put you into a better mood. Joke with your partner. Whatever it takes, move yourself out of the frustration you feel. When you become emotionally relaxed, balanced, and focused, you are ready to climb again.

Achieving Emotional Balance

There are many ways to achieve emotional balance. Because you are going to be on the rocks, you need something which is quick and easy. I offer two suggestions.

Grounding

The first method of regaining your emotional balance I call grounding. Your objective is to feel your feet firmly anchored to the rock.

Concentrate on feeling the strength and stability of the rock under your feet. Let all other thoughts disappear. Your feet will begin to feel heavy, almost planted to the ground. After a few minutes you will feel a strong connection to the rock. Once you have this feeling, your emotions will be balanced and you will be ready to climb.

Breathing

The second method of achieving emotional balance is through breathing. Your objective is to relax your abdomen, which in turn will calm your emotional state.

Inhale slowly and deeply. Follow your breath as it fills your lungs, then let it fill your abdomen. Hold your breath for a couple of seconds, then exhale slowly. When you exhale, empty your abdomen, then your lungs. Feel the tension flowing down your body and out of your feet as you exhale. It should only take about six of these breaths to relax you and recenter your emotions.

A few months ago I noticed myself climbing very poorly all day long. I became more and more frustrated, which of course made my climbing worse. So, in between climbs, I sat down and took some deep breaths and let my mind wander a bit. Then I tried to think of what was bothering me. Why was I so upset that I was not climbing well? For me climbing is a game that I love, but still a game. I climb with an emphasis on enjoying myself, not performing well (although performing well naturally helps me enjoy myself!). But everyone has their off days and I decided to use this one to climb without looking for excellence. Instead, I concentrated on enjoying my motion over the rock. As soon as I realized this I was able to laugh at myself and everything was all right again.

Positive emotions can push you through a crux just as negative ones can make you fail. Exhilaration, that sense of being on top of the world, can give you an "I can do it" attitude. Nothing will seem too hard. Failure is no longer an option to you; everything you try works.

Climbing Desire

Your will is also a very important component of a good climb. Sometimes pain unexpectedly becomes a part of your climb. Your fingers feel like they are on fire, your forearms just want to burst. Use your will to push you through the hard moves ahead to a resting spot, regardless of your pain. Accomplishing a climb against pain, through sheer willpower, is very satisfying. You have extended your limits beyond what you thought was possible, and succeeded.

Your Climbing Environment

The settings you get to play your games in are spectacular. High cliffs amid mountains - in places such as Yosemite and the European Alps. Smaller **crags** beckon in the Verdon, at Joshua Tree, and countless other places throughout the world. Even boulders have their appeal, though they may sit squarely in the heavy industrial section of your home town and lie covered in graffiti.

Weather dictates when you can climb. At many cliffs, rock climbing in winter is out of the question. Instead, you may like to take up ice climbing (climbing up frozen waterfalls) or alpinism (a sport which combines snow, ice, and rock climbing to reach the top of a mountain).

If you are fortunate enough to live in a moderate climate, you will be able to climb year-round. Many climbers plan their vacations according to seasonal patterns. As you become more enthralled with climbing you may join their ranks.

Before you know it you may find yourself traveling across the country, even to foreign countries, to climb. Climbing rocks can be a very cosmopolitan sport, bringing you into contact with many people from different countries. Climbing creates bonds

which extend past language barriers and cultural differences.

On the other hand, you may prefer a less crowded atmosphere. Many climbers do not like long **"approaches,"** or hikes to the rock. There is a lot of **backcountry** (wilderness area which is rarely entered by man) in the world which contains some incredible, rarely climbed, cliffs. If you love the solitude of nature you can locate these remote peaks and climb untouched rock.

Learn About the Area You Intend to Visit

You must bring the right type of climbing equipment when you visit an unfamiliar cliff. Every rock outcrop has different features, and may require different types of gear to climb it. Does the cliff have many cracks, or is it mostly face climbing? Is the rock hard, or is it soft?

You already learned that, unfortunately, the type of rock has little bearing on its features. Instead, rock features are determined by how the rock was formed and how much, and what type, of weathering it has undergone.

A good way to find out what type of climbing is in a given area is to consult other climbers. Many climbers travel to faraway cliffs, and you may find someone who can tell you everything you need to know about a given area. (Your longtime climbing partner may have been to the area many years back and never told you about it.) Ask every climber you meet for information.

Guidebooks are also an excellent resource - well worth the investment. They give you an overview of the area, telling you how to get there, what the common rock is, and what gear you need to bring. They also get very specific, describing all of the areas routes in detail. You can quickly find just the right climb for you.

How You Can Get Started

You may have already tried climbing a few times, but you want to become more involved. Here's how:

First purchase your own Newcomer's Kit (see page 24). You will need the gear in this kit throughout your climbing career. If you are tight for money you can begin with just a pair of rock climbing boots. Sometimes you can find a pair of used boots (that fit) for sale; check the bulletin board at your local climbing shop. I recommend that you don't buy any of your other gear used. You don't know its history; it is probably weaker than it looks. You need to be able to trust your life to your gear so it is worth paying a little extra to get this trust. Altogether a Newcomer's Kit will cost you around $200. (Some mail order companies are packaging newcomer kits for around $160. Mountain Tools and Colorado Mountain Equipment are two such companies. See page 357 for their addresses.)

The next thing to do is find a climbing partner. Hopefully you already have a friend who climbs, but if not, don't worry, end of your climbing career!

There are several ways to proceed. You can enroll in a climbing course (which might be a good idea anyway) and expect to meet your future partner there. This may or may not happen, but if you do find a partner here rest assured that he will know as little about climbing as you do. This means you will be teaching each other, which is not a bad way to go, but it does take longer to learn the basics this way.

Teaching Others

Once you have gained some climbing skills, you may want to teach your friends how to climb. This can be a lot of fun, and it can provide you with climbing partners.

However, you should be careful about how you teach someone to climb. Your goal is to interest the prospective climber in climbing, not to scare them away. Many people that I've spoken with informed me that they tried climbing once, but found it too scary. After further questioning they revealed that they felt rushed: they didn't trust the equipment enough to feel comfortable on a high cliff.

I have taught several friends to climb. I have learned from these experiences that I, the instructor, need to pay careful attention to my pupil. My goal is to show him new things, thereby keeping his interest, but to do it slowly enough that he doesn't feel overwhelmed. For example, some of my friends had a desire to climb immediately, without learning all the basics. I satisfied their needs by toproping a climb, which they climbed while I belayed. After they tried climbing for a while, they invariably wanted to learn the basics (how to belay, rappel, tie knots, etc.). Other friends where intimidated

by the rock and desired to learn the basics first. Once they learned these skills, and understood what was happening, they felt comfortable climbing.

Another thing is that not everyone wants to immediately climb tall cliffs. Some do, but most of the friends I have taught like to stay on short cliffs until they gain confidence in the gear.

The underlying principle is to respect your student. Don't try to scare or impress him; rather, respond to his needs while maintaining a safe environment.

You can advertise for a partner on the bulletin board at your climbing shop. Be sure to state your level of experience and amount of available time. Ask the salespeople as well; if nothing else they can give you some suggestions. If you find someone who is interested, find out how much experience and what equipment they have. Go to a practice area the first day you climb together so you can make sure that you want to climb with this person.

You can also join a club such as the Sierra Club. Here you can gain immediate access to experienced climbers. You will be able to make friends with these climbers and enjoy much more interesting outings than if you enroll in a climbing school. Climbing is much more fun and challenging when you are with experienced friends.

Another way to find a partner is just to go climbing alone. Drive to your local cliffs and hang out. You are bound to bump into some friendly climbers who are willing to take you up the rock. Be careful about whom you climb with though. It is hard to tell how safe and experienced a climber is until you begin climbing with him, and then it might be too late! Don't climb with anyone who seems to be more interested in their gear than in actually climbing. Someone like this may sound very knowledgeable on the ground but is often an incompetent climber.

Try and "feel your prospective leader out" through conversation. Watch him as he prepares for the climb. Does he show you how to belay and tie to the rope? Does he anchor you, the **belayer,** into the rock? If he doesn't, ask him why. If he is experienced he will appreciate your concern and give you a good answer. If his answer doesn't satisfy you, get out of there. Climbing with people you have just met is a more adventurous than other possible ways to learn climbing, but you may meet really neat people, and you are sure to learn a lot.

So now you have your Newcomer's Kit and someone to climb with. The next question is where do you climb?

The answer is naturally dependent on your geographical location and the type of cliffs available. If you don't know where to go, ask in the climbing store. Hopefully the salesperson will sell you a guidebook to your area, giving you such vital information as where the good climbs are, how to get there, and their level of difficulty.

Before you follow any routes, that is, **clean the pitch** behind your friend, who is leading, you need to know the following things: how to tie a few knots, belay, and rappel. The only way to learn these things is to practice them until they become automatic. *There is no substitute to practice!* Your friend can teach you these things: if he can't, don't climb with him!

One way to learn the basic climbing motions is to toprope climbs. This is the safest way to climb, providing your anchors are well placed! Climbers of all levels toprope rocks. It is an excellent way to develop your techniques, learn new moves, and practice without the danger of being on the lead. See below for more on toproping.

Buying Your Gear

If you have decided to try climbing, you need some climbing gear. But before you buy this gear I recommend that you send for the eight mail order catalogs on pg. 357. In these catalogs you will find a wide variety of gear, so you will have a better idea of your buying options.

I have organized your most likely gear needs according to the standard types of climbs I have been describing. For example, if you are going to toprope climbs you should buy the gear I have listed under toproping. Note: before you begin leading, read the chapter Your Rack, pg. 39, for more information on the gear you need.

Remember to make changes to this list depending on the rock and ethics of your area. If you are in an area which does not use bolts, for example, you will need to buy a larger variety of chocks (for placing in cracks).

All the items of gear listed here are thoroughly described and discussed later in this book in the sections bearing their names. See each section for details.

You will be reading many new terms on the next few pages. You will probably not be able to understand everything you read. Remember, the terms in boldface are in the glossary, and if you don't know what some of the gear is, it is all described in detail later in this book.

Note: *you must learn how to use climbing equipment properly before you climb!*

Game #1: Bouldering

You need very little gear to boulder. A pair of climbing boots, a **chalkbag,** and some chalk are standard bouldering equipment for most climbers. You also need a length of 1" flat webbing with a buckle to hold your chalkbag around your waist.

You may also want some tape (for your fingers) and a toothbrush (to clean caked chalk off the rock).

Estimated cost: $150.

Newcomer's Kit

Here are a few things that you must have to do roped climbing. This is a good kit to have when you are taking a rock climbing class or if a more experienced friend has offered to take you on a climb, but you must bring your own gear.

Things you need: one pair of rock climbing boots, a chalkbag, some chalk, a harness, a descender/belay device combination (a **figure eight,** for example), and a **large pear locking carabiner.**

Two more items are helpful for practicing knots: a five-foot length of sling, and a five-foot length of tubular webbing (called a runner).

Estimated cost: $200.

Game #2: Toproping

When you begin to toprope climbs you are entering the world of roped climbing. Besides offering tremendous climbing possibilities, handling rope requires you to learn how to set up anchors (see pg. 53). You should learn from a more experienced climber, someone whose abilities you can trust. In case you have forgotten how to get in touch with an experienced climber, I refer you back to page 23.

The security of your toprope depends upon how well you have placed your anchors. You must be sure they are **"bombproof"** - that they cannot possibly pull out. You can usually trust two good bolts (you may still want to back them up with a chock), a runner around a strong **natural anchor** (such as a big, secure tree), or three to four well-placed chocks. You can see the emphasis here is on placing multiple anchors; if one fails you must be sure there are others in place to back it up. *You must have a secure anchor!*

The equipment you need for toproping is inclusive of your Newcomer's Kit. This means I assume you already have your boots, harness, chalkbag, etc. To toprope you must also have a partner to belay you. There are ways to belay yourself, but you need to be more experienced before you learn to use those.

The following is the minimum gear you need. It will suffice if the rocks in your area already have two good bolts on top of a natural anchor (a strong tree, etc.) is handy. Buy one 165-foot, 11-millimeter climbing rope, one ten-foot and two five-foot lengths of one-inch tubular webbing (for runners), and two **oval** and four **"D"** style carabiners.

If you need chocks to place your own anchors (your area does not use bolts and there are no natural anchors), then you need to spend a bit more money. You should buy three or four **wedging chocks,** preferably in every other size offered. (You can flip them from their width to their depth to fit the sizes in-between.)

You could also purchase one or two **passive camming chocks** (**hexentrics** are the cheapest). See the chapter called passive camming chocks for details (page 233).

Estimated cost: $370-410.

Game #3: Basic Leading

You have already done some toprope climbing and you know how to set an anchor. You have **seconded** (belayed the leader and then cleaned the pitch by removing the protection) some climbs with a more experienced friend leading. Now you are ready to do some leading of your own and you need the proper gear. Here is the equipment you will need for basic **(easily protected)** lead climbs.

In addition to your Newcomer's Kit you will need: a rope; six oval carabiners; twenty "D" carabiners; one **double runner** (a ten foot length of

one inch tubular webbing, looped); eight runners (five foot lengths of one inch tubular webbing, looped - you can double loop them to serve as **quickdraws**); one set of large wedging chocks (you may want to double up - buy two of - the small sizes so you can place two small chocks close to each other for added security); four hexentrics - the larger sizes will probably be more useful to you initially but it depends upon the rock in your area; and finally, enough slings to rig all the unwired chocks you have. (Sling lengths are on page 297.)

As you continue to lead you will need to replace some of your equipment occasionally. Runners and slings usually go first. You will also need to resole your boots (I tend to have mine done every six months; I climb twice a week).

In addition, you will want to increase your supply of gear as you progress. You will begin to get an idea of what you need from your own experience and by talking with other climbers you meet. Read the next section (Advanced Leading) and buy your gear using the two principles I present there as your guideline.

Estimated cost: $380.

Game #4: Advanced Leading

By the time you are doing advanced leads you will probably already know what equipment you need. However, there are two principles you should follow. The first is to increase the depth of your protection; you must be able to place protection on many different kinds of rock. The second is to streamline your entire protection system. This means getting rid of excess weight (instead of tying your runners into loops, use **sewn runners,** which are lighter and often stronger). By following these two principles you will develop a versatile and efficient rack.

To increase the depth of your rack you need many different types and sizes of chocks. The idea is to have protection for a variety of rock and types of climbs. Once you have a versatile rack you can climb some of the larger walls which have varied routes: perhaps starting with a finger crack, going to a chimney, and ending up with a face climb.

You will need some **active camming chocks,** which are very versatile. These are spring-loaded, mechanical devices which use camming pressure to secure themselves in a crack. You can place an active camming unit very quickly, which makes them useful on hard climbs. They are also able to hold firmly where nothing else will.

Before you buy an active camming chock, you should carefully check its size range. Certain designs permit more expansion than others, while some are smaller as a complete unit so that you can fit them into pockets in the rock. You may get the widest range of sizes by buying sets from different manufacturers. (See the Active Camming Chock chapter, page 65.)

You may also want: two sets each of small and large wedging chocks; 4-5 **Tri-Cams;** at least one other rope (perhaps a small 9 millimeter rope for rappelling; or, you may want to switch to **double ropes**); and another pair of climbing boots (you may want a pair of specialty boots, geared to edging, friction, wide cracks, artificial climbing walls and training, or **thin cracks**).

The second principle, streamlining your equipment, will increase your overall efficiency. You are looking for light weight and low bulk without losing strength.

Use sewn runners instead of knotted ones. Quickdraws (small runners) are in order also; these are excellent for using between your **protection-clipping carabiners.** You should buy a couple of **load limiters** (see chapter on Slings and Runners, page 291); they are very handy on long **runouts** with dubious protection. Supplement your standard "D" carabiners with lightweight **small pears.** Half of them should have **bent gates** for quickly clipping into a rope.

You may want to start making first ascents. This means that a drill and some bolts may be in order (this depends on the climb). You will of course need **hangers** for the bolts. (Buy some extra hangers because some cliffs have bolts with no hangers. You must place your own; remember to take your hangers with you when you're done!) To speed your climbs you should buy a pair of ascenders.

Because you will be climbing harder routes you may find yourself with cuts on your fingers and hands. To stop the bleeding and cover the wound, and protect the entire finger tip, you can put some **superglue** on your fingers. You may also want to use some **Tincture of Benzoin** to harden your hands before encountering rough rock.

Remember that these are just suggestions. Your area and the type of climbing you are interested in dictate the type of gear you will buy.

Estimated cost: $500 + .

Newcomer's Aid Climbing Kit

It was only a few years ago that newcomers to rock climbing learned to aid climb before learning to free climb, if they learned the latter at all. The opposite is true now, due in part to the general increase in climbers and the damage that aid climbing does to the rock. But placing aid is an art, and it is still essential for many big wall routes, as well as some shorter ones.

The Newcomer's Aid Climbing Kit is the equipment that every aid climber must have to start with. To attempt aid climbing you and your partner, between you, must come up with the Basic Aid Climbing gear listed below.

You still need such items as a pair of climbing boots; a harness; at least one **locking carabiner;** and a belay/descending device. In addition, you need a pair of **etriers;** a **daisy chain;** two **Prusik loops** (loops of six millimeter sling which you wrap around your rope and use to ascend it); and a large gear sling to hold all of your partner's chocks and **pitons** (machined pieces of metal designed to support you when you hammer them into the rock).

If you have the money and are sure you want to aid climb, you can buy some additional items. One pair of gloves (fingerless); one pair of knee pads; one pair of hand held ascenders; a **helmet;** and a **Fifi hook** will do the trick.

Estimated cost: $225-270.

Game #5: Basic Aid Climbing

You can do some basic aid climbing (practicing the skills) with your Newcomer's Aid Climbing Kit and the Basic Leading gear. However, such a limited selection of gear will prevent you from doing all but the shortest, and easiest, aid climbs. This is because aid climbing involves placing a piece of protection every few feet. You need a lot more equipment than you would on a free climb. My selection will work well for practicing with (climbing short, easy routes to learn how it is done) and for some mixed free/aid climbing. It is also a good base from which to build a wider range of gear. Naturally, as you continue to develop your skills and increase your experience you will know what else you need to buy.

After practicing aid climbing with your basic leading rack, you may decide to become more involved in aid climbing. To do so you'll need at least 30 carabiners (half ovals, the rest "D"s). You will also need four hooks and 10 **hero loops.** You need at least 10 **Horizontal** and 10 **Angle** pitons, three sets of **copperheads,** and a **hammer** to place them. You can use chocks as aid (by placing them in the rock and using them as you would pitons). In fact, at first you may want to do this exclusively because you already have some of the gear (from basic leading). Add a set of large wedging chocks, two sets of small wedging chocks, and at least one set of active camming units.

Estimated cost: $425.

Game #6: Advanced Aid Climbing

Advanced aid climbing does not necessarily include being on a big wall. However, I am combining equipment for the two here, because most big wall routes you climb will have at least a few pitches of aid, some of it fairly advanced.

Do not jump right into advanced aid climbing! Rather, take it one climb at a time; as you increase your experience increase your equipment as well.

As you become more advanced you should increase your efficiency. You are already dealing with a lot of gear here; it takes really good equipment management to be efficient.

Take only as much gear as you will need. Although you will be hauling a lot of your gear up after you in a **haulbag,** the more weight you have the slower you will go. Cut down on bulk as well. You don't want to have so many bags to haul up the rock that you need **sherpas** to help you out! Everything should have its place in your haulbag. (See how to pack a haulbag on page 207.) This will change according to the pitch you are going to climb: you may need to use the gear you stowed on the last pitch. Be organized!

Advanced aid climbing requires a lot of equipment. You need approximately 80 carabiners; three ropes; two **pulleys;** one haulbag; a **portaledge** for every member of the party; 5 sets of copperheads (a length of wire with copper swaged on one end); and many pitons. The types of pitons you need are: 20-30 Angles, 20 Horizontals, 15 Knifeblades, 10 **RURPS,** a number of **Bongs** (for offwidth protection - the number you use depends on how much offwidth climbing there is on your route), and ten

Leeper Zs. Many routes include **dowels** or **rivets** so you need a selection of **rivet hangers.** You also need around 30 hero loops (see Slings and Runners for more information); 20 runners; and 10 hooks (two Fifi hooks, 6 sky hooks, and two seam hooks). You should have a bolt kit (includes a drill, drill holder, a selection of bolts - your discretion - and an appropriate number of hangers.) You should bring some extra hangers if the bolts on your route do not have any.

You should also bring a large selection of chocks. Take a few sets of large and small wedging chocks, active camming chocks (**three camming chocks** as well as **four-cams**), and possibly some offwidth protection if your route demands it (**Big Bros** or some other type of large chock).

Your personal gear includes a harness; a helmet; a pair of rock climbing boots; a pair of fingerless gloves; kneepads; and a **double gear sling.** Also: three etriers, three ascenders; three prusik loops (as backup for the ascenders); a **headlamp;** and a hammer. Naturally you also need a sleeping bag, food, water, cooking gear, clothes (be prepared for both hot and cold/wet weather), sunglasses, first-aid kit, duct tape (to hold everything together), superglue, athletic tape, and various bags to store everything in.

The route, your personal preferences, and the amount of money you can get together for the climb all play a role in dictating what equipment you need and can bring along. Planning an aid route is an intense exercise in organization. When you are on a big wall you need to have everything with you. It is quite a job to pop down a thousand feet, gather the gear you forgot, and jug back up to your camp!

Estimated Cost: $2000 + .

Where to Store Your Gear

You should be careful where you store you climbing gear. You don't want to damage it by placing it in a damp environment where it might rust or rot!

The best place to store climbing gear is cool, dry, dark, and clean. Such a place may be a closet, cellar, garage, or even an attic.

Final Words

As a rock climber you must know your equipment as well as you know your own body. You must be aware of its strengths and weaknesses. Your life depends on this gear. When you know it thoroughly you will be able to use it with resourcefulness and skill.

The main body of this book will teach you about your gear. You will learn its uses, strengths, and limitations. You will also learn how to care for it, repair it if need be, and determine when to retire it.

This book will give you the knowledge about your equipment that is essential to becoming a good rock climber.

But being a good rock climber takes more than knowledge about climbing equipment. You must also know how to move over rock. And the only way to learn this is to practice, practice, practice. So get out there and do it!

Where To Buy Your Gear

You can buy climbing gear from three different sources: climbing stores, mail order companies, and other climbers. In addition, climbing magazines are a good resource for locating the mail order houses (for the addresses of some climbing magazines, see pg. 359).

The Climbing Store

Climbing stores are important to rock climbers. A good store is owned and staffed by climbers, people who know the local climbing scene. You can get a lot more from a climbing store than just equipment: you can learn where the best local climbing is, what equipment you need to climb there, and any pertinent local news, such as access problems. If you are looking for a climbing partner, ask the salespeople in the store. If they don't know someone offhand they will point you to their climbing bulletin board, or maybe let you start one.

The Bulletin Board

The bulletin board is the climber's information center. Climbers use it to advertise for climbing partners and to buy and sell used gear amongst themselves. Most climbing stores have a bulletin board; if your local store doesn't, ask them to put one up. If they object, point out that they will actually increase their business by providing useful services for climbers.

Gear Selection

The selection of gear at a climbing store varies. Some stores stock only **chalk, chalkbags,** and a few token **climbing boots**. Other stores are more complete, offering boots, **harnesses, ropes, chocks,** and all the other gear you will need. The stores with complete gear selections sometimes have small **artificial climbing walls** upon which you can try out a pair of boots. They may also have a rope from which to test the store's harnesses; hanging in a harness will quickly tell you how well it fits.

Another nice thing about climbing stores is that when you need to buy gear, you can do so immediately. You don't have to wait days, or even weeks, for your purchase to arrive in the mail. The exception to this occurs when you want to buy more pieces of a particular item than the store carries in stock. This happens most frequently with **carabiners**, but occasionally with chocks, **pitons, bolts,** and **runners**. Or the store may be out of a particular size. But you won't need to wait very long, perhaps only a week if the store is professional. And, if you aren't happy with something you bought, you can take it back immediately to exchange it or receive a refund.

On the negative side, climbing stores are usually more expensive than mail order companies. A climbing store is great for buying a few items, but for collecting your entire selection of gear, consider buying through the mail. But before you decide on either one, add up the prices each offers on the gear you need. Include tax, shipping, and any relevant discounts (examples: REI has a membership discount; some mail order companies offer a 5% discount if you buy a quantity of gear). The bottom line is price versus delivery (immediate gratification is great).

This brings us to the issue of selection. Although, as I said before, some climbing stores offer a wide range of climbing equipment, mail order companies often stock equipment that you will not be able to get locally. You can find the widest equipment selection in mail order catalogs, so order as many of these as you can find. The best place to locate these mail order companies is in climbing magazines. Manufacturers, retailers, and mail order companies all advertise in the different climbing magazines. (For your convenience I have included the addresses of 8 of these companies on pg. 357.)

Climbing Magazines

Climbing magazines do more than just provide access to equipment dealers. They also keep you in touch with the activities of the general climbing community, nationally and internationally. Just as your local climbing store seeks to be the center of the climbing scene in your area, so the climbing magazines are centers of the entire climbing scene, as a whole.

Climbing magazines offer gear updates and reviews, which help you keep track of what is happening in the fast-moving equipment industry. They provide information on training, as well as on improving your climbing skills. They provide inspiration and motivation through pictures and profiles of various big-name climbers. The magazines even have sections describing new routes, from local areas to the harder climbs in the big climbing centers of the world (such as the Verdon, Mt. Arapiles, and Yosemite). Summed up, climbing magazines are an important part of the climbing community because they keep you in touch with what everyone else is doing.

Mail Order

Order as many climbing gear catalogs as you can find. This will make you a more sophisticated shopper. Instead of buying the first carabiner you see at your local climbing shop, you will have the option of carefully evaluating many different carabiners. And when you finally do decide to buy a certain carabiner, you will know that you have found the best for your needs.

After looking through your catalogs, you may find that your local climbing shop still has the best equipment. More than likely, however, the store will offer some of the gear you want, but not everything. And the only way you can get the other gear is by mail.

Mail order companies usually offer good prices. They make their sales by attracting climbers away from the local stores. But note that a particular set of chocks with a cheaper price in a catalog may not be cheaper in the end. This is due to shipping costs. And remember that it takes a few days to receive the gear (although mail order companies respond quickly, often delivering in less than a week). Also, if you decide you don't want an item you ordered, it will take some time to return it and receive a response, much longer than through your local climbing store. One last thing: many mail order companies won't accept requests for specific colors. They fill your order in their huge, factory-like stock rooms where they send out gear as fast as they can. This means that they usually give you the first piece of gear on the pile. This is only true of ropes, harnesses, **webbing**, chalkbags, and other nylon products. However, you can successfully ask the company to meet a general requirement, such as a bright color, a dark color, or a plain color.

Buying Used Gear

You can buy used climbing equipment from other climbers. Climbers put their gear on the market for a variety of reasons. Some of them give up climbing, due to an injury, lack of time, or a change in personal goals. Other climbers never really start climbing before they quit, and they end up with a lot of almost-new equipment to sell. Still others decide to re-equip themselves, and want to sell their old gear, making room for the new. Whatever the reason, used climbing equipment is always around. The trick is to find the equipment that you want, in a condition you can use.

Finding used climbing gear can be hard. Sometimes you are lucky, and meet a climber who is selling the gear you want. But usually you must simply keep an eye on the bulletin board at your local climbing store, hoping that someone will offer the equipment you need. You might consider actively seeking gear by putting a wanted request on the bulletin board and by asking every climber you meet if he knows of any gear for sale. You will find what you want sooner of later: perseverance is the key. Other places to find used climbing equipment are: in the parking lot below the cliffs (dedicated climbers are always trying to sell used gear for cash to spend on food) at a swap meet, a flea market, or in a garage sale. Keep your eyes open; you may be surprised to find some good deals in odd places.

The advantage of buying used gear is its low price. You can often find almost-new climbing equipment for half its original price, or less. And if the price is not right you can bargain. If the seller is desperate, he may go for your offer, no matter how low it is.

Buying used gear does have its problems. Besides being difficult to find, used equipment is often of poor quality. And quality is essential in climbing gear: remember, your life is at stake! Before you buy any used climbing gear, I recommend that you read the chapter in this book describing that piece of gear. Pay special attention to the section entitled Care, where I discuss the problems the gear usually develops.

Don't worry so much about gear that is not directly involved in stopping a fall. These items include: climbing boots, chalkbags, chalk, **extractors, gear slings**, gloves, **hammers**, headlamps, knee pads, **sit bags, portaledges, haulbags**, training equipment, tape, **superglue**, and **tincture of Benzoin**. Of course you should carefully inspect any gear before you buy it: if it has any cracks, rips, or other structural problems, don't buy.

More inspection is in order if you want to buy chocks, carabiners, pitons, **copperheads**, pulleys, bolts, and **hooks**. These items are all vital; their failure could lead to serious problems. If you suspect a weakness in any one of them, don't buy it! Note that **wedging chocks** and **passive camming chocks** are both made of durable, solid pieces of metal: if they don't have any obvious problems you shouldn't hesitate to buy them. However, be careful about their **slings**: unless the slings are definitely new you should replace them.

All used nylon equipment is suspect. This includes ropes, webbing, cord, harnesses, **daisy chains**, and **etriers** (although these last two are not as crucial because they shouldn't be the only gear supporting your life). Nylon weakens with age and use. It is usually difficult to determine exactly how old and worn a piece of nylon gear is. Examine all nylon equipment thoroughly. Look for abrasion, cuts, stiffness, and sun damage. With ropes, pull the entire rope through your hand, feeling for soft spots in the core. A soft spot means that the rope's core is damaged (see pg. 285). If nylon gear has any of these problems, don't buy it.

Other critical items of gear include helmets, **ascenders, descenders**, and **belay devices.** Although these items are made for strength and durability, they all perform critical life-supporting functions. For instance, if your descender breaks while you are rappelling you will have nothing but your hands to keep you from dropping to the ground far below. Unless you are somehow convinced that this gear has hardly been used, if at all, and you see no weaknesses in it, don't even consider buying it. Remember that your life depends on this equipment; is saving a few dollars worth the risk?

Buying climbing equipment is a lot of fun. It is also a very important aspect of this gear-dependent sport. Get to know the sources of your gear (the climbing manufacturers, stores, and mail order companies). Becoming familiar with these sources will broaden your possibilities; you will no longer need to buy a certain brand of carabiner simply because it is the only one you can find. There are many manufacturers making quality equipment today. Let them fight for your business by making better and better gear, and at lower prices.

Buying Strategy

My strategy for buying climbing gear involves studying a wide selection of equipment. I like to know all of my options: why should I only buy the gear in my local climbing store when there might be other, higher quality gear somewhere else, and perhaps at a better price? So first I send off for as many gear catalogs as I can find. When these arrive (it often takes a month or two) I study them carefully, comparing the gear I want and its prices until I have a solid understanding of the market. During this time I also learn as much as I can about the gear, by reading reviews (in climbing magazines) and talking with other climbers about the gear. Then I visit my 3 local climbing stores and check their gear selection and prices. Because I have already studied the market, I can immediately decide how good the deals are at the climbing store, which is especially useful during gear sales.

If I need a piece of gear to climb with tomorrow, I'll buy it at the climbing store. But I try to plan in advance, so I have the option of ordering through the mail if the prices are better.

Summed up, my overall buying strategy is to *collect information first*. With information on the gear I am seeking I have more options. I'm more likely to be satisfied by the products I buy.

How to Move Over Rock

For me, moving over rock is the most exciting aspect of climbing. It *is* climbing. Although I feel satisfied when I reach the top of a route, my real thrill is being on the rock, in the *process* of climbing. It is a sensuous experience; my entire being is dancing along, enveloped in movement.

You can't learn how to rock climb from a book. Books, such as this one, are excellent for learning about rock climbing gear: what it is and how to use it. But climbing is very different! The only way to develop your climbing skills is to get out on the rocks and do it! I feel that learning by trying, instead of by reading, is not only much more fun, but also teaches you more about your body. You are forced to pay attention to your body, to feel your arms and legs, your fingers and toes, and to develop your sense of your balance through motion.

To help you get started, I discuss the pure fundamentals of moving over rock: relaxation, breathing, footwork, short moves, rhythm, and mental attitude. I also demonstrate, in illustrations following this text, the common climbing techniques. (Note that I illustrate various crack jamming techniques in Starting Out, on pg. 5.) This information will be enough to get you started. Climb on small, low angle boulders at first. Deliberately try different movements. Combine the techniques if you want: swing your body one way, then the other; let your spontaneous creativity tell you what to do.

Basic Principles Of Moving Over Rock

Be relaxed! Relaxation is the first key to climbing well. If you are relaxed everything else will fall into place. Climbing a vertical wall can be a frightening experience, for sure, but if you can stay loose and flexible, you will climb it much more easily. If you notice that you're getting tense, take several deep breaths (as described on pg. 21), and shake your limbs, one by one, holding onto the rock with the other three. Deep breathing helps drain the tension from your body, and restore your mental balance. Shaking out your limbs will increase the blood flow to your muscles, which oxygenates and relaxes them.

Breath deeply and rhythmically not only when you are tense, but also as you climb. This is especially important if your limbs start to twitch, or do what is called the "sewing machine." Twitching means that you need more oxygen, which is where the breathing comes in. Usually your legs will twitch first; if both your legs and arms are twitching, watch out, you're probably about to fall! If you're in such dire straights, quickly find a good rest stance, a place to relax. Shake out your arms and legs, and calm yourself before you continue climbing.

When you are relaxed as you climb, your eyes will wander around, dancing over the rock. Let them! Encourage them! Wandering eyes will find previously hidden holds. For instance, you may be stuck, unable to find a way up the rock. But then your eyes pick up a rock knob jutting out just a foot away; with it you can easily continue your upward progress.

Good footwork is critical to good climbing. Use your feet, not your hands, to keep you on the rock. Your legs are much stronger than your arms. Your natural tendency will be to crush the rock between your fingers: after all, it can be scary up there at first! But remember that you're wearing special rock climbing shoes for a reason. Give them a chance to show you how well they grip the rock. When you give them your confidence, you will find yourself standing on smooth, slightly protruding rock, or even nickel-thin edges. Where you could *hang* onto such a small edge for only a few seconds, you can *stand* on the same edge for several minutes.

Make short moves. When you look for the next edge upon which to place your foot, look close by. And the same is true for your hands. Although you will probably want to reach up as high as possible, don't. Instead, look for the intermediate moves. You will climb more efficiently, and much smoother, if you make short steps.

Develop a smooth rhythm. Climb as if you were swimming: one stroke, or move, should flow into the next. Remember to use a basic law of physics that states: "a body in motion tends to stay in motion." Every time you stop moving, you must spend more energy to get started again. Of course, sometimes you will need to stop and rest. Use these rests fully: they are ideal opportunities to examine the route ahead, to figure out, in advance, how you will flow over the next section.

Mental attitude is the key to climbing. Keep everything in perspective; if you can't climb a rock today, don't dissolve into frustration. The same rock will be there for you to try tomorrow! Try to stay in a learning frame of mind: accept new information, wherever it comes from (a lizard may show you something about climbing!), and use it to improve yourself. Above all, be safe, and have fun!

Climbing a slab

Climbing vertical rock

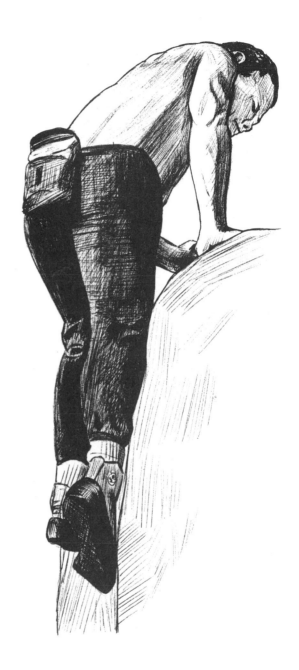

Climbing overhanging rock

Mantling

Stemming   *Liebacking*

Using an Undercling

Heel-hooking (toe-hooking is the same, but with the toes)

Your Rack

A rack

What Is A Rack?

In its broadest sense, a **rack** is all the gear that you carry with you and use to protect yourself while leading a climb. On a **free climb** this may include your **chocks, carabiners,** and **runners** (loops of **webbing**), while on an **aid climb** this might include all of the above and possibly **pitons, copperheads,** and **hooks,** among other things. Climbers also call your **gear sling,** when it is full of gear and ready for a lead, a rack.

In the chapter Starting Out (see pg. 5) I set forth some general ideas for buying equipment. These were just to show you what you could expect to buy depending on the type of climbing you were doing and the level of development you had reached.

However, developing a rack is more involved than just arbitrarily buying gear from a list, so in this chapter I will describe how you can collect a rack that is suited to your needs. If you aren't familiar with the gear I describe, remember that each piece has a chapter to itself, where I expound on it in detail.

Note that your rack has nothing to do with some other, very important pieces of equipment. It does not include your **climbing boots,** your **chalk** and **chalkbag,** your **harness,** your **rope,** and other such essentials. It includes only the equipment that you use to connect your rope to the rock when you are leading a climb, and a gear sling to hold that equipment.

Buying Your Rack

Your rack is very important to you. It is the gear that you have bought and collected, but only after considerable thought - and some expense! Your rack is your creation, a creation that you made not only in response to the rock you want to climb, but also as an extension of your ideas about how you want to climb it.

Because a rack is so personal, you are the only one who should decide exactly what you are going to include in it. You can, and should, listen to the ideas of others, but ultimately your rack is yours alone. Every climber has a different idea about what should go on a rack, but you are the one who is going to use your rack, so you had better be happy with it!

Although you will orient your rack to your preferences and values, you must first of all respond to the rock. Buy equipment that you will be able to use at the cliffs where you expect to climb! Many climbers first climb with other, more experienced climbers before they buy a rack. This allows them to try their partner's equipment, to experiment with his gear and to see what works best, and where it works. From this experience they begin to develop some ideas of their own. So try to find an experienced climber to partner with, but if you can't, don't despair: you can develop a good rack by careful observation of the rock itself and of what other climbers are using at the cliffs.

Before you buy gear for your rack, find out what the rock's general features are. These features will determine what equipment you need. First of all, are there many **face climbs** (cliffs without cracks)? Climbers must usually place **bolts** to **protect** a face climb, and if your local cliffs are mostly bolt-protected, you will find it easy to prepare a rack. All you need are several **quickdraws** with which to attach these bolts to your rope. A quickdraw is a runner that has a carabiner on either end.

A quickdraw

Here is a synopsis of the basic crack shapes, and the type of chock that will hold in them. Note that the first two cracks, vertical and horizontal, are

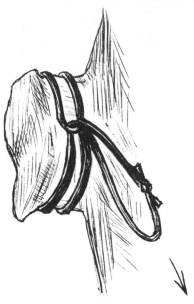

A runner looped over a chickenhead

Some face climbs have protruding rock knobs called **chickenheads**. You can connect your rope to a chickenhead, and in so doing protect your climb, by looping a runner around the rock, as illustrated above right.

Most rocks have faces that are split by cracks. If the rock in your area is like this, you need to buy some chocks in addition to carabiners and runners. Chocks take the place of bolts. They are devices that you place into a crack and then connect to your rope. If you fall your chocks are designed to safely stop you.

Different types of chocks hold in different shapes of cracks. There are 3 basic types of chocks, each having its own chapter in this book. These types are: **wedging** (pg. 325), **passive camming** (pg. 233), and **active camming** (pg. 65). For you to buy the right type of chock, you need to find out what kind of cracks are in your area, and what size they are. Once you know this, read each chapter on chocks (first see wedging, pg. 325, then passive camming, pg. 233, and finally active camming, pg. 65).

general types, and have any of the shapes that follow.

Vertical Cracks
Vertical cracks split the rock from the ground up. Vertical cracks can be of many shapes, some being easy to protect, others not. The chock that you use to protect a vertical crack depends on the crack's shape.

Horizontal Cracks
Horizontal cracks split the rock horizontally, parallel to the horizon. Like vertical cracks, horizontals can be of many shapes. However, horizontal cracks are usually harder to protect, often requiring either passive or active cams, or two wedges rigged in opposition (see pg. 329).

Irregular Cracks
Irregular cracks are very common. These deep cracks have uneven sides that continually widen and then narrow. Irregular cracks are the easiest to protect. You can use all types of chocks in them, in-

cluding wedging, passive, and active camming chocks.

Note: I list wedging chocks only under irregular cracks, because these are the cracks they are designed to fit. Don't let this give you the illusion that wedging chocks aren't useful: on the contrary. Irregular cracks make up most of the worlds cracks, and so wedging chocks are extremely useful, a must for any crack climber's rack.

An irregular crack

Parallel Cracks

Parallel cracks have parallel sides. They are harder to protect because they have no rock protrusions that will easily hold a chock. Wedging chocks are useless in a parallel crack; passive cams sometimes work; active cams work well.

Flaring Cracks

The sides of a flaring crack expand either outward or downward, and sometimes both. Flaring cracks are even harder to protect than parallel cracks. Wedging chocks are useless, Tri-cams (a type of passive cam) sometimes work, and active cams usually work.

Piton Scars

Piton scars are cracks that have been radically altered by climbers hammering in and removing pitons over many years. Piton scars come in different shapes, depending on the type of pitons used and how much the crack has been enlarged. Usually piton scars are shallow, flaring cracks of up to 4 inches long, so they have an abrupt beginning and end.

A piton scar

Piton scars are difficult to protect because they are often too shallow for an active cam, and wedging chocks won't hold on their flaring sides. You can sometimes use a small wedging chock, a Tri-cam, an active wedging chock, or a narrow-headed active cam (such as a 3-cam) in some piton scars.

Note that sometimes rock naturally forms into cracks that are similar to piton scars. These cracks are called slots.

Grooves

Grooves are shallow cracks, often flaring. They are different from piton scars because they extend many feet. Grooves are hard to protect. Like piton scars, protecting a groove requires the use of a chock that fits the crack's shallow shape. Such chocks include: active wedges, narrow active cams (3-cams), and sometimes small Tri-cams.

Pockets

Pockets are small holes in the rock. Although not cracks, pockets can sometimes be protected by wedging chocks (see pg. 325).

A Crack's Size

All the crack shapes that I just described appear in different sizes; just which sizes determine whether or not you can place a certain chock in the crack. So the next thing you must consider is the size range of the chocks you buy.

If there are mostly thin cracks in your climbing area, buy small chocks that will fit these cracks. Most cliffs have a variety of crack sizes, as do many **routes,** so you should buy a range of chocks that will fit a wide variety of cracks.

But before you buy any gear, you have one more thing to consider. Which chocks will uphold your values, the way you like to climb, and still be effective on the rock? For example, you may decide that you want to rely as much as you can on simple, inexpensive chocks for protection. This is to support your idea that a good climber is someone who is able to work with the rock, who is able to protect himself from falling with simple tools that require careful attention to the rock's features. Or you may decide that you want to lead really hard climbs as soon as possible, and that to do so you need many active cams, which are quick and easy to place. These are just two simple examples; most climbers create a complex rack, one that is oriented to the area they climb in, to their values, and to providing protection in a wide range of situations.

A Sample Rack

Evelyn is a gung-ho climber. She has been climbing several years, and likes to try any moderate route, from a bolted face climb to a wide range of cracks. She lives around granite, which offers the variety of climbing that she seeks.

Evelyn originally bought the equipment for basic leading (see pg. 49). But she has since developed her own preferences and ideas for what gear should be a part of her rack. These tastes have been thoroughly influenced by her climbing environment: by the rock she climbs, the people she climbs with, and her own beliefs.

Her rack includes 10 oval and 20 "D" carabiners. She uses the ovals for holding her chocks on her rack and rigging anchors, and the "D"s for clipping to protection. She has 10 single runners (made of 1-inch tubular webbing), 2 double runners, and has recently bought 4 6-inch sewn slings (for quickdraws).

Evelyn originally bought herself a set of large wedging chocks. She has since added to this by doubling-up on the smaller sizes (buying two each of the smaller chocks), and by buying several of the larger small wedging chocks (she has a special weakness for thin cracks). To deal with the parallel and flaring cracks that are common in granite, she has Tri-Cams #1, 2, 3, and, for the off-fist crack, a #7. She also has the larger Hexentrics (#7-10), which she finds helpful for hand and fist cracks. She doesn't need the small hexes, because she owns a #3/8 Alien. For the occasional larger flaring crack she has #2.5 and #3.5 Friends.

Evelyn finds that this rack fits her needs, and the rock, well. It is lightweight and yet offers enough size range and versatility to let her easily protect the climbs she attempts. It is certainly not an all-encompassing rack, but, at approximately $450, it is inexpensive, especially considering that she doesn't need to add to the rack (unless, of course, she decides to attempt harder routes that demand more specific gear, such as cracks which require several #2.5 Friends).

Organizing Your Rack For A Climb

I am going to assume that you now have a rack. Whether this rack is your partner's, your brand new creation, or just some odd chocks and carabiners that you put over your shoulder, it doesn't matter. The point is, you have a rack and you are ready to lead a climb.

What parts of your rack do you bring on this particular climb? Maybe you need the entire thing, but maybe you will only use a few of the chocks and carabiners, in which case you would waste your energy carrying your entire rack up the cliff.

So what do you bring along? Observation is the key to answering this important question. You start by looking carefully at the route you are going to climb, and deciding exactly where you are going to place your chocks. Count how many bolts are on the route, if any, and prepare a quickdraw for each. If the climb follows a crack, try to see exactly where you are going to place each chock. Count the total, and make sure you bring slightly more than enough (you will need extra chocks of different sizes in case some don't fit the crack). Remember to bring 3 or 4 chocks and a few extra carabiners and runners for your anchor.

Sometimes you won't be able to see an entire climb from the ground. This will prevent you from making an exact count of the bolts and potential chock placements. You can still get a rough estimate of these points of protection by guessing how high the climb is. Most climbers place their protection approximately every 15 feet, although you can of course increase or decrease this distance as you see fit. So if you think the climb is 80 feet high, you will know that you need carabiners and runners for possibly 5-7 bolts, or chock placements, and an appropriate number of chocks. And you need enough carabiners, runners, and chocks to set up an anchor when you get to the top.

Note: *it is better to bring too much gear up a cliff than not enough!* Don't feel embarrassed because you are carrying a huge pile of chocks up a cliff, when some other climber just climbed the same route with only 5-6 chocks. Bring as much equipment as you feel comfortable with. When you are beginning to lead you won't be able to know, from looking, exactly what chocks you need on a climb. And you don't want to get near the top of the rock and find yourself out of gear!

As you become more experienced you will learn to bring just enough gear for the climb, but not too much. This is a fine line: too much gear weighs you down and saps your strength, while too little gear leaves you unprotected. Your ability to determine how much gear to bring will improve naturally, as your confidence and your climbing skill increases. Be patient and forgiving with yourself.

Racking Your Gear

After determining the kind of protection, and how much of it you need, you are ready to start racking your gear, that is, putting equipment onto your gear sling (the bandolier-like loop with which you carry your gear, see pg. 185).

The first step is to decide whether you want to use a gear sling at all. You may not if you don't need to bring much equipment, and you have a harness with **racking loops**. You can attach your gear to these loops, which will keep it available yet out of your way.

Many climbers don't like using their harness to carry their gear. Others carry their chocks on their gear sling and their quickdraws and free carabiners on their harness. You may want to alternate between these two methods, depending on the climb. Experiment to determine what you like best.

At the base of the cliff, separate the gear you are bringing on the climb from the gear you are leaving behind. You may want to do this by making several piles, or you might just put the appropriate gear directly onto your gear sling, in the order that you want it. Putting your chocks on the gear sling is easiest if you hang the sling from something: for example, your neck, a tree branch, or a hook.

The order in which you connect your gear to the gear sling is important. You need to put your rack together in such a way that you can quickly and easily identify each piece of gear and remove it from your gear sling. Establish a system of organization that you can use every time: this way you will know where each piece of gear is even before you look for it, which is very handy, as it saves you from inefficient fumbling.

There are some useful basics to learn for organizing your gear onto your sling. Keep the heavy equipment behind the lighter stuff. The heavy equipment will push the lighter gear forward, because it wants to sit at the lowest point in your gear sling, which is the middle. This means that you should put small wedges first, then large wedges (both are types of wedging chocks), then small hexes, large hexes, then small to large Tri-cams (all of which are passive cams), and finally small, then large active cams. You should also put your wired chocks in front of the heavier, bulkier cord-slung chocks. But still keep the types of chocks together (for example, put the wired wedges before those with cord, which are themselves in front of the wired hexes).

Next, consider how you want to attach your holding carabiners. Holding carabiners are those that you use to hold your chocks to your gear sling. The answer to this arrangement depends on two things: whether or not you can determine what chock you need by looking at the crack, and how you like to group your chocks.

Many climbers who are experienced at placing chocks are able to glance at a crack and know exactly which chock will fit it. This is an important skill because it allows the climber to place a chock quickly, which saves both his time and his energy. However, until you are experienced at using your chocks you will have to fumble through the chocks on your rack before finding one that fits a particular crack. If you are at the "fumbling stage" of your climbing development you will want to rack your gear differently than if you can immediately spot the correct chock for a crack.

If you can't find the correct chock immediately, you will need to try several of them until you get the right one. Therefore you should separate your chocks into groups of 3 or 4, according to type and size. For example, keep several small wedges on one carabiner, a few medium ones on another, and 2 or 3 large ones on a third. Then start over again, using the same method of grouping, with your passive cams, if they are your next largest and heaviest chock (remember, the heavy ones to the rear). The key is to clip the carabiners that are holding these chocks (your holding carabiners) to your gear sling with their gates opening up and in (toward your body).

This rig allows you to estimate a crack, take off a group of chocks, try them until you find one that fits, place it in the crack, and then remove the carabiner and other chocks, which you clip back in its place on your gear sling.

If you can glance at a crack and know immediately what chock will fit it, then you have two basic options. You can group your carabiners, as before, or you can carry each chock on its own carabiner. If you decide to group your chocks, position your holding carabiner so that its gate opens down and out (away from your body).

Grouped chocks on a carabiner that opens up and in: the ideal rig if you need to try different chocks to find the one that fits

Group chocks on a carabiner opening down and out: this rig works if you can quickly spot which chock to use

Positioning your holding carabiners down and out allows you to quickly remove the chock you need, leaving the carabiner, and the other chocks, hanging from your gear sling.

Carrying each chock individually lets you use any one of them without having to first fumble with the other chocks, trying to get them out of the way so you can open the carabiner's gate. Position your carabiner with its gate opening up and in, so that you can easily remove it from your gear sling.

Carrying your chocks individually emphasizes a problem: it limits the number you can comfortably carry on a climb. If you bring a lot of chocks (more than 10) your carabiners will spread themselves out along your gear sling, making a bulky and un-wieldy load. But if you don't bring very many chocks, you may not have the one you need to fit a placement!

Usually you will find it best to carry your chocks individually only on short climbs in which you won't need many chocks, and are certain about the sizes you need. You may want to carry a couple of active cams individually, because they have a good size range, and the rest of your chocks grouped.

If you carry your chocks individually, you won't need to bring many free carabiners, just 4 or 5. But you will need more free carabiners if you group your chocks, because the carabiners provide a con-nection between your chock (once you've placed it) your runner, and your rope.

Take along enough carabiners to rig your ex-pected number of placements. For instance, if you are going to climb an 80-foot crack, and you want to place 7 chocks, then you need 14 carabiners, two for each chock (with a runner in-between). Bring along 4-5 extras for establishing an anchor at the top of the pitch. No matter how many free carabin-ers you bring, carry them in chains of 3-4, positioned in front of your chocks.

If you are climbing a bolted route you will want some quickdraws. If they are over 6 inches long the best way to carry them is to clip one of the carabin-ers to your gear sling (with its gate positioned up and in), and the other carabiner to the first, as illus-trated above.

Rigging your quickdraws in this way saves your energy: it is harder to unclip two carabiners from your gear sling than just the one. And, unless it is a short quickdraw (4-6 inches) the second carabiner will hang around your legs, getting in the way of

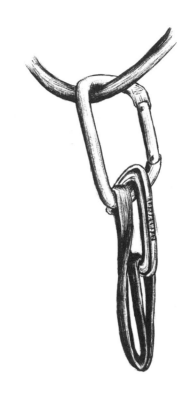

A quickdraw attached to a gear sling

your climbing, so you must clip it up, out of the way. Once you have attached the carabiner to your protection you can either unclip the second carabiner and attach it to your rope, or, if you are getting tired, you can clip your rope directly to this second carabiner.

Sometimes you will want to pre-clip a quickdraw to your rope. This means that you attach one of the quickdraw's carabiners to your rope before you begin to climb, leaving the other carabiner con-nected to your gear sling.

This rig allows you to quickly clip your rope to a bolt or chock, without wasting much time or energy. Using this rig is helpful when you must make a hard move, where you need all your energy for climbing, or when the first bolt of a climb is high off the ground and you want to connect your-self to it quickly.

Carry small runners (the ones that you cannot fit over your head and one shoulder) either pre-at-tached to carabiners, as I just described, or tied with a **Girth Hitch** (see pg. 46) onto your gear sling.

A short runner tied to a gear sling with a Girth Hitch

Larger runners you can carry as bandoliers. Put these runners on after you have put your rack on, or you won't be able to take them off! These runners should be tight enough that they won't slide off your shoulder. If they are too large, see if you can double them and still put them on. If this isn't possible you will have to accept the fact that they may slip off your shoulder as you climb. This is irritating because such large runners can impede your movement.

Another important item to carry on your rack is a **belay/rappel device.** You might have two separate devices, one for each purpose, or one unit that does both. Whichever you have, you need to carry it up the cliff so you can **belay** your partner up after you and still be able to **rappel** down, if that becomes necessary.

You should also consider carrying two loops of **accessory cord,** tied with a Girth Hitch to either your harness or your gear sling. These loops are for use as **Prusik knots** (see pg. 76). It is possible for you to fall into a place from which either your partner must haul you up or you must prusik up the rope. Your loops of accessory cord will help you out of these situations.

Wearing Your Rack

Now you are ready to put your gear sling on. You can wear it over either shoulder, but you may want to position it so that the hand you use most frequently is the one that removes your equipment from the sling. For example, if you are right-handed, sling your gear under your left arm. Remember that some climbs will dictate which way you must sling your gear. This is especially true on **liebacks,** where the rock gets in the way of your gear.

Aid Climbing Racks

Racking your gear for an aid climb is different than doing so for a free climb. While aid climbing you do use chocks, but you often must also use pitons, copperheads, bolts, **rivet hangers,** and hooks. Because aid climbers travel along routes that are impossible to climb free, the cracks are much, much smaller and the faces are entirely sheer. If they weren't, it wouldn't be an aid climb. So, to make progress you must use your gear to build a ladder up the cliff. And the rungs of this ladder must be close enough for you to step from one to the other.

The result is that an aid climber's rack is very large, much larger than a free climber's rack. To carry this massive amount of gear you will need a large gear sling, such as the **tiered gear sling.** A tiered gear sling has two sets of slings, one set on each side of your body. Each set itself consists of two slings. This arrangement gives you four places to hang your equipment.

The tiered gear sling's design not only allows you to carry a lot of gear, it also balances the gear spread around your body. This is very important when you are carrying so much weight. To further distribute the weight, intersperse your chains of free carabiners throughout the tiers of your rack. Put the free carabiners on the rack last; use them to adjust the rack's weight until you are balanced.

Organizing your aid climbing rack is similar to organizing a free climbing one. Put the lightest pieces of equipment in front, and the wired gear before those that are slung with cord. Because you will be carrying so many pitons you should group them onto holding carabiners. Position the holding carabiners so that their gates open down and out; you need to be able to sort and remove the correct piton quickly and easily.

How many pitons you can carry per carabiner depends on the types of piton you choose: each type has a different size and shape. You can usually put either 2-3 normal **Angles**, 3-4 small Angles, 5-6 **Knifeblades**, 4-5 **Lost Arrows**, 1-3 **Leeper Z** pitons, lots of **RURPs**, or 1-2 **Bongs** (depending on how large they are), on each carabiner. Be sure to reverse your Horizontals and Angles when you place them on the carabiner. This allows them to sit as close to the other pitons as possible.

Pitons reversed on a biner so they fit better

Because your copperheads are so light, you should carry them in the front of your rack, up by your rivet hangers (wire loops which you place over **rivets** - see pg. 101). Group 4 or 5 of them on each holding carabiner, with the carabiner opening either down and out or up and in - your preference (as with chocks, which way you position the carabiner depends on whether or not you can spot the right copperhead immediately). Carry your hooks (see pg. 227) wherever it is convenient for you, preferably in a location you can reach without too much fumbling.

Racking For Multi-Pitch Routes

A **multi-pitch route** is a long climb, one that contains many pitches. Climbing a multi-pitch route is much more complex than climbing a shorter rock, partly because it requires the climber's serious commitment. When you are a few hundred feet up a cliff you can't just have your belayer lower you down so you can rest! You must continue the climb until the top, or make a series of rappels to get back down. Climbing a multi-pitch route requires at least a thorough knowledge of basic climbing skills: you should also have some climbing experience before you embark on such a route.

You will find that it is also harder to decide what equipment to bring on a multi-pitch climb. You can't see the higher sections of the route, so there is no way to guarantee that you have all the gear you need. However, you can get a good idea by looking at the route description in a guide book and by talking with climbers who have completed the route. But as a general rule, multi-pitch climbs require a large rack: you must prepare for a variety of rock features.

Cleaning the Pitch

When a climber leads a route, someone, usually his partner, climbs up after him and retrieves all the gear that he placed. This is called **cleaning the pitch,** and is a very important job (see also pg. 51). The climber who is cleaning the pitch has the responsibility of retrieving all the gear without dropping it (it would be expensive to leave some behind!), and putting it on his gear sling in an organized, orderly fashion. Keeping the gear organized is important, because it saves time: having to reorganize your rack after every pitch of climbing is very slow and tedious!

Important: when you clean a chock, remove it (or, if it's a bolt, unclip the carabiner) and re-attach it to your gear sling *before* you unclip the second carabiner from your rope. This way, even if you drop the second carabiner, the entire rig (chock and quickdraw) will remain attached to your rope. There is nothing worse than watching a quickdraw and your (or your partner's) favorite chock go bouncing down the cliff in the middle of a climb!

Leading

A climber leading a route

For most climbers, leading is the most exciting and challenging aspect of rock climbing. Leading a climb is being the first climber from your group up the rock. You, the **leader,** are the one who places the **protection,** who makes the decisions about how to accomplish the climb. It is up to you to forge ahead, not only to overcome any obstacles but also to establish a net of protection that will keep your partner safe.

The leader is on the **sharp end** of the **rope.** The "sharp end" is the term climbers use to describe the danger of leading. For if you slip and fall, you will plummet until your rope catches you, and this often means at least a 10-foot fall! The reason for this is that when you lead a climb, you place a piece of protection, connect your rope to it, and then climb past the protection, above and beyond it. And if you fall, you will drop twice as far as the distance you had climbed above your **anchor,** and a little more besides (due to rope stretch). Although your equipment will stop your fall (if you used it correctly!), you might still be in danger of landing on a rock ledge and injuring yourself before your rope can catch you. Of course, if you protect the climb properly you will have protected yourself against this possibility. But sometimes good protection is impossible, whether because there is nowhere to put your chocks or because you didn't bring the right equipment (a mental error!). This potential danger is what makes leading so fascinating: you are climbing the line between safety and danger, and your success rests entirely on you alone! But when you succeed, when you reach the top of a climb, in that instant nothing else can compare!

However, before you can successfully begin leading, you should have a good understanding of how to place protection, how to **belay,** how to **rappel,** how to rig an anchor, and, of course, how to climb.

All of these skills are involved; they may take you many years to learn thoroughly. But you can start leading on easy climbs as soon as you know the basics of each. Then the more leading you do, the more your skills will improve.

Because this book is about rock climbing equipment, I discuss the various techniques involved in leading under the appropriate gear chapters. You will find the basics of Moving Over Rock in the chapter of the same name, on pg. 33. I cover mental and physical preparation in Starting Out (pg. 5), as well as route information. I discuss rappelling in **Descenders,** pn pg. 157, and belaying in **Belay Devices,** on pg. 87. I cover the basics of rope management in Ropes, pg. 269. There are three different types of chocks, **Active Camming, Passive Camming,** and **Wedging,** and I discuss placing each in their respective chapters on pgs.

65, 233, and 325. I discuss **aid climbing** techniques in the chapters **Etriers** (pg. 173), **Daisy Chains** (pg. 153), **Ascenders** (see pg. 75), **Pitons** (pg. 241), **Copperheads** (pg. 147), and **Pulleys** (see pg. 259).

In this chapter I discuss the actual sequence of leading, for both **free** and aid climbing, and the way a leader and a **belayer** communicate. In addition, I describe the principles of and some specifics about how to rig an anchor.

The Sequence of Free Climbing

The sequence for free climbing is simple. With a two-man team, it goes like this:

Your belayer anchors himself while you, the leader, get ready to climb (by studying the **route** and figuring out what you need on your **rack**). Both of you tie the rope to your **harness,** with a **Figure-Eight knot** (see pg. 200).

When you're ready, you say to your partner "on belay?" If he's ready, he will reply "belay on." This means that he's in position and ready to catch you if you fall, *from that point on.*

You, now that you're confident that your belayer is ready, say "climbing." To recognize this statement, your partner replies "climb on." Now both of you know that the one is climbing, the other belaying, and that you both know what is going on, which is vitally important!

You begin to climb, and your belayer pays out rope as necessary. Important: as a belayer, don't hinder the leader by not letting enough rope out, but at the same time don't let too much rope out, or the leader will fall farther than necessary. Pay attention to the leader, and help him as best you can by allowing him to forget the rope is even there, until he needs it.

As you climb you connect your rope to pieces of protection for security. It's a good idea to position your protection close together at the beginning of the **pitch,** and then spread it out as you put more rope between you and your belayer (which reduces the **fall factor,** see pg. 270). Note if you're the belayer: the leader will need some slack in order to clip the rope to a piece of protection. You should be ready for this, and pay out the slack quickly so the leader spends little energy pulling up the rope.

Protection: The Basic Concept

Your protection system is your safety net. When you lead a climb, you bring it with you, and build it as you go. There are several links in this system, and each is very important, because if one fails the entire system may collapse. The links include an anchor tied to your belayer (two links), who holds your rope (another link), which is attached to you, via a harness and a knot (three links - your body is a link because it also absorbs some of a fall's force).

Another series of links, just as vital, are those that connect you, through your rope, to the rock. The first in the series is the piece of protection, which is something such as a **bolt, piton,** or chock that is anchored in the rock. To this you connect the next link, a **carabiner.** You cannot connect your rope directly to this carabiner, because the movement of the rope (caused by you climbing) would jerk the carabiner so much that its gate might open and the rope escape. Or the rope might leverage the piece of protection out of the crack (if the piece was a chock or lightly-placed piton). To solve this problem, and to keep your rope running straight, you connect a **runner,** with another carabiner on its end, to the first carabiner. You can clip your rope to this second carabiner.

When you, the leader, reach the top of the pitch, you set up an anchor (see pg. 53). When you are securely connected to this anchor, *and not before,* shout down "off belay!" In response, your belayer yells "belay off!", but only *after* disengaging the rope from his belay device. Now both of you know that you are no longer on belay.

At this point you switch roles with your partner. You become the belayer, and he becomes the climber. You pull up the slack in the rope, and ready yourself to belay (by clipping into your belay device, and getting into a comfortable stance). Your partner gets ready to climb by putting on his shoes, chalking up, stretching, or whatever it takes. When he's ready he asks you "belay on?" If you're ready, you reply with a positive "belay on!" Your partner then yells "climbing!" and you return with "climb on!" Now your partner can begin to climb up to you, and to remove the chocks you placed as he comes to them.

Important: when you are belaying a climber from

above, make sure you're connection to your anchors is tight. If there is any slack in the connection, and your partner falls, you will be pulled from your stance!

A piece of protection, with carabiners and runner, connected to a rope.

When your partner reaches the **belay station,** he connects to the anchors. Secured, he says "off belay" and you reply "belay off." Now both of you either prepare for the next pitch, or, if you are at the top of the rock, disconnect the anchors and walk down the back of the rock to the ground (although sometimes the only way to return to the ground is to rappel from this last belay station).

There are three other signals that the person climbing can use when addressing you, the belayer. The first is "slack," which means pay out some rope, give me some slack! If there is too much slack, the climber will shout "rope," which means take in some rope. And if the climber yells "tension!" take in as much rope as you can and get ready to hold a falling climber!

You can also climb with 3 or more climbers, although progress is naturally slower. The steps are basically the same, although you'll find it easiest to use 2 ropes. Tie the leader and his belayer together with the first rope. Then connect this belayer, who

will be the second climber, and *his* belayer (the third climber) together with the second rope. This way you avoid having to lower a rope for each climber, which is good because a rope might snag on the rock.

If the route is straight, and up to, but no more than, vertical, then the second climber up can **clean the pitch** (remove the protection). The third climber is not climbing without protection since he is anchored from above by the leader. But if the route traverses, or overhangs, the last climber up *must* be the one to clean the pitch (the second climber "clips through" the protection, that is, he unclips a chock from the rope he is being belayed with - from above - and then clips it to the rope hanging below so that the third climber can remove the chock. If the second climber removed the protection, and the next climber fell, this climber would swing way off route, either to the side or out into space! Returning to the route could be very difficult and, even worse, time consuming. Remember, speed is important, especially on the taller cliffs. Summed up: when 3 people climb a vertical route, the least experienced climber goes third - he is protected by a **toprope** and doesn't need to waste energy removing the protection. On an overhanging or traversing route he goes second and the last climber up cleans the pitch.

The Sequence of Aid Climbing

The sequence in aid climbing is different from that in free climbing. This is because leading an aid pitch takes much longer than leading a free pitch. Consequently, to speed the process, the second climber up will clean the pitch while ascending the rope with ascenders **(jumaring)**; this is much faster than if he were to climb the pitch (note however that cleaning an aid pitch while climbing it will teach you a lot about aid - if you are on a small practice aid climb, I recommend you do this to gain experience). In addition, you may also have a **haulbag,** in which case you will need to set up a hauling system (see below).

When you aid climb you use the same basic signals as if you were free climbing. All the shouts of "on belay," "climbing," "tension," etc. apply equally to aid climbing. So I won't go through that again. Instead, assume that this is going on while I take you through the basic sequence of aid climbing.

Your belayer is anchored, has you on belay, and you begin climbing. (Note: if you have a bag to haul, you need to bring the haul line up with you; tie it to the back of your **swami belt.**)

You place your aid as you go, and eventually you reach the top of the pitch.

You set up your anchors and clip yourself to them. Then you securely tie the rope (the one connected to your partner) to the anchors. Finally, you set up a hauling system.

When you are ready to haul, you shout down to your partner exactly that: "ready to haul!" He will release the haulbag from its anchors, and make sure that it doesn't snag on the rock as you begin to haul.

While you are busy hauling, your partner will be ascending the climbing rope, and cleaning the pitch.

When you have hauled the bag up to your perch, connect it to some secure anchors. Your partner should follow soon after, and when he reaches you, he should connect himself to the anchors as well.

Now the two of you can consolidate the gear you need for the next pitch, and one or the other can begin leading.

If you have a three, or more, member team, you will need three ropes. Lead with one, and trail the other two (from your swami belt). When you reach the belay ledge, tie off all three so that the haul line is set up for hauling, the climbing rope is ready for one of your partners to ascend (with an ascender) and clean the pitch, and the third rope is secured and hangs free. Your third partner ascends up this rope quickly and begin to lead the next pitch while your second partner is still cleaning the previous one. (This requires more equipment, however, as you can't use the gear that is still being cleaned down below!)

The Sequence of Climbing Solo, But Roped

You can free climb and aid climb alone. However, this is an advanced skill, and you should be an experienced climber before you try it.

Roped solo climbing is not too different from climbing with a partner. Obviously, the big difference is the absence of the belayer! In addition, you must use two ropes. But you can rig an effective self-belay, by tying one rope to anchors at the beginning of the pitch, and running it through a specialized ascender (called a **self-belay device**) connected to your harness (for more detail on this ascender, see pg. 82).

The sequence is basic. Rig your anchor, which must be secure, tie your rope to the anchor and through your self-belay device, tie the additional rope to your swami belt, and proceed up the cliff.

Place protection or aid as you climb, clipping your anchored rope in (if you're free climbing use extra protection since your ascender can't stop as long a fall as a belayer could; in case you fall your self-belay rig won't have to absorb so much force).

When you reach the belay ledge, rig a secure anchor, tie both ropes securely to it, and use the free hanging rope to rappel down to your previous anchor.

Connect your ascenders to the climbing rope (the one going through the pieces of protection), so you won't fall. Clean the anchor, begin ascending (on your ascenders) the climbing rope, and clean the pitch as you ascend.

When you're at the belay station, pull up your rappel rope and begin this process again, up the next pitch.

Hauling a bag up after you involves an extra step, but is not too complex. The only difference is that, after you rappel back down to the previous belay ledge, you tie the haulbag to the rappel rope, which becomes the haul line. When it is securely connected, free the haulbag from the anchors. Then, clean the pitch as usual. When you reach your new anchors, haul the bag up to the ledge.

If the pitch traverses or overhangs, things are a little more complicated. Going up is no problem, but getting back down to the previous belay ledge is difficult. If the pitch is long, you must trail two ropes, tied to each other; if the pitch is short, one long (165-foot) rope will do. The idea is to rappel down the rope, end up below the belay ledge, and then ascend up and over to the ledge. If you have a haulbag you need to be careful not to snag it on the rock as you lower it away from the anchor, into position directly below the next belay ledge.

Communication

I cannot over-stress the importance of clear communication between climber and belayer! As I have said, both of you must know exactly what is going on, what your job is, and what the other's job is. If you begin climbing when your belayer is not belaying you, you are *unprotected*!

The signals that I previously described are the only ones you need to know. They are standard among rock climbers everywhere (of course, they aren't always in English!). However, there are times when for some reason your partner won't be able to hear you, even when you shout with everything you've got (note that the farthest-carrying sound you can make is "BO"). Perhaps the wind rips every word from your lips, or maybe you are beneath a large overhang and your partner is high above, effectively out of hearing. Regardless of the reason, the result is that the two of you cannot communicate verbally. The best way to deal with such a situation is to plan a solution out in advance, and to stick with this plan. Some climbers communicate through tugs; for example, two tugs from the leader means "off belay," while a replay of two tugs from the belayer means "belay off." However, the problem with this method of communication is that one of the climbers may have to tug the rope to free it from the rock. And since the other doesn't know what is really going on, he responds by replying to the imaginary signal. Obviously, this is not a good solution!

One more effective, but slower, method of communicating with your partner is to belay him until he begins a steady pull on the rope. This means that he has reached his belay ledge, has anchored in, and is on belay. Only now can you disengage your belay, clean your anchor, and begin climbing. Although this is a slow method, it is also safe, providing both of you stick to the plan.

Rigging Anchors

When you lead a climb, you connect your rope to various pieces of protection as you proceed upward. These pieces of protection will stop you if you fall (providing you rigged them correctly). So obviously they are vital to your security! However, even more vital than these individual pieces is the anchor you tie into when you reach the top of the climb. The reason for this? As your partner cleans the pitch, he removes each piece of pro, which diminishes the connection between the two of you and the rock. And when he climbs onto the belay ledge, your anchor is the only thing keeping both of you safe. If one of you falls from the belay ledge,

or the surrounding cliff (which might happen when you begin leading the next pitch, before you are able to put in another piece of pro), the anchor must be strong enough to hold the force of your fall, or both of you will plummet to the ground! Clearly, when you do any roped climbing you must make it your first priority to establish a secure anchor!

An anchor consists of several distinct parts, or links. First there is the initial connection to the rock, the piece of pro. This can be many things, perhaps a loop of **webbing** around a tree, a bolt, or maybe a chock. Usually you will use more than one piece of pro to increase your anchor's security. The next link is a carabiner connected to each piece of pro. Then to each carabiner you clip a length of webbing, or perhaps some of your rope (if you don't have enough webbing), which forms the next link. The final link consists of two carabiners with their **gates opposed,** or a **locking carabiner,** with which you secure your rope to the webbing.

An anchor

As I said, you can use many different pieces of protection to establish your connection to the rock. A tall, strong tree or a large, secure boulder may provide excellent security. (If you have any doubts about this, back up the tree or boulder with *at least* one additional piece of protection!) However, trees and solid boulders are often scarce on a bare cliff, so you will usually find yourself rigging various configurations of bolts, pitons, and chocks into a solid anchor. None of these three types of protection are as strong as a good tree or boulder, so you should *always* combine several different pieces together!

As a general rule, two good bolts are secure. One good bolt, a bad bolt, and a good chock (to back up the bad bolt) are also secure. Two solid, well-placed pitons are good, but it is usually hard to determine how well-placed a piton is. Consequently, always back up such an anchor with a chock or two. If you are using just chocks, then you need *at least* three of them, each well-placed. And, if you use chocks on a multi-pitch route, you will need to position them so they will hold both a downward

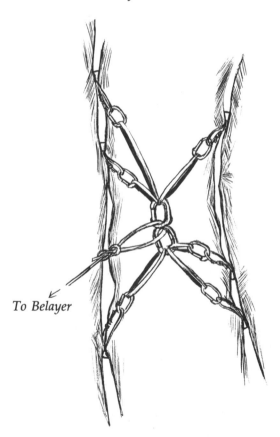

A multi-directional anchor made of chocks

pull and an upward pull (this lets you use the anchor to belay your partner while he leads the next pitch). Such an anchor is known as **multi-directional.**

To save time, rig the chocks this way from the beginning, instead of repositioning them after your partner reaches the belay station.

Now you know how many pieces of protection it takes to rig an anchor. But making a strong anchor is more complex than simply throwing these pieces together any old way. You have two other things to consider: the angle of the webbing (or rope), and the anchor's equalization.

When you connect two pieces of protection together, their meeting point forms an angle.

This is true not only for two distinct pieces of protection, but also for a loop of webbing, such as one you might use around a tree.

The idea behind using more than one piece of protection is that each piece will have to support only part of the load. And the more pieces of protection, the less load each must support. This seems sound enough, but there is a problem. If the angle of the webbing is equal to 120 degrees, then each piece of protection supports the *entire* load.

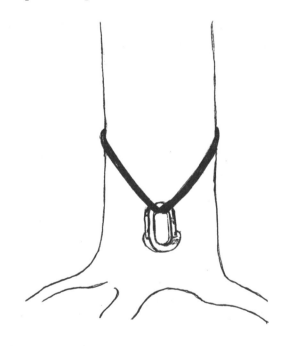

The angle of the webbing wrapped around a tree

And if the angle is more than 120 degrees, each piece ends up with *more* than the entire load (each piece of protection must also support the load caused by the other pieces)!

Obviously, this is not desirable! Instead, if you can position the pieces of protection so that the webbing forms an angle of 90 degrees or less, you will succeed in reducing the load on each anchor. The closer you get to 0 degrees the lower the load.

A wide, 120 degree angle: a very weak anchor!

You can change the webbing's angle by altering its length. The farther apart your pieces of protection are, the longer you need your webbing to be. Note: a quick way to get the correct webbing angle is to use webbing that is as long as the distance between the anchors.

Another important thing to consider is equalizing your anchor. This means that you rig the anchor so that each piece of protection (assuming you are using more than one) supports an equal share of the load.

There are two advantages to an equalized anchor. First: the load is distributed evenly over each piece of protection, which reduces the load on each, and the chance that they will fail. The second advantage becomes apparent when you imagine that one piece of protection does fail. If the anchor were not equalized, the load (which would probably be you or your partner) continues dropping until the second piece of protection catches it. However, because the anchor wasn't equalized, this piece of pro is loaded **dynamically** (a falling body is a dynamic load), which vastly increases its chances of failure as well!

There are two ways to equalize your anchor. You can set up a simple equalized rig, or you can establish a more complex self-equalizing rig. The simple rig is safer and stronger (because it has more

backup built in), but it may take longer to set up, depending on the situation. It also requires more pieces of webbing than the self-equalizing rig.

Below are two common examples of a simple equalized anchor.

An equalized anchor with three pieces of protection

An equalized anchor with three pieces of protection

There are two basic ways to make a self-equalizing rig. The first is ideal if you are using two pieces of protection. Connect a carabiner to each piece of pro, twist a loop of webbing and clip it to these two carabiners. Now clip two carabiners (with their gates opposed) over the "X" formed by the webbing.

A self-equalizing anchor with three pieces of protection

A self-equalizing anchor with two pieces of protection

If one piece of protection fails, the two carabiners will slide down to the end of the webbing, where they will remain secure. However, this will put a mild dynamic load on the other piece of protection, which may cause it to fail. To reduce this potential problem, use as short a loop of webbing as possible, but remember to maintain the proper webbing angle!

You can also connect more than two pieces of protection with a self-equalizing system. For clarity, I demonstrate with three pieces, but you can use the same design with more.

As always, clip each piece of pro with a carabiner. Now take a single loop of webbing and connect it to each carabiner. Next, clip a carabiner over both sides of the webbing, but only at the intervals between the points of protection, as illustrated below. Connect your rope to these two carabiners (oppose the carabiners' gates). Notice that these two carabiners are outside the loop of webbing. If all but one point fails, they will slide free. To prevent this, clip a third carabiner to your rope and into the loop of webbing.

Anchor Chains

Some two-bolt anchors have short lengths of chain connecting the two bolts. Such chains are called "anchor chains." An anchor chain is designed to replace the runner that you would otherwise need to clip, via carabiners, to the bolts. Anchor chains save time and gear: to set up the anchor, simply connect your rope to the anchor chain.

An anchor chain

Tying Your Rope To The Anchor

The connection between the anchor and your rope must be secure. This means two things: one, that you use two carabiners with their gates opposed, or a locking carabiner, at this connection. And two, that you use a strong knot to tie your rope to these two carabiners.

Because you are already tied into one end of your rope, you need a knot that you can tie using just the middle of the rope. The Figure-Eight-On-A-Bight (see How To Tie The Figure-Eight-On-A-Bight, on pg. 201) and the **Clove Hitch** (below) both work well. The former is stronger, while the latter is easier to adjust.

How to Tie the Clove Hitch

The Clove Hitch is an easy knot to tie. Simply bend the rope so that you have two loops, as illustrated below.

Beginning the Clove Hitch

Finishing the Clove Hitch

Notice that the two loops are twisted the opposite way.

Slide one in front of the other, clip into a carabiner, and pull tight.

Basic Principles Of Leading

Leading a climb is a complicated business. There are many things to be aware of, such as how much gear you need to bring (see Your Rack, pg. 39), when to place a chock, whether you have enough chocks to set up an anchor, keeping rope drag to a minimum, going fast enough to save your energy, and making sure you don't fall. Because of this complexity, you should start by leading easy climbs, climbs that are well within your ability. As you lead more climbs, you will begin to take these many variables into account automatically, and you will be able to increase the difficulty of the climbs you can lead, until you are leading climbs that are on the very edge of your ability.

But how do you determine what climb is appropriate for you, at your current level of skill? Climbers use a **rating system** for this purpose. After a climber makes a first ascent (puts up a route) he gives the new climb a name and a rating. The name helps others identify it, while the rating reflects his impression of the climb's difficulty. Of course this is only one climber's point of view: sometimes climbs have ratings that, by a consensus of other climbers, are way off mark. But usually the rating will give you a good idea of the climb's difficulty, which will help you decide whether it is the one you want to climb. For a thorough discussion of the rating systems (unfortunately there are more than one!) see pg. 345.

Efficiency and speed are two vital ingredients of a successful climb. Efficiency increases your speed, and speed is important because of weather and fatigue.

If you are climbing in the high mountains, or somewhere else where there are many storms, weather can be a dangerous element. A rain storm may quickly turn the cliffs into slick, non-climbable surfaces. A cliff is also the worst place to be in a lightning storm! Your chances of getting zapped are uncommonly high. And a storm may also bring cold weather, which can be fatal if you're not ready and willing to wait until climbing is again possible. Climbing quickly will help you avoid the possibly dangerous consequences of being caught in a storm.

Fatigue is another important element you should consider. The longer you stay on a cliff, the more energy you will lose, and the more fatigued you will become. So again, a speedy ascent will get you off the cliff quicker, and reduce your chances of becoming dangerously tired.

However, climbing too quickly will also bring on fatigue! You don't want to rush up a cliff only to burn out with 3 pitches still to go. Instead, *pace* yourself. If you can pace yourself well, if you can develop a rhythm, you will be much more efficient, and faster, than you would be otherwise.

You will also save energy by not placing too much protection. Every time you put another chock in, or clip to a bolt, you spend valuable climbing energy fiddling with your gear. It is hard to hold onto the rock with one hand and two feet while trying to unclip a carabiner from your **gear sling**! Do it only when necessary. Find the balance between spacing your protection too far apart and putting it too close together.

It is critical for you to find a good rest position from which to place a piece of protection. Try to let your feet support your weight, to give your arms a rest. If you are successful you will have a lot more energy left for the climbing yet to come. (The same applies if you are cleaning the pitch - find a rest stance before you remove the protection.)

Another important part of efficiency is bringing only the gear you need, and using it correctly. Of course, it can be hard to decide exactly what you need to bring on a climb, particularly a long one, but if you study the guide book carefully, and talk to climbers who have done the route, you will gain enough information. Using your gear efficiently is another matter. At first you will spend many hours fumbling around, figuring things out. But this will change with practice; the more leading and general climbing you do, the more efficient you will become.

I must make one last point regarding leading. With more and more people coming out to climb the cliffs, congestion is becoming a problem. In some places, the popular routes (which are inevitably the best, most spectacular ones) often have a line of climbers waiting their turn. This cannot be helped, and you should use common courtesy when dealing with other climbers in such a situation. Respect the others, and expect them to respect you. The important thing is to realize that climbing can be a fatal game, and that by rushing or angering other climbers you may cause an accident!

If you are on a long route, you may find that there is a party of climbers above or below you. If they are above, be ready to avoid falling rocks, and wear a helmet! If they are below, don't dislodge any rocks; if you do, immediately yell "ROCK!"

Sometimes you may be climbing faster than another party that is above you on the same route. Or there may be a faster party coming up from below. Whichever way it works, the best way to avoid problems is for the faster party to be courteous to the slower group, and to wait to pass until the slower climbers are at a large enough belay ledge. Neither of you want to interfere with the other; this will just make problems, which is certainly the last thing you need on a climb!

Leading a Runout

Three minutes earlier I had been staring up at this spot where I am now perched. I was studying this section of the cliff because I knew it was the crux, the hardest part of the climb. And I knew that it was unprotectable.

I remember noting that there were only two places to anchor a rope on this 120-foot rock. I scrutinized them carefully. The first was a shallow groove positioned 20 feet off the ground. From there, it was another 40 feet to the next anchor, which was a bolt. Between them was the hardest part of the climb. And although I would be tied to my climbing rope as I crossed this area, a fall might be fatal, for the ground would catch me before my belayer could.

And now I am balanced at the beginning of the expanse, at the edge of the empty rock desert that lies between the two anchors. The ground below is strewn with jumbled boulders. Falling on those jagged bones is not an option; I can't allow it. But if I continue upward, the possibility of such a fall may become a reality.

This morbid fantasy is keeping me glued to the rock: I haven't moved in the last two minutes.

I glance down at my rope. I can see it trailing below me as it travels to my belayer, who is staring up at me with a puzzled look. I can feel his question as though it were a shout: "what's the problem?" I ignore his unspoken demand for an answer.

Slightly over halfway between myself and the ground I can see the two carabiners that connect my rope to the rock. They signal the first anchor. Without them I could easily forget this small piece of safety exists, due to the bulging rock between us. Perched where I am, this lone connection will save me from the boulders below, should I fall. But with one more upward step, my security will be gone.

My mind wanders back. Yesterday I was at the beach, swept away by the majesty of another beautiful day. I remember it clearly: an almost-empty cove bathed in off-white sand, surrounded by coastal apartments that gazed with indifference at the white teeth of a cold, green ocean. The wind whispered by, sometimes gaining enough force to lick my face, intimately. I could see palm trees waving, bending; occasionally their rustling reached my ears.

With a jerk I pull myself back to the present, back to the rock. But I find that reality has become existential. Questions are flitting through my mind, hundreds of them. They are soul-searching, life-directing questions; they imply unanswerable thoughts. I can hear one in particular, a stubborn creature that refuses to be satisfied: "is climbing a rock worth risking my life . . . ." I have no answer.

My calves are cramping. I shift my weight onto one leg and lift the other one off the rock to shake some blood into it. This done, I return the revived limb to its stance and shake the other leg. I can't keep this up for long. Fatigue will soon take hold, and dictate my quick return to the hard earth below.

Some other climbers are walking by. They stop to watch. I feel embarrased; I hear them muttering amongst themselves. I can't make out the words, but I know they are not impressed. My mind shuts them out, and I am only vaguely aware of their receding voices as they wander off.

I need to shake my legs again. As I do this, I glance upward to size up the next section of rock. I have done this innumerable times already, but once more seems necessary. Again I glance up at the bolt, the lone anchor that offers salvation to anyone with enough daring to make the unprotected upward journey.

Daring! It isn't daring, it's foolishness. The rock preceeding the bolt offers nothing but fear, misery, and death. How can anyone be expected to push past such obstacles?

Again I am questioning. My presence on this cliff is useless, it serves no purpose. I should retreat; I should pass the lead over to my partner and let him make the dangerous journey, if he desires it. Myself, I should have nothing to do with it!

But something keeps me here. Retreating seems like a pleasant option, yet I sense that I cannot retreat. To retreat would be to hide from my fear, to let it overcome me. Fleeing from this rock would be fleeing from myself. When all the others, when my belayer, when the climbers that walked by, when all these people forget that I was defeated, I will still remember. And this memory will haunt me, will jar me awake, will tinge my confidence with a rotteness that will grow and fester. I cannot let this happen.

I push myself upward. My hands are sweating, my grip on the rock is tight. But I am determined. Fear is hounding me, but I am not letting it get beyond my outermost consciousness. I feel tense as I climb, as I link move after move, but the bolt is getting closer. I vaguely notice that I am too high, that death is a certainty should I fall. But I am a rocket that has been launched, and I cannot be recalled.

I make a final move, and reach upward to grab the bolt. It's poor style - but my breathing is fast, my hands shaky, and my feet are slipping. With a final effort I feel one hand close over the hard metal. Its solid, cold presence is sanctuary, safety, security; these words mingle in my brain, becoming a relieved sensation as I connect my rope to the anchor. I hear a cheer from below, but it seems far off. My heart is in my ears, pounding with a machine-gun intensity. Ebulient relief mixes with joy: I have done it!

Looking back, I see that it was not the climb that I conquered. Instead, I overcame myself. The rock was merely an equalizer: while it offered no help or mercy, it demanded nothing. I intruded upon it, and this intrusion brought forth all the uncertainty and fear that was lying dormant within me. Climbing the cliff externalized my emotions. Once they were in the open I was able to push beyond their immediate reality.

For the first time in my climbing career the danger of falling was real, death was a possibility. Previously, I had always found enough protection to maintain my sense of security. Up to this point, I had thought that my safety lay in my climbing gear. But now I realize that this is false, that ultimately a climber's ability is his only security.

What About Falling?

A falling climber

Unsupporting space rushes past you. You grasp for a hold, but your fingers find nothing. Your body is twisting, spinning, as you begin the long plummet to the hard earth below . . . .

Falling is a scary idea! And it may be the one thing that keeps you from learning to rock climb. But it doesn't have to. With modern equipment, and the knowledge to use it correctly, you can *safely fall off the cliff!* Although it may sound strange, many climbers actually accept falling as a necessary part of their sport. Because a climber knows that he will survive, he is willing to fall. And this willingness allows him to constantly push his limits, to try climbs that are on the very edge of his ability.

It wasn't always like this. Only a few decades ago (before the mid-1950's) the opposite was true. If you fell, your safety wasn't guaranteed. It was very possible that your rope would break. Early climbing ropes were made of natural fibers, mate-rials that weren't strong enough to support the tre-mendous load of a falling climber.

But the advent of nylon changed the world of climbing. Nylon is a synthetic fiber developed dur-ing World War Two. What makes nylon unique, and useful for climbing, is its high tensile strength combined with superb elasticity (stretch). There are other strong ropes: for example, you can use a steel cable if all you want is strength. But, although cable is certainly strong enough to stop your fall, it doesn't work for climbing. Cable doesn't stretch, and the shock of being brought to a sudden stop would probably break your back! An elastic mate-rial, such as nylon, will catch you gently, slowly stopping your fall.

When climbers learned that they could fall safely, providing they rigged their equipment properly, their attitude toward climbing changed. They had learned from bouldering (climbing on safe, small boulders) that the way to free climb har-der routes was to push themselves beyond their previous abilities, to climb with everything they had. But before the nylon rope, they hadn't been able to do this while leading a climb: to stay alive they were forced to remain cautious. The develop-ment of the nylon rope allowed climbers to discard their caution and to lead free climbs that were at the very limit of their abilities. Such routes were harder than any previously imagined. The idea of what was possible, the definition of the word "climbable", was altered forever.

"From then on, falls in controlled situations began to be accepted as a legitimate tactic in free climbing. Going all-out with good protection was acceptable because the rope could be trusted not to break. This change in attitude was to have a far-reaching effect in raising the standards of Amer-ican free climbing."
- Royal Robbins, *Climbing* #111, December, 1988, discussing his first free ascent of *Open Book* (at Tahquitz), in the mid-1950s.

There Are Times Not To Fall!

At the beginning of this chapter I stated that, when you use modern climbing equipment properly, fal-ling is safe. And this is true, to a point. If your rope is properly rigged and anchored above you, as it would be if you were toproping or following a climb, and your partner knows how to belay, you can fall safely. But once you begin to lead routes, to climb above your protection, the situation changes. You can still fall safely, but only if you have placed your protection properly. If, for instance, you didn't correctly place your last chock into a crack, the force of your fall may yank it free, and you will keep falling. Or, if you climb too far above your last piece of protection, you run the risk of falling onto a rock ledge, or even the ground, before your rope has a chance to catch you. However, these are mental mistakes which are avoidable; when you rock climb you pay for your own errors.

Some climbs have "runouts," sections of rock which offer no protection. On such routes your safety lies entirely in your skill as a climber. If you don't feel comfortable in such a dangerous position, don't climb that rock! You can climb wherever you like, and if you crave danger, you can easily find it on the cliffs. On the other hand, you can also climb in almost-guaranteed safety. There is room for everyone.

If you are a newcomer to rock climbing, let others look for danger. You can develop your climbing skills in total security by toproping climbs, or by following a more-skilled partner up the rock. Don't lead a route until you have confidence in your climbing abilities, and you can use climbing equipment properly!

Overcoming Your Fear Of Falling

The single most important way to overcome your fear of falling is to develop trust in your equipment. And the only way you can learn to trust your equipment is to fall on it. Hanging from a rope won't seem so scary once you have proved to yourself that it will hold you.

Your partner may assure you, in very eloquent terms, that there is no way the equipment (which is probably his) will break. Don't believe him! Test his gear by hanging on it: tie into the rope, climb 4 feet up the rock, have him pull the rope tight and belay you, and then jump! Swing on his rope; let it support you as you run across the rock; jump up and out, away from the cliff. Repeat this exercise until you are assured that his rope, and anchors, will safely hold you. Only when you are convinced of the rope's strength will you begin to trust it, and to lose your fear of falling. Once you prove to yourself that you can fall without dire consequences, what reason is there to be afraid of it?!

How To Fall

There is a right way to fall. The wrong way is obvious: you don't want to go head first, or to roll end over end! No, the best way to fall is to keep your body upright, feet below you, arms flapping for balance, and legs slightly bent to absorb the force of your landing.

The steepness of the rock will alter the way you should fall. If you fall on a low-angle slab, and lose your footing, you could easily find yourself sliding down head first. To avoid this, begin running backwards, or backpedaling, down the cliff as soon as you feel yourself start to fall. If you fall from vertical or overhanging rock, you will plummet faster but safer. Instead of contending with a slab which threatens to trip you at the slightest mis-step, you will find yourself floating gently, albeit quickly, through the air. You should promote your entry into space by pushing out, off the rock, as soon as you begin to fall. Remember that you won't land *on* the rock, but swing *into* it. So keep your feet and hands slightly in front of you, ready to absorb the impact.

The key concept to falling properly is to *go with* your fall. This demands a zen-like commitment: embrace the danger wholeheartedly. Instead of clinging desperately to the rock, push yourself into the fall. This demands trust in your equipment, but once you've begun falling you really don't have any choice!

You can use visualization to train your body to respond properly when you fall. (You could achieve the same result by practice-falling onto your anchored rope, but this would be expensive: you would quickly need to replace the damaged rope; see Ropes, pg. 269.) Visualize yourself falling from a slab, and then from a vertical cliff. Mentally rehearse your appropriate actions on each as I described them above. After just a few visualizations your body will "remember" what to do when you actually begin falling.

Falling Is Instructive

The way to grow, the way to learn, is to make mistakes. If you always stay safely within your limits, you won't be able to expand your vision and improve your abilities. Obviously, if you fall off the rock you made a mistake. But this event also gives you a great opportunity to learn something new. Actually, it's not only an opportunity, but almost a necessity. It's hard to retreat when you're hanging halfway up the cliff! And so you're forced into addressing the question: "why did I fall?" If you can answer this question, and with perseverance, you will, your climbing abilities will improve. Additionally, you may find yourself more willing to make mistakes in the rest of your life, because now you can see how to learn from them.

Key Point
"Despite their easy, quick placement characteristics, it is possible to screw up an active camming chock's placement."
See page 69

Active Camming Chocks (Spring-Loaded Camming Devices; SLCDs)

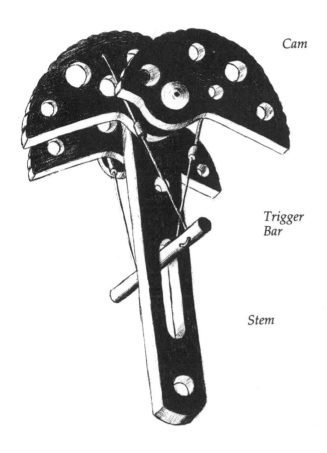

Cam

Trigger Bar

Stem

An active camming chock

What Is An Active Camming Chock?

As you climb a crack, you place **chocks** into it. These chocks anchor into the crack and, when you connect your rope to them with **carabiners,** protect you if you fall. There are three types of chocks on the market, and they are known as **wedging** (see pg. 325), **passive camming** (see pg. 233), and active camming chocks.

An active camming chock is the most technolog-ically-advanced type of chock. A spring-loaded mechanical device, the active cam is quick and easy to place into a crack, yet it holds very securely. It is the spring that gives the active camming chock its name; to use the chock you actively move its parts.

An active camming chock contains either three or four quarter-circle metal cams which are connected to the rest of the unit by an axle (or two). This axle is in turn held in position by a stem containing a trigger mechanism. When you pull the trigger the cams rotate in, narrowing the width of the chock, and allowing you to place it into a crack. When you release the trigger, the spring-loaded cams open firmly against the sides of the crack, where they anchor securely.

The Theory Behind The Design

An active camming chock uses friction to anchor itself in a crack. Friction is a gripping force that operates when objects touch each other. The harder these objects push against each other the stronger the friction between them becomes, sometimes making them immovable.

A falling climber needs a very secure anchor to halt his descent. Active cams are designed to provide that security: they increase the amount of friction holding them in a crack as the load on them (pull from the falling climber) increases. They accomplish this with three or four cams which rotate securely into the rock as their stem is pulled out by the falling climber's rope. This rotating motion is called camming.

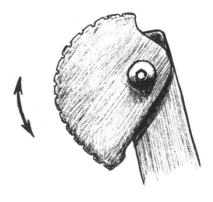

How a cam rotates

Active cams hold very well in hard rock, but not as well in soft rock. This is because the tremendous force the active cam exerts while holding a fall (the camming force is double the fall's force) can break the softer rock. In some sandstone cracks, for instance, you will sometimes see track marks of an active cam that broke the rock and slid out. Hopefully the unfortunate climber had other good protection to hold him!

An active cam's area of contact with the rock remains the same, no matter the position of its cam (open, closed, or somewhere in-between). This constant area of contact is called the cam angle.

A wide chock won't fit into a shallow crack

The cam angle

The cam angle determines both the chock's holding power and its size range, or the width of crack it can fit. The chock's holding power and size range have an inverse relationship. A smaller camming angle has more holding power than a larger one. But a small camming angle means the chock has a narrow size range. Besides fitting a larger number of cracks, a chock with a wide size range holds better in flared cracks.

The next important point in the active cam's design is its width, or axle distance, which is called the camming zone. If the camming zone is small you can place the chock into a shallow crack. But if the camming zone is too wide, you are restricted to using only deep cracks.

Although the narrow active cam can fit into more cracks, a wide active cam has more stability. So you should use a wide, stable active cam if possible, but if most of the cracks in the cliff are shallow, you'll need narrower active cams.

The active cam's stem also affects its stability. As you climb past the chock you just placed, your rope tugs it this way and that. A short, solid stem is more likely to feel the rope, and leverage the axle, moving the active cam this way and that. This leveraging can have dangerous consequences: the chock may "walk" into the crack, losing its secure position. To keep your rope from leveraging an active cam, always connect a **quickdraw** between the rope and the chock. The **runner** allows your rope to move around without affecting the chock.

Despite potential stability problems (which are negated if you use a runner) solid stems are good on active cams. Manufacturers can connect a solid stem to the chock's axle very securely: they simply drill a hole through a solid stem and insert the axle. The solid stem not only makes a strong connection; it also makes retracting the trigger bar very easy. (This is especially important for removing over-cammed chocks: you can pound on the stem with a hammer!)

Many active camming chocks have flexible cable stems, rather than solid stems. Flexible stems reduce leveraging problems. They also allow you to place your active cam into a horizontal crack without worrying that the stem will break when loaded over the crack's edge. (I discuss this feature in more detail under Placing Your Active Camming Chocks, pg. 69). However, flexible stems are weaker than solid stems. And they aren't nearly as durable: a solid stem may survive repeated falls with little damage, whereas a flexible stem's cable will often kink (especially if it was in a horizontal crack), which seriously weakens the chock. A final point: manufacturers must solder the cable to the chock's axle, and obtaining a strong, reliable soldered connection with cable is very difficult because the air between the cable's individual wires makes the solder harden inconsistently.

A final issue in the active cam's design is the number of its stems. While some active cams come with a single stem, either solid or flexible, that is attached to the center of the axle, others have two stems, both made of flexible cable, that attach to the axle's ends.

Although it seems like two stems would be stronger than one, they often aren't, simply because they are made of cable (which is weaker than a solid metal bar). However, since the two cables are usually positioned closer to the cams (at the ends of the axle), they provide more support to the axle, which would otherwise have to support more of the load emanating from the each cam.

A double stem often absorbs a load unevenly, because first one stem, and then the other, is loaded. The result is that the axle twists, unstabilizing the entire chock, perhaps even causing it to shift out of position and pull free. In an effort to alleviate this problem, manufacturers use flexible stems on all their double-stemmed active cams. However, this is only partially successful. Uneven loading won't be a problem if you can anticipate the load's direction and place your active cam so that its stems are loaded simultaneously, i.e. if you're protecting a straight, downward fall, angle the active cam so that both stems point down.

A final problem with two stems is that they increase the active cam's camming zone. As I have already discussed, this makes the unit useless in shallow cracks.

From this discussion I hope you can see that specific active camming chocks are designed for specific jobs. You should carefully select the active cams that will work best for your needs, which will be dictated by the rock you are climbing. This is one of the reasons why I think that you should buy active cams only after you have learned how to use the simpler passive and wedging chocks. Once you have such experience, you will be able to decide which active camming chocks you need.

Types

There are two basic types of active camming chocks: four-cam chocks and three-cam chocks.

Four-Cam Chocks

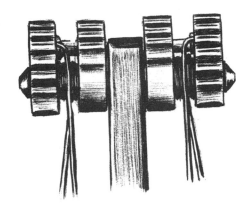

An active camming chock with four cams

Active camming chocks constructed with four cams provide excellent holding power in deep cracks. They are usually fairly wide (the notable exception is the Alien), which makes them stable. They fit only the deepest piton scars and slots, but work well in any parallel or flaring crack which is deep enough to house the device.

Three-Cam Chocks

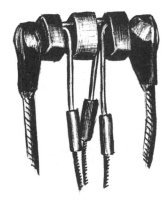

An active camming chock with three cams

Active camming chocks utilizing three cams are narrower than those with four. They work well in shallower cracks, such as grooves and piton scars, fitting where most four cams won't. They aren't as stable as many four cams, so you should use them only when you can't get the wider chocks to fit.

Active Wedging Chocks

A wedging chock (see pg. 325) is a piece of metal which wedges between the sides of a crack. An active wedging chock incorporates two such wedges into one device. These are easy to operate, spring-loaded and triggered devices.

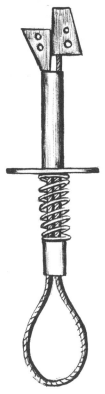

An active wedging chock

An active wedging chock acts like a pair of stacked wedges (see pg. 329). It will hold in parallel cracks because a load on one pushes them both harder against the sides of the crack, increasing their holding power (friction).

Active wedges are very small and narrow. They fit where no other chock will: into thin, parallel cracks, and even into slight flares. Al-
though each active wedge has a good expansion range, these devices are so small that this range doesn't give them much versatility. Example: a #1 Lowe Ball fits cracks from 3 to 6 mm. wide. This is a 2:1 expansion range, much better than the range of other chocks. But the difference is only 3 mm., which is a very small difference, discernable only to the experienced eye!

Considering their thin size, active wedges are quite strong. Their strength ratings vary from 800 to 2400 lbs., depending on the size of the device and the manufacturer.

Naturally, the active wedge's strength is not the only factor keeping it securely in place. The way you place the chock is much more important. Because they are so small, active wedges are unstable. The best placements are even-sided cracks that don't allow the chock to move one way or another. If one side of the crack extends beyond the other, you must place the chock carefully because it could rotate out of position after you climb past it.

A bad placement: the active wedge could rotate out

Sample Wedging Chock Specifications			
Name	# of chocks	Strength (lbs)	Expansion (in)
Metolius Sliders	5	1200-1700	.25-.65
Lowe Balls	3	800-1700	.118-.473
Go-Pro Rock 'n' Rollers	5	1000-2400	.26-.80

Placing Your Active Camming Chocks

Active camming chocks are very quick and easy to place. Some climbs are so exhausting that you can barely hang onto the rock, much less place your protection. An active camming chock will come to your aid in these situations. You can place them easily; they won't waste your time or energy. Active camming chocks are easy to size: after using them just a few times you will rarely pull the wrong one off your **rack.**

Poor Placements

Despite their easy, quick placement characteristics, it is possible to screw up an active camming chock's placement! For instance, if you don't position the chock in the direction of potential loading, and then you fall, the chock will swivel around with the fall, losing its secure position, and possibly pulling free. In a straight vertical crack be sure to angle an active cam's stem diagonally down and out. This will support a load from below (if you fall) as well as one directed out of the crack, which might occur if you fell on a piece of protection located above this chock.

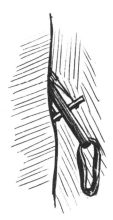

A diagonally-angled active cam in a vertical crack

You can jam an active cam in a crack that is too small for it (this is called "over-camming"), which makes it very difficult to remove later. When you place your active cam, watch to see that the crack doesn't force the cams into their tightest position. If it does, pulling on the trigger later won't release

the cams because they won't be able to rotate further.

Note: to remove a severely over-cammed active camming chock, loop the wire cables of two wedging chocks over the trigger bar, then loop a runner through them. Yank on this runner with one hand while you use the other hand to push the stem into the crack. Perseverance is the key.

You can also place too small an active cam in too large a crack. Only Chouinard's Camalots are secure in a fully-opened position. *All other active cams currently on the market are not strong or stable enough in the fully-opened position to offer you any security.*

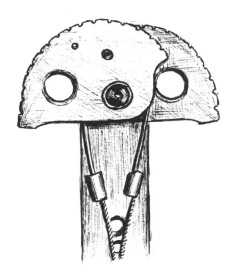

An active cam in a fully-opened position

After you've placed your chock, but before you clip your rope to it, check that all its cams are equally loaded. If one cam is extended further than the others, the entire unit will lose stability and may wobble and "walk" into the crack later.

This ability to sometimes walk further into a crack makes it difficult to remove an active cam. These chocks can walk so far into a deep crack that you can't reach them, or can't reach their trigger bar, which is just as bad. To remove active cams that have walked away, you need an **extractor** (see pg. 181) and lots of patience.

Active cams walk into cracks for a variety of reasons. You may have placed the device perfectly but have too short a sling to absorb the jerks from the rope as you climb. With too short a sling, every time your rope moves it yanks the active cam's stem, which swivels the chock, which starts the cam on its inward journey.

strength cord, then clip your runner and rope to this cord. Although this setup is still not ideal, it is far better than loading the stem over a rock's edge.

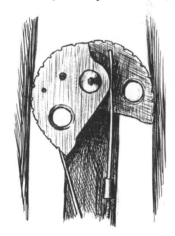

Cams that aren't equally loaded may walk the chock into a crack

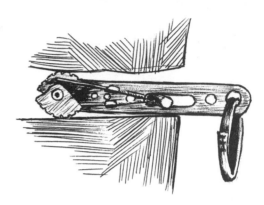

*A solid-stemmed active cam in a horizontal crack: **Don't Do This!***

Equally frustrating, the cams on your chock may not be equally loaded. This makes the chock unstable and even more likely to walk. Finally, the size and shape of the crack itself may cause an active cam to walk. This is especially true if the crack gets wider as it deepens, or if the active cam is too small for the crack it is placed in.

Keeping your active cams from walking is actually easy. Always examine the device when you place it. If you can't see it you won't be able to determine if it is the right size for the crack, equally loaded, and stable. Always add a runner to your active cam (see pg. 72), even if it already has a small runner tied to it. This additional runner will prevent your rope from jerking the active cam out of position as you climb. This will also reduce rope drag on you.

Using a Solid-Stemmed Active Cam in Horizontal Cracks

Note that solid-stemmed active cams are not made for horizontal or diagonal cracks. Rigged normally, a solid stem that juts out of such a crack will severely bend when a load is placed on it.

If you must place an active cam in a horizontal or diagonal crack, thread its forward hole with high

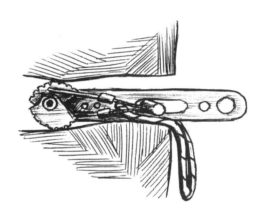

How to safely use a solid-stemmed active camming chock placed in a horizontal crack

Color-Coded Active Camming Chocks

Manufacturers color code their active camming chocks according to size so you can determine which one you want to pull off your rack at a glance. Some active cams have stems encircled by colored plastic sheaths while others (e.g. Wild Country's Friends) use colored slings. These slings will wear out, but when they do you can replace them by tying a 2-foot length of the same color of one-inch **tubular webbing** onto the chock.

It will take time to familiarize yourself with the meaning of your color-coded active cams. However, before too long you will know what size red stands for, or blue. And then a simple glance at your rack will tell you what chocks you have available at any time in your climb.

Specifications

Size Range

Active camming chocks have a larger size range than either passive cams or wedging chocks. It is easier to find the correct active cam on your rack: you can approximate the size and find that the chock will still fit.

Active camming chocks fit a very wide range of cracks. They go from very thin, 1/2-inch cracks to wide, 7-inch cracks.

Strength

The strength of any active camming chock varies with its design. In general, they range from 1600 to 3300 lbs, which is usually enough to hold your fall. If you anticipate an abnormally hard fall (a high fall factor, see pg. 269), then use two chocks anchored within a foot or two of each other.

Weight

Active camming chocks, compared with the other types of chocks, are fairly heavy. They weigh anywhere from 2 to 13.2 ounces. Their weight dictates how many active cams you will want to bring with you on a climb.

Sample Active Camming Chock Specifications			
Name	# Of Cams	Strength (lbs)	Expansion (inches)
Chouinard Camalots	4	2200	1.2-4.6
Hugh Banner Quad Cams	4	3087	.74-2.65
Colorado Custom Hardware Aliens	4	1600-3000	.35-2.17
Metolius 3-Cam	3	1600-2400	.40-1.35
Wild Country Friend	4	2860-3300	.75-3.95
Wired Bliss TCUs	3	2200-2400	.4-2.5
Yates Big Dude	4	3500	2.5-7

Materials

The materials that manufacturers use to construct active cams are very important. A material's characteristics determine the chock's strength and durability. Therefore, manufacturers pay special attention to the materials they use to construct their active camming chocks.

With any piece of gear, manufacturers struggle to reach an effective compromise between strength and light weight. To achieve the best result, they work with aluminum alloys as much as possible. Aluminum alloys work well where a lot of material can be used; the more aluminum, the stronger it will be. The cams of active camming chocks are made from aluminum, as are their solid stems, if they have them. For the small or thin pieces, such as cables, axles, and end fittings, manufacturers use steel or steel alloys.

The soldered connections are very important. The best solder is part silver - most manufacturers use an alloy containing 56% silver in their solder. The soldering job should look smooth, clean, and neat. If it doesn't, the connection is probably weak, so don't buy that chock.

When you examine an active camming chock, make sure that its parts work smoothly. You should be able to easily retract the trigger bar, which will narrow the cams. When you release the trigger the cams should quickly spring back into their original position. Examine the cams themselves. They should fit fairly snugly onto their axle, with no sideways wobble. The axle end fittings must be tight.

General Safety Guidelines

Placement Is Everything!

Your active camming chock will not stop your fall unless you place it in the crack properly. Line it up in the direction of anticipated force and make sure each cam is equally supporting the total load on the device.

Don't Use Your Active Cam Fully Opened!

Unless you are using a Chouinard Camalot, don't use your active camming chock fully opened (as a wedge). In this position it is neither strong enough nor stable enough to stop a fall.

Always Connect a Runner to Your Active Cam!

Connecting a runner to your active cam keeps it from walking into a crack. Walking occurs from your rope moving about as you climb, which leverages the chock's stem, shifting the device. Once out of position, an active camming chock may not hold. It is also difficult to remove. The device can continue walking deeper into the crack as you progress up the rock.

Care

Active camming chocks contain many moving parts. This means that they require a certain amount of care to keep them operating smoothly.

Use your common sense: try not to knock your active cams on the rock and don't drop them. Although strong, active cams are more fragile than your other chocks, which don't have moving parts. You should also be sure to place your active cams properly or they may break if you fall.

Keep your active camming chocks clean. Don't lay them in the dirt; instead, put them (and the rest of your gear) on your pack or a clean rock. Inspect and clean your active cams occasionally, perhaps every three months (but this depends on how much you climb).

Cleaning

Because an active camming chock has many small parts, it can be difficult to clean. However, you should be able to do the job with patience, a rag, some solvent, and a small brush.

You can give the cam a light cleaning by wiping it with a dry rag. This will get the superficial grit off. For a more thorough cleaning, you'll need to use a solvent and a thin brush, such as a toothbrush. Spray the solvent on the axle area, including the springs and cams. Now take your brush and scrub every part of the device you can reach. Use your dry rag to wipe the parts you can't reach with a brush. You can thread your rag under cables and into the thin gaps between the cams.

Once you've scrubbed your active cam you must remove the solvent. There are two ways of doing this. One is to leave the cam in the sun and simply let the solvent evaporate. This takes about ten minutes, depending on how much sun there is and how much solvent you sprayed on the device. The

other way is to boil a pot of water, and place your active cam into it for 30 seconds. Hold the device in the water by its sling, if it has one, so that the sling doesn't get wet. It's no big deal if it does, but the sling will take longer to dry. Once you remove the cam from the water it will dry very quickly; the hot metal will evaporate the water.

Lubrication

There are two times to lubricate your active cams. When an active camming chock first begins to stick, its cams will have trouble opening. If, after you lube them, the cams still don't open easily, this means that you need to clean the device. The second time to lubricate your active camming chock is directly after cleaning it.

It's easy to lubricate your active cam. Simply spray or squeeze the lubricant onto the cam's springs and between the joints where the cams meet the axle. Wait for the lubricant to dry (leave it for ten minutes) and your chock is ready.

When to Retire Your Active Camming Chock

Your active camming chocks should last a few years. The cables may be the first to wear, probably fraying and possibly breaking. Even one broken strand in the cable reduces the active cam's strength, making it effectively useless for stopping your fall. With such a damaged device, you have no choice but to send the unit to the manufacturer for repair (contact the manufacturer for prices, see pg. 353), or to retire it.

You should also check all soldered connections frequently. Although manufacturers are careful to maintain high-quality soldering, the solder may still crack. If any part of the active cam cracks you must retire the chock.

Other problems that will force you to retire an active camming chock include: cracked or severely worn cams, cracked, bent, or kinked stems, and bent axles.

Modifications And Tune-Ups

Your active cam's trigger cables may wear out after several years. The manufacturer will be happy to repair the device, so contact him (see pg. 353). Or, if you have a pair of #17-B4 Nicopress swagers, you can repair you own. You need 1/16-inch steel cable, the length depending on the number of trigger cables you want to replace (remove and measure them). You also need some aluminum swages (the metal that actually forms the swage), the number again depending on how many active cams you intend to repair.

To replace the trigger cable, cut the cable to the correct length and insert it through the trigger holes (half through one hole, half through the other). Pull the cable tight and swage it to the solid rod that connects to the cam. Try to make both trigger cables the same length, or you will end up awkwardly pulling an uneven trigger bar.

Accessories

Brush

A brush is helpful for cleaning your active cams. Any small brush will work, even a retired toothbrush.

Lubricant

You should use some type of dry lubricant on your active camming chock. Graphite and teflon both provide a good dry base. LPS 1 is a good brand name lubricant to try.

Nicopress Swager

You can buy a #17-B4 Nicopress Swager from some hardware stores or A5 (a climbing company).

Solvent

Hardware and paint stores sell solvents. Kerosene is a good solvent, as are most degreasers, such as Engine Brite.

Swages

You can buy aluminum swages from some hardware stores or A5.

Wire

Hardware and electrical stores sell 1/16-inch wire.

Some Active Camming Chock Manufacturers

Chouinard, Colorado Custom Hardware, Hugh Banner, Liberty, Metolius, Wild Country, Wired Bliss, and Yates all manufacture active camming chocks. See pg. 353 for the manufacturers' addresses.

Key Point

"Ascenders have two common uses in rock climbing: for ascending a fixed rope (self-belaying) and for hauling."

See page 81

Ascenders (Jumars; Jammers)

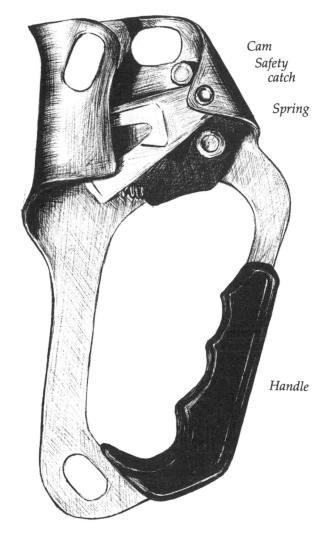

Cam
Safety
catch

Spring

Handle

An ascender

What Is An Ascender?

Using an ascender is an advanced technique. It is fairly simple to actually use the device, but setting your **ropes** up properly so you can use it takes a thorough understanding of your equipment. If you are a beginner, use this chapter to familiarize yourself with ascenders for the time when you have enough experience to use them.

Ascenders are used as part of an ascending system. An ascending system is complex: it contains equipment which is rigged a certain way, and probably includes a rope and three ascending devices (knots or ascenders). A number of different systems have been developed over the years, each with countless variations. I will demonstrate one, the Mitchell system, shortly. Feel free to research and experiment with other systems to find the one that works best for you. The book *On Rope* by Padgett and Smith presents a good overview of several ascending systems (see Bibliography).

An ascender is a mechanical device which you use to ascend a rope. You attach a long sling, or an etrier (see pg. 173), to the ascender, into which you put your foot. With a hand on each of your two ascenders and a foot in the sling below each, it is possible, with a little practice, to ascend a rope.

Naturally, the rope must be anchored above you for you to ascend it. One member of your party must climb up and anchor the rope in position. Then you can begin to ascend.

To use the ascender, you must first place it on your rope. There is no one way to put an ascender on a rope; each type of ascender is put on in a different way (I will cover each one under Types). Once you have it on, you can easily slide the ascender up the rope. But when you pull down on it, the ascender will securely clamp to your rope. This allows you to climb the rope, one step at a time.

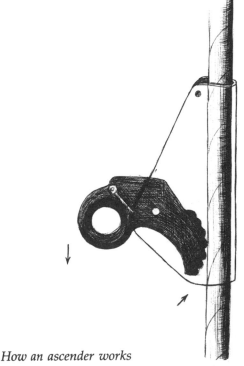

How an ascender works

You can see from the illustration that an ascender will grip your rope from only one direction. This means that it won't work if it is upside down. This probably won't happen, but you need to be aware of the possibility so that you can avoid any setup which might lead to it. For example, on a **traverse,** if your rope broke ahead of you, you might fall head first. Your ascender would not catch you! Therefore, if there is any chance that you may end up upside-down you should use at least two safety knots which will slide up your rope and be able to clamp on both upward and downward pulls. The **Prusik knot** does this well.

The Prusik Knot

You can use a Prusik knot to ascend a rope. It grips from both upward and downward pulls, which makes it very safe. However, it is inefficient compared with mechanical ascenders. The Prusik doesn't easily slide upward; you must push it, loosen it, and keep pushing it to make any progress.

The knot is very simple to construct: all you need is a loop of **sling** or **runner.** The Prusik holds best with 6-7 mm **kernmantle** nylon cord - when you are climbing with a 9-11 mm climbing rope. Thinner ropes require thinner cord, and vice-versa. A thin cord on a thick rope will jam easily and is awkward to use.

You can use your chock slings as Prusik material in an emergency (**Kevlar** does not work very well for Prusiks; both nylon and **Spectra** are better). For example, if you were **rappelling** and something went wrong, and you needed to ascend your rope (but you didn't bring any ascenders or cord). If you brought **chocks** that are slung with cord, you could use those. Their slings make very good emergency Prusiks. You don't need to remove the chock from the sling; you can simply thread it through the loops that are formed as you tie the knot.

To tie the Prusik, you need at least a two foot long loop of accessory cord. Simply wrap the loop several times around your rope, as shown, taking care that each wrap goes through the previous one. Two wraps hold well although you might want the better grip provided by three wraps if your rope is wet or muddy.

How you attach your Prusik depends on which ascending system you use. You can substitute a Prusik for an ascender in each system, although the knot won't be as efficient because it is harder to slide up the rope.

Be aware that the cord you use for your Prusik will abrade rapidly. You must check it for abrasion before you use it and again after your climb. If your Prusik somehow works loose and you slide down your rope on it, the cord can disintegrate! You *must always have a backup!* Never make a long ascent up a rope with just one Prusik knot; use three.

This rule applies to ascenders as well. Never

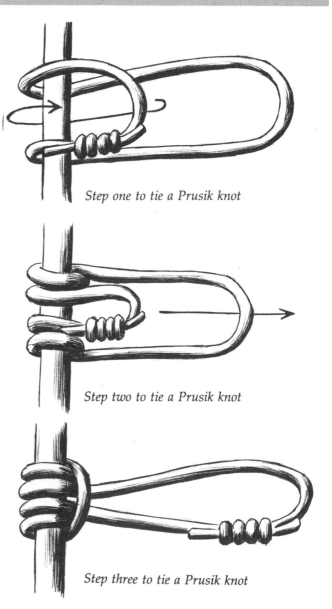

Step one to tie a Prusik knot

Step two to tie a Prusik knot

Step three to tie a Prusik knot

use one ascender: use either three ascenders or two ascenders and a Prusik. It can be slow going, pushing all these devices up the rope, but safety is everything.

The Prusik is only one knot of several which can be used to ascend ropes. For further information on these various knots, I recommend you read Bill March's *Modern Rope Techniques* (see pg. 361).

Ascenders come both with and without handles. Handles provide a comfortable grip but they are bulky, and they weigh more. Although a handle makes it easy to move the ascender, it may lead you to use your arms too much (ascending a rope is easiest when you can use your legs to progress upward).

Handleless ascenders are ideal for attaching (with a carabiner) to your **chest harness**. This is because their lack of a handle makes them difficult to grasp; tied to your chest the ascender will follow you up the rope, needing only a slight push as you go. They also work well as a ratchet device in some hauling systems (see pg. 261).

A combination of handled and handleless ascenders works well: use two handled ascenders for your hands, and one handleless ascender for your chest. You can also substitute the ascenders with three ascending knots, such as the Prusik. Or you can use a combination of ascenders and ascending knots (two ascenders and a Prusik knot, for example).

Brief History

The first ascending device was the Prusik knot, developed by Dr. Karl Prusik. He initially developed the knot to repair violin strings, but he soon saw how useful it was for climbing. Because of the ethics practiced at the time (each member of the climbing party had to climb the rock, none could just ascend the rope), Prusik knots were at first used only for crevasse rescue and by climbers who were stuck out in space under an overhang.

This changed in the 1950's, when climbers began to explore Yosemite's big walls. These climbers found that they could climb faster and save energy if only the **leader** climbed the **pitch.**

A climber in the 1860s

The second climber ascended the rope with Prusik knots. Since then, on long climbs ascending the rope has become the acceptable way to progress for everyone but the leader.

The first mechanical ascenders were made by Jumar in the late 1950's. They were immediately popular, despite some problems (they tended to be brittle and popped off the rope too easily). In 1969, the manufacturers Gibbs and Dole began selling the Gibbs ascender. This was a much safer device, as it completely encircled the rope. However, it wasn't as efficient as the Jumar.

Since those early days, many manufacturers have made ascenders. They have refined designs and produced much safer, more efficient, and durable devices. But the original Prusik knot is still considered an *essential* safety device, the knot that will hold when all the gadgets fail.

Types

There are three types of ascenders. I am going to refer to each type by the name of a well-known manufactured model which demonstrates that type's mechanical principles. For instance, I refer-red to the first type of ascender as the jumar. Jumar manufactured the most popular mechanical ascender at one time, and its ascender typifies the principles behind the other ascenders of the same type (although there are variations between each individual ascender). Other companies who make excellent jumar-type ascenders include: Petzl, CMI, Clog, and Kong, among others.

The second type of ascender is represented by Gibbs. Rock Exotica manufacturers excellent gibbs-type ascenders.

The third type of ascender is represented by Petzl's Shunt. The Hiebler is an older shunt-type ascender.

Jumar-type

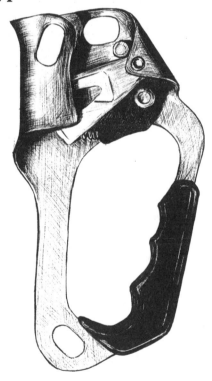

A jumar-type ascender

The jumar-type ascender has a shell which is open on one side. This makes it easy to put the jumar on to, and take it off of, a rope. To do so, you must swing open the cam. But to open the cam you must first move a safety catch. The safety catch is designed to keep the cam in position when the jumar is attached to your rope; if the cam opens, the rope can easily escape. You must be able to operate the

safety lock with one hand. Try it out in the store; it's best to find out if you can one-hand the lock before you buy the jumar!

The jumar's cam is held against your rope with a spring. This spring ensures that the cam is always next to your rope, ready to clamp tight. However, it also means that in use your rope will suffer from abrasion more than it otherwise would. The jumar's teeth will be worn as well, so eventually you will have to replace the cam (see pg. 84).

Jumars are very efficient. They easily slide up your rope with minimum wasted motion. You can quickly take a jumar off the rope to pass a knot, and then put it back on again, all with one hand (although this does take a little practice). This ease of use is very important on long ascents for which you have tied two ropes together and must ascend past the knot.

Jumars are ideal for **jugging** (ascending) big walls. After the leader has ascended to the next **belay ledge** and anchored the rope, the second climber can use his jumars to ascend the rope and **clean the pitch.** Using ascenders in this manner is fast and saves energy, both of which are essential on long climbs.

The jumar concentrates your weight onto a small area of your rope. This means the jumar can easily damage it. Because of this, the jumar is not safe to use for protecting yourself against falling from above your anchor (see Leading, pg. 49); the force of your fall may slice your rope in two!

Jumars come both with and without a handle. This makes them useful with many types of ascending systems. You must buy jumar ascenders as a pair; each ascender is designated for either your right or your left hand. Each thumb must be on a jumar's open side so that it can swing the cam open.

Jumars are made to fit all standard climbing ropes (8-11 mm). Their actual range varies, but is anywhere from 6-14 mm. You can only use jumars on single ropes.

Note that if your rope's sheath is accidentally cut, it may slide down the core. Jumars do not grip core fibers well. A gibbs grips them much better.

A jumar is safest when you keep it parallel to your rope. Its shell only partially surrounds the rope, and a lateral twist combined with an upward and outward pull can pry the ascender off the rope. This is most likely on diagonal ascents, such as overhangs and traverses, where your jumar and rope are no longer parallel. To fix this problem, clip a carabiner to your jumar's lower hole, and then to your rope. Be sure to keep the safety lock in position!

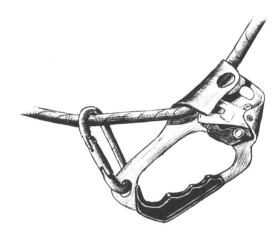

A carabiner clipped to the lower hole of your ascender and around your rope will keep the ascender safely parallel to the rope

The jumar doesn't hold well on icy or muddy ropes. If you are ascending such a rope you must keep your jumar's teeth clean. Ice or mud builds up fast and fills the gaps between the teeth. This makes the cam smooth, and it won't grip the rope.

You can make your jumar grip hard-to-hold ropes better by tying your sling to the top hole. When you pull down on the sling, the entire ascender will rotate, creating an "S" bend in the rope. But before you do this, make sure the safety catch is in position!

Gibbs-type

Gibbs-type ascenders are very different from jumars. The shell of the gibbs-type ascender completely encircles the rope. To put it on and take it off your rope you must dismantle the entire ascender. This is easy to do but it takes two hands.

The parts of the gibbs are connected with either wire or chain to prevent you from losing them. Unlike the jumars, none of the gibbs ascenders have handles. Some of them come with springs to hold their cams against your rope. Those that don't will slide before they clamp the rope, which is undesirable when you are self-belaying while solo roped climbing (see Technique pg. 82). On the positive

side, the lack of a spring reduces rope abrasion.

The gibbs grips the rope in a less concentrated way than a jumar. Its teeth, if it has any, are comparatively wide and blunt. Consequently, the gibbs won't damage your rope as easily as jumars. This means that you can use a gibbs for self-belaying while climbing. Note: the Rock Exotica ascenders were all made specifically for self-belaying and are the safest to use. They grip the rope between a curved cam and curved shell, instead of the curved cam and flat shell design used by the Gibbs and jumar-type ascenders. This means that Rock Exotica ascenders spread the load on the rope; the result is very high holding strengths.

One result of the gibbs' wide, blunt cam design is its ability to grip muddy or icy ropes fairly well. The same design also allows the gibbs to grip a rope's core fibers. This ability is vital if the sheath of your rope has somehow slid down, exposing its core. Although unlikely, this is not an unheard-of event. It usually happens on an older rope whose sheath has been cut through somehow.

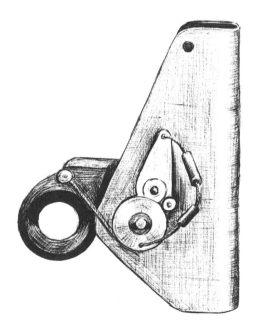

The Gibbs - one of the gibbs-type ascenders

All these features make the gibbs a safe backup device to your other ascenders. It works well attached to your chest or waist while you use two jumars with your hands. Some ascending systems require a gibbs at either the foot, knee, or shoulder, or in all three places.

On the negative side, gibbs ascenders are not as efficient as jumars. They do not slide up your rope as easily. And they are very awkward for passing knots: you must use both your hands, which is a very difficult thing to do while hanging from a rope.

Shunt-type

The shunt-type ascender works on a different principle than the other two types. It uses an exaggerated "S"-shaped camming action to clamp the rope.

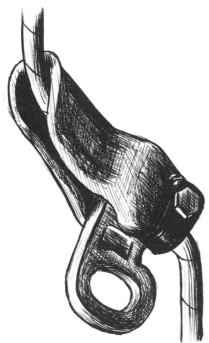

A shunt-type ascender clamping a rope

Only two models of shunt-like ascenders have been sold. The first was the Hiebler clamp, which is no longer available (although you may run across a used one). The other is Petzl's Shunt, which is still being sold, though primarily as a safety device for rappelling. However, you can use Petzl's Shunt both to ascend and descend ropes.

Regarding Hiebler ascenders: there is a good reason they are no longer sold. They pop off the rope very easily! Removing the Hiebler from the rope requires the same motion as ascending with

it. The two movements are distinct only in that you must twist the Hiebler to take it off your rope. Climbers have had Hieblers come off while they were ascending. Therefore, always use a Prusik above or below a Hiebler!

Why use a Hiebler at all? Because it provides an excellent grip on muddy and icy ropes. And its exaggerated camming action also clamps your rope's core fibers well.

Petzl's Shunt works on the same principle as the Hiebler. However, it has a much safer design because it encircles your rope more securely.

You can use the Shunt with either one or two ropes. The Shunt is the only ascender with two-rope capacity.

Unfortunately Shunt-type ascenders are not efficient. They put such a bend in your rope when they grip it that you lose 3 inches every time you move the shunt.

The Ascender Box

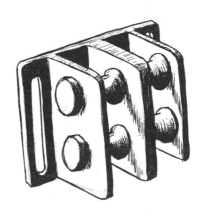

An ascender box

An ascender box is not actually an ascender. It is simply a box with rollers inside that is ideal for using with some ascending systems. Its job is to keep your upper torso close to the rope as you ascend. The rollers allow your rope to run freely, with minimum friction.

The ascender box connects to your chest or waist harness. To use it, thread your rope and the sling of your upper ascender through the box. The upper ascender's sling threaded through the box keeps your foot from swinging wildly out to the side, which makes it easier to ascend. The rollers inside the box allow your rope and sling to run easily, without friction.

Note: webbing does not work well with ascender boxes. Use an 8-9 mm static nylon cord. The cord will suffer heavy abrasion, so you must check it before, during, and after an ascent.

Technique

Ascenders have two common uses in rock climbing: for ascending a fixed rope **(self-belaying)** and for hauling. I will describe a popular way to use each one. In addition, I will demonstrate a way to use a gibbs-type ascender for self-belaying while **solo-roped climbing.** I am showing this so you understand the difference between simple self-belaying as you ascend a rope already in place, and the

very advanced, and much more dangerous, type of self-belaying in which you climb without a rope in place. Remember that when you use a self-belay while solo-roped climbing you must put in your own protection as you climb.

Ascending A Fixed Rope

There are many ways to ascend a rope already in place. The following one is called the Mitchel system: it is simple, works well, and is a good starting point for learning how to ascend. If you plan on doing a lot of ascending, you should learn other systems as well. They will give you more options. The best way to do this is to discuss ascending with other climbers.

Remember that you always need redundancy in your system; if one part fails, another part must be there to hold you. For instance, by running both your rope and the sling from your upper ascender through a **carabiner** clipped to your chest or **waist harness,** you have a backup. If the sling breaks, the harness will slide down your rope and jam on your lower ascender. (An **ascender box** instead of a carabiner is more efficient, but it is also an extra piece of gear to carry. See pg. 80.)

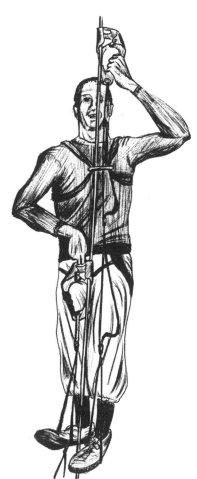

A climber using the Mitchel system

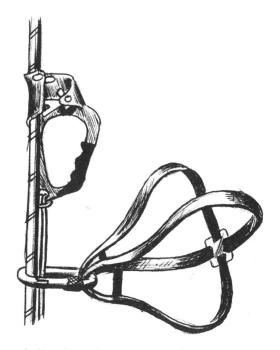

The rope and sling from the upper ascender running through a locking carabiner on a chest harness. A half-circle screw link makes a stronger connection, and an ascender box is more efficient

Besides providing a backup, using a chest harness increases your efficiency. It keeps your upper body close to the rope, which keeps you vertical as you move up. This puts most of your weight on your legs, which is where you want it. Your legs are stronger and can support you much longer than your arms can.

The length of your slings depend on many factors: your height, leg length, arm length, the ascending system you are using, and the position you feel most comfortable in. The best sling length will allow you to move with as little wasted effort as possible. When you use the Mitchel system, the sling to your upper ascender should end just above your chest harness. This shorter sling should alllow you to easily reach your lower ascender.

You can use your **etriers** in place of slings. This is ideal if you are on an **aid route,** because you need etriers anyway (you can use them for both **aid climbing** and ascending). They are also very adjustable: simply step into the next loop to adjust the height of your ascender. See Etriers, pg. 173.

Hauling

You may need to do some hauling for one of two reasons. First, you may be on a multi-day climb in which you must haul up your bag full of food and equipment (see Haulbags, pg. 207). Second, your partner may fall and be injured, in which case you will need to haul him off the cliff.

Ascenders work well for hauling. They act as a rachet-type device, allowing you to let go of your rope between pulls. Here is a common hauling method. For a more in-depth discussion of hauling, see Pulleys, pg. 259.

Self-Belay While Climbing Solo

You can use some types of ascenders for belaying yourself while you are climbing solo, but roped. This technique is very advanced, and requires a thorough knowledge of your equipment. *Unless you are an experienced climber, don't use a self-belay!*

The best ascender to use for self-belaying is one of the three Rock Exotica ascenders: either the Soloist, the Big-wall Soloist, or the Rescucender.

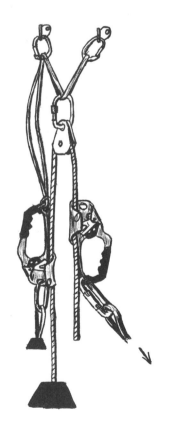

The Yosemite method for hauling: it has a 1:1 ratio (the hauling force is equal to the weight being hauled)

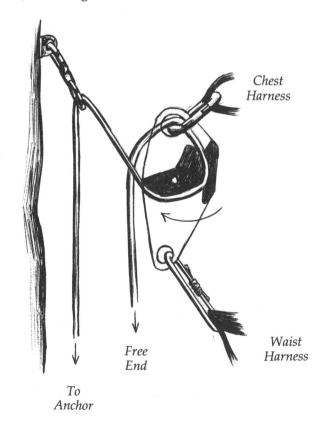

Chest Harness

To Anchor

Free End

Waist Harness

How the Soloist holds a fallen climber

These ascenders were designed specifically for self-belaying techniques.

Most ascenders are not designed to support a fall. *Never use any jumar-type ascender for self-belaying.* A jumar ascender (see below) concentrates the entire force of your fall on one or two of its teeth. This much force in so small an area will cut your rope in two!

Specifications

You will see only two specifications for ascenders in a catalog: strength and weight.

Strength

An ascender's strength rating tells you its maximum strength *in ideal conditions.* This strength varies anywhere from 1500 to over 5000 lbs. However, *most ascenders will cut your rope long before they themselves break!* This means that you should never load your ascender close to its strength rating.

The amount of load an ascender can hold without damaging your rope varies. The wider and smoother the cam, the less it will damage your rope. The Rock Exotica Soloist can support loads of more than 2500 lbs., whereas a typical jumar-type ascender breaks the rope at around 1600 lbs.

Weight

Ascenders must be fairly light because to use them you must push them up your rope. It can be very tiring pushing a heavy ascender up a long rope! Remembering to keep your weight on your feet and off your hands will help. Ascenders usually weigh from 6 to 20 ounces.

Materials

Manufacturers make ascenders from aluminum alloys and steel. For climbing, you need a lightweight yet strong ascender. Aluminum alloys work best for this purpose. Many manufacturers incorporate steel rivets into their ascenders for added strength. This is good, because aluminum alloy rivets are too small to provide enough strength.

The way an ascender is constructed is important because it affects the ascender's durability. Manufacturers use various methods of construction. Casting is one method, used only with Jumar ascenders. The metal is poured into a mold, then allowed to cool. Cast construction produces more brittle metal; therefore the Jumar's shell can crack easily.

CMI extrudes their ascenders. These ascenders are durable and strong, showing the value of the extrusion process.

Another way to obtain durable ascenders is to mill them. Milling is the process of forming the metal by grinding it. Rock Exotica mills their ascenders.

Petzl rolls their ascenders from sheet metal. Sheet metal has no voids, meaning that it won't crack easily.

General Safety Guidelines

Backup!

Always backup your ascender! This means using three ascenders. Or you can use only two ascenders, but backed with a Prusik knot.

Most Ascenders Don't Stop Falls!

Be aware that most ascenders are not designed to stop falls. Therefore don't use any ascender to belay yourself, unless you know what you are doing. *Never use a jumar-type ascender for self-belay!* Gibbs-type ascenders work much better, but even they may cut your rope.

Overhangs!

An ascender will not hold you if it is upside-down! Anytime there is a possibility that you could flip upside down, you should tie two Prusik knots as a safety backup.

Care

Because your ascenders have so many moving parts, you must take extra care to keep them clean (see Modifications and Tune-Ups for cleaning instructions). There are two additional things you must do: check for cracks and check for corrosion.

Check For Cracks

Check your ascenders regularly for cracks. Unfortunately, most cracks are too small for the eye to see. The best thing you can do is avoid dropping or knocking your ascenders against the rock. If you do drop one, give it a thorough inspection. You must decide whether you should retire it. A brittle cast ascender should be retired after a hard knock; a stronger milled ascender may be okay. But this depends on many things, such as how old the ascender is, how many times you have already dropped it, and how cold it is (a cold ascender is more likely to crack than a warm one). If you have any doubts about your ascender's integrity, retire it!

Corrosives

The best defense against corrosives is to wash your ascenders off. Cleaning your ascenders regularly will keep them free from all sorts of corrosives (see below).

If your ascender has some corrosion on it you will need to do some sanding. Use a semi-fine grade of sandpaper, such as 220, and lightly sand the corrosion off. When you have finished, wash the device, then air dry.

When To Retire Your Ascender

Ascenders have many small parts which can break. If a part on your ascenders breaks, call the manufacturer and ask him what to do. Is the ascender repairable? How much will it cost to repair? And how long will it take?

You may decide that it will be cheaper, or save you valuable time, to simply buy a new ascender. If this is the case, be sure to discard your retired ascender - you don't want to use it by accident!

Modifications and Tune-Ups

Ascenders are complex devices with many moving parts. Each part must operate smoothly for the ascender to function well. Because of this you will probably find that the easiest way to repair your malfunctioning ascenders is to return them to their manufacturer. For a fee, he will fix them. It may be some time before you get your ascenders back, however. Sometimes the actual manufacturer is in Europe, and the ascender must be sent there to be repaired.

The first part of your ascender to wear out will probably be its cam - the teeth wear down from rope abrasion. However, you should be able to make many long ascents before this happens.

You need to tune-up your ascenders occasionally. How often you do this depends on how much you use them. Any time you hear squeaks, see that a part doesn't operate smoothly, or notice that the ascender is dirty, you should get to work.

Cleaning

Here's how to keep your ascenders clean. For a basic cleaning, wash them in warm water. If they are really gritty remove the grime with some degreaser (spray it on, scrub it off). Try to keep the degreaser off any enameled parts; it will weaken the enamel. The degreaser will evaporate, but you should wash your ascenders with soap and water just the same.

Use a mild soap, especially if your ascenders are enameled. Rinse your ascenders with plain water when you're done with the soap. Wet soap that dries becomes solid and can impede the motion of your ascenders' moving parts.

Wipe your ascenders dry. You probably won't be able to reach all the parts, so let them air dry. After you have dried your ascenders you should lubricate them.

Lubrication

The parts you need to lubricate are the cam and safety catch pivot points. Never use an oil-based lubricant; every dirt particle within a yard of oil wants to stick to it. Instead, use a dry lubricant such as graphite or teflon.

Accessories

Wire Brush

Bring a small wire brush on your winter climbs; you'll need it for cleaning the mud and ice from your ascender's teeth. If you forget to bring the brush, or it is too hard to get to, try to knock the ice off your ascender with your hand and rope. If you have one, use an **extractor;** it will work well.

Your brush also works for removing the degreaser you use to clean your ascenders.

Lubricant

Not just any type of dry lubricant will do. Use a lubricant that has either a graphite or a teflon base. You could use a silicon-based lubricant, but it is not environmentally sound (it's even worse than the other two!). Don't use an oil-based lubricant; it will attract dirt and jam the ascender.

Degreaser

For heavy-duty cleaning, you need a powerful degreaser. Gunk Engine Brite seems to work well.

Sandpaper

A medium to fine grade of sandpaper is helpful for removing corrosion. 220 grade works well. You can buy it at any hardware store.

Soap

You should use a non-abrasive soap to give your ascender a good clean. Something as basic as a hand washing or light dishwashing soap will work. You probably already have that in your kitchen.

Some Ascender Manufacturers

Clog, CMI,Gibbs, Jumar, Kong, Petzl, and Rock Exotica manufacture ascenders. See pg. 353 for manufacturers' addresses.

Key Point

"You will use either a rope or a runner to connect yourself to the anchor; whichever you use, make sure that it is taut. If there is any slack in the connection. ... You may be pulled right off the belay station!"

See page 94

Belay Devices

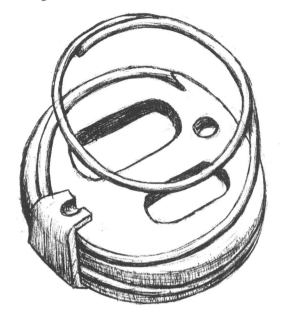

A belay device

What Is a Belay Device?

Falling is now a part of climbing. With modern equipment and techniques you can fall and trust that you will be safely stopped. But it is not the equipment alone which stops your fall, it is also your partner, the **belayer**. If you fall he keeps your lifeline, the **rope,** from slipping through his hands. This would be very hard, often impossible, if he was simply holding a rope attached to you. To make it easier and safer to stop a fall, climbers have developed various belay techniques. A belay technique is a method of using the rope to stop your fall. I will discuss two fundamental belay techniques in this chapter, the **waist belay** and the **belay device.**

Note: you must know how to belay other climbers (no one always climbs alone!). Some of the time you will be climbing and some of time belaying your partner.

Although there are now many different belay techniques in use, one of the first, and most effective, was the waist belay. You should learn to waist belay before you learn to use a belay device because you can rely on the waist belay if you forget or lose your device.

Part of the attraction of the waist belay is that you belay with only your rope; no other pieces of gear are necessary. Simply wrap the rope around your waist, holding one side with your braking hand and the other with your guiding hand. This technique is explained in detail on pg. 94. When your partner climbs, you can easily feed the rope out to him. If he falls, all you have to do to stop his fall is to cross your braking hand over your body, as shown below.

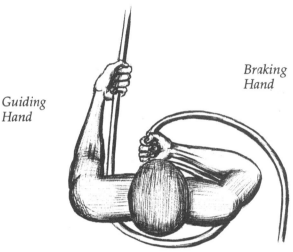

Guiding Hand

Braking Hand

Holding a fall with a waist belay

The waist belay technique produces what's known as a **dynamic belay.** By letting the rope slip through your hands as your partner falls, you use a dynamic belay to gradually bring him to a stop. A **static belay,** on the other hand, abruptly stops his fall.

A dynamic belay puts less strain on your equipment than a static belay. By gradually stopping your partner's fall, the fall's force is slowly spread through your gear. If the rock you and your partner are climbing is weak and crumbly, or doesn't have any secure places to fit your protective **chocks,** then you want to put as little strain on your **protection system** as possible. This is the time to use a dynamic belay.

A static belay is good for those times when the falling climber would crash into a ledge or the ground if he was not stopped immediately. Of course, his protection must be well-placed and strong or it might pull out when the static belay takes effect. And you, the belayer, must be well **anchored** (see pg. 53); you must be able to absorb more force than if you were using a dynamic belay.

Although the waist belaying technique is simple, effective, and puts little strain on your gear, it has three main problems. First, because the technique is dynamic, on severe falls the rope around your waist will slip. As a result, you will probably suffer rope burns on your body and hands. If you use a waist belay, remember to wear gloves (see Gloves, pg. 189) on your hands and extra clothing underneath the rope. Second, it takes a lot of strength to stop the falling climber. A lightweight belayer, for example, finds it very difficult to catch a heavier climber using only a waist belay. Finally, during a fall the rope can slip out of the belayer's control. The fall's force may pull it over or under the belayer. You can guard against this by running the rope around your waist through a **carabiner** clipped to your waist harness. Or you can make sure that the **sling** connecting you to your anchor is between the rope around your waist and the direction the rope might be pulled off of you.

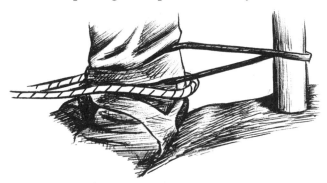

Anchor sling positioned to keep the rope from sliding over belayer's head

These three problems lead to one conclusion: *the waist belay must be done right,* or it might fail and could injure both the falling climber and the belayer.

To deal with these three limitations, climbers have developed various belay devices. A belay device is a metal apparatus connected to your **harness** through which you run your rope. Your rope makes two or three sharp turns as it runs through the device; holding the rope allows you to easily stop a fall.

Belay devices give a static belay on low loads (short falls). On higher loads (usually above 500 lbs.) the device will give a dynamic belay. The result is a good balance. On short falls your partner won't fall farther than necessary because of the sta-

tic belay. And on longer falls the equipment will suffer as little damage as possible due to the dynamic belay.

The belay device is free of the waist belay technique's problems. Since you don't run the rope around your body, you can't suffer any rope burns (except for your hands, if you hold a horrendous fall!). Using a belay device you can easily stop the fall of a much heavier person. And you don't have to worry about the rope slipping out of your control because it is securely locked into your device.

Using A Belay Device

All belay devices work in a similar manner. You must push a **bight** of rope through the device and clip it to your **locking carabiner,** which is connected to your waist harness. Once you lock the carabiner, your belay device and your rope are safely secured.

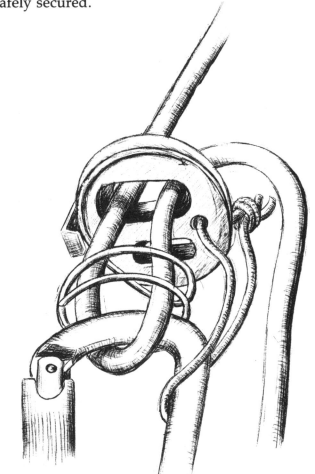

Clipping into your belay device

This secure connection is vital. If it should fail you wouldn't be able to stop your partner's fall. Be sure to use a locking carabiner: a carabiner without a lock might open accidentally. If you don't have a locking carabiner, use two carabiners with their gates opposed (see pg. 130).

Two carabiners at this connection, whether locking or not, will increase your belay's stopping power. In other words, when you push a bight of rope through your belay device and clip it to your waist harness with two carabiners, your belay will become more static. You will find this useful if you anticipate having to hold a severe fall, such as when you are at a **belay station** halfway up a cliff and your partner, who is climbing, is unable to place a piece of protection. If he falls, all the force of his fall will come directly to you, and you must have a very strong belay to stop him. You will also need more holding power if your rope is wet. A belay device doesn't stop a wet rope as easily as it stops a dry one.

To keep your rope running smoothly through your belay device you should keep the device 3 to 8 inches away from your locking carabiner. Much closer or farther than this makes it difficult to manage your rope.

You can use a holding loop (as illustrated on pg. 88 at the beginning of this chapter) to keep your belay device at the correct distance. The loop will prevent the device from travelling along the rope. This is particularly important when you are belaying from above, as gravity will try to pull your belay device out of your control.

Nylon cord or wire can be used for this holding loop. However, nylon may rub on your rope, and nylon on nylon builds up heat quickly, and melts! To avoid this problem, use a wire loop. You will have to swage the wire in place, which is easy if you have, or have a friend who has, a swager. If you don't, your local hardware store can swage it for you. Cord is your economical choice.

Rappelling

Many belay devices can be used for **rappelling** as well as belaying (see Descending, pg. 157). However, if you use your belay device to rappel, be extra careful. Unless the device was originally intended for rappelling (such as the figure-eight, see below) it is not as safe as most rappel devices. This means that you must descend slowly, in a controlled manner, and use a **Prusik knot** for backup (see

pg. 76). *Never **sport rappel** (fast, bouncy descent) with a belay device!*

Types

There are four different types of belay devices: **belay plates, figure-eights, tubers,** and one type that has no common name. This last type consists of two similar devices: the **Bankl Plate** and the **Seilbremse.**

Belay Plates

A belay plate

Belay plates are metal rings or disks of various shapes and sizes. They have a hole, sometimes two, through which you feed your rope. They are very simple, small, and effective. Belay plates are lightweight: the smallest ones are simply metal rings. The larger ones are more complex and a little heavier, but make up for this with more durability.

The Sticht belay plate was the first one on the market, and is very popular. It is a round disc with two holes in it for your ropes (if you are using one rope, use only one hole!). You can buy the Sticht with a steel spring attached. This spring keeps the Sticht from jamming onto your locking carabiner when you hold a fall. To keep the spring from tangling with your slings and runners, you can clamp it down under the metal hook that is on one side of the Sticht.

Other belay plates have a simpler design. Some of them look like the Sticht, with a two-holed plate, but without the spring, while others are single-holed rings. The two-holed belay plates are more versatile, but sometimes heavier (by only an ounce, at the most).

Belay plates can be awkward to use. Some designs bind your rope, and make it difficult for you to feed the rope through, especially when you are lowering a climber. The square-edged designs bind more than those with curved edges.

Although you can use your belay plates for rappelling, there are two reasons not to: heat and abrasion. On small devices like belay plates, heat builds up very quickly. This is especially true if you are using a small belay plate, as compared to a larger one, such as the Sticht. Even if you rappel very slowly, your device will heat up. This heat is a problem because whenever you stop, your belay plate will melt some of your rope's fibers, which weakens your rope. Abrasion is also a problem on a rappel because your rope may wear through your belay plate. Before you rappel with the plate, look it over and make sure that its finish is in good condition. The finish on many belay plates makes them tough enough to withstand rope abrasion. (See Materials for more on this; pg. 97.) If the finish is worn, don't use the device to rappel!

Different belay plates are designed for different-sized ropes. Some plates have only one hole, which means they can only be used with one rope. The hole will fit either 9 mm or 11 mm ropes. Other plates have two holes, and can be used with two ropes. One hole may fit 9 mm and the other 11 mm (which will let you use either a single 11 mm rope or double 9 mm ropes), or both holes may be 9 mm or both 11 mm. All these combinations cater to you, to fit the rope technique you want to work with. The most versatile design is the 9 and 11 mm double-holed plate, because you can easily use it for both a single and a double rope technique.

Figure-Eight

The figure-eight was designed for rappelling (see pg. 158), but many climbers use it for belaying as well. You can belay with your figure-eight in two ways. The first is similar to the way you would use a belay plate. The second is like using the device to rappel.

Using the figure-eight as a belay plate gives good braking power. That means the belay will stop a harder fall before it allows the rope to slip through the device. To use it like this, simply push a bight of rope through the figure-eight's smallest hole and clip the bight to your harness with a locking carabiner.

To make it easy to push the bight through, use a

figure-eight with a large smaller hole. Don't use the large hole of the figure-eight for belaying! It is too large to have any stopping power.

Using the figure-eight as if you were rappelling gives less holding power than if you were to use it as a belay plate. To set it up for rappelling, simply

A figure-eight

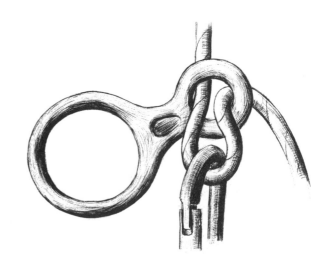

Belaying with the small hole of the figure-eight

push a bight of rope through the large hole and over the outside of the smaller hole. Then clip your figure-eight to your harness with a locking carabiner.

Tubers

A Tuber

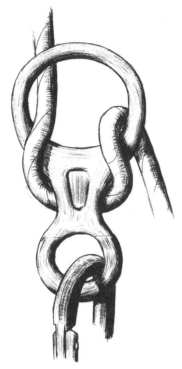

Belaying with the figure-eight in rappel mode

The advantage of using the figure-eight for belaying, and the reason that so many climbers do, is that it works great for rappelling. Then you only need one piece of gear for both operations, which saves weight, bulk, and time (to find and connect different devices).

The main problem with using a figure-eight as a belay device is that it will twist your rope. This is particularly true if you use the rappelling setup, although the belaying setup produces twist as well. A twisted rope can be horrible to deal with: it kinks.

Be careful to keep your figure-eight close to your waist. You cannot tie a holding loop to the device, so you must rely on your concentration to keep it in place. This is especially important when you are belaying from above, because the figure-eight will take every opportunity to slide down your rope.

A tuber is a small cylinder of metal. It has ribs around the outside, and a loop of cord over one end and through a small metal tube that divides the tuber's middle. The ribs are designed to dissipate heat and the cord is intended to be looped around your carabiner to keep the tuber from sliding up your rope. The metal divider keeps your ropes separated, which helps with rope management.

The tuber is designed to keep your rope from twisting while you belay. It does this by providing a long, smooth tunnel for the rope to run through. This avoids the curves and bends that cause the rope to twist in other devices (such as the figure-eight).

You can use the tuber for rappelling as well. It dissipates heat better than belay plates do, because of its longer shape and heat-absorbing ribs.

However, the tuber is slow to use. Getting the rope through the long cylinder takes time, longer than with other devices. This is no problem if you are belaying someone who is climbing slowly, but if he speeds up you might not be able to keep up with him. Then the climber would have to fight the pull of the rope as he climbed.

Bankl Plate And Seilbremse

The Bankl Plate and the Seilbremse are very similar to each other, and work on the same principle. The Seilbremse is more common in the U.S.; it is the one you will probably see in your local climbing store.

The Bankl Plate

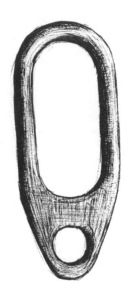

The Seilbremse

Using the Bankl Plate with 2 ropes

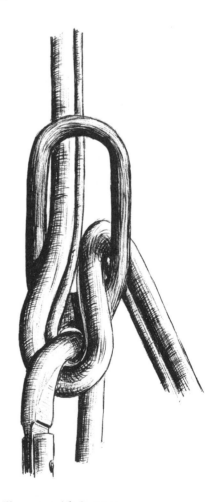

Using the Seilbremse with 2 ropes

As you can see, the difference between the two is in the Bankl Plate's wider design, with two holes instead of one. The holes are to let you clip your locking carabiners to the device. This design means that if you want to use two ropes, you must use two carabiners. These two carabiners keep the device from twisting, but that is not a big advantage.

With the Seilbremse you can use two ropes with one carabiner because the device has a long hole that allows both ropes to run easily around the one carabiner.

Now that you know the differences between the two devices, I shall discuss their similarities. I will refer to the Seilbremse and the Bankl Plate together, calling them the Seilbremse.

You can use the Seilbremse both to rappel and to belay. To set up either, simply clip a bight of rope and the device to your locking carabiner.

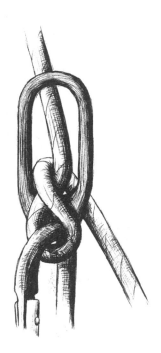

The Seilbremse ready for belaying only

The Seilbremse ready for either rappelling or belaying

Another way to use your Seilbremse works for belaying only. Clip the bight of rope as before, but this time cross the brake side of the rope over the other side, and then back around.

This setup provides more braking force than the first way, but also permits more rope abrasion, which is why you shouldn't use it to rappel. Nylon runs against nylon, which is never good for your rope (heat and abrasion problems).

The Munter Hitch

The Munter Hitch (also called the Italian Hitch) is a belaying knot. It allows you to belay your partner with just the rope and a locking carabiner. Because the Munter Hitch has a high braking force, but is still a basic method of belaying, you should learn how to use it; you can belay effectively even if you lose your belay device. See pg. 132 to learn how to rig the Munter Hitch.

The Munter Hitch can be awkward to use, because it sometimes jams on the carabiner. However, you can avoid this problem by using a large pear locking carabiner (which has a large enough end that the knot won't jam). An additional problem with the Munter Hitch is that your rope will suffer slight abrasion because the knot forces it to rub itself, and nylon quickly abrades nylon.

Technique

Belaying properly is simple. Once you learn how, you will be surprised at how obvious it is. For most newcomers, getting the concept right at the beginning is difficult. You're sure you're doing it right but then your partner screams at you for being unsafe! Don't worry, we all do this at first. Practicing with your partner on short, easy climbs allows you to figure out the details of belaying before the climbing gets more serious.

You will use the same belay technique to protect a partner whether he is climbing either above or below you. The only change is in rope direction: you feed it out if the climber is above you and take it in if he's below.

Tip: when you lead a climb you must belay your partner up from below. Before you can do this you must pull all the slack rope up after you, until you feel your partner who is tied to the other end of the rope. To save your energy and time, pull this slack up before you clip the rope into your belay device. Many climbers neglect this, and waste time laboriously pulling the slack through their belay device.

There are two fundamental points regarding belaying. First, as the belayer, you must anchor yourself in the anticipated direction of load. In other words, if your partner is climbing up from below you, anchor yourself so that, if he falls, he doesn't pull you down from your belay station. Note: regarding multi-pitch climbs. When your belaying your partner from the side of a cliff, and he begins to lead the next pitch, you must secure yourself from both an downward and upward pull. The downward pull may occur if he falls before he can place a chock: there is nothing to keep him from falling below you. The upward pull may occur if your partner falls after he has placed a chock for protection. See pg. 53 for more about rigging anchors.

The second point to remember when you are belaying pertains to your anchor connection. You will use either your rope or a runner to connect yourself to the anchor; whichever you use, make sure that it is taut. If there is any slack in the connection, and your partner falls, he will pull you with him until the rope or runner pulls tight. You may be pulled right off the belay station! See pg. 57 for more about tying into your anchors.

I will demonstrate the proper belaying hand motions with a waist belay, while belaying a climber from below. The same hand motion applies for all belay devices.

First, grasp the rope with your brake hand.

When your partner climbs up, let the rope slide out. This pulls your brake hand to your hip.

Now comes the trick. Extend both your arms and grasp both lengths of the rope with your guiding hand. Make sure you keep holding the rope with your brake hand. Now slide your brake hand up to your guiding hand, *without* taking it off the rope.

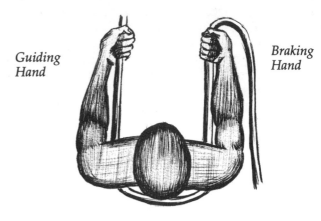

Guiding Hand   *Braking Hand*

Grasping the rope with your brake hand

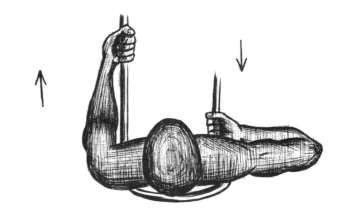

Feeding the rope out pulls your brake hand to your hip

Sliding your braking hand up to your guiding hand

You are now ready to let out more rope.

It sounds simple, and it is. But so many climbers do it wrong: they take their brake hand off the rope when they move it up to their guiding hand. Often, they even reach over the guiding hand. This is a very bad practice. If your partner fell at the moment you did this, he would be unprotected.

Be methodical about your belaying. Use the same basic hand motion every time you belay. Eventually, you will be able to belay properly without thinking about it. This is why it so vital that you do it right from the beginning.

Special Note: Don't restrict your braking to whichever hand you like using the most. Try to become an ambidextrous belayer. This flexibility is necessary if you are belaying next to a rock wall. In such a situation you cannot use the hand that is against this wall as your braking hand. You won't be able to effectively brake with it: the wall is in the way.

Removing Yourself From The Belay System

In the event of an emergency (perhaps your partner is injured during a fall), you may need to go for help. But this is impossible while you are connected to the belay system: if you move, the rope will be free to drop your partner to the ground. To deal with such emergency you should know how to properly remove yourself from the belay system.

The first step to removing yourself from the belay system is to "lock off" your belay device - to prevent the rope from slipping through it. You can accomplish this by tying a knot in the rope. Different belay devices require different knots. The Overhand knot (see pg. 175) works with belay plates and tubers, while with either a Figure-Eight or a Seilbremse you must first push a bight of rope through the device's far end, and then tie a Half Hitch in the rope as illustrated.

Once you have locked off your belay device, attach a Prusik knot (see pg. 76) to the rope, just above the device. Connect a **quickdraw** between the Prusik and your anchor.

Now unlock the rope from your belay device, and let it slide out until the Prusik knot tightens (lowering your partner slightly). You can now disengage your belay device from the rope, which ef-

A locked-off Figure-Eight

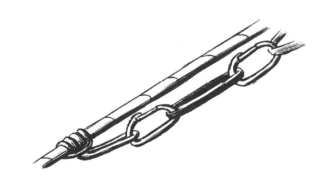

A quickdraw connecting a Prusik knot to the anchor

fectively frees you from the belay system.

Before you go for help, increase your partner's security by adding two more Prusik knots between the rope and anchor. In addition, tie the section of rope that lies slack between the anchor and Prusik knots to the anchor with a Half Hitch (using a bight, or loop, of rope).

Specifications

Strength

Your belay device must be strong. If it fails, you may not be able to catch your partner if he falls.

Fortunately, not all the stress of a fall will end up on your belay device. The stress will be absorbed by other equipment, such as your rope, carabiners, **runners,** etc. Also, the more points of protection you have between you and your partner, the less stress your belay device will receive. You must also realize that the stress of a fall does not directly affect your belay device: it will hit your locking carabiner (through the bight of rope) the most. And the bends in the rope will absorb a lot of the stress.

A good minimum strength for a belay device is 3000 lbs. Not every manufacturer will list the strength of his device; if you really want to know you must call him and ask. See Appendix for manufacturers' addresses and related information.

Weight

Some belay devices weigh as little as half an ounce, whereas others weigh 5 ounces. This difference in weight tells you important information: how much metal is in the device. Generally, the more material in the belay device, the longer it will last. If you really want just the bare minimum, a lightweight belay device will work. But for durability and overall usefulness, the heavier belay devices are best.

Materials

Durability is important in belay devices. They must be able to withstand lots of rope abrasion. As a general rule, the more metal you have in the device, the longer it will last. Small belay plates will wear out long before large figure-eights.

The finishing process is particularly important, because of abrasion. Manufacturers know that rope abrasion is a problem, and they pay special attention to the device's finish. Small belay plates usually have a very good, tough finish. A figure-eight's finish is very important because of its rappelling function. Any nicks on its surface may have sharp edges which will cut your rope. Always look out for such nicks and edges. If you see any, file them down.

Manufacturers usually use aluminum alloy in their belay devices. This is a strong, lightweight metal. It abrades quicker than harder metals such as steel, however. Therefore, the finish on an aluminum belay device is very important, whereas the finish on a steel belay device is much less important. A good example is the Bachli Seilbremse, which is made of steel. Its finish isn't very good, but it doesn't have to be. The steel will last for many years.

Another thing to consider is heat buildup. Aluminum alloys build up heat much quicker than steel. And a thin strip of metal will heat up more quickly than a wide band. Therefore, when buying an aluminum belay device, which you know you will be using for rappels (where heat builds up quickly) make sure you buy a large device, such as a figure-eight.

General Safety Guidelines

Don't Remove Your Braking Hand From The Rope!

Never take your braking hand off the rope when you are belaying someone. The climber could fall at that instant, and he would be unprotected. When you belay a climber, his life is in your hands.

Don't Use A Belay Device For Sport Rappelling!

Unless you are belaying with a device that was made for it, *don't use your belay device for sport rappelling!* It will build up heat much too quickly, and will suffer heavy abrasion. Both of these things could severely damage your equipment, maybe enough to cause it to fail mid-rappel!

Check Your Locking Carabiner!

Your locking carabiner is the only thing that keeps your belay device attached to your waist harness. If you forget to lock the carabiner, it may open and the belay device come off. Remember, *you are responsible for your partner's life when you are belaying him!* Be careful.

If you don't have a locking carabiner, use two carabiners with their gates opposed (see pg. 130).

Check Your Waist Harness!

Make sure your waist harness is closed properly. You must double the webbing back through the buckle. If you don't, the harness can easily slip open.

Care

Caring for your belay device is easy. Look it over after every climb. If it has a crack, retire it immediately. If it has any protruding sharp edges, sand them down.

Blunt Sharp Edges

To blunt the sharp edge of a nick or cut, you can use either a very fine (600 grade) sandpaper, or a fine emery cloth. Be careful when you sand the edges; you don't want to scratch too much of the finish off the device. Sand just enough to blunt the edges, no more and definitely no less.

When To Retire Your Belay Device

If your belay device doesn't develop any cracks it should last a long time. How long depends on how much you use it, and how hard. The reason for retiring a belay device is usually that its finish has worn off. The finish of most belay devices will last for a few years (if you are a weekend climber). This depends on how much rope abrasion the device is subject to, and how well it handles this abrasion.

Aluminum devices wear quicker than steel ones. If you see that your aluminum belay device no longer has its finish and is starting to wear, retire it. When it has reached this point, it is not nearly as strong as it was when new. It could fail anytime (probably it won't, but you never know). Your steel belay device will last long after its finish has worn through. Retire it when the metal gets thin. This is a judgement call; if you aren't sure you can take your device to a climbing shop and ask the most knowledgeable salesperson there.

Accessories

Cord

If your belay device has a hole for a small loop of cord, you need to buy an 8-12 inch long cord. Different devices have different size holes; use whichever diameter cord fits the hole in your device. The cord doesn't have to be very strong. Its job is simply to keep your belay device close to your locking carabiner.

Wire

You may want to use wire as a holding loop instead of cord. If so, go to a hardware store and find some wire that will easily fit through the hole in your belay device. Laid wire is best (the kind that is made of many small twisted strands).

Swager

You need a wire swaging tool if you are going to use a wire holding loop. The best such tools are Nicopress swagers. Your hardware store may stock them, if not, you can order a pair through A5. However, they are expensive, and to avoid this expense you may be able to have someone at the hardware store swage your wire loop for you.

Sandpaper Or Emery Cloth

Sandpaper or emery cloth is vital for blunting sharp nicks and cuts. Whichever you buy, it must be a very fine grade (600 grade sandpaper is good). You can buy both sandpaper and emery cloth at any hardware store.

Some Belay Device Manufacturers

Chouinard, Clog, CMI, DMM, Latok, Sticht, Wild Country, and Yates manufacture belay devices. See pg. 353 for manufacturers' addresses.

A Belayer's View

I have an indelible image etched into my mind. It is as clear and sharp as a photo. It is full of frozen drama, of unfolding action; it contains the kind of terror that stems from uncertainty. It is an image that I will never lose.

I can change the angle of the image. First I am close, almost touching, underneath. Then I am above, but watching from a great distance. Finally I'm off to one side, exploring a previously unknown perspective. The image has a sterile, surgical remoteness to it. I am almost borrowing it from a stranger.

He is falling from a high cliff! My climbing partner is in the air! I should have been ready for this, having already belayed many other climbers. But falling is a sudden thing, something you can never be ready for. The sudden rush of air, the blur of rock, the fear of empty, unsupporting space: it comes as a surprise to everyone.

A climber steels himself, prepares himself to fall. When he begins a climb he knows that he may slip and find himself plunging down. This knowledge gives him an edge. It forces his entire being to focus on survival. He takes everything into account.

But it had happened without warning. I was belaying from some small boulders at the base of the cliff, basking in the pleasant afternoon sun. I was enjoying this day: the clear sky and soft breeze were relaxing. But my suddenly-airborne partner was a cloud crossing the sun. At was as if the ash and smoke from a distant volcano had covered my world, had painted it a dull grey. If I had been paying attention I could have dealt with his fall easily. But my mind was wandering, and I was surprised.

I was like the student startled out of a daydream by the teacher. He is staring at me, his eyes accompanied by those of forty-nine other students, all of them demanding an answer. I want to know what the question is, but there's no time. I must act.

But I could not act. There was nothing more I could do. All the preparation was done: physically I was ready. I had the rope in my hands. It ran through my belay device, a tool designed to control the rope and stop just such a fall. This threw me off guard. What must I do? Surely I must respond. I felt confused. I must do something, and quickly. It occurred to me then that I was the bottom line. If I didn't stop my partner's fall, nothing would. This realization filled me with apprehension. The sudden responsibility was stifling. What if I failed?

But something shoved this senseless thought from my mind. In its place a calm certainty entered. I knew what to do. I must hold the rope tightly, pulling it back against my hip. In this position I had the ability to stop a falling weight many times heavier than my partner's. I was reassured. I was ready after all.

I could do nothing but wait. It seemed like an eternity. My partner was stuck in space, fossilized, imprinted in the petrified air. It is this image that will never leave my mind. I was waiting for the moment when my partner's fate would be decided. I felt my stomach tighten into a knot. The tension was inescapable.

Then it was over. There was a gentle tug on my waist as the rope pulled taut. Its fibers stretched, absorbing the force of his fall. All the inner tension seemed to drain out of me and into the rope, which grew tighter and tighter. For an instant I thought that the tension was too much, that the rope would burst. I felt as though a giant wave was roaring up from the ocean and trying to pull me back into its depths. But I fought it, I withstood it, and suddenly it receded. The tension subsided from the rope, leaving nothing but its thin length stretched along the rock wall. It lay there, stiff and motionless, providing the connection between a fallen climber and his life.

My partner had descended about twenty feet. He was hanging comfortably in his harness. Although shaken, I knew from his vehement cursing that he was alright. I felt relieved.

I had never held such a fall before. Of course I had pictured it many times, but reality was not like I had imagined. I had always known that I would be ready. But I wasn't. Now I know that there is no way I could have been. It is impossible to be ready for a fall's immediate suddenness. All I can do is train myself until my responses are such an integral part of me that I will act unconsciously. My partner may fall anytime and I must be able to respond, because I support his safety net: I keep him alive.

Bolts

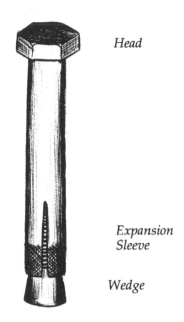

Head

Expansion Sleeve

Wedge

A bolt

What Are Bolts?

A bolt is a **multi-directional**, permanent **anchor.** It is a thin metal rod that you, or another climber, place into a pre-drilled hole in the rock. Because it is strong and multi-directional (you can safely load it from any direction), a bolt is one of the most secure anchors available to connect you to the rock. Usually bolts have **hangers** attached, and it is to the hanger that you connect your **carabiner** (and then your **rope**). To place a bolt you need a hammer, wrench, or glue (depending on the bolt), and of course the drill to make the bolt hole. I discuss all this gear in this chapter.

Bolts are an explosive issue. Sure, they offer great **protection:** clip your rope to a bolt and you're probably safe, even if you take a long fall. However, bolts (with one exception, see pg. 103 below) and their holes are permanent additions to the rock. Once you place a bolt, the only way to remove it is to chop it with a bolt cutter or yank it out with some incredibly high-powered machine. And then you still have the bolt's hole to deal with. So bolts permanently deface the rock.

Climbers recognize this, and respond by placing a bolt only when it is absolutely necessary. If you can connect your rope to the rock by putting chocks in a crack, then you don't need a bolt. Often crack-less face climbs will have nubbins (or **chickenheads** - small rock knobs that stick out from the cliff) that you can wrap a **runner** around, providing you with protection. But if a climb is so solid and sheer that neither one of these options is open to you, and a fall could, at best, seriously injure you, then you can consider placing a bolt.

However, if you are a beginning rock climber, you should never put a bolt in the rock. You should assume that most of the easier **routes** in your area will have already been climbed. And if another climber was able to succeed on a route without a bolt, or with the bolts that are in place, then there is no need for you to add a bolt. If you feel that you can't climb the route without placing a bolt, then the climb is above your level and you shouldn't try it! Placing an unnecessary bolt is a sure way to anger your climbing community. When you have gained more experience, and know the local climbers and their ideas about bolts, then you can consider finding a new route, upon which you might legitimately need a bolt.

Types

Bolts

There are many different types of bolts on the market. However, most of these are meant for construction use. They are not designed for climbing; some of them aren't strong enough to hold a fall. All the bolts I discuss in this chapter are used by climbers, and they are suitable for climbing.

Simply: climbers use either of 2 types of bolts: specialized expansion bolts and chemical bolts. Expansion bolts are more common in the USA, and work well in hard rock. Chemical bolts are more popular in Europe, because they hold well in the softer rock found there.

Expansion Bolts

An expansion bolt is a bolt that anchors into the rock by expanding against the sides of a pre-drilled hole (note that all bolts require a pre-drilled hole).

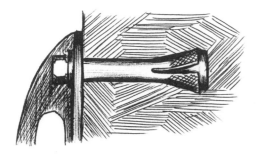

An expansion bolt in the rock

Two styles of expansion bolts are available, hammer-ins and torque-ins. To place a hammer-in bolt you must hammer it into the rock, while to place a torque-in bolt you simply twist it in with a wrench.

In addition, each style of expansion bolt (hammer-in or torque-in) has several variations.

Expansion Bolt Type Guide

The variety of expansion bolts may seem confusing at first, so I have made this chart for easy reference:

Hammer-In	Torque-In
1) Compression:	1) Pull-type
a) Screwtop	2) Push-type
b) Buttonhead	
2) Wedge	
a) externally threaded (stud-type)	
b) internally threaded (self-drive)	

Hammer-In Bolts

The first type of hammer-in bolt I will discuss is the compression bolt, or Rawldrive (made by Rawl). This bolt has a split shank; in other words, its metal length is divided into two sections which bow in the middle.

A buttonhead compression bolt

When you hammer a compression bolt into the rock, its split shank squeezes together, forcing the shank sides to fit into the hole. The compressed shank anchors the bolt tightly by exerting a constant pressure on the surrounding rock.

Compression bolts can have either of two head designs: the screw-top or the buttonhead.

Buttonhead compression bolts have a permanent, slightly-rounded head.

Because it's stronger, the buttonhead design works better for rock climbing than the screw-top. Remember to put a hanger on the buttonhead before you hammer it into the rock, because once inserted, the bolt is permanent.

The screw-top has threads that accept a removable nut.

A screw-top compression bolt

This design allows you to place a hanger on a bolt which has already been anchored into the rock - i.e. as you climb. Then your partner can remove the hanger when he **cleans the pitch** behind you. Note that the screw-top's threads make its design slightly weaker than the buttonhead.

While compression bolts hold securely in hard rock, such as granite, they don't work as well in softer rock, like sandstone and limestone. This is because the constant outward pressure they exert is too much for the soft rock: the bolt constantly pushes against the rock, slowly widening the hole it's in, but then it is unable to expand enough to fill the newly-enlarged hole it has created. Regardless of the rock you put it in, a compression bolt will lose its grip slightly over time, although it will hold very well for several years in hard rock.

Rivets And Rivet Hangers

A **rivet** (also called a **dowel**) is a basic, coarse-thread, construction bolt, of the type you can buy in a hardware store, hammered into a hole in the rock. Rivets don't have a high-grade construction, so they aren't strong, durable anchors like bolts.

Rivets are not designed to support a fall, just body weight, so climbers use them only for aid climbing.

Use a rivet when you are confronted with an existing empty, 1/4-inch hole (the best holes are made by #14 Rawl drills, whose diameters are just fractions larger than 1/4 of an inch). Your rivet should be a grade 5 (coarse thread) steel hardware bolt, 5/16 by 3/4 of an inch long. To use the bolt, hammer it into the hole. The threads of the oversized bolt will bind in the hole, anchoring the rivet.

A rivet in the rock

To use your newly-placed rivet, you need a **rivet hanger.** When placed, the rivet should protrude from the rock slightly, allowing you to slip a rivet hanger behind it.

A wire rivet hanger on a rivet

A **hero loop** (a short runner made from 1/2-inch by 24-inch webbing - see pg. 295) will often work as a substitute rivet hanger. Another good substitute is a wired **wedging chock:** slide the wedge an inch up its wire sling, slip the newly-formed loop over the rivet, and push the wedge tightly against the rivet.

The RP keyhole hanger also works on rivets, because you can slot the hanger into place.

An RP keyhole hanger

The other type of expansion bolt on the market is the wedge bolt. It is surrounded by an even-sided sleeve that is split at the bottom. To secure the bolt, you must place a wedge (a small metal piece that comes with the bolt) onto the end of the sleeve and hammer them both into the pre-drilled bolt hole. The wedge expands the sleeve into the rock, where it holds securely.

There are two models of wedge bolts, those with external threads and those with internal threads. The externally-threaded wedge bolts (also called stud-type bolts) are the easiest to place, and are usually stronger than those with internal threads.

An externally-threaded wedge bolt

The internally-threaded bolts are also called self-drive bolts, because you actually use the bolt to drill the hole in the rock.

An internally-threaded wedge bolt

However, drilling with the bolt means that, if the bolt dulls, you won't be able to use it. And the bolt will dull in hard rock. In fact, you may go through several bolts before you make a deep enough hole. This means that you will use perhaps three bolts to drill one hole! A expensive and time-consuming process.

Additionally, when you use a self-driving bolt you will find that it's hard to determine how deep to make your hole. This is because the bolt sits on the end of your hand-powered drill, and you can't see exactly when the bolt is flush with the rock.

Another disadvantage of the self-driving bolt is that you must drill a large hole to fit the bolt into. For example, the bolt may be only 5/16-inch in diameter, but you must make a hole that will fit the bolt's sleeve, which may be 3/8-inch. And, considering the large size hole, the bolt you use is much weaker than the full 3/8-inch expansion bolt you could use for that hole.

Rawl and Star are two reliable wedge bolt manufacturers. They each make both internally and externally-threaded wedge bolts.

Using A Piton As A Bolt

Some rock is so soft that a bolt won't hold well. In such a situation you can use a baby angle **piton** (see Pitons, pg. 241). To make the piton as secure as possible, you will need three different drills: 1/4, 3/8, and 1/2 inches (in diameter). The distance you drill with each size depends on the quality of the rock. For example, in really soft rock, such as some sandstone and limestone, make most of the hole with your 1/4-inch drill. A rough guideline: first drill about 1/2-inch into the rock with the 1/2-inch drill. Then, use the 3/8-inch drill to deepen the hole another inch. Finally, use the 1/4-inch drill to finish the hole, making it as deep as the piton's blade (approximately 3 inches). This method will allow you to insert the baby angle, which narrows at one end, and provide it with a consistently tight fit.

To make the anchor really strong, pour some polyester glue into the hole. Put glue on the piton as well. Finally, hammer the piton into the hole, making sure to keep its eye down and not to bottom it out (don't let it hit the bottom of the hole - it helps to test the hole depth first by inserting a bolt drill and comparing the distance it went in with the piton).

Torque-In Bolts

A torque-in bolt is a bolt with a standard, wrench-fitting bolt head. To anchor the torque-in bolt simply tighten it with a wrench. There are two types of torque-in bolts on the market, the pull-type and the push-type.

Using a baby angle piton as a bolt

The pull-type torque-in bolt is similar to a wedge bolt. Both have an expanding sleeve that surrounds the bolt and locks it into the rock when a wedge forces the sleeves apart. The difference between them is that the wedge bolt expands when you pound it with a hammer, while the pull-type bolt expands when you torque it with a wrench (it pulls the wedge into itself).

A pull-type torque bolt

Pull-type torque-in bolts are one of the easiest kinds of bolts to place in the rock. They are also strong and hold well, although this depends on the individual model used. The Rawl-Bolt, Metolius bolts, screw-out bolts (Rawl, Star, and USE are popular manufacturers of these), and sleeve bolts (again: Rawl, Star, and USE) are all popular types of pull-type torque-in bolts.

The push-type torque-in bolt is only slightly different than the pull-type bolt. While pull-type bolts expand by pulling a wedge in, push-type bolts expand their sleeve by pushing it out. You torque a screw, or the bolt (depending on the design), into the sleeve, which enlarges it.

USE Diamond and HME are the two main push-type bolt manufacturers. USE makes the taper bolt, which is illustrated on the next page.

The taper bolt is difficult to place well, because you can only turn the bolt a set number of times

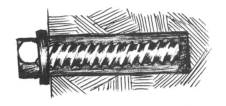

A taper bolt (a make of push-type torque bolt)

A chemical bolt, glued into the rock

(the number of turns depends on the type of bolt - ask for instructions when you buy it). Any more or less turns and the bolt won't be at full strength! This is a problem. It means that you must drill your hole to exactly the right size: if it's too deep you will turn the bolt too much to place it, and if it's too shallow, you won't be able to turn it enough.

HME's bolt looks like this:

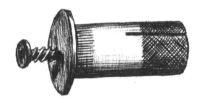

HME's push-type torque bolt

This bolt is reusable! To anchor the bolt in the rock you slide it into a pre-drilled hole, turn its allen screw (you need an allen head wrench), which expands the bolt's sleeves and locks it into the rock. Your partner can take it out when he cleans the pitch by simply loosening the allen screw, which frees the bolt. Although this HME bolt is expensive, you'll find it works very well on routes that have a great many existing bolt holes (such as some El Capitan routes).

Chemical Bolts

Chemical bolts are the other type of climbing bolt on the market (the first is the expansion bolt, which we have just been discussing). Chemical bolts are simple, roughly-threaded metal rods that take their name from the chemical glue you must use to anchor them into the rock.

Because they are glued, chemical bolts are very strong. The glue often becomes harder than the rock, and it strengthens with age! Also, chemical bolts have a higher pull-out strength (loaded from straight out) than shear strength (a perpendicular load), an uncommon characteristic in bolts (it's usually the reverse). See Specifications, pg. 110, below. Chemical bolts work very well in soft rock,

because the glue surrounding the bolt spreads the load over a wide area. Expansion bolts, on the other hand, concentrate the load in one small place (around the expanded part), which easily damages soft rock (that's why expansion bolts work better in hard rock). Chemical bolts also withstand the weather better, because the glue blocks any water from entering the bolt hole. Of course, the exposed part of the bolt may still corrode, but you can prevent this by using a stainless steel bolt.

Chemical bolts have some problems; this makes them useful only in certain situations. For one thing, it takes 10-20 minutes for the glue to set, so you can't use a chemical bolt while you're **leading** a climb unless you have a comfortable place to stand for this long. Because such good stances are rare, you are limited to using chemical bolts while rappelling, where you are anchored by a rope. And putting the glue capsule into the bolt hole is difficult on overhanging rock, because if you don't immediately block the hole, the capsule will slide back out. In addition, you must clean the hole very well before you put the glue into it. If there are any dust particles left in the hole your glue won't bind to its maximum ability when it dries. Finally, you must use a power drill to place the bolt, because you must spin the bolt at 300 rpms for the glue to mix properly. Power drills, although easy and fast to use, are heavy and expensive. Also, you must bring an adapter bit for the drill, so that the bolt will fit into it properly. You can either buy an adapter that will only fit one size of bolt (cheaper), or an adapter that adjusts to fit many differently-sized bolts (more expensive).

Hangers

Climbers commonly use a hanger made of sheet metal, with two holes in it, that is bent 90 degrees, as illustrated on the next page.

A typical climbing hanger

SMC, Leeper, Metolius, and Petzl all make this type of hanger. It is very strong, and works well for all rock climbing situations. Before you place a bolt, make sure that its hanger can sit flat against the rock.

A poorly-placed hanger will leverage the bolt out

but they are not as suitable for rock climbing. For example, some hangers are bent horizontally, instead of lengthwise. These work best if your carabiner lies flat against the rock.

The hanger well-placed: flat on the rock

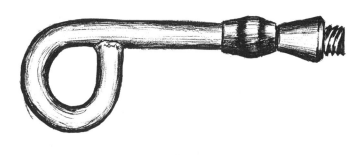

A Metolius eye bolt

If the hanger doesn't sit flat on the rock it will leverage your bolt.

Metolius makes an eye bolt which doesn't need a hanger.

In the past, climbers used other eye bolts, but they all proved to be weak. This is because the bolt's eye is welded together, and since welds are never consistent performers, the weld is a weak link. However, the Metolius bolt is well made, and very strong. Don't buy any other eye bolts, unless you see positive tests conclusively proving the bolt's strength.

There are many other hanger designs available,

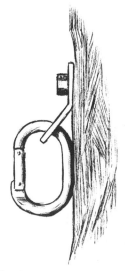

A carabiner in a horizontally-bent hanger

If your carabiner doesn't sit flat on the rock, it will leverage the bolt, weakening it.

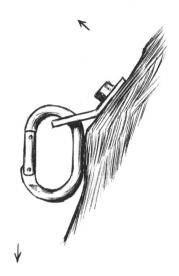

A carabiner leveraging a bolt, because of the hanger design

Other hanger designs that are unsuitable for rock climbing are those that force you to tie your rope to them, instead of clipping to them with a carabiner. These hangers are intended for caving, not rock climbing. They aren't sold in climbing stores, but you may see them occasionally in mail order catalogs: I mention them here so that you won't accidentally buy and use them.

A hanger that you must connect your rope to

Bolt Drills

There are two types of bolt drills on the market: hand-powered drills and battery-powered ones. Manufacturers of hand-powered drills intended for rock climbing include Rawl and Dakota. Electric drills are cordless pneumatic hammers. They save both time and energy. The most popular electric drills are made by Bosch and by Hilti.

Hand-Powered Drills

Unlike what you might expect, a hand-powered drill is not a tool you crank (like a brace and bit). Instead, you pound a chisel-like drill into the rock with a hammer. I'll explain it in more detail below. There are two different hand-powered drill rigs currently available: the Rawl system and the Dakota system.

The Rawl system consists of a drill, a drill holder (an aluminum rod with a rubber grip), and a drift pin. You should attach a length of cord to the drift pin, so you don't lose it.

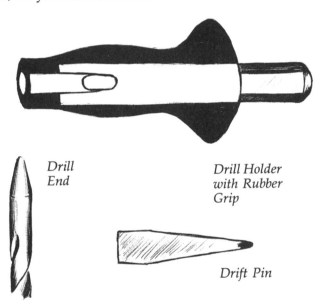

Drill End

Drill Holder with Rubber Grip

Drift Pin

The Rawl drill system

To use the drill you must push it into the holder, where it will fit tightly. Removing the drill is more difficult: you must push the drift pin into an ejection slot, which will release the drill. However, sometimes this is hard to do, and you must really hammer at it.

You should use the standard #14 drill holder, because it will accept 1/4, 5/16, and 3/8-inch drills. Rawl also makes several other drill holders, but you won't need these.

The Dakota system has a similar drill and holder, but no drift pin. Instead, the holder has three allen screws which you tighten to secure the drill in the holder, or loosen to take it out. These screws allow you to gently free the drill from its holder, without it shooting out. However, be careful not to loosen the allen screws too much or they will fall out and you will probably lose them! An allen head wrench comes with the holder, and is connected to it with a cord. If you use the Dakota system, be sure to bring extra allen screws.

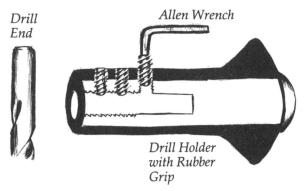

The Dakota drill system

There are two styles of Dakota drill systems made: the Quint and the Quad. With the Quint you can use 1/4, 5/16, or 3/8-inch drills, while with the Quad you can only use 5/16 and 3/8-inch drills. You can use 1/4 and 5/16-inch self-driving bolts with both, although you need a separate adapter to do it.

A Bolt Bag

A bolt bag makes it easy to carry all the parts you need for bolting. You can put bolts, hangers, glue, spare drills, a drill sharpener, drill holders, allen screws, batteries, blow tube (plastic tubing for blowing out the hole), and anything else you might like to bring along, in the bag. The best bag design has some loops sewn inside, where you can put the drills and drill bits, and a separate easy-access compartment for your bolts.

To use a hand-powered drill you need a hammer, because you must pound the drill, in its holder, into the rock. Hammering a hole for a bolt is very strenuous, and in hard rock takes around 15-20 minutes per hole.

The drill is a simple device: it looks like a carpenter's drill bit. The drill is a metal rod, sharpened at one end, with flutes along its length. A flute is a groove, and three different types of drill flutes are made: no-twist, slow-twist, and fast-twist. While you don't absolutely need a twisted flute, it helps because it removes the rock dust from the hole as you drill.

A drill with a no-twist flute

A drill with a slow-twist flute

A drill with a fast-twist flute

There are two types of drill tips you can use, chisel ends or pointed ends. Chisel ends have a sharp, flat edge. They last longer than pointed ends because the entire edge absorbs the wear.

A chisel-end drill

Pointed-end drills have a sharp point. This point makes it easy to start a hole, but once you have the hole going the tip wanders a lot, so you may want to switch to a flat-end drill.

A pointed-end drill

The drill's body must be the same size, or smaller, than the tip. If the body is larger, it will easily bind in the hole. After you have used a drill several times the sides of its tips will be worn down, thus becoming smaller than the body, and binding in the hole.

Your drill will be dull after you make a few holes. How many holes depends on the hardness of the rock (drills obviously last longer in softer rock) and the drill tip you use (carbine-tips last longer than plain steel ones). Regardless, you will have to sharpen the drill, so bring a sharpener with you when you go climbing. You may also want to carry 1-3 extra drills up your climb, just in case.

Battery-Powered Drills

A battery-powered rotary hammer (pneumatic drill) makes drilling much quicker and easier. The Bosch 11213 K "Bulldog" and the Hilti TE 10A are currently the best battery drills for rock climbers on the market. They are heavier than a hand-powered drill (weighing 7-9.5 pounds), and much more expensive (around $500-600!) but they are so much faster that if you plan to drill many holes, this tool more than makes up for its cost.

A battery-powered drill will cut a specific number of holes before its charge wears out. The number depends on the drill - I have stated each drill's capacity below. You may have to bring a spare battery along if you are climbing a long route in which you think you'll have to place many bolts. You will have to buy the extra battery separately, and they are expensive. In short, a battery-powered drill is expensive high-tech gear that requires money, care, and planning to use properly.

The Bosch weighs 7 pounds, 12 ounces, and will drill approximately 10 3/8 by 3-inch holes per battery charge (in granite). It takes almost two hours to recharge the battery. A spare Bosch battery weighs just under 5 pounds.

The Hilti weighs 9 pounds, 10 ounces, and will drill around 23 3/8 by 3-inch holes per battery charge (in granite). You can recharge the Hilti's battery in just over two hours. A spare battery for the Hilti weighs 5.5 pounds.

Because the Hilti is able to drill more than twice as many holes per battery charge, it eats drill bits. So be sure to carry a few extras with you on a climb, because the high-speed power drill will dull them quickly.

A Bosch drill

A Hilti drill

Rig Your Power Drill For Bolting On The Lead

If you want to make the first lead of a climb, and must use a battery-powered drill to place bolts, you must consider how you're going to get that drill up the cliff.

The easiest way to do this is to bring the drill along in a holster, as if it were your climbing hammer (see Hammers, pg. 191). Wear the holster on your **swami belt,** and attach a leash in your drill (in case you drop it, so that it won't fall far). Make the leash out of a strong cord (remember, a power drill weighs up to 9 pounds), such as 5-6 millimeter static cord (see Slings and Runners, pg. 291). Tie the cord through the drill's handle area with a Bowline (see pg. 202).

The heavy drill hanging from your hip will change your balance, so you'll have to learn to adjust for it. But once you're used to it, you can pull your drill out of its holster and make a hole, quickly, and with no fuss. Many climbers find that it's easiest to hold the drill upside-down, as illustrated below, but you should experiment to find the most comfortable grip for you.

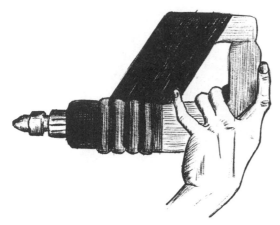

Holding a power drill

Technique

The most of explosive debate raging in the American climbing community concerns the proper approach one should make to bolting a climb. Actually, this debate doesn't really concern the entire climbing community, just those advanced climbers who put up routes (make the **first ascent** up a cliff, putting in the necessary bolts). And this debate is restricted to the U.S.A because the rest of the world has already decided how to place bolts - by **rappelling** down from the top of the cliff to place the bolts before anyone leads the climb.

That is one approach, bolting a route from the top down. The other approach, the **traditional** method, is to bolt the route from the ground up. This involves finding a "no hands **stance**" (a place with large enough footholds that you can actually let go of the rock with your hands), or hanging from hooks.

Both sides have their reasons and give their arguments, which I discuss in more detail on page 15. In this section let's consider how to actually place a bolt, regardless of whether you do so standing precariously on some minute rock edges, or hanging comfortably from a rope.

Placing A Bolt

Placing a bolt involves following a 4-step sequence. First, locate the spot where you want to place the bolt. Second, drill a hole in which to insert the bolt. Third, clean the hole in preparation for placing the bolt. And fourth, insert the bolt into the hole.

A climber placing a bolt while hanging from hooks

Where To Place The Bolt

Before you can begin drilling a bolt's hole, you must decide exactly where you are going to place the bolt. This is not always easy to do, as you must evaluate many different factors. First, the bolt must be easy to clip to when you are climbing the route. One problem with placing a bolt from rappel is that often you won't know exactly where to put the bolt. If you're not careful, you'll end up with a hard-to-reach bolt placed between several difficult moves where it's difficult, if not impossible, to clip your rope in! If, on the other hand, you are *leading* a new route, it will be obvious where each bolt needs to go. If possible, position every bolt so that you can reach it easily, without stretching too far (the best distance is about 2/3 the reach of your arm). This will make both placing a bolt and clipping your rope to it easier.

Once you know the approximate location in which you want the bolt, you must determine if you can actually place it there. First, check the rock to make sure you will be bolting to a solid section of cliff. You don't want to place a bolt on a section of rock that may break off one day! Next, look for cracks, other bolts, or flakes in the area. Your bolt must be at least 10 bolt diameters away from any of these potential hazards. If the location looks good so far, tap the rock with your hammer (or something solid) to make sure it isn't hollow. Don't hit the rock too hard, though, or you will weaken it. If you are still convinced that this is a good place to locate a bolt, clean away any loose flakes or knobs, so you can drill directly into the most solid part of the rock.

Practice Placing Bolts

Before you bolt your first climb, you should place at least one bolt, just for practice. Since this is just practice, you don't want to place the bolt on a cliff. Instead, go to your local climbing area and find a small piece of rock, about 12 inches by 12 inches by 5 inches. Make sure that the rock is solid, that your bolt will hold in it. Take the suitable rock home with you, where you can place as many bolts as necessary - until you know what you're doing.

Drilling The Hole

Drilling is the tricky part. Be sure you drill the bolt hole perpendicular to the rock. If you angle it to one side, the bolt will be weaker. When you drill, stay in the hole, without bouncing your drill around. If the drill bounces the hole will get bigger, which will ruin it because then your bolt won't hold. You must make a perfectly-sized hole!

Be sure to drill the hole to the correct depth. A bolt that uses a wedge to lock itself (many types of expansion bolts) won't lock if the hole is too deep.

However, this is usually not a problem, since you will be trying to keep your drilling time short! Instead, too shallow a hole is more likely. If you drill too shallow a hole, the bolt, when placed, will protrude too far from the rock: this will increase the leverage on it, resulting in a weak bolt.

The best technique for drilling depends on which drill you are using, the hand-powered or the battery-powered type.

A wedge bolt in a hole that's too shallow

Using A Hand-Powered Drill

Using a hand-powered drill requires a certain technique. Hit the drill repeatedly with medium to light strokes. After every hit, rotate the drill, so that you don't bind it in an uneven hole. Make sure you rotate it at least 180 degrees during your drilling, not just back and forth between the same two settings. A good method is to rotate the drill clockwise 1/8 of an inch between each hit.

As you drill, dust buildup becomes a problem, because too much dust will bind your drill. Occasionally remove your drill from the hole and blow out the dust. You can also wet the end of your drill with saliva and rotate it around in the hole. This will gather the dust into a paste that will stick to the drill, making it easy to remove.

To start a new hole, crosshatch the rock with your drill until you make an indentation that allows you to keep your drill in the same place. Then, hammer away, being careful to keep your drill in the same position, always perpendicular to the rock.

Using A Battery-Powered Drill

A power drill is incredibly fast: it takes only about 50 seconds to drill a bolt hole in hard rock! Compare this to the 15 minutes it takes with a hand drill!

Drilling is simple: put the tip of your drill against the rock and push the power button on. Starting the hole is the most difficult part, because the drill is pneumatic, which means that it hammers on the rock. Go slow at first, and hold your drill in a firm grip so that it doesn't jump around. As the hole gets deeper you can relax. At this stage, don't push the drill into the rock: let it work for you. The pneumatic hammering alone will get the job done. Just hold the drill steady.

Cleaning The Hole

After you've drilled the bolt hole, and before you place your bolt, clean all the dust out of the hole. This is especially important if you are using a chemical bolt, because the glue won't bind to the rock if there is dust in the way.

Clean the bolt hole with your blow tube (a 12-inch length of surgical tubing). Put the tube in the hole and blow through it. Keep your eyes closed or away from the hole (it helps to have a long blow tube!) so the dust doesn't get in them.

Inserting The Bolt

If you're using an expansion bolt, this is a good time to coat it with some polyester resin. The resin will protect it from corroding. Coating is easy to do: smear the resin over the bolt with your fingers. Once you have coated the bolt, insert it in the rock, according to the next few instructions.

Inserting A Compression Bolt

When you insert a compression bolt, make sure to position its bowed shank horizontally (perpendicular to the expected direction of the load, which is usually down).

If your hole is too shallow for the compression bolt, you may bottom out (hit the bottom of the hole, which makes the bolt bounce out slightly). If this happens, don't hammer the bolt again! Leave it if it seems secure (tug on it); if it's weak, try to remove it. Failing that, try to push it all the way in. If that doesn't work deform the bolt so that no one else can use it. You will have to locate and drill a new hole. Remember that minimum environmental impact is the ethic: if you are screwing-up bolt placements, you should practice some more at home!

Inserting A Wedge-In Bolt

To place a wedge-in bolt, regardless of whether it is of the hammer-in or the torque-in variety, you must first place the bolt's wedge in the end of the bolt. Push it in just far enough to grip, but not any farther, or you'll expand the sleeve and it won't fit into the hole. Now insert the bolt into the hole, and hammer, or torque (with a wrench), it into place. Note that torque bolts require only a few turns, around 3-4, to reach full strength. An exception is the HME push-type bolt, which you need turn only once.

Inserting A Chemical Bolt

Place the glue capsule or cartridge into the hole. Place the hanger on the bolt and insert it. Then, with your electric drill, spin the bolt down into the hole. This is necessary to break the capsule and mix the glue; you must spin the bolt at around 300 rpms. (drill at full power). Stop drilling (spinning) when the bolt and hanger are flush with the rock. You should remove the drill from the bolt immediately, before the glue has a chance to set. During this time you can move the bolt by hand with no problem to position it correctly, but don't touch it after the first minute, or you'll weaken the bind!

Specifications

Bolt Length

The length of bolt you need will be determined by the hardness of the rock you are going to place it in. In hard rock, such as granite, you can use a short bolt, about 2 inches. In softer rock, such as limestone and sandstone, use a longer bolt, from 3-3.5 inches long.

Bolt Width

The bolt's width determines both its strength and the time it will take you to drill the hole. The wider the bolt, the stronger it is, but the longer you must drill.

In the past, climbers used 1/4-inch bolts almost exclusively. However, these bolts are fairly weak, and are not suitable for modern rock climbing, in which climbers take many falls. Instead, use a bolt of either 5/16 or 3/8-inch diameter. Use the 5/16-inch bolt in hard rock when you can't drill easily. The 3/8-inch bolt provides excellent strength; you should always use it in soft rock; it provides the best anchor in hard rock, so you should use it there too unless drilling is difficult.

Bolt Strength

There are two aspects to a bolt's strength: shear strength and pullout strength. Shear strength is the load a bolt can withstand from a perpendicular direction.

Pullout, or tension, strength is the load a bolt can withstand along the axis of its shaft. This rating is always less than the bolt's shear strength, except with chemical bolts.

Shear loading

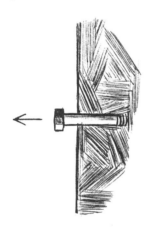

Pullout, or tension, loading

Naturally, how strong a bolt placement actually is depends on how well it is placed, and in what kind of rock. Manufacturers test their bolts after embedding them in concrete that is usually rated to 4000 pounds per square inch (psi), which is the compressive strength of the material. Rock, on the other hand, has varying compressive strengths: from 4000 to 40,000 pounds in granite, 1000 to 20,000 pounds in sandstone, and 1000 to 5000 pounds in limestone. Naturally, a bolt will hold better in harder (more compressed) rock. In addition, the people who place test bolts are expert bolt setters, who have been doing this for years. And until you become as experienced, you won't be as consistent in your bolt settings. Therefore, a manufacturer's strength rating will not show you how much of a load your bolt will actually hold on the cliff. Instead, unless you are drilling on obviously hard rock (you'll know!), assume that your bolt is weaker than the manufacturer's ratings. However,

unless you made a poor placement or the rock is extremely soft (again, you'll know!), the bolt should easily hold a fall.

Hanger Hole Size

Most hangers have two holes in them, one small, one large. The small one is the important one, because it is the hole through which you place your bolt. If the bolt is too large for the hanger, it won't fit in this hole. The larger hole is for clipping your carabiner. All the hangers sold by climbing stores and mail order companies have holes large enough to accept your carabiners.

Hanger Strength

A hanger must be at least as strong as the bolt supporting it. Perhaps the weakest climbing hanger on the market is Petzl's, which is rated to 3960 pounds. This is an adequate strength, although you may feel more comfortable with a stronger hanger, such as SMC's, rated at 4500 pounds.

Sample Bolt Specifications

Manufacturer/Type	Size (inch)	Shear Strength (lbs)	Pullout Strength (lbs)
Expansion Bolts			
HAMMER-IN:			
Rawl/Rawldrive	5/16 x 1.5	4850	3500
Stud-type	3/8 x 3	4100	3400
Star/Self Drive	3/8 x 1.6	4400	2140
TORQUE-IN:			
Rawl/Rawl Bolt (pull-type)	3/8 x 3	8155	5590
Metolius/Metolius Bolt (pull-type)	3/8 x 3.25	7000	6000
Chemical Bolts			
Rawl/Chem Stud	3/8 x 3.5	7340	7820
Hilti/HVA	3/8 x 3.5	5700	7260
Molly/Parabond	3/8 x 3.5	4063	6580

Materials

Bolts

Problems are arising now from the old, 1/4-inch steel bolts that climbers put into various cliffs only a few years ago. These bolts have corroded, and are extremely weak and untrustworthy. Consequently, climbers have had to replace them with new bolts. The result is spectacular rock covered in metal and old bolt holes (although climbers usually try to hammer the bolt into the rock and fill the hole with resin).

To avoid adding to this problem you should use stainless steel bolts and hangers. Stainless steel is strong and resists corrosion. Also, be sure to use the larger 3/8-inch bolts, or at least the 5/16-inch ones. Again, durability is the issue. Every bolt you place is permanent; it must be able to offer security for countless climbers coming up the route after you.

Note: you can make a bolt and hanger even more weather-resistant by coating it with polyester resin before placing it (see pg. 110). Some climbers have tried epoxy, but epoxy corrodes steel, so refrain from using it.

General Safety Guidelines

All Bolts Are Not The Same!

Not every bolt you clip into will provide you with a bombproof anchor. Some bolts aren't well-placed, while others have weakened with age.

Rarely will you be able to visually inspect a bolt: usually the hanger is in the way. However, if the bolt looks severely corroded or bent, its shank sticks out too far (it should only protrude enough to accept a hanger), or it is placed in cracked rock, don't trust it!

Always Use At Least Two Good Bolts At A Belay!

One bolt never guarantees security, and at a **belay station,** you must have foolproof anchors. Therefore, *always clip in to at least two good bolts!* If you can't find two good bolts, use a chock to back up each of the bolts you use.

Accessories

Bolt Bag

You can buy a climbing-specific bolt bag from A5, or you can improvise your own. For example, you might use a fanny pack, or even an empty **chalkbag.**

Bolt Drills

You can buy both hand-powered and battery-powered bolt drills from many climbing mail order companies and climbing stores, while you can get one or the other from some bolt manufacturers and hardware stores. You can also buy spare parts, such as holders, drill bits, and batteries, from the same sources.

Blow Tube

You can buy a 12-inch length of surgical tubing at most pharmacies.

Polyester Resin

Most paint and hardware stores sell polyester resin. Buy the small can so that you can easily carry it with you.

Some Manufacturers That Sell Bolts

Some manufacturers that sell bolts and bolting equipment include 5.10, Dakota Bolt Works, HME, Metolius, Petzl, Rawl, SMC, and Star. See pg. 353 for the manufacturers' addresses.

Boots

Upper

Rand

Rand

Sole

A rock climbing boot

What Is A Rock Climbing Boot?

A rock climbing boot is unique among boots and shoes. Its most surprising feature is its totally smooth rubber sole which, amazingly enough, grips rock incredibly well. This boot often has a wide rubber "rand" that covers your toes, runs around the sides of your foot, and encircles your heel. The boot's uppers, extending from the sole, up under the rand, and to the top of the boot, are usually made of leather. The lacing system of most climbing boots is very long, stretching from your ankles almost to your toes.

The result of this design is precise foot control. While wearing these boots you can keep your feet in place on a steep, smooth slab of granite, locked tightly in a crack, or while balanced on a "credit card-thin" edge of rock. As you can see, rock climbing boots allow you to walk in places that are otherwise inaccessible.

Is A Rock Climbing Boot Important?

Rock climbing boots are arguably the most important piece of rock climbing equipment you can own (your **rope** is the other). With a pair of these contemporary, sophisticated climbing boots you can easily walk up rock that would otherwise be impassable. Climbing boots have improved so much that today, with a little practice, many beginning climbers can successfully negotiate the hardest known routes of just three decades ago!

Footwork is the most important skill a rock climber can learn. Climbing rocks takes endurance, and your legs, being far stronger than your arms, can support you for a much longer time. Many beginning climbers declare that "if my arms were just a little stronger I would have no problem climbing that route." But actually, all they need to do is learn to support their weight with their feet instead of their hands!

The reason many climbers have trouble with their footwork is that rock climbing boots can support them on improbable pieces of rock. How can you trust your feet to hold you on rock that seems to be as smooth as ice? Trust is the key word here. If you trust your boots you will put more weight on them. Rubber uses friction to hold itself to the rock, and the harder you press it, the tighter it will hold. So keep your body, and therefore your weight, over your feet!

It takes time and practice to learn good footwork. As you become more experienced, small indentations and edges where you can put your feet will seem to appear on previously smooth rock. You will learn to trust your feet, and to move with small, economical steps whenever possible. When this is not possible, you will know that you must use more of your arms to help you move quickly to the next secure stance where you can get your feet back under you and rest. But this takes practice. Although you may understand how to use your feet right now, without many hours of practice using them you will not really be able to use them well.

Technique

Before discussing the boot in detail, I will briefly discuss four basic foot climbing techniques - four ways to use your feet on a climb. These four techniques all have many variations, and any climb may require you to use only one of them, or all four. These techniques will give you the basic knowledge you need to begin developing trust in your feet. This discussion will demonstrate just how valuable the climbing boot is.

The first technique I will describe is called **frictioning,** or **smearing.** Climbers smear smooth rock, such as some granite slabs, where there are no sharp edges or protrusions to stand on. When you smear smooth rock, such as some granite slabs, where there are no sharp edges or protrusions to stand on. When you smear, you re relying totally on friction to maintain your grip on the rock. To get the most friction you need boots with flexible soles that can put as much rubber in contact with the rock as possible.

The second technique is called edging. Many types of rock have edges that climbers can use to support their weight, some so small that they are about the width of a credit card. When you edge

Frictioning (smearing) smooth rock

the rock you use the inside or outside edge of your climbing boot to keep yourself on a thin edge of rock.

Edging the rock

Toeing is the third technique, and it is essential for climbing pockets. A pocket is a small, somewhat round indentation in the rock, which is usually limestone or lava tuft. To stand in a pocket you must support yourself with your toes. This is very strenuous because your foot leverages your body weight, increasing the strain on your toes.

Toeing a pocket

The fourth technique is called jamming, and works only while climbing cracks. There are many different sizes and shapes of cracks, each of which requires a different method of jamming. However, the principle is always the same. Rotate your foot sideways, so that it is thin enough to insert far into the crack. When you have inserted it, try and return it to its normal position. It won't go far before it tightens securely.

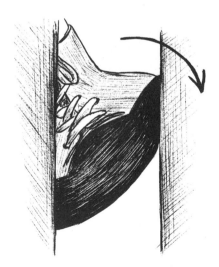

Jamming a crack

Types

There are three basic types of rock climbing boots on the market: high-tops, low-tops, and slippers.

These days high-tops and low-tops have very similar performance characteristics, while the slipper is quite distinct.

Note: the term "rock climbing boot" is generic and includes all three types.

The High-Top Boot

The boot

The high-top boot has tall uppers which cover your ankles. It looks like a basketball shoe.

Uppers serve several useful purposes. First, they protect your ankles from rock abrasion. This is particularly useful when you are climbing wide cracks into which you must put your entire foot, and possibly some of your leg, to get security. Next, uppers provide support for your ankles. This support saves your ankles on long, fatiguing climbs and again, while climbing wide cracks where you must keep your foot from rotating out of position.

High-tops, because they encircle your upper foot securely, are also good for climbing pockets. They cup your heel and support your ankle, which makes it easier to stand on your toes.

Uppers increase a high-top's lateral stability. This stability keeps your foot from rotating off a thin rock edge.

A good edging high-top has a laterally stiff sole in addition to stiff uppers. Note: a tight-fitting high-top edges better than a loose one, so tighten your laces as much as possible, especially around the ball of your foot, before you climb.

A high-top's tall uppers inhibit your ankle's flex-

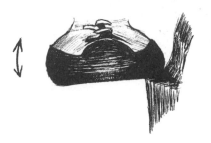

Lateral rotation

The shoe

ibility. This flexibility is important when you are trying to friction the rock and climb thin cracks. To increase your ankle's flexibility, lace the high-tops only 2/3 of the way up. This will make your high-top function more like a low-top.

An Aid Climbing Boot

You don't need normal rock climbing boots to **aid climb**. In fact, on long aid **routes** you may prefer a stiffer boot, like a hiking boot. (This is particularly true on **big walls.)** Such a boot will keep your **etriers** from biting into your feet, so you will be more comfortable.

Unfortunately, a hiking boot doesn't grip the rock very well. This is only a problem when you need to leave the security of your etriers to **free climb** a section of rock (a free section). (If there are many free sections on your route, consider bringing along a pair of standard climbing boots.) You can solve this problem by purchasing a pair of Fire Big Wall Boots, which are made for aid climbing, but have climbing-boot-rubber soles. Or, you can saw the front half of your hiking boot's sole off, and replace it with climbing rubber (see Resoling, pg. 124). Either solution will work well.

The Low-Top Boot

Also known as a shoe, a low-top rock climbing boot has low-cut uppers, similar to those of a tennis shoe, which are cut below the ankle.

By having a stiff upper, yet at the same time cutting it below the ankle, low-cuts offer both support and flexibility. Because the short upper is stiff it will give your foot enough support to edge well. At the same time, because the upper is cut low, you have good ankle rotation. This rotation will help your friction and thin crack climbing.

However, without protective ankle covering, low-cuts aren't good for climbing wide cracks. If you do use a low-cut boot to climb a wide crack, you may reach the top of the crack with bruised and bloodied ankles!

Few low-cuts are made with a complete rand. Many have only a toe and heel section, with perhaps a small rubber strip around the front half of it.

The Slipper

Climbing slippers are appropriately named; they really are like house-slippers. A climbing slipper's upper is very flimsy, and cut low around the top of your foot. Often the slipper is held to your foot only by a built-in elastic strap which fits around your heel. Some slippers are a little more substantial than this, having short laces as well. Note: if the elastic strap digs into your heel, put some tape on your foot for protection.

Slippers offer your foot excellent sensitivity and flexibility. These characteristics make slippers very good for friction climbing. They allow you to feel

The slipper

every indentation in the rock, and know how much you can trust your foothold.

With almost non-existent uppers, slippers give you excellent ankle rotation. This makes them good for climbing thin cracks in which you need to really twist your foot to secure it in place.

Slippers are excellent for strengthening your feet. Their lack of support means that your foot must work that much harder to keep you on the rock. Gradually your foot will adapt to this increased load by getting stronger in the ankles and the smaller foot muscles and tendons.

There are some problems with slippers, however. Because they don't have supportive uppers and lacing, they can slide around on your foot. For this reason, it is imperative that you get a tight fit when you buy a pair. Buy your slippers one size smaller than your regular rock climbing boots (whether high-top or low-top). However, if the particular model of slipper you are buying is known to stretch (ask the salesperson), you should consider buying them two sizes smaller.

The same lack of support that makes slippers excellent training tools also means that when you begin climbing with them your feet will quickly become fatigued. You don't want to be halfway up a long climb with feet which are too tired to continue! Until you build up your foot strength, use slippers only on short climbs (they work great for bouldering). Note: if you have strong feet and want to build up their endurance, wearing slippers on a medium to long climb is good training.

Slippers are not very durable. Their light construction makes them very prone to wear.

Most slippers have almost no rand. The rand may be only a thin strip of rubber covering your heel, and a small patch covering your toes. This means that slippers aren't great for **toe-hooking** and climbing wide cracks (anything wider than your toes), and work only with some **heel-hooking,** depending on the rock.

Make a special point to walk only on rocks when you are wearing slippers. They have thinner soles than both high-tops and low-tops and will wear out faster. Above all, *don't step on glass!* Glass could easily puncture your soles (and then your feet).

Brief History

Because rock climbing is a by-product of mountain climbing, the first rock climbers wore mountaineer's hiking boots. They were very stiff, with

A climber in the 1860s

leather uppers and ridged soles. They worked well for long hikes, easy climbs, and even the hard edging climbs of that era. But they were miserable for friction and crack climbing.

To deal with this problem, some rock climbers started using straw-soled shoes. Straw was much more pliable than stiff leather hiking boots, and provided a better grip. However, the straw-soled shoes didn't last long: the rock tore them apart.

Then, in the late 1940's some rock climbers began wearing tennis shoes, which had become cheap and commonplace after the war. Tennis shoes gripped the rock fairly well, although they were too soft to edge well.

Galibier, a French company, manufactured a pair of stiff-soled climbing boots in the 1950's. These had blue suede uppers and were the climbing shoe of choice for many years.

Galibier introduced the E.B. in the 1970's. With its relatively soft, frictioning rubber, and a rand that covered the toes, instep, and heel, the E.B. provided the early model for today's climbing shoes.

In the early 1980's a company called Boreal revolutionized the climbing boot industry with their introduction of the Fire (pronounced Fee-Ray). This climbing boot was made with sticky rubber soles which were able to grip (friction) the rock incredibly well. With the Fire, novice climbers could undertake routes that were previously inaccessible to them. And the expert climbers were able to open up a whole new, very difficult, level of climbing.

Now, in 1989, the climbing shoe industry is very competitive. Many companies produce excellent rock climbing boots. The trend is away from high-tops and toward low-tops. The footwear companies are producing more specialized shoes, some made for edging, some for friction, and some just for cracks. Many climbers like to buy a different pair of boots for each type of climbing, but this is not really necessary, as they all work well enough on all types of rock features. But it's fun to have toys!

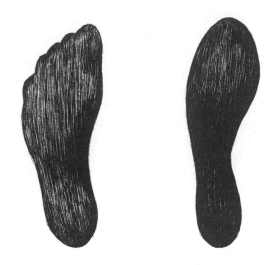

My bare foot compared to my climbing shoe. The sizes are proportional.

Getting A Good Fit

Rock climbing boot manufacturing technology has become so sophisticated that you cannot buy a bad pair of boots. Although the boots are often specialized, perhaps edging better than they friction, all of them will easily grip most rock features. You may hear a novice climber blame his shoes for his failure to climb a route, but you may then see a more skilled climber effortlessly floating up the same route in a junky old pair of E.B.s! In other words, the differences between one climbing boot and another are so subtle that a beginner won't be able to make use of them.

So instead of wasting your time looking for the most expensive boot, spend it trying on cheaper models. Fit is the most important thing for you to consider when you buy a pair of climbing boots. For the best performance, your boots should fit you *exactly*. If they're too large your foot will slide around. Too small and they will be so painful that you won't want to climb in them. Here's a tip for you downhill skiers: my friends that both climb and ski tell me that their tight-fitting ski boots feel about the same as their climbing boots.

A climbing boot should fit your foot like a glove: every toe should touch the end of your boot. However, this doesn't mean your toes should be painfully crunched! Your heel should sit well in the boot, and you shouldn't have empty space between the boot and your foot.

Many rock climbing boots are made to fit specific types of feet. For example, some manufacturers only make a narrow boot. While such a boot may have the characteristics you want, if you have wide feet you won't be able to wear it.

The best way to find the right boot is to make successive approximations. Start by determining exactly what you want your new climbing boots to do. If you are a beginner, you just need a basic, versatile, all-around boot. But if you're more advanced, maybe you want a specialized crack, edging, or friction boot.

If you want a specialized boot, consider what kind of climbing is common to your area. A good crack climbing boot won't help if there are no cracks to climb! What kind of climbing do you like doing best? Do you want to work on face climbing, for instance, because you haven't done much of it? These are the kind of questions you should ask yourself before you begin your search for a good rock climbing boot.

The next thing to do is to start looking at climbing boots. Look through your catalogs (if you don't have any, order them!) and tour your local climbing stores. Find all the boots that could possibly work for the type of climbing you want to do.

When you are satisfied that you have found enough models of boots that fit your requirements, find out which ones fit you. For instance, are they narrowly-cut, wide, or do they fit average feet (is there such a thing)? The best way to check this out is to try the boot on, so go to your local climbing store and do exactly that.

Ordering Climbing Catalogs

To order a climbing catalog, either call or write to the manufacturer or mail order company with your request. I have suggested 8 mail order companies to order from initially: their addresses are on page 357. In addition, you can find the mailing addresses of some U.S. and foreign climbing gear manufacturers on pg. 353.

If you find several climbing boots that fit you, you must choose between them. Find out as much information about each one as you can. A very important thing to learn is whether or not the boot will stretch. Generally, unlined leather stretches. Buy such boots in a very tight fit. Now consider durability. Will the boots quickly fall apart, or will they last a few years. You will need to resole them occasionally, so they should be able to withstand the cobbler hands (most high-tops and low-tops can, but slippers usually can't).

Once you have nailed down the facts regarding fit and durability, you can go to actual performance. Which shoe is known for really performing well on the types of climbs you want to make? A good way to find this out is to read the rock climbing boot review in a climbing magazine. Climbing magazines usually review the new line of boots yearly, and offer good performance information. For climbing magazine addresses, see pg. 359.

Price may be a factor in your selection of climbing boots. Don't always go for the cheapest boot because it may be the first to fall apart. Then again, an expensive high-performance boot won't be much of an advantage to you if you aren't climbing extremely hard routes. These days you can get a good pair of new climbing boots for around $100. However, climbing stores and mail-order companies occasionally have specials, so you might find a pair for $80. But you have to wait for the special. You can also buy used boots, although it is almost impossible to find a pair that fits, but maybe you'll be lucky.

Ordering Climbing Boots Through The Mail

The only problem with ordering climbing boots through the mail is that you can't try on the boot before you buy it. Of course, if the boot doesn't fit, you can always return it for another size. However, this takes time.

But you can help the mail order company send you the right boot the first time around. First, if possible, go to a climbing store and try on the boot you intend to buy. Find a boot that fits, and send its size along with your order. If your local climbing stores don't have the boot you want, then you should send the following information with your order: the size of your old boots, a tracing of your foot's outline (only one foot, and wear socks if you wear them when you climb), whether or not your feet are narrow, medium, or wide, and how tight you like to fit your boots. This information will increase your chances of getting the right boots, the first time.

Materials

There are six parts to a rock climbing boot: the sole, last, upper, rand, lining, and laces. Each part affects how useful the boot as a whole will be for any particular type of climbing you do.

Sole

The sole of a rock climbing boot is smooth, flat rubber. Yet it has incredible gripping properties, holding on slight bumps and textures that no other sole would be able to grasp.

The secret to this incredible holding ability is the correct mix of rubber. Manufacturers have spent many years coming up with more effective rubber compounds. Their resulting recipes are kept secret.

The ability of rubber to grip rock comes from two attributes: friction and interlocking. Friction is the gripping force which occurs when two objects rub along each other. The harder you push, the more friction results. (This is the reason why you want to keep your weight above your feet.) The more the surface area of one object is in contact with the other, the more friction results. This is where interlocking comes in. Interlocking is the rubber's ability to conform to the shape of the surface it's on, without tearing. Maximum interlocking gives maximum surface area contact between the rubber and the rock (the surface it's on). The more contact between the two surfaces, the more friction acts on them.

The trick is to make a rubber compound which

has good interlocking ability (increasing friction) yet which won't tear. When you slip, the rubber is tearing, ripping off the rock. You can see the tears if you look at your soles; the tears are the ridges that run from side to side across them.

Sticky Spanish rubber has a good reputation and is used with slight variations by many companies. There are many other good mixes around, including 5.10 Stealth rubber which is claimed by many to be the best. I use Stealth rubber and have found it to be excellent for friction climbing. It seems to be too soft for hard edging however; it rolls off the edge.

These days manufacturers make a number of specialized rock climbing boots. They may be intended for friction, edging, pocket, or crack climbing. You need different characteristics in the boot's sole for each of these different types of climbing.

Friction climbs require that the sole be both flexible and sensitive. Flexibility is important because you want as much of the sole to be in contact with the rock as possible. A good way to tell whether the sole of the boot is designed for friction climbing is to bend it. You must be able to bend the sole fairly easily, both lengthwise and across the width. Try a few models of boots so that you can get a feel for this. A sensitive sole allows you to feel the rock through your foot. This information helps you make the most use of each foothold, telling you when you should make position adjustments. It will also let you feel when your foot is about to slip.

A good edging boot stays stiff and motionless on a credit card-sized edge while it supports your foot. To do this it must have a sole that is laterally stiff, or stiff across the width of your foot.

Your boot's sole should taper from wide at your toes to thin at your heel. This design keeps your heel from leveraging your boot off a hold. It also puts more of your weight directly on the rock, which means you are less likely to slip. The less frequently you slip the longer your boot's sole will endure.

You should note that severely-tapered soles require you to hold your heel high to get a good placement on the rock. Some boots remedy this by providing a thick heel last that lifts your heel for you.

Sole Durability

The durability of your rubber soles depends on how you use them. Stiff, hard rubber lasts longer than flexible, soft rubber when you are climbing edges. Soft rubber lasts longer on friction climbs because the rubber is able to flex more and spread the area of contact over a larger portion of the sole. The wear on hard rubber is more localized and so a hard sole doesn't last as long.

Sole Thickness

Thin boot soles are more sensitive than thick soles, and work better for edging. However, they don't last as long as thick soles.

Boots and shoes have thicker soles than slippers. Both boots and shoes usually have 4-6 mm thick soles. Slippers have 3 mm soles.

Sole Shape

The shape of the rubber sole's edge is important. A straight, square-cut edge will not hold well on small rock ledges. Remember, the rubber flexes under load, therefore a rounded, or beveled, edge will hold on rock edges much better. Think of it as a wall's buttress: if a wall goes straight up it tends to be wobbly, it has no support at the base. A buttressed wall, on the other hand, has a curved line which gives it support.

A sole's beveled edge

Bi-Density Soles

Boot soles are sometimes split into two sections, separated laterally at the instep. These soles are known as bi-density soles.

The front, or toe section, of the bi-density sole is made of normal sticky rubber. The rear, or heel section, is a lighter, less sticky type of rubber. The advantage of this design is that the lighter rubber in the back allows the boot to remain very flexible. This means the rubber on the front section can be stiff for edging while the lighter back section reduces the boot's overall stiffness to make it good for friction climbing.

The Midplate

In the past, manufacturers used the same rubber recipe for all types of boots. No longer. Edging shoes have stiff rubber soles which are sometimes even supported by a midplate. A midplate is a strip of metal, carbon fiber, or stiff nylon which fits in the front section of the sole. It makes the shoe very stiff laterally, which is vital for easy edging.

A midplate makes a shoe too stiff to friction well. To solve this problem, some manufacturers make shoes with removable midplates.

Rubber alone can be very stiff and work well for edging. Yet boot manufacturers are not satisfied with rubber alone: they are starting to insert sole stiffeners. These are "plates" of a stiff material; some manufacturers use carbon fiber, some nylon, and some plastic. The idea is to give lateral support for edging and yet retain longitudinal flex for friction climbing. This increases the boot's versatility somewhat, although the plates do reduce sensitivity.

To increase the boot's applicability to friction climbing some plates are designed to be removed. This eliminates any potential sensitivity problems. If you buy a boot of this type make sure that it is well-constructed. Try wearing it with both the plate in and out of the boot. Does it feel comfortable either way?

The Last

The last is the climbing boot's inner sole. A foot-conforming last has advantages: it fits better, slips less, and gives you more control. An orthopedic last conforms closer to your foot than a simple flat last. Most modern climbing boots have at least some foot-conforming features, usually an arch.

Lasts come in two shapes: asymmetrical and symmetrical. Symmetrical lasts come to a point in the center of the boot, between your big toe and little toe.

A symmetrical last crams your toes into the boot's point. Few manufacturers use a strictly symmetrical last: it is too uncomfortable and doesn't allow for a good fit.

Asymmetrical lasts come to a point on the side of your big toe.

An asymmetrical last is comfortable because it follows the natural shape of your foot.

The Rand

The rand is the strip of rubber that wraps around the lower part of your climbing boot. A complete rand covers your heel, the sides of your foot, and your toes.

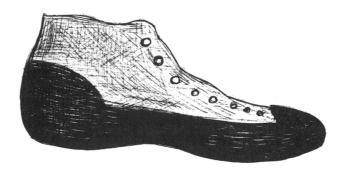

A complete rand

The complete rand is versatile. You can climb many different types of cracks, and do toe hooks and heel hooks with the complete rand. Because of this it is used on general purpose boots, boots that work well on many types of climbs.

The purpose of the rand depends upon where it is located on your boot. On the sides, the rand adds stability to your foot and protects your boot's upper. Over and around your toes, the rand protects them and gives them friction, qualities essential for jamming your toes into cracks. These protection and friction characteristics also help you hold a toe hook in position.

A rand's toe profile is important. If it's narrow you will be able to fit your foot into thin cracks. If it's sharply pointed and stiff, it will work well for pocket climbing.

The rand around your heel is useful for heel hooking and jamming your foot in a wide crack. Heel rands also cup your heel, which helps to keep it from slipping around in your boot.

Specialized boots often don't have complete rands. The rand is only put in necessary places, such as around the toes and up the heel (usually only a thin strip), or even just around the toes.

The Uppers

A climbing boot's upper is the material, usually leather, that extends up your foot from the sole. If the boot has a rand (most do), the rand covers the lower section of the upper.

The upper's shape is important. A stiff upper that covers your ankle protects your foot in cracks and adds stability for better edging control. However, it also inhibits your ankle flexibility, which makes it difficult to friction and climb thin cracks. The reverse is obvious: a low-cut upper frees your ankle for maximum rotation, making it excellent for friction climbing and wedging in thin cracks. Unless it is really stiff, a low-cut upper is not ideal for edging problems. It is never good for wide cracks because it doesn't protect your ankles. An upper that is cut down around your achilles tendon but still covers your ankle gives you flexibility and protection.

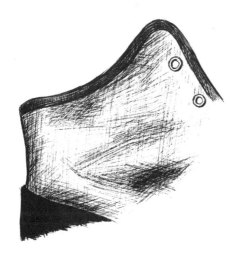

An upper that's cut down around the Achilles Tendon

Uppers are usually made from leather, a good material because it weathers well and lasts a long time. Its stretch allows it to conform to your foot; it will gradually fit better.

Uppers are also made out of canvas and cordura nylon. These materials don't last as long as leather, nor do they protect as well. But they are stiffer, and do weigh less.

The Lining

Most rock climbing boot uppers are lined. This lining stiffens the upper, adding stability and reducing stretch.

Boots may be lined with canvas or with Cambrelle (a synthetic material). Both linings work well, although Cambrelle absorbs sweat more readily than canvas.

Climbing boots that aren't lined will stretch. Before you buy an un-lined boot, make sure that it fits very tightly. After a month of climbing the boot will have stretched to fit you perfectly. But after using the boot for six months to a year it will have stretched even more; it may become too loose to use.

The Laces

Laces are important because they control the tightness of your boot. The tighter it is, the less it slips, and the more control you have.

There are two effective lacing systems in general use. The first is the one you probably use when you wear tennis shoes. It is the single lacing system.

The second is the dual lacing system. This system uses two laces, one for the front of your boot, the other for your boot's rear and upper.

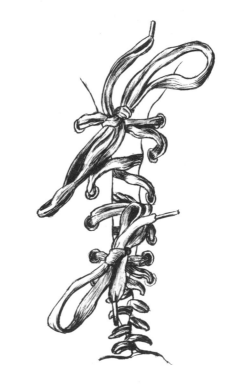

A dual lacing system

The advantage to the dual lacing system is this: you can vary the fit of your boot to the type of climbing you intend to do. On edging and wide crack climbs you should tighten both laces as much as possible. This will keep the boot from slipping, and allow its upper to give your foot lateral support. For friction and thin crack climbing you can tighten the lower lace but keep the upper one loose. The loose upper lace allows you to rotate your ankle fully, which is vital on friction climbing and toe-jamming cracks.

Your boot's eyelets are important, no matter which lacing system you use. The upper eyelets are protected by metal rings, the lower ones are not. These metal rings allow you to pull your laces together tightly, without fear of ripping through the hole. There are no rings protecting the lower holes because there isn't enough room and you don't need to pull them tightly together (you can tighten them before you put the boot on, and they will stay tight for a long time).

Climbing Boot Size Conversion Chart

The following chart approximately compares U.S. climbing boot sizes to European sizes. Note that climbing boots are often hand made and so each boot has a slightly different size. In addition, boot manufacturers make their boots in slightly different sizes, i.e. a Kamet size 37 boot is comparable to Dolomite's size 38 boot. And finally, climbing boots are often a half to one size smaller than street shoes. To guarantee a good fit, you'll simply have to try a boot on.

U.S. - men	U.S. - women	European
5	6.5	37
6	7.5	38
7	8.5	39
8	9.5	40
9	10.5	41
10	11.5	42
11	12.5	43

Care

Rock climbing boots are fragile tools. You must treat them well to get the most out of them.

Don't Walk In Your Boots

Rock climbing boots are not made for walking or hiking. You will reduce their life span if you walk in them. This doesn't mean you must take them off to walk the fifty feet to the next climb, but it does mean that you should avoid hiking in them.

Keep Your Soles Clean

The cleaner you keep the soles of your climbing boots, the better they will stick to the rock. Scrubbing the rubber with water cleans it well enough; you can also use your spit if you don't have enough water with you for the job. To do a thorough job, rub the sole with a rag soaked in solvent.

When **bouldering** and **toproping** you can put a small, square piece of carpet down at the beginning of your climb. Before you begin, step on the rug and rub your boots clean.

Wire Brushing

Rubber gradually oxidizes, losing its fresh, sticky rock-grabbing grip. To remedy this you can wire-brush your boot's soles and rands. This removes the oxidized rubber, revealing a fresh rubber surface that performs like new.

You will shorten the life of your soles if you wire-brush them too frequently. Brush only when you feel that it is really necessary, maybe once every few months.

Shoeper Stik

Another way to make your oxidized rubber soles stickier is to apply some Shoeper Stik. Shoeper Stik is a resin mixture that comes in two spray bottles. Bottle A is a cleaner (a mixture of alcohol) and bottle B is the resin.

The cleaner alone will add some life to the soles of your boots. The resin works best in moderate weather: too hot and it melts everywhere, too cold and it congeals. It wears off as you climb so you may need to apply several coats throughout the day.

Be careful where you step once you've applied the resin. Dirt sticks to it like flies to flypaper. Don't use the resin on new boots. There are two reasons for this: first, you shouldn't have to and second, the resin will deteriorate the soles' gripping ability.

When To Resole

You will need to resole your climbing boots occasionally. Buying a new pair every time the soles of your old ones wear through is just too expensive.

When any part of a boot's sole wears through to the last, it is time to resole. The area that usually wears through first is the inside section along the big toe.

I recommend that you have a professional cobbler resole your boots. This recommendation is based on experience. I have both used a cobbler and done the job myself. I found that resoling the boots myself took so much time and money that for only a few dollars more I could get a professional job. Ask at your local climbing store for a good climbing boot repair shop in your area.

If you are handy with tools and have a day's worth of time to spare (spread out over three days, to allow for drying, if possible), then you may want to resole your own boots. If so, read the next section on tuning up your boots.

Modifications and Tune-Ups

Rand Separation

If your boot's rand separates from the upper you can easily glue it back together. You'll need some Barge all-purpose cement, a rag, and some solvent.

Dip the rag in the solvent and scrub the separated areas clean. Wait for the solvent to evaporate (it should take only 2 minutes, maximum). When the areas are clean and dry apply a thin layer of glue to each surface. It's sometimes hard to get the glue deep into the separation. If this is the case, don't worry; just apply the glue as well as you can. Once you have finished applying the glue, wait for it to set (it takes 10-15 minutes). Be careful that the two sides don't touch during this set up period. You might want to break a toothpick and put it between the rand and upper to keep them apart. After the glue has set, firmly push the two sides together. The harder you push, the better the bond. Let your boots sit for a day so the glue can really set up.

Sole Separation

Sometime part of your boot's sole will separate from either the rand or the lining. You should fix this quickly or it will get worse. The repair is simple and takes only a few minutes.

First, clean the separated rubber with some solvent. Use a rag to scrub the rubber clean, then wait for the solvent to dry. When the rubber is clean and dry, fill it with Aquaseal. Try to keep the Aquaseal in the separation. You can wipe of any excess with a dry rag.

Set your boots aside for at least a day. This will give the Aquaseal time to set.

Aquaseal is the best material on the market for patching your boots, but it won't last forever. If the seal breaks, patch it back together again (this can get tedious but it saves your boots).

Resoling

5.10 is the only company currently selling resoling kits. I used their kit to resole a pair of my boots,

and had mixed feelings about the result. Overall, the job was successful. The soles have stayed together for 5 months now, and, besides occasional sole separations, which are easy to fix, they look as though they will stay on until they wear through. However, I found that the actual job took more of my time than I expected, and was fairly difficult at some points (notably removing the old soles).

So that you can understand the details of resoling, I will paraphrase 5.10's clear instructions here and offer my own comments as we go along.

The kit comes with a sheet of rubber (either normal 5.10 rubber or 5.10 Stealth rubber, your pick), a tube of Barge cement, and instructions.

The tools you need for the job are: an Exacto knife (or similar thin-bladed knife), a pair of pliers, an electric belt sander or a drill with a 2" grinding wheel which fits into it, some solvent, a rag, and an oven, electric stove top or similar heat source. You may also want some Aquaseal to patch up any mistakes (see Sole Separation, left).

You should always resole both boots at the same time, usually twice a year or at the end of your climbing season.

The first thing you must do is remove the old soles from your boots. This can be a bit of work and requires patience. You will need to heat the old soles to de-laminate the glue. You can do this by holding them over a burner on your stove top. Wear cooking mitts, because it will get hot. Once the soles are hot you can begin pulling them off with a pair of pliers. I found that I had to reheat the sole many times before I could pull it entirely free. The best rhythm seemed to be to heat, pull as much as possible, and then heat again, only now heat both the outside and the inside of the sole.

When you're removing the old soles you want to avoid pulling off any sections of the midsole. The midsole is the surface you are going to glue your new soles onto so you need it to remain flat. If you do pull off some of the midsole, fill in the hole left with Aquaseal. This also applies to the edge of the rand. You need it to be as flat as possible. The Aquaseal takes a day to dry, so allow for this in your schedule.

One of the reasons that I recommend you have a professional resole your boots is this: when I pulled off one sole, it took some of the thread sewn into the midsole with it. If a cobbler were doing this job he could have resewn the thread, but I had to leave it unsewn, which weakens the boot's construction.

Once you've pulled the old soles off you must prepare the boot to receive the new ones. As the instructions tell you, draw the old sole patterns on the sheet of rubber provided. Cut the sheet in half, leaving as much room as possible between the two sole patterns. The rubber cuts easily when you saw the Exacto knife back and forth, and pull the two sides apart (have someone pull them for you, or sit on one side of the rubber with your knee and pull the other side with one hand).

Before you can glue the new rubber onto your boots you must roughen both surfaces. Use your electric sander or grinder to do this. Roughen the entire sheet of new rubber. Be careful when you roughen the midsole; it is fragile and you don't want to tear it up.

After you've roughened the two surfaces, clean them both with your rag dipped in solvent. Let them dry. Now you are ready to glue.

Apply the glue to both the new rubber and the bottom of your boots. Use your finger to smear on a thin layer of glue, very thin - as thin as you can - but completely covering both the new rubber and the mid-sole. Let the glue dry for 2 hours.

Take each boot individually through the next few steps. Heat both surfaces, your new sole and the boot bottom, for 15-30 seconds. You want the glue to heat as evenly as possible. One good way is to put your boots into a hot oven. Be careful not to leave them in for long, or the glue securing the boot's rand will start to melt! You can use a stove top burner as 5.10 recommends, but it's hard to get the glue to heat evenly, which means that some sections of the sole may not bind as well as the rest. When you have heated both glued surfaces, and while they are still hot, carefully roll them together, from one end to the other, leaving no gaps or wrinkles in the surface.

Squeeze each boot and its new sole together as firmly as you can. The harder you push, the better it will bond. Cobblers put each boot on wooden "feet" and hammer the soles on. You can fill them with newspaper and hammer, or squeeze them together with a large pair of pliers. Make sure you press the boot's edges particularly tightly.

You should wait a day for the glue to dry before you trim off the excess rubber. Use your thin knife for this job. Try to cut the rubber as close to the rand as you can. This will save you some time-consuming grinding.

When you have a boot trimmed, sand or grind the sole into shape. Be careful not to heat up the rubber much, because it might de-laminate. Grind the entire sole so that it has a rough texture. The most important thing is to bevel the edges of your soles inward, so that they will be able to edge well.

Boot with untrimmed sole

You can experiment with just how beveled you want your edges. Bevel them only slightly at first and try your boots out. If they roll off small rock edges, bevel them further.

Accessories

Aquaseal
Aquaseal is good for filling in any sections of your boot's sole that are coming apart. You can buy it at water sports stores: it is usually used to repair wetsuits.

Carrying Bag
A bag to carry your rock climbing shoes in.

Glue
Barge cement is excellent for shoe repairs. You can buy it at many shoe stores, and all shoe repair shops.

Laces
Naturally you will have to replace your old and worn boot laces sometime. If you had single laces and want to continue with them all you have to do is measure their length, then buy the same size.

If you want to switch to the double lacing system you'll have to estimate the lengths. You can easily do this by lacing one boot to the height that you want the first lace to go and then tying the lace. Use the lace from your other boot to tie the first boot's upper holes (those not used by the first lace). You'll need to shorten both laces, the lower one more than the upper. Mark the distance with a piece of tape. Take the laces out and measure from one piece of tape to the other. These are the lengths you need.

You probably won't find the exact lace length you need but you should be able to get close. I have medium feet (Fire size 9.5); I use 22-inch laces on the lower half and 36-inch laces on the upper section.

Pliers

You need a pair of pliers to resole your boots. You can get them at any hardware store, and most supermarkets.

Replacement Soles

Two companies are selling rubber soles: 5.10 and Cocida. 5.10 sells a resoling kit that allows you to do the job yourself. They offer either their regular rubber or Stealth rubber. Cocida sells their resoles alone for you to take to your cobbler. Cocida offers three different soles: one for edging, one for friction, and one for training/bouldering.

You can buy 5.10 soles at most climbing shops or order directly from the company. Not all climbing stores sell Cocida soles, but you can easily order them from One Sport, their distributor (see pg. 353 for addresses).

Shoeper Stik

Shoeper Stik can be hard to find. Try a climbing shop. If not, ask around at shoe repair shops.

Solvent

You need solvent to clean your climbing boots' rubber soles. The 5.10 company recommends Trichloroethane, but I used kerosene with good results. You can get both at most hardware stores.

Thin-Bladed Knife

A thin-bladed knife is helpful for resoling your rock climbing boots. An Exacto knife also works well. They are cheap, and can be found at any stationary or hardware store.

Wire Brush

This is an excellent way to rejuvenate your oxidized rubber. Most paint and hardware stores sell wire brushes. Buy a size that you feel comfortable scrubbing with; it takes too long to use a small brush, and a large brush can be awkward.

Some Climbing Boot Manufacturers

Asolo, Boreal, Calma, Camp, Dolomite, Five-Ten, Kamet, Merrel, Mekan, La Sportiva, One Sport, and Scarpa all manufacture rock climbing boots. For the manufacturers' addresses, see pg. 353.

Carabiners
(Karabiners; Snaplinks; Mousquetons; Biners; Crabs)

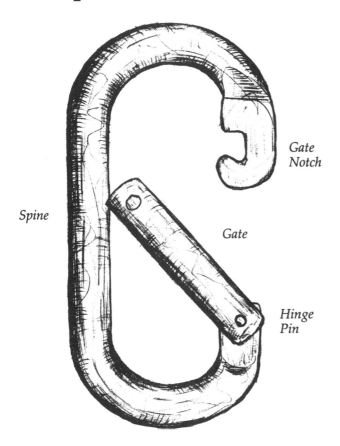

A carabiner

hold hard falls, yet light enough for you to easily carry a **rack** of them up the rock.

Before you buy a carabiner, make sure the gate opens and shuts properly. The gate notch must have a dip in it to catch the pin (rivet).

In the illustrations below, notice how the pin's position changes when the carabiner is loaded and then unloaded. This is due to the biner's flexible body. You cannot open the biner gate when its pin is in the loaded position. For more information see Opening Under Body Weight, on page 136.

Good gate notch design

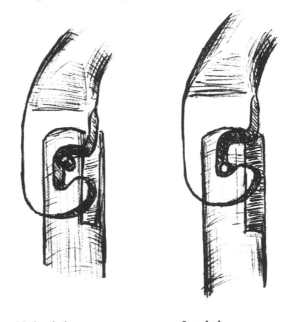

Unloaded   *Loaded*

What is a Carabiner?

At its most fundamental level the carabiner is merely a metal link used to connect two pieces of gear. For you, and all other climbers, however, the "biner" is much more. It is your connection to the mountain and to your lifeline (the rope). The biner links your entire climbing **protection system,** which keeps you safely attached to the rock if you fall.

It is the carabiner's spring-loaded gate which makes the biner so useful to you. You constantly need to connect and disconnect various bits of gear, and to do so quickly. The job of the gate's spring is to keep the gate shut so that nothing escapes.

It is important for the biner to be strong while remaining lightweight. It must be strong enough to

Bad Gate Notch Design

A gate notch which has no groove to catch the pin is unsafe. When you load the biner the pin may slide right out of the gate notch, opening the biner's gate.

Manufacturers are aware of this problem, so you will probably never see it. The gate notch design is something you should check if you are thinking of buying some biners of uncertain origin (something I don't recommend!).

Note: many modern carabiners have a "blind gate." This means that the metal surrounding the gate notch protrudes slightly from the rest of the carabiner. You can see a blind gate in the previous

Bad gate notch design

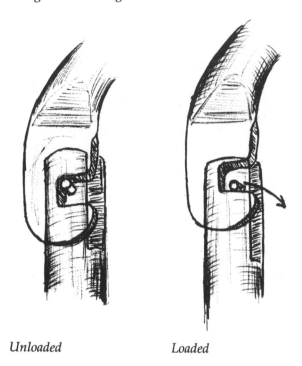

Unloaded   Loaded

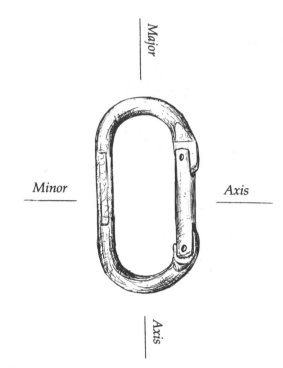

Oval biner with major and minor axes

gate notch illustrations. A blind gate lets you feel which way the gate opens, which makes it faster and easier to position the carabiner properly.

Major and Minor Axis

All carabiners have a major and a **minor axis.** The **major axis** runs through the length of the biner while the minor axis takes the horizontal path, running through the gate. You must make sure to load a carabiner along its major axis only, because it is much stronger than the minor one. If you load the biner's minor axis you run the very probable risk of breaking the gate, which could send you crashing to the ground below.

Three-Way Loading

You really weaken your biner when you load it from three different directions. The reason is that some of the three-way load ends up along the minor axis, which, as you just learned, stresses the biner's gate.

It would be impossible for me to describe all the gear configurations and climbing situations in which you might load a biner from three directions. There are too many and they always vary slightly from one another. I have shown you a common one below, with the best solution to the problem.

Remember, when you load a biner from three-ways you run the risk of breaking it, which could cause you to fall.

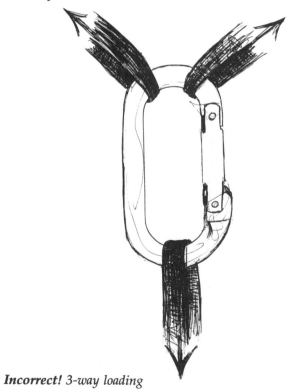

Incorrect! *3-way loading*

Brief History

A climber in the 1860s

Climbers first began to use carabiners in 1910. Otto Herzog, a climber from Munich, Germany, saw that members of the local fire brigade all had pear-shaped karabiners. He realized that these links might be very useful for climbing some of the harder **routes,** routes where protection was needed. (In those days climbers used only a rope attached to a partner, sometimes looped around a tree or **chockstone** — if they used any protection at all.)

Although some climbers in the Alps were using carabiners as early as 1910, it took the Second World War to popularize their use. The military on both sides, in outfitting its mountain divisions, supplied its men with factory-made carabiners. Although of poor quality, these biners spread the idea to climbers everywhere.

After the war, carabiners became a standard part of the climber's protection system. However, since then, their design has improved tremendously. Pierre Allain, of Paris, France, manufactured oval models which were popular back in the 50's. Yvon Chouinard, who founded today's Chouinard Equipment company (pronounced shoo-NARD), developed the "D" shape which gave much more strength for its size and weight than previous models.

Types

There are four types of carabiners. There are the **oval,** the **"D",** the **large pear,** and the **small pear** shapes. You will learn that the shape of the carabiner determines not only what type it is, but also its best use.

Keep in mind that I am only describing the best way to use each type of biner. You can interchange the biners with adequate results (use a "D" where an oval would be more advantageous).

Manufacturers don't always call their carabiners by the same names I am using here. For instance, Camp makes a "D", as they call it, which is actually a small pear. You will notice this mostly with small pears being called "D"s. I have used the name small pear because its asymmetrical shape is similar to large pears, and there is no other official name.

The Oval

Oval carabiner

The oval is the most versatile carabiner. Climbers use ovals to hold their gear on their rack and for **carabiner brake rappel rigs.**

Ovals are also very good for making a secure connection to a **belay station** or in setting up a **toprope** (by putting two biners together with their **gates opposed,** and then clipping the **rope** and **runners** to them).

Using two biners with gates opposed makes for a very strong connection. For one, you are using two carabiners, and two, each gate opens on a different

Carabiner brake rappel rig: This complex setup consists of two pairs of oval biners connected to a locking large pear.

side so the chance of your rope or webbing getting out of this connection is very small. Climbers sometimes use the oval biner for clipping into their protection on a climb, although the "D" works better, because it is often stronger and always less likely to flip over, out of position. (More on this in a moment.)

A word of caution: the oval's design contains a

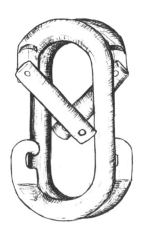

Two ovals with their gates opposed.

weakness. Because a load is positioned between the oval's sides, its weight is distributed evenly to both of them. This means that the oval's weaker gate side must support as much weight as its stronger spine, or solid, side. The biner's gate is weak because it is only connected to the body by two small rivets, called pins. These two pins must support as much of the biner's load as its spine. Obviously, the oval's design makes it fundamentally weaker than the other types of biners, which are asymmetrical in shape, allowing the spine to carry more of the load.

The other problem with the oval is that it has a tendency to spin. When you clip your protection with an oval you must keep an eye on the biner; its gate must remain in the **down and out** position. The gate must open down (the hinge pin is above the gate notch) to reduce the chance of your rope coming out. If your biner's gate faces into the rock, brushing against a rock knob or edge may be enough to open it.

Sometimes the movement of your rope as you climb will rotate the oval, putting its gate against the rock.

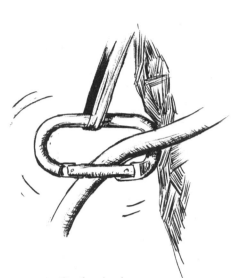

*Oval clipped down and out
(Be sure to close the gate!).*

Oval spinning

Oval gate opening on rock edge.

Despite these problems, the oval remains one of the most useful carabiners you can own. With the ability to hold your gear, use with gates opposed, make a biner rappel rig, and even clip into your protection, the oval is a must for your rack.

The "D"

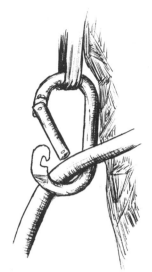

"D" carabiner

The "D" carabiner's main advantage is its strength. This strength comes from its "D" shape, which angles the biner's load onto its spine. Keeping most of the load on the "D"'s spine keeps it off the gate, and makes for a stronger biner. This means that the manufacturer has the option of using less material, for light weight, while still keeping a good strength rating.

The "D" is excellent for clipping into protection.

It is not as likely to spin as the oval, and so you don't need to worry about the gate flipping around to the wrong position.

The "D" does not work very well for holding your gear and using with its gates opposed. The angles of the "D"s corners force all the **chocks** and other gear that you're carrying onto each other, jumbling them together and making them impossible to separate quickly. This interferes with your efficiency. One common solution is to use one "D" per chock.

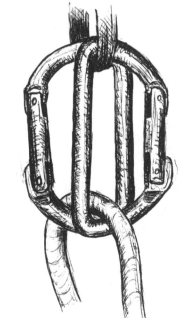

While being very secure, this arrangement binds the rope.

With their gates opposed, "D"s provide a strong connection but they also bind the rope. It is the angle of the corners that causes this, and the only solution is to not use "D"s with their gates opposed if you want your rope to run freely. (Use Ovals!)

"D"s come in several sizes. The large "D"s are made with locking devices (I will discuss locking devices (I will discuss locking devices in detail in the next section). The large locking "D"s work well for clipping your belay/rappel device to your harness. However, they do not have a very large interior space. This is their one limiting factor. A locking large "D" is an excellent replacement for the two ovals you might use at secure connections, such as anchors and topropes.

The Large Pear

Large pear carabiner

Note: At first glance, you may not notice the difference between the "D" and the large pear (or the small pear). However, there is one important difference. The large pear has an asymmetrical shape, that is, one end is bigger than the other. This shape is unique to the large and small pear biners.

Large pear carabiners are ideal for jobs which require a strong biner with a large interior space. For example, large pears are excellent for clipping a **descender** or **belay device** to your **harness**. Large pears also work well with the **Munter Hitch** belaying knot. If you don't know this knot, learn it! It's very useful.

You cannot afford for your **rappel** or belay device to come unclipped! For this reason large pears are sold with **locking sleeves**. The locking sleeve screws or slides along the biner's gate. In one position it

locks the gate, while in another you can work the gate with no restrictions.

A locking sleeve which slides is spring loaded. It shuts automatically, so to operate it just hold it

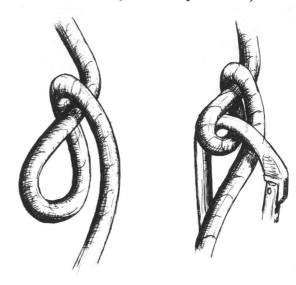

Beginning the Munter Hitch   Finishing the Munter Hitch

open long enough to move the gate. The problem with this design is that it doesn't stay open; when you use it you must constantly hold it to keep it from shutting. However, you don't ever need to remember to close it, which is a big plus!

Sliding locking sleeve   Screw locking sleeve

A locking sleeve which screws shut stays open when you want it to. Unfortunately, you may find that the sleeve is open when you need it shut, simply because you forgot to screw it closed. You must always double check this locking sleeve to make sure it is in position!

Sharp Threads

Anytime you buy a carabiner (or any other piece of gear) with a screw sleeve, make sure its threads are flat. Sharp threads will easily cut nylon, such as your rope and webbing. Most manufacturers are themselves experienced climbers, and they usually take care of this potential problem. However, I recommend that you always check the threads just to be sure.

You can use large pear biners for clipping to your protection, but there are plenty of reasons not to. For one, large pears are much more expensive than "D" biners, which I recommend for this job. The locking sleeve of the large pear tends to get in the way, snagging on rope and webbing and becoming a general nuisance. Also, large pears are large, and weigh more than the smaller standard biners. You must carry all your gear when your climb, and adding to the weight of your rack when you don't have to just doesn't make sense.

You should have at least one large pear carabiner to secure your rappel/belay device to your harness. You may want an additional one to replace the two ovals (with opposed gates) that you would otherwise use for secure connections.

The Small Pear

Small pear carabiner, straight-gate

Small pear biners have an entirely different use than their larger brothers. Climbers use small pears for clipping into their protection in place of "D"s. Small pears replace "D"s because they are lighter, have at least as large a gate opening for easy clipping, and still retain a fair amount of strength.

Small pear biners come with either straight or bent gates. A bent gate (also called a dog leg) is advantageous for quickly clipping onto your rope. Its bent shape acts as a hook; it is most useful on the rope-clipping end of a runner (the length of webbing between your rope and chock).

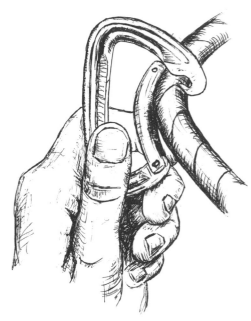

Clipping a rope with bent-gate small pear is easy. Notice how the gate notch hooks over the rope and draws it into the gate.

The bent gate also gives the manufacturer a way to make the biner's gate opening larger. Where a straight gate would hit the spine quickly, making the gate opening smaller, a bent gate is able to open wider.

The bent gates do have one problem. *They can open if the rope crosses back over the gate.* As long as you never to cross your rope back over the bent gate, you will have no problems.

For difficult routes, a bent gate small pear biner is the ideal rope clipping tool.

The small pear biner is not versatile. Because of its asymmetrical shape you cannot use it for much besides clipping to your protection and **anchors**. It is also fairly expensive, so before you fill your rack with small pear biners, make sure that you really need them.

Small pear carabiners are really useful for **leading** hard climbs. When you get to this advanced level, a rack full of small pear biners will increase your efficiency by allowing you to quickly connect your rope and protection. The best **quickdraw** set-up is a straight gate "D" or small pear for clipping to your chock and a bent-gate small pear for clip-ping to your rope.

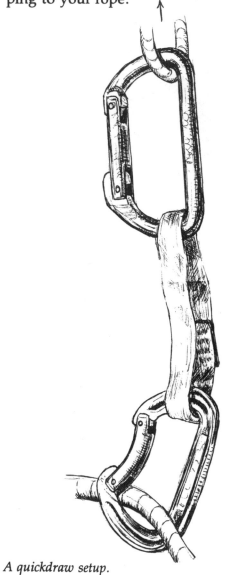

A quickdraw setup.

Small pear carabiners cost more than ovals and "D"s.

An Alternative Carabiner Design

The 3-D Carabiner
Stubai's 3-D biner has an unusual twisted shape. The ends have a bend in them, meaning that the spine is on one plane while the gate is on another.

3-D biner

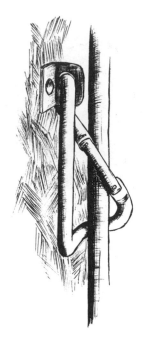

3-D clipped to bolt with rope running through it. Notice how the 3-D biner allows the rope to run freely. Any other single biner would bind the rope to the rock.

The 3-D is useful when you want to use only one biner to clip a bolt. It's twisted shape allows your rope to run freely through it, without any possibility of being pinned to the rock. This saves your rope from possible abrasion and cuts. Obviously, a cut rope would send you to the ground very quickly!

The 3-D also comes as a large pear (with a lock-ing sleeve). It can be very useful for toproping, as it won't bind your rope to the rock.

In both of its shapes, the 3-D is not a versatile biner. Its shape makes it awkward for uses other than some bolt clipping or toproping situations. At around $10, the 3-D also costs much more than a standard biner.

Alternative Gate Designs

The Key-Lock
The Key-Lock system offers an interesting alter-native to traditional carabiner gate designs. It re-places the gate notch with a solid end, and the pin

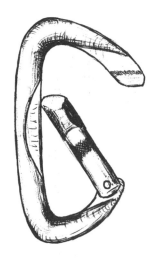

The Key Lock

Side view of Key Lock

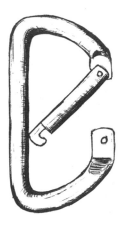

The Reversed Gate Notch

with a slot. The solid end fits right into the slot, just like a key fits into a keyhole.

By eliminating the pin at the end of the gate, this design is slightly stronger than traditional gate designs. And by getting rid of the large, heavy gate notch, the biner is very lightweight. With no gate notch, there is no possibility of snagging your gear as you clip into it.

The Key-Lock system is patented by Kong-Bonaiti. So far it is used only with the small pear biners shape. It costs about the same as most small pears.

The Reversed Gate Notch

The Reversed Gate Notch is simply a reversal of the traditional gate design. The gate notch is on the gate, while the pin is where the gate notch was.

There isn't much advantage to this design. It slightly decreases the chance of your snagging your gear. It offers no added strength or security.

The Reversed Gate Notch is patented by Camp, and costs about the same as most small pears.

The Diagonal Gate

Bonaiti makes a "D" carabiner with a gate which opens diagonally. The biner's body is slightly twisted at the hinge pin and gate notch, so the gate can swing past the biner's spine.

The diagonal gate design permits the gate to open to its maximum size, a clear advantage for clipping large amounts of gear. Because of its specialized design, this biner costs more than standard "D" biners.

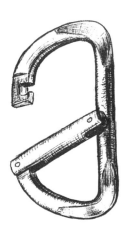

The Diagonal Gate

Screw Links

Other names: Maillons, Maillon Rapide, Quick Links (a misleading name!).

The screw link is slightly different from the carabiner. This difference lies in its gate design, which is a metal sleeve (much like a locking sleeve) that screws open or closed.

The screw link's gate design offers both advantages and disadvantages. It gives the link tremendous strength, due to the lack of pins in the gate. Therefore, manufacturers can make the screw link much lighter than, but just as strong as, high strength steel carabiners.

The big problem with the screw link is that it takes time and energy to unscrew its gate. When you are trying to clip into your rope or protection you cannot afford to waste either your time or your energy trying to open a screw link.

In conclusion, the screw link is ideal for long-term, strong connections. Use it to connect your rappel device to your harness on a really long rappel.

There are three types of screw links: the oval, triangle, and half-circle shapes. Much like the different types of carabiners, each type of screw link has a different purpose.

The Oval Screw Link
The oval screw link provides a basic link between two pieces of gear.

X-ray view of an oval screw link

The Triangular Screw Link
A perfect device for three-way connections, the triangular link has three major axes.

Triangular screw link

The Half-Circle Screw Link
Another great device for three-way connections. The half-circle design has more interior space than the triangular link. It was specifically designed for the large amounts of gear cavers use on an ascent or rappel.

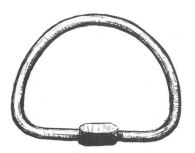

Half-circle screw link

Where To Buy Screw Links
You can find screw links at both hardware stores and some outfitters. Outfitters stock screw links which are specifically designed for recreational use. These links are stronger and lighter than those sold by hardware stores. They also tend to have larger gate openings, which may be important to you, depending on the size of the gear you need to connect. Regardless of where you shop for your screw link, find out its strength rating *before* you buy it.

Specifications

A carabiner's specifications are valuable tools. They can help you cut through all the manufacturer's hype (the "latest design") and get to what is really important: the carabiner's actual performance. The specifications we will examine are: opening under body weight, gate-opening dimension, gate-open strength, overall strength, and weight.

A manufacturer will generally print in his catalog all the numerical values for the specification headings I discuss in this book. These are all the ones you need to know. If he fails to provide this information, call him and ask for the details you need. You can find the telephone numbers of most popular manufacturers in the back of this book. Another way to find the spec values is to inquire at your local climbing shop. If no one there knows, ask them to call the manufacturer for you.

Opening Under Body Weight
Occasionally you need to open a carabiner which is supporting your weight (when you are aid climbing this occurs fairly often). Given a biner's strength, you might think this would present no

problems. However, when a certain load is reached, the biner's body expands to the point where the pin snugs up against the gate notch. Once this happens you can't open the carabiner.

A biner's gate-open strength equals the amount of load it can handle before its gate locks shut. Usually this amount is around 250 pounds.

> ## Caution
> Always have a back-up system in place when you are opening a carabiner that is supporting your weight!

Most rock climbers don't weigh 250 pounds. But any equipment you carry with you will add to your weight. Take these extra pounds into account *before* you start climbing.

A biner's value for opening under body weight does not always appear in the manufacturer's catalogs. If you have any doubts about this value you should call the manufacturer (before you climb!).

Gate-Opening Dimension

The gate opening dimension is the size of the carabiner's gate when it is open. You need to be able to cram loads of webbing and rope into the biner, so the wider the gate opening the better. The smallest size I've seen is 13 millimeters, which is just two millimeters larger than a standard 11 millimeter climbing rope.

If you plan on using extra-large ropes (above 11 millimeters), or need to clip to a thick aluminum rod (of a stretcher, for instance), both of which you might do in a rescue, make sure to buy biners which can accommodate these larger sizes.

Gate-Open Strength

A biner's gate-open strength rating is really for reference more than practical use. You should NEVER use a biner whose gate will not close. The forces generated by a twenty-foot fall (not an uncommon distance) will commonly be 1500 pounds, and sometimes more. Most carabiners with their gates open fail at 1200-1800 pounds. This doesn't leave you any safety margin. By the way, any time your biner's gate starts to stick, immediately repair or discard it. See Modifications and Tune-Ups page 140.

There is a chance, albeit a very small one, that your biner's gate may open after you have clipped it to something. As I said earlier, keep your biner's gate opening turned down and out from the rock.

Its outward position keeps the gate from being pushed open by any rock edges or protrusions, and its downward opening position lessens the small chance that your rope may somehow find its way out of the gate.

Strength

Your carabiners must be strong. Their many functions are all intimately tied up with your protection system. A good minimum strength rating is 4000 pounds. Remember, typical falls generate at least 1500 pounds of force, while some can be as high as 3000 pounds. Your biner's strength rating needs to be high enough to include a good **safety margin,** a buffer to absorb other possible weakening factors. These factors include such things as **dynamic loading** (the load is applied quickly, as in a fall) and possible contact between the rock and the carabiner.

> ## Steel
> Steel carabiners are strong. You should use them if you are in a rescue situation, or whenever you need to put a heavy load on a carabiner. Steel biners weigh a lot more than aluminum alloy ones.

Unfortunately manufacturers do not always tell you how they have determined their carabiner's strength rating. Their rating may be the highest test's result, or an average from all the carabiners they tested, or, best of all, the lowest test result. And you need to remember that a biner gradually loses a little of its strength to wear.

The only reason you need to know this is so you don't try to load the biner to its tested limit. It will be strong enough for normal climbing purposes, but don't overload it. If you anticipate a heavy load, use two biners at every connection, or steel biners.

Weight

You need lightweight carabiners. It is amazing how just a few extra pounds resulting from a large rack full of biners makes climbing so much more difficult.

The heaviest ovals and "D"s on the market weigh around 2.2 ounces. This figure is decreasing as manufacturers design smaller "D" and pear shapes which can still retain their strength.

Carabiner Specifications

Manufacturer/ Type	Rod Dia.[1]	Gate Opening	Wt. (ounces)	Strength (lbs.) Gate is: open	closed
Chouinard					
Oval	11R	.665"	2.2	1540	4400
"D"	9F	.630"	1.7	1320	5060
Quicksilver	8F	.780"	1.6	1500	4620
Big-D Locking	11F	.840"	2.6	2200	6160
SMC					
New Oval	11F	.720"	2.18	1500	5060
Light "D"	9F	.740"	1.7	1200	4620
Locking "D"	11F	.820"	2.6	1800	5500
Wild Country					
Almost Oval	10F	.740"	1.7	1034	4400
Microlite 9	9F	.750"	1.4	1100	4400
Camp					
Classic	10T	.840"	1.7	1450	5500

[1]The rod dia. refers to the diameter of the rod stock used. Also, R = round; F = flat; T = T section; these are the cross-sections of the rod's shape.
For more information, see the Materials section.

Materials

Carabiners are made from rod stock of either steel or aluminum alloy, with steel pins. These pins are very small (about three millimeters in diameter). In fact, they are so small that they wouldn't provide enough strength if they were made of aluminum alloy.

Aluminum alloy is a good material for carabiners because of its light weight and high strength. If you compare aluminum with steel you will find that the aluminum alloy is actually the stronger of the two, taken pound for pound. You may respond that it takes much more alum-inum alloy to equal a pound's worth of steel, and this is true. To exceed the strength of a steel carabiner an aluminum alloy link would have to have much more material in it. Naturally this is impractical; however, aluminum alloys have proven their worth to climbers for many years.

Rod Stock

Beyond the materials, you must consider the cross section shape and the size of the rod stock. Besides having obvious implications for the weight, bulk, and strength of the biner, the stock's shape and size affects your rope. The thinner the rod stock, the more damage to your rope. (The rope bends unevenly, permanently stretching the fibers on the outside of the rope's bend. These stretched fibers lose much of their load absorption properties, and are likely to break under stress. See the Rope chapter.) If you must fall repeatedly on the same place in your rope, use two biners instead of one. This will widen the bend in the rope, reducing damage.

Another thing: you must use thin slings (such as 11/16", maximum) when you are using biners made from thin stock. Wider slings put stress on the biner's gate, weakening it (the 3-way loading principle).

Spectra slings work really well, being both thin and extremely strong.

There are three different cross section shapes being used for biners: round, flat, and T-section.

Round rod stock   *Flat rod stock*   *T-section rod stock*

The round rod stock was commonly used in the past, but is now used by only a few manufacturers. It is usually used in at least 11 millimeter stock (sometimes 12 millimeter — as with the HMS Kwik, a large pear biner). Being thicker than the other stock shapes, the round stock is bulky and heavy. However, it is fairly strong and doesn't damage your rope as much as thinner stocks.

The flat rod stock is currently the most popular stock used by manufacturers. It is less bulky, and lighter weight, than the round stock shape. The diameter of the flat stock varies anywhere from 8-11 millimeters. It is flat only on the outside; the inside corners are rounded to reduce rope damage.

T-section stock combines medium strength and light weight. It has wide corners to reduce rope damage, but then thins out along the stem of the "T" to reduce weight. The diameter of T-section stock varies from 10-11 millimeters. It is excellent stock for lightweight, medium strength biners. Manufacturers usually use it with small pears.

Durability

A carabiner's durability is determined by its method of construction. You can take as a given that the best aircraft quality aluminum alloys will be used to construct these carabiners. The big factor still to consider then is the method of construction.

While there are many variables involved in constructing a carabiner, manufacturers have made it an exacting science. They are able to provide a consistent method of construction, repeating the same proven techniques exactly in each biner. Unless you want to become a manufacturer, you will find it unnecessary to learn all the different construction techniques used. Instead, you will be interested in results.

On this basis I recommend that you rely on the reputation of the manufacturer when deciding whether his equipment will be durable. Find out how long a manufacturer has been in business. Inquire at your local climbing shop; the climbers there deal with gear every day and have a lot to say about the various manufacturers. You should also find out what other climbers think about a manufacturer's gear. Always keep your ears open around other climbers: they usually know valuable tips about the various manufacturers. All the manufacturers that are listed at the end of this chapter (see pg. 142) produce quality carabiners.

General Safety Guidelines

These safety guidelines are for emphasis, not instruction. If you don't know how to use rock climbing equipment, get an instructor! (If you don't know how to get an instructor, whether a friend or a professional guide, refer to Getting Started, page 5.)

Loading the Carabiner!

Remember back at the beginning of this chapter that I mentioned the biner has both a major and a minor axis? In case you can't quite recall what we talked about there, I'll recap.

The major axis runs through the length of the biner and is the strongest way to load it. The minor axis runs through the biner's width, which means that one part of the load is on the gate. Stressed along the minor axis the gate will fail from a very small load. So your job is to keep the load along the major axis.

This seems like it would be fairly simple, and it usually is. However, there are times when you may

need to load your carabiner from three directions.

Try to avoid three-way loading, but if you can't, at least follow this principle: Make your three-way loading as close to two-way as possible. The linking carabiner will still be weak, but not as much as if the load comes from three very different directions at once.

To supplement the strength of a three way link you can use two biners. Use ovals with their gates opposed; you'll have extra strength and security.

Down and Out!

Any time you use a single carabiner, always make sure that its gate opens down and out. What this means is that the gate must be out, or away, from the rock; the biner's hinge pin must be on top so the gate opening is at the bottom. Any other position is less secure.

When you use two biners with their gates opposed, they should look like this:

No Edges!

Never position your carabiner so that it is on a rock edge. The edge will concentrate all the biner's load onto the one point where it touches the biner. If you're lucky the biner will only bend; however, it may well break. Besides costing you a carabiner, you are flirting with disaster when you load one over an edge of rock.

No More than Two Carabiners in a Row!

Never clip more than two carabiners in a row for any life-supporting function. Because a middle biner won't flex, it may force its way out from one of the other two.

Instead of a third biner, use a quickdraw to connect two biners.

Care

Carabiners don't ask for a lot of care. Just a little common consideration. If you give them this, your biners will give you good service for years.

So what is it you need to do? There are three basic things.

Keep Your Biners Clean

Keeping your carabiners clean seems like an obvious thing to do. But I have seen countless climbers, and I am guilty of it myself sometimes, dump their rack of biners into a pile of dirt before or after a climb. Don't do this!

Dirt gets into the spring well and in the hinge connecting the gate to the body. This creates problems that you just don't need to deal with. The spring will start to stick, as will the hinge itself. Often, the gate won't open all the way. You cannot use a carabiner that has these problems because it is not safe.

If you have somehow let your biners slip into the dirt you need to clean them up. Look under Modifications and Tune-Ups, below, for directions.

When to Retire Your Carabiner

The time will come when you should retire a carabiner. It is difficult to determine this time in advance, however. Some biners have lasted twenty-five years, and still show no signs of weakness! Others only last a couple of years before they must be retired. Because of this wide variation, every case is different and I cannot accurately estimate when you must retire yours. I can, however, give you some basic guidelines.

History

You need to be able to recall the general history of your biners. This is hard to do because you have so many of them and they all look alike. But if you can remember it, the history of your biner will help you decide when to retire it.

Has your biner supported any severe falls or suffered any hard knocks on the rock? If it has, retire it now or thoroughly examine it, and I mean with *an X-ray machine*. (Of course not many of us have access to X-ray machines. Unless you do, retire your suspect biner *now!*) Minute cracks can develop in the metal which you will not be able to see, but which can be the source of sudden biner failure.

Don't Drop Your Biners

Never drop your carabiners, especially not onto rock! Although biners are strong, they cannot handle sharp, hard impacts — they may shatter. This shattering takes the form of very minute cracks, often invisible to the eye but weakening the biner's load capacity.

If you suspect your biner of cracking, throw it out! You shouldn't keep it around the house because you might pick it up someday and use it.

Avoid Corrosives

Corrosives eat aluminum. Don't let them eat your biners. Keep all kinds of acids away from the metal; acid and your biners should never be in the same room together.

Unfortunately for all of you who aspire to climb those cliffs by the sea, sea salt eats carabiners. To prevent this, wash the salt off your biners with fresh water once you have finished a climb. While you're at it, wash off all of your metal equipment. A few minutes of washing will save you a lot of money later replacing half-eaten gear!

Replace If It Breaks

If any part of your biner breaks, replace the entire biner! A broken carabiner has no use in climbing.

Inspect

Inspect your carabiners before you climb. If you suspect any problems, or see any reason for failure, retire the biner. Upon examination you might find things like cracks or severe corrosion, as I already discussed. Light corrosion you can fix. Severe corrosion and cracks are grounds for retirement!

Anodized Carabiners

Carabiners usually come with a bright metallic finish, but anodized biners are available from certain manufacturers. Sometimes the biner is colored, sometimes it is left with a metallic finish. Black is a fairly common color for large pear biners (this is to accommodate military (teams). REI sells its standard ovals and "D"s in a variety of colors, such as gold, blue, and red.

Anodizing helps the biner resist corrosion, which is particularly protective while seacliff climbing. Colors make identification easier, as more climbers use plain, non-colored biners and the colored ones stick out like a sore thumb.

The anodized finish does wear off after extensive use. It usually comes off first in the biner's corners, as this is where the rope runs, causing the most abrasion. Besides nicks and scratches, the biner's body should stay anodized for quite some time.

Modifications and Tune-Ups

The only real modifications you can make on your biners is to add personal markings to separate your biners from the other guy's. I'll tell you just how to do this a little further on.

Biner problems you can repair are somewhat limited as well, including only cleaning, lubricating, and smoothing burrs and other rough spots. The time and money it would cost you to try to repair more serious problems is just not worth it. You may as well consider the biner a loss and buy a replacement. But if your biner problems are minor, read on.

Cleaning

Any time one of your carabiners gets dirty, especially if there is dirt in its hinge or spring well, you need to clean it. This is very important if its gate doesn't open all the way, or gets stuck.

Often you can clean your biners adequately by simply wiping them with a damp rag. If a gate is sticking or you somehow can't get the dirt off with a rag, clean the biner with a solvent. Kerosene, paint thinner, engine degreasers, and other common solvents will work.

Pour some solvent into the biner's spring well. Solvents work best when you can scrub the dirt; it is very difficult to scrub the inside of the spring well! The best thing you can do is let the solvent soak for around half a minute. Then open and close the biner's gate rapidly to break the dirt apart. Pour out any remaining solvent and try working the gate again. You may have to repeat this a few times.

When all the dirt is gone, remove the solvent by dropping the carabiner into some boiling water for twenty to thirty seconds. Be careful when you take it out, the carabiner will be hot. I like to hook the carabiner with a fork. You will not need to dry it, the carabiner will be so hot the water will quickly evaporate. As a finishing touch, lubricate the gate.

If none of this works you're going to have to retire the biner. You just can't take a chance with a gate which may stay open, or not open all the way.

Lubricating

When your biner's gate starts sticking you need to lubricate it. Make sure you use a dry lubricant! Dirt and dust sticks to wet lubricants. If you use those your biner's gate will be clogged in no time.

Lubricate your biners in a clean place protected from the wind. Lubricants are fairly toxic so you should work in a location, such as a garage, where you won't continue to be assaulted by the vapors after the job. Put a drop of lubricant into the spring well, and then one on each side of the hinge pin.

Work the hinge back and forth to spread the lubricant around. You should wait for the stuff to dry (it takes around five minutes) before you stow it.

Smoothing

You don't want any sharp metal edges on your biner. They might cut your rope or webbing. The normal action of the rope passing through the biner makes it unlikely that any edges will develop, but if they do, you need to do something about it. Buy a piece of fine sandpaper and use it to take the edge off a nick.

If your biner is nicked you must decide whether to keep it or throw it away. If the metal has a severe cut you should toss the biner because it is definitely too weak. Blunt any small, sharp edges with your sandpaper.

Be careful when you blunt an edge. You must not weaken your biner by filing its body down! Just a quick pass or two over the edge with your sandpaper should do the trick.

Identification

You should identify your biners so that you don't mix them with your friend's. The easiest and safest way to do this is by wrapping tape around the biner's gate or body. Use different colors of tape, or distinctive widths which will quickly identify your biners.

Cut your tape into short lengths, just enough to go one and a half times around the carabiner. This small overlap will hold the tape securely without being bulky enough to be in your way. You might put the tape on your biner's spine (solid side), where it is unobtrusive, or you might prefer to mark the gate — specifically the gate's opening end.

Note: don't mark your carabiners by filing grooves into them! Weakening your biners is a high (and unnecessary) price to pay for permanent identification.

Accessories

Dry Lubricant

You should occasionally lubricate your biner gates to keep them from sticking or squeaking. Don't use WD-40; it is petroleum based. Oil-based lubricants will attract dirt and clog the gate.

Any dry lubricant will work well. You can find one for a few dollars in a hardware store. Teflon and graphite lubricants work well. A decent teflon lubricant is Tri-Flow, which costs around five dollars a can.

Solvent

You will need solvent to clean grit out of the biner's spring well. The problem with solvents is that, although they may soften the grit up, you must brush the grit to actually clean it out. It is very difficult to brush the grit in a biner's spring well! The only solution is to buy the most powerful solvent you can find (make sure it won't damage your biner!). I have used an engine degreaser called Gunk Engine Brite, which you can buy in any hardware store.

Identification Tape

Taping your carabiners can save you from losing some by mixing them with your buddy's during a climb.

Vinyl tape (such as duct tape) works best, but any tough tape will do. You may want different colors. Your local climbing store might sell tape but you can also find some good stuff at most hardware stores.

Sandpaper

Buy a sheet of 320-400 grade sandpaper. You want such a fine grade so that you don't make any large scratches in your biner's finish. Hardware stores sell sandpaper.

Some Carabiner Manufacturers

Bonaiti, Camp, Chouinard, Climb High, Clog, Contat, DMM, 5.10, Lowe, Omega Pacific, REI, Salewa, SMC, Stubai, and Wild Country manufacture carabiners. See pg. 353 for manufacturers' addresses.

Chalk

Various chalk containers

Why Chalk?

Climbers use soft, powdered gymnastic chalk to keep their hands dry. Climbing is a strenuous business. It quickly produces sweaty hands, and sweaty hands slip on rock!

What Is Chalk?

Chalk is powdered magnesium carbonate. Manufacturers make their chalk into a very fine, exceptionally dry powder.

Most climbers prefer white chalk because of its dry quality. However, some companies sell colored chalk, which, unfortunately, is not as dry. Despite this, you may prefer colored chalk because it blends in aesthetically with the rock. Some climbing areas favor colored chalk to keep the visual impact down. Rocks spotted with white chalk marks may stay that way for months.

There are many different colors of chalk available; you should be able to match the color of your chalk to the color of the rock in your area. North American Mountaineering sells Etho Chalk, which currently has the widest selection of colors.

I encourage you to experiment with both white and colored chalks. You should determine your preference: maybe you prefer no chalk at all.

Does Chalk Damage The Rock?

The sweat from your hands erodes the rock more than chalk alone. However, the combination of sweat and chalk is even more damaging to the rock. (For more information, read D. MacGowan's article in *Climbing* 101, entitled: "Reliving the Chalk Wars: A Geochemical View.")

You must realize that the passage of any element, whether it is rain, another rock, or a human, erodes the rock. Rocks exposed to the surface of the earth are constantly being eroded; climbers are also eroding agents. As long as we keep our impact at a moderate level we are merely playing our part in shaping the earth. Be balanced: don't splatter the rocks with chalk, but, at the same time, don't be afraid to use it!

Anesthetic Properties

Chalk has a mild anesthetic effect on cuts. If you cut or scrape your hands in a crack, for instance, smear some chalk over the cut. The pain will diminish slightly, and the chalk will provide some protection against further irritation.

How Much Chalk Should You Buy?

If you intend to do a lot of climbing you should buy a large quantity of chalk, because it is cheaper. Chalk is sold in many different sizes, including:

    small, uncrushed 2 ounce blocks
    1 pound boxes of eight 2 ounce blocks
    small 2 ounce bags of powdered chalk
    large, 2-3 pound bags of powdered chalk.

A company called Bison makes Chalk Balls™ which they sell through various climbing stores. These are 2 ounce balls of powdered chalk which are held in thin nylon netting. The netting is designed to prevent the chalk from spilling, which means that it should last longer than loose chalk.

I cannot tell you how often you will need to buy chalk, because everyone uses it at a different rate. It also depends on how much chalk you spill, or how much seeps out of your **chalkbag.**

Accessories

You must have a chalkbag to hold your chalk. See page 145.

Key Point

"A toothbrush is an excellent tool for cleaning over-chalked or dirty holds."

See page 146

Chalkbags

A chalkbag

What Is A Chalkbag?

The chalkbag is a bag that holds climbing chalk. Not just an ordinary bag, a chalkbag is designed to give you quick access to your chalk while you climb. The rim is reinforced with wire, which keeps the bag open. It closes with a drawstring. The inside of the bag is lined with pile (a fleece-like material); this helps keep the chalk in the bag.

You will find it most convenient to wear your chalkbag around your waist. The bag has two small loops through which you can thread a length of **webbing.** Any webbing will work, as long as you make sure it fits (wrap it around your waist; be sure to leave some extra length - see Belt, pg. 146). Most climbing stores sell one-inch **flat webbing** with a plastic buckle sewn in; this works very well.

To close a chalkbag you must pull its drawstring shut. It has a small plastic or nylon spring-loaded toggle which keeps the drawstring in place.

Different Chalkbags

There are three different chalkbag designs on the market: fingertip bags, kidney bags, and standard bags.

Fingertip Bags

For climbers who want a small, lightweight bag which will stay out of the way there are fingertip bags.

A fingertip chalkbag

These bags don't hold very much chalk, which means you must check the bag for chalk everytime you go climbing. Larger bags hold enough chalk for many excursions; how many depends on how much chalk you use.

Kidney Bags

Misty Mountain makes a kidney-shaped chalkbag. It is designed to keep the chalk in the bag when you forget to close it, then slide down the rock on your rear. Losing chalk like this happens to some people more than others. Try to avoid it because spilled chalk is ugly and needless.

A kidney chalkbag

Standard Bags

The standard chalkbag is large enough to store a lot of chalk. It is nothing special, but is cheap and does the job very well. It is the most popular type of chalkbag on the market.

A standard chalkbag

Features

A zippered key pocket and a toothbrush holder are two handy chalkbag features.

A chalkbag with a key pocket is more expensive than simpler designs. The key pocket may be on the side of the bag or underneath it. A key pocket is strictly a luxury feature.

A toothbrush holder is much more useful. The toothbrush is not for your teeth; it's to clean the rock. This is useful on new climbs where the rock is covered in a thin layer of dirt, and also on difficult but popular climbs. The holds on a difficult climb are usually very small; you need to get the best grip possible. With many climbers attempting the climb, its holds can become caked with chalk. *A hold caked with chalk is slippery.* A quick scrub with your toothbrush before you climb should solve the problem.

Materials

Most chalkbags are made from either tough cordura or nylon cloth. I have also seen older chalkbags that were made of some sort of plastic. I don't recommend these bags: they are ugly and heavy, and the plastic will wear out in the sun.

Some chalkbags have a section of more flexible nylon in the middle or at the top. This is to allow the drawstring to close the bag. In other bags the drawstring pulls the inside lining shut.

The inside of many chalkbags are lined with pile. Pile lining helps keep your chalk from flying around.

Chalkbag drawstrings are made from simple cotton cloth with a plastic or nylon locking device, called a toggle.

Although I haven't had any problems with them, I have many friends who find that the spring inside the toggle gradually wears out. Once it does, the toggle will not keep the bag closed tight enough to prevent the chalk from leaking out. This is easy to fix: simply replace the toggle (you can find them at most outdoor stores). If you can't manage to buy a toggle you can keep using your chalkbag normally, but wrap it in a plastic bag when you put it in your pack.

Accessories

Belt

A length of flat one inch webbing works very well as a chalkbag belt. Most climbing stores sell one inch flat webbing with durable plastic buckles. You can also use a simple length of cord tied with a **Square Knot**. The best way to determine the belt's length is to put the chalkbag on the belt, wrap it around your waist, and adjust the tension until the chalkbag is at the angle you want.

Some manufacturers sell **runner**-strength chalkbag belts. If you run out of runners while on a climb, you can use this type of chalkbag belt as a runner. However, I don't recommend doing this because you will be stuck carrying your chalkbag in your hands, or perhaps throwing it down the cliff!

Toothbrush

A toothbrush is an excellent tool for cleaning overchalked or dirty holds. A regular toothbrush with stiff bristles works very well. For cleaning hardpacked dirt, you may need a brush with a wood handle and metal bristles.

Toggle

If the spring in your chalkbag's toggle wears out you need to replace the device. Toggles are cheap, and you can buy them at most climbing shops.

Copperheads (Mash Heads; Mashies; Bashies)

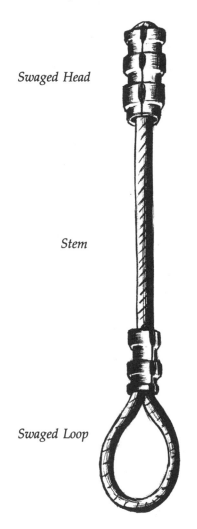

Swaged Head

Stem

Swaged Loop

A copperhead

is well-placed a copperhead usually looks very mashed and bashed!

The heads have varying shapes. Some are long, thin, ribbed cylinders. Others are similar, having the cylindrical shape but without the ribs. Still others are square and blocky.

A cylinder-like head with ribs

A cylinder-like head without ribs

A square blocky head

What Is A Copperhead?

A copperhead looks vaguely like the snake of the same name. But this is not where the gear's name comes from. No, the name originates from a copper, or aluminum, hunk of metal (the head) that is attached to a thin, flexible wire cable. Climbers hammer the heads into cracks in the rock, where the metal expands to merge with the stone and provide a secure anchor. It is from this hammering that copperheads get their various other names (Mashies, Bashies, and Mash Heads). By the time it

What Do Climbers Use Copperheads For?

Copperheads are **aid climbing** tools. This means that you will use copperheads on sheer climbs that offer no natural holds. After you place a copperhead (usually by hammering), you will connect your **etriers** to it and climb up them, hoping that the copperhead will support your weight, and it usually will. In fact, if you placed the copperhead well it will be very secure. However, if you placed it poorly it won't be as secure, but will still probably hold. *Always test a copperhead placement before you commit all of your weight to it!* Placing a copperhead well takes a lot of practice. I shall present some general guidelines for placing a copperhead under Technique, pg. 149.

Copperheads are essential for most modern aid climbs. They fit into naturally shallow cracks in the rock such as U-shaped grooves. They also work well in some old **piton scars** that have widened through repeated use, but are too shallow to accept more **pitons.**

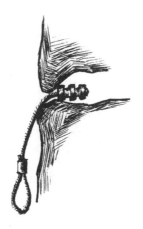

A copperhead wedged in a crack

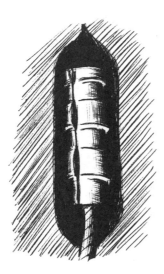

A copperhead in a wide, shallow piton scar

for a piton. You can protect this crack by using both the copperhead and the piton, as illustrated below. (You can sometimes use a small wedging chock in place of the copperhead.)

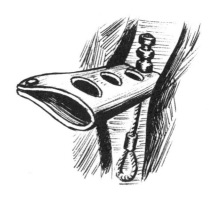

A piton and a copperhead in a wide but shallow crack

Using A Copperhead As A Chock

Although copperheads are made to be hammered into the rock, sometimes you can place them without a hammer. When you place a copperhead in this manner you are using it as if it were a **wedging chock** (see pg. 325). A wedging chock fits into a crack and anchors itself between the crack's sides.

Important: Copperheads are designed to support your body weight, not your fall! A copperhead's strength as a **chock** depends on its size and condition (as well as its placement). A new, 1/2 inch by 1 inch copperhead can hold as much as 4000 lbs., which will hold most falls. However, smaller copperheads can be considerably weaker. Conclusion: use copperheads as chocks only as a last resort (if you really need some protection and you are out of your normal wedging chocks, or you don't have any small enough to fit the crack you are climbing).

Sometimes you will come across a vertical crack that is too wide for a copperhead yet too shallow

Note: you will find many such wide but shallow piton scars on popular (trade) **routes.** More than likely the first climbers to do the route found very thin **seams.** These seams were often shallow, becoming solid rock just a few inches in from the surface. As climbers hammered their way up the cliff, their pitons, repeatedly placed and removed over time, gradually widened these previously-thin cracks. Because the cracks ended just a few inches into the rock, the pitons widened but didn't deepen them. The result is the awkwardly-sized, ugly piton scars that travel up many rock faces today, scars that force you to use the afore-mentioned technique of combining a piton and a copperhead to get a secure placement.

Brief History

A climber in the 1860s

> Copperheads were refined from the original aluminum mashies, which were aluminum squares developed around 1965. They had a hole in the center and a loop of webbing tied through this hole.
>
> Bill Forrest made the first actual copperheads in 1968. His design is still used today: a ribbed-cylinder head on a wire cable. His copperheads were a big improvement over the mashies: the copper was more durable and gripped the rock better than the aluminum, and you could remove these placements later.

Technique

Placing A Copperhead

It takes practice to place a copperhead well. It must hold securely but also be easy for your partner to remove. Practice on short, out of the way climbs before you get yourself on a long, more committing route where a mistake could be fatal!

You must hammer a copperhead into position for it to provide security in a crack. The thin, pick-

end of your hammer works best for this job. You can also use a blunt, 5/8-inch chisel, although this means carrying an extra, weighty piece of gear up the cliff.

As I mentioned before, copperheads are designed for shallow cracks where pitons won't hold. Naturally, if the crack is thin you will need a thin copperhead; use the wider, square copperheads in wider cracks.

A crack's width is important. Your copperhead should just fit into it. If your copperhead slides in too easily it will require more hammering to make it fit, which will spread the metal too thin, weakening the placement. Of course, a copperhead can also be too wide for a crack. But this is fairly obvious: you won't be able to fit it in.

Placing a copperhead

Now begin hammering. Lightly tap an X into the head with opposite diagonal blows. Tap these Xs in a sequence similar to the one shown below. The idea is to evenly settle the head's entire length into the rock. Hit it just hard enough for the head to expand without breaking apart.

When the head has filled the crack, tap its edges against the crack's sides. This will give the placement further security by increasing the head's bite into the rock.

Finally, give the head a few light blows from above and below. This will settle the placement.

Important: you can over-place a copperhead by hitting it too much. This weakens both the head's

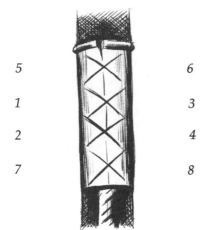

X-ing a copperhead

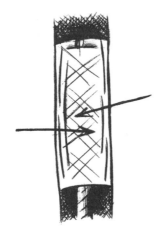

Widening a copperhead

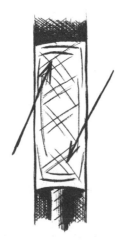

Settling a copperhead

connection to the cable and the rock around the copperhead. It can also make the copperhead difficult to remove, which may force you to leave the head stuck in the rock.

Also important: you can under-place a copperhead by not hitting it enough. An under-placed copperhead may slip out of position simply because it isn't biting the rock securely.

The ideal copperhead placement grips the rock evenly along its entire length.

Testing A Copperhead

You need to test a copperhead before you commit all of your weight to it. You can easily do this by clipping a carabiner to the copperhead and pulling it gently from side to side, and then down. The copperhead shouldn't move. If it seems secure, connect your long etrier to it. Gingerly step on the most convenient rung, gradually adding more weight. Keep a constant eye on the copperhead. If when it is supporting most of your weight it still hasn't moved, it probably won't. This isn't a guarantee, but it's the best you get.

On some routes you will come across copperheads that other climbers placed and didn't remove. Can you trust such placements? Sometimes. There are many factors affecting the security of previously-placed copperheads. These include: how well the first climber placed them, whether or not his partner tried to remove them, but failed, and in so doing weakened the placement, how long they have been in position, and how many other climbers have used them since they were placed. The issue is complex!

Testing previously-placed copperheads is similar to testing your own placements, except the first step: examining the copperhead. Careful examination of a copperhead is vital before you tug on the placement with your carabiner. It should be free of rust. Its wire cable should be completely intact. It should look well-placed, as I described previously. If it meets all these requirements to your satisfaction, then you can tug on it with a carabiner. Continue with the rest of the testing procedure as you would with a copperhead you just placed.

As your experience increases so will your ability to determine how well a copperhead is placed. Unfortunately, even the experts are sometimes surprised! However, if you go slow and pay attention to all the details that I have mentioned, you should have no problems.

Removing A Copperhead

If your partner didn't over-place the copperhead you should be able to remove (clean) it easily. Connect a **cow's tail** (a **runner, daisy chain,** or chain of **carabiners,** see pg. 191) to both your hammer and the copperhead. Swing your hammer up and out. This should easily rop the copperhead free.

Note: if your partner over-placed the copperhead you may yank the cable right out of it, leaving a mess of metal in the crack. If it looks like this will happen, don't try to remove the copperhead: it is considered bad etiquette to do so. Leave it for someone else to use. Removing the cable alone will make the copperhead useless to everyone - both you and future climbers.

If the cable does come out of the head, try to clean the remaining pieces of the head out of the crack. If you're lucky, a few hammer blows from above and below will do the trick. If not, remove as much of the head as possible and then continue your climb.

Specifications

Size

Copperheads vary in width, but they are basically thin devices, ranging from 1/8-inch to one-inch thick. Their length dimensions are less important, but are generally 6-12 inches long.

Strength

Manufacturers don't list the strength of copperheads. The reason for this is that a copperhead's actual placement strength depends upon how much you mash the copperhead when you place it in the rock. What may have begun as a 4000 lb. copperhead can, through over-placement, quickly turn into a 500 lb. chunk of metal! However, if you are timid when you hammer the copperhead you will under-place it, which is just as bad as over-placing it.

Copperheads are designed to hold your body weight. Use them for this purpose and you won't have to worry about their strength: they should support you easily. Of course this depends upon how well you place them!

Materials

Some heads are made out of copper and others are made out of aluminum. Copper is more durable than the softer aluminum. The aluminum, however, is more malleable. As a result, manufacturers make small heads out of copper: they want the thin metal to be as durable as possible. They use aluminum for the larger heads, which have enough metal to provide reasonable durability.

General Safety Guidelines

Test Before You Commit!

After you place a copperhead, test it to make sure it will support your weight. This is easy to do: clip one of your etriers (see pg. 173) to the copperhead and, while your other etrier supports most of your weight, lightly step into its lowest rung. Gradually put your weight on the copperhead, observing it while you do. Look for movement. If it doesn't move, and you feel confident that it will hold, commit yourself to the new etrier and continue your climb.

Care

Copperheads are made to be abused. They like to be hammered, nicked, and flattened. Don't be afraid to knock them as thoroughly as you can, if that's what it takes to get a good placement.

Sometimes, but not often, you can reuse a copperhead. If it isn't too mangled by the previous placement, give it a try.

Make Your Own

Copperheads, at around $1.50-2.50, are inexpensive. But only if you buy a few. If you begin to use a lot of them this price will eat away at your finances. As a cheap alternative to these commercial copperheads, you can make your own.

You should always buy the square-blocky copperheads commercially. This is because their heads are soldered onto their wire stems, and you must have excellent soldering skills to achieve a strong enough connection. You must also know the correct solder to use for joining these materials. For example, if the head is of copper and the wire of steel you would use a different solder than if the head was aluminum and the wire was of steel alloy.

Definition: Swager. A swager is a tool for shaping or bending metal. Swaging is the process of shaping or bending this metal so that it permanently joins another piece of metal, in this case, the head.

If you want to make your own copperheads you will need a Nicopress swager. A swager enables you to swage the head (the swage) to the future copperhead's cable. Nicopress swagers are recognized as the best tools for this job because of their consistent performance. Other swagers are not always so reliable.

To construct a copperhead, you need a length of wire and two pieces of metal to swage. One piece is the head, while the other connects the end of the cable in a loop. See "Accessories" below for more details.

Double back the cable and swage the head onto it (make sure that a little cable protrudes from the swage). Be sure to squeeze the swager tightly for a secure fit. Now form a small loop at the other end of the cable and tightly swage the second piece of metal around it. Test this loop by pulling on it. It shouldn't move or slide around at all. (If it does, throw the faulty copperhead away: it isn't safe to use.) Once the copperhead passes this test, you are finished.

Accessories

Swages

You can buy the metal for copperhead swages at A5 (see pg. 353 for address). They sell both aluminum and copper swages, already sized (from 1/8 to one-inch), in lots of 100. Call them for more information.

Swagers

If you want to make your own copperheads, you will need a pair of swagers. Nicopress swagers work the best, but they are very expensive (about $150). Buy them only if you are a frequent aid climber: they are too expensive to be justified if you aren't. You may want to split the cost with your climbing partners and share a swager.

You will need different swagers for different size heads (according to A5): Nicopress #64 swages #1, 2, 3, and 4-sized heads; #63 swages #3, 4, and 5-sized heads. The #17-B4 tool swages only #0 heads but costs just $35. You can order Nicopress swagers through A5 or you might be able to find them at a hardware store.

As an alternative, some hardware stores will swage your copperheads for you. Make sure they use a Nicopress swager, and they let you watch the work.

Wire

The size of the wire used determines the size of a copperhead. If you want a thin copperhead, use thin wire; the same is true for thick copperheads.

Determining the correct wire size is easy. Subtract the doubled width of the swage from the size of copperhead that you want to make. The result is a rough estimate of the wire size (although you will double back the wire, it will compress to a single width when you swage it). Example, if you want a 3/8-inch copperhead, and your swage's doubled width is 1/8-inch, then you know you need a 2/8-inch (1/4-inch) wire.

Some Copperhead Manufacturers

A5, Chouinard, Fish, and climbers parked at select climbing areas (the Camp 4 parking lot in Yosemite is filled with copperheads for sale) manufacture copperheads. See pg. 353 for manufacturers' addresses.

Daisy Chains
(Anchor Chain)

A daisy chain

What Is A Daisy Chain?

A daisy chain is a large loop of **webbing** (a **runner**) that has been sewn into many smaller loops. By clipping your **carabiner** to any of the different loops you can quickly adjust the daisy chain's length. This is very useful in **aid climbing** and for quickly setting up **anchors.**

To use the daisy chain (daisy) for aid climbing, first attach it to your **harness** (see Harness, pg. 195). You can do this with a **locking carabiner** (the easiest method) or with a Girth Hitch knot.

It's easy to tie the Girth Hitch. Push the loop on one end of the daisy through your harness' swami belt (waist belt) and leg loops. Then thread the rest of the daisy through this end loop.

Using a Girth Hitch to connect a daisy chain to your harness

Now that you are secured to the daisy you can clip it (with a carabiner) to a **piece of aid** (a **chock, piton,** or **bolt** that you use to support your weight). When you are clipped in you can lean back and rest, letting the aid hold you. If you want to be positioned closer to or farther from the rock, clip the aid to a different loop in the daisy.

Most aid climbers use the daisy chain in conjunction with **etriers.** To do this, clip an etrier (which is a rope ladder, see pg. 173) into a piece of aid, and then clip in your daisy chain. Now you can test the piece of aid, by jerking on it, without fear of losing it; if it comes out, your daisy chain will keep it from plummeting to the ground.

You can also use your daisy chain as a **"cow's tail."** Clip the daisy, which you have already tied to your **waist harness,** to the piece of aid (with a carabiner). This setup will keep you near the rock, preventing you from flipping over backward, which is particularly helpful when you are climbing steep walls and overhanging rock. You can make a cow's tail from a sling, runner or even a chain of carabiners. However, the daisy chain makes the best cow's tail, because it is the easiest to adjust.

You can also use a **Fifi hook** (see pg. 228) to quickly attach your cow's tail to a piece of aid. The hook is easier to use than a carabiner because you won't waste time opening and closing a gate.

Most daisies are runner strength (the only one that isn't is the adjustable daisy, which I discuss below). This makes them good for setting up your anchors because you can quickly adjust them to the necessary length (for more on anchors, see pg.

53). You can also use your daisy as a runner, (although you would only do this if you were desperately out of runners).

Daisy chains are very safe connectors. This is because every loop in the daisy is backed up. To demonstrate: if the sewing connecting one of the loops was to rip out, you would not become disconnected. Instead, you would be secured to a slightly larger loop, one made up of the two loops that had been joined before the stitching ripped.

This process of loops ripping out could conceivably (but not likely) happen to all of them, at which point the entire loop of webbing would act as a runner, and you would still be connected to your protection.

Note: the daisy is similar to a **load limiter** (see pg. 295) in this way; under heavy loading they both rip their stitching to form a runner.

An adjustable daisy chain

Adjustable Daisy Chain

Some manufacturers sell adjustable daisy chains. These strips of webbing have a sewn loop on each end and a cam buckle (a buckle that is spring-loaded and locks when you pull from one direction) connected to one of the ends.

The cam buckle allows you to quickly adjust the length of your daisy chain. To either shorten the loop or lengthen it, just pull on the webbing.

Make Your Own Daisy Chain

It is easy to make your own daisy. All you need is one long strip of either 11/16 or one-inch-wide tubular webbing. This webbing's length depends on how many loops you want in your daisy. A 10-foot runner will give you about six loops. A 20-foot runner will give you 10 loops. You can get a couple more loops into the runner if you make each loop really small. Don't make the loop too small - it must still be easy to clip!

Making the loops in your length of webbing is just like making an etrier (see Etrier, pg. 173), only with smaller loops. First, tie your length of webbing into a loop with a Frost knot (see pg. 175). Make sure there are no twists in the loop. Now begin a series of Overhand knots (see pg. 175), which you tie until you reach the end of the webbing. Before you tie each knot, pull one side of the webbing up slightly, so that when you tie the knot a permanent loop is formed.

A do-it-yourself daisy chain has some negative points. It is bulkier, heavier, and weaker than a commercially-made one.

On the positive side, the do-it-yourself daisy is easy to make, taking just a few minutes. Once you know how to rig one, you can quickly do so anywhere, even on the side of a cliff, if necessary. The do-it-yourself version is also cheaper than a commercially-available daisy.

Care

Although your daisy chain is essentially a runner, you should give it special care. This is because it is both more expensive than a runner and has a more specific purpose. Try not to use the daisy as a common runner because it will soon wear out.

Making a daisy chain with Overhand knots

Accessories

Webbing

If you want to make your own daisy chain you must buy some tubular webbing (see Slings and Runners, pg. 291). You can buy webbing from any climbing shop or climbing mail-order company. Don't buy it from non-climbing/rescue sources (the quality may not be as high)!

Check your daisy's stitching occasionally. Sunlight and rock abrasion will gradually deteriorate the thread, weakening the stitching. When the thread looks thin, faded, and generally worn you should discard the daisy. And, if any one area of your daisy becomes severely worn (over fifty percent of its fibers are damaged) you should retire it.

Key Point

"... rappelling is very dangerous. Many rock climbers avoid it if at all possible."

See page 166

Descenders (Rappel Devices; Abseil Devices)

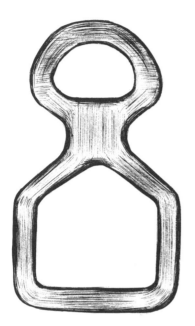

A descender

A climber rappelling

What Is A Descender?

A descender is a mechanical device that, when you rig it properly to your rope and harness, allows you to quickly and safely descend your rope. Making such a controlled descent is called **rappelling.**

Descenders use friction to control the speed of your descent. Friction is created when one surface, such as a **rope,** slides along, or through, another surface, in this case a descender. You can increase the friction by tightening the two surfaces together, or by increasing their area of contact. Increasing the friction will slow you down. All the devices and techniques in this chapter make use of this principle.

How To Rappel

Your body position is important when you rappel. With your feet on the cliff you must lean out, perpendicularly, away from the rock. In this position you can walk down the cliff, as though it were a vertical sidewalk. Leaning out into space, far from the security of your handholds on the cliff, is a scary thing to do, but as you relax you will discover that this position is the most secure way to descend.

As you rappel, let your rope, **harness,** and descender hold you. Trust them. Keep your hands on the rope, as illustrated above, and your arms relaxed and slightly bent.

The first few times you rappel, you will probably want to grip the rope tightly with both hands. This is fine, but there's no need to take this precaution. Your control comes not from your hands but from the friction of your rope bending through your belay device and then wrapping around your hip. Use your hands to simply guide the rope. This works best if you keep your fingers in a loose circle, which will prevent you from gripping the rope.

Try to keep a slow, steady pace as you descend. This will help you stay in control of your descent. Also, avoid bouncing on your rope. Bouncing is fun but it damages the rope and increases the possibility that the rope may be abraded, even cut, by the rock above.

Types

Four basic types of descenders are manufactured: the **figure-eight,** the **bobbin,** the **rappel rack,** and the **Seilbremse (Bankl Plate).** All of these descenders are safe devices that are designed specifically for use in rappelling.

A figure-eight rigged for rappelling

If you want more friction, loop a second bight of rope over the small hole. (For example, you will need the added friction if you are carrying a heavy load or rappelling on a thin rope.)

A figure-eight

The Figure-Eight

The figure-eight device is named after its shape. It is a one-piece, metal device that is very easy to use and maintain. It is currently the most popular rappel device in the U.S.

To use the figure-eight, push a bight (loop) of rope up through the device's large hole and down over the small one. Now clip the small hole to your harness with a **locking carabiner.**

A figure-eight rigged for added friction

The figure-eight is one of the safest rappel devices on the market. There is no way, unless something breaks, that your rope can come undone from a properly-rigged figure-eight. With a little practice, rigging the figure-eight to your rope is easy. It's also very obvious when you make a mistake, so you aren't likely to rig the device incorrectly.

The figure-eight works just as well with two ropes as it does with one (for more on rope technique, see pg. 277). You will descend slower, however, which makes it difficult to get going when you are at the top of the rappel (the rope's weight beneath you pulls the rope tight, which increases friction). Rig two ropes through the figure-eight the same as you would one rope.

Sometimes you need to "lock off" your descender. Locking off lets you use both your hands freely, without worrying about your rope slipping through the device. This is useful if you want to take a picture, disconnect some gear from the cliff, or clean the rock to prepare it for climbing.

There are two locks: a soft, or quick, lock, and a hard, or full, lock. A soft lock comes undone when you take your weight off of the descender, whereas a hard lock will remain secure until you unlock it.

You can lock the figure-eight off easily while halfway down the cliff. For a soft lock, simply cross your rope under the device's large end, and hold it there.

A figure-eight with a soft lock

To make a hard lock, loop a bight of rope up through the figure-eight. Then tie a **Half Hitch Knot** in it, as illustrated.

The figure-eight has the additional advantage of being a fairly good belay device (see pg. 87). Its applicability for two essential jobs, rappelling and belaying, make the figure-eight a versatile climbing tool.

Using the figure-eight does present you with some problems. Because of the way the rope wraps

A figure-eight with a hard lock

through the device when you rappel, it twists as it pulls through. If the end of your rope is piled on a ledge below you it will kink as you descend because it cannot untwist. Twist damages your rope: it either unwinds the core fibers or winds them too tightly. You can reduce this damage by letting your rope hang inert along the rock after you have used a figure-eight device to rappel down it.

Because of the figure-eight's smooth sides, your rope may slide up from the small end of the device and jam over the large end. In essence, the rope forms a **Girth Hitch,** right in the middle of your rappel! The only way to undo this knot is to take the tension off the section of rope above the knot. The easiest way to do this is to rig a **Prusik Knot** above your jammed figure-eight, connect your harness to it with a piece of **webbing,** and let it suport your weight. Now your jammed rope will easily slide free. If you're strong enough you won't have to use the Prusik knot: simply lift yourself up, off your jammed figure-eight, hold yourself there with one arm and undo the know with the other hand. This is much more strenuous, but also much quicker.

You cannot adjust the maximum amount of tension that your figure-eight applies to the rope. This means that it's difficult to descend a medium to long rope (300 ft. or more) with a figure-eight because the rope's weight at the top would prevent it from feeding through the device. The figure-eight works best on short, 150-200 ft. descents.

You cannot engage and disengage your rope from the figure-eight without removing the device from your locking carabiner. This is unfortunate because it takes more time to rig.

As you rappel your figure-eight will rapidly become hot. This is because it is made from aluminum alloy, which conducts heat quickly. Even after a short, 30-foot rappel your device will be quite hot. This is hard on your rope, because when you stop your descent the hot metal can burn your rope's nylon fibers. In addition, if you descend too rapidly and the figure-eight really heats up, the combined heat and friction may be enough to stop your descent.

Despite these problems, the figure-eight continues to be one of the most popular descenders on the market. It is fairly lightweight and has little bulk. Combined with its almost fail-safe design and capability to function as a belay device, the figure-eight is a very good tool.

Figure-Eight Variations

There are two variations on the basic figure-eight design. One is similar, but smaller, to the standard one. The other has "ears." Both are situation-specific tools that, although they will work for all-around rock climbing, are much better when used in their particular specialty.

The Small Figure-Eight

The small figure-eight is very lightweight. This makes it useful for alpine ascents, where you may need a rappel device but you don't want to carry much weight. However, because of its small size, the small figure-eight heats up very quickly. Being thinner, it also can't withstand as much abrasion as a standard figure-eight. Because of these two problems, don't use the small

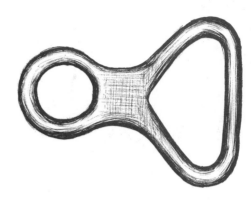

A small figure-eight

figure-eight for **sport rappelling!** The lack of abrasion resistance also makes the small figure-eight less durable: it won't last as long as a standard figure-eight.

The Figure-Eight With Ears

The figure-eight with ears (also known as a rescue figure-eight) is a safer device than the standard model. Its ears are designed to keep your rope from slipping over the large hole and forming a Girth Hitch during rappels, as I described above.

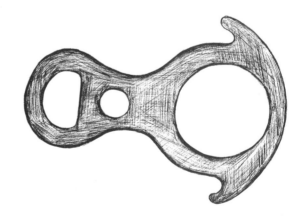

An eared figure-eight

Because it's so safe, this type of figure-eight is useful for rescue operations. However, it is both heavier and bulkier than standard figure-eights. Because of this I recommend that you use the standard model for rappelling.

The Bobbin

The bobbin is a very popular European descender. It consists of two pulley-like wheels (called sheaves) connected between two aluminum sideplates.

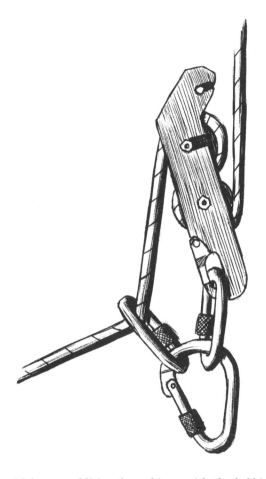

Using an additional carabiner with the bobbin

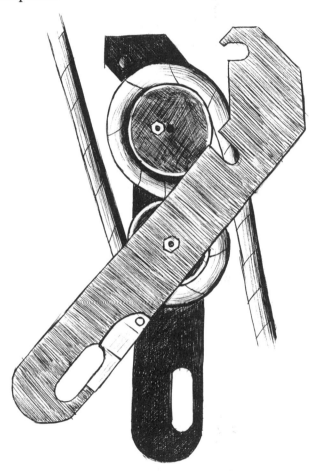

The bobbin

The bobbin's easy-to-use design is a great feature: you can rig it to your rope without first detaching it from your harness. Simply swing one of the sideplates up, thread your rope around both pulleys, and rotate the sideplate back down. One sideplate has a safety catch which clips onto your locking carabiner.

Some climbers feel they get more control by threading the free side of their rope through an additional waist **carabiner.**

Although the rope abrades the carabiner as you rappel, you may decide to use the bobbin this way. Experiment with different methods and use the one with which you feel most comfortable.

The bobbin's design allows your rope to run straight, without twisting, so it won't kink while you descend. To slow your descent, thread your rope over the bobbin's top pin, thereby increasing the friction between the rope and bobbin.

To descend faster, reduce the amount of rope friction by threading your rope through the bobbin as shown below:

Note: don't use this reduced-friction rig for descending unless the device won't work without it. There are really only two reasons this might occur: if you are using a thick rope or if you are rappelling down a long rope (the weight of a long rope hanging below you will increase the friction in the device).

To rig a soft lock on your bobbin, push a bight of rope through the locking carabiner at your waist. Loop this bight over the entire device.

To get a hard lock on a bobbin, rig the soft lock. Now thread another bight of rope through the first, and drop this over the bobbin.

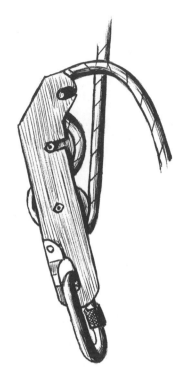

A rope threaded over the bobbin's top pin

A soft lock on a bobbin

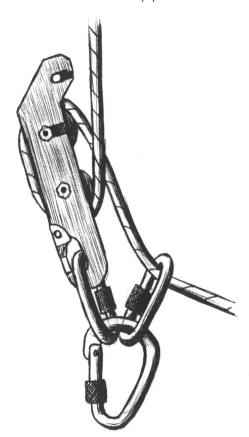

A bobbin rigged for reduced friction

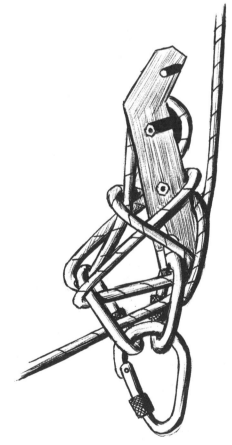

A hard lock on a bobbin

Some bobbins have double sheaves to accommodate two ropes (for more on double ropes, see pg. 177).

Bobbins have some negative points. For instance, at the beginning of a long rappel they are awkward to use. To get started you must feed the rope through the device, otherwise you won't go anywhere.

A bobbin is a long device and can get in your way when you are climbing. Clip it to the back of your harness until you are ready to descend.

Petzl makes a unique bobbin called the Stop. It looks similar to other bobbins, but has a handle attached at one side. When you descend you must close this handle with one hand and feed the free side of your rope through with the other.

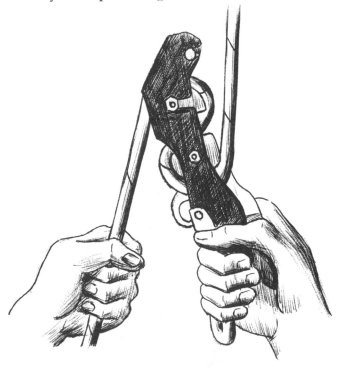

Holding the Stop's handle to descend

When you want to stop descending, let go of the handle. This movement gives the equivalent of a hard lock (although the old models creep slightly).

Letting go of something when you want to stop is an unnatural motion. In a tense situation your impulse will probably be to grip, not to release. Therefore, the Stop bobbin takes some getting used to. Bear this in mind when you use the Stop bobbin!

You can disengage the stop feature by clipping a second carabiner to the bobbin's handle.

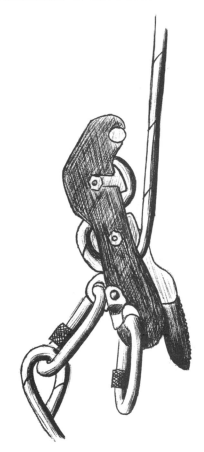

A second carabiner clipped to disengage the Stop

The Rappel Rack

The rappel rack is a descender, but it isn't meant for rock climbing. It is much too heavy and bulky. It's also very long: if you were to hang the rappel rack from your harness it would interfere with your climbing. Rather, the rappel rack works better for the long rappels more common to cavers. I am discussing it for the benefit of anyone wishing to make such a rappel, which can be down a big wall, such as El Capitan, just as easily as in a cave.

The rappel rack consists of a "U"-shaped vertical length of metal rod, which is called the rack. Various regularly-spaced horizontal brake bars are mounted along this rack.

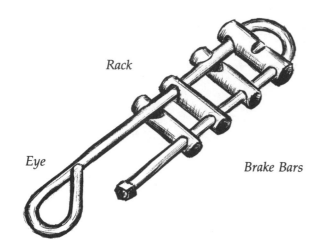

Rack

Eye

Brake Bars

A rappel rack

To rig the rack for descending you must put your rope over the first brake bar and through the "U"-shaped rod. Now swing the other brake bars into position, one after the other, each time flipping the rope through the "U".

A rope rigged through several brake bars

The rack is a very adjustable descender. This is what makes it excellent on long descents, undoubtedly the best device there is for such a job. At the top of the descent you can put the rope through only a few bars, which provides very little friction. This is necessary because, as I have already stated, the weight of a long rope increases the friction on the device when you are at the top of a rappel. As

you descend, the rope's weight will play a decreasing role in slowing you, so that you will need to swing more bars into the rig. In this way you can adjust the friction as necessary, the amount you need depending on the rope's weight.

Another way to adjust the rack's friction is to vary the distance between the bars. The closer they are to each other, the more they bind the rope.

You can buy the rappel rack with either steel or aluminum brake bars. Steel bars are hollow, to reduce their weight. They dissipate heat well, but your rope will run over them very quickly, so you must practice using them before trying a long descent. Aluminum bars build up heat very quickly, but grip your rope better, requiring less practice to use them well.

Because you will not be using the rappel rack for climbing, I won't discuss it in any more detail. If you want to make long rappels, and therefore need to buy a rack, I recommend that you read Padgett and Smith's book *On Rope* first. This book is written for cavers, who frequently make long descents and use the rack as an integral part of their equipment. The book contains a detailed description of the rappel rack, including how to modify your rappel rack to fit your individual needs.

The Seilbremse And The Bankl Plate

The Seilbremse (pronounced sile-brem-sah) and the Bankl (pronounced bank-l) Plate are two very similar descenders. Each has a large hold through which you can insert your rope and a smaller hole through which to clip a carabiner (actually the Bankl Plate has two carabiner holes).

For rappelling with one rope, both devices are rigged in the same way. First, clip a locking carabiner to your harness and through the device's small hole. Now push a bight of rope through the large hole and clip it into the carabiner.

To rig the Seilbremse for two ropes, simply follow the same steps as you did for one.

To rig the Bankl Plate for two ropes, you need an additional locking carabiner clipped through your harness and through the second carabiner hole. Rig the second rope into the device as a mirror image of the first. Both ropes will run out the center of the large hole together.

All the other features of the Seilbremse and Bankl Plate are very similar, so to make things easy I will discuss both devices as if they were one. I shall refer to them as the Seilbremse, because, unlike the Bankl Plate, the Seilbremse is sold here in the U.S.

The Seilbremse   *The Bankl Plate*

The Seilbremse is a small device, smaller even than a standard figure-eight, which you can rig without removing from your harness. This setup increases your security, since once you put the de-

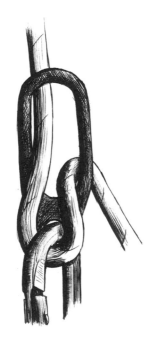

Rappelling with one rope

vice on, you have no reason to take it off, which negates the chance that you'll use it later when it isn't rigged for rappelling, which might result in an accident. And because you have no need to alter its position, the Seilbremse allows you to use your time more efficiently on other necessary jobs.

The Seilbremse is made of steel, which distributes heat better than aluminum. Unfortunately the metal around the large hole (the rope hole) is thin; it will heat rapidly during your rappel.

The Bankl Plate rigged with two ropes

The Seilbremse won't twist your rope when you rappel with it. This is very advantageous; it keeps your rope from kinking up, and from being damaged by the twisting motion, as I've already discussed.

You can use the Seilbremse for belaying (see pg. 92). This versatility makes the device more attractive: rock climbers need their gear to perform more than one job.

You should be aware of the Seilbremse's one big drawback. Its design forces the rope to run through your locking carabiner. When you rappel, your rope not only abrades the Seilbremse (whose steel body can easily withstand the abrasion), but the rope also abrades your locking carabiner. Unless you use a steel carabiner, which is both heavy and expensive, your locking carabiner won't last very long. As it wears it grows dramatically weaker. And when your carabiner grows weak you can't use it for anything; you must retire it. Compared to other descenders, the Seilbremse eats carabiners.

Technique

Rappelling is a skill that every rock climber must have. If you are climbing a long, hard **route** and aren't able to reach the top, rappelling to the bottom is your only option. Many routes ascend peaks which, once attained, present no easy way down. Again, rappelling is your only alternative.

In addition, many people take up rappelling for sport. It can be an exhilarating activity: speeding down the side of a cliff, or even through empty space (a free rappel).

However, *rappelling is very dangerous*. Many rock climbers avoid it if at all possible. First of all, rappelling is one of the few things you can do while rock climbing in which you must trust your life to a weak anchor system (see pg. 53). Also, most of us don't belay each other as we rappel, because this is often impractical, and it always takes too much time.

Practicing rappelling on a short cliff from which you can walk down presents no problems. You can set up a very safe anchor system, with multiple anchors, and even belay your partner, the rappeller, with another rope (*always belay anyone who is just learning to rappel!*). And when you've finished practicing, you don't need to leave any gear behind because you can walk down from the top of the cliff.

When you're climbing a taller cliff, rappelling is often the only way to descend. You don't want to leave much gear behind, so you will use only one, maybe two, anchors. *Unless these anchors are* **bombproof,** *this is very dangerous!* Therefore, your anchors must be totally secure! If you aren't certain of this, leave some gear behind. The cost of losing your gear is nothing compared with injuring yourself or even dying!

On many routes, climbers have solved their anchor problem by placing **bolts** at every belay ledge. These bolts (usually two per anchor) are not always

as secure as they seem, so look carefully for signs of weakness before you use them (see pg. 108).

Retrieving Your Rope

On many routes you must retrieve your rope once you've finished your rappel. An easy way to accomplish this (do it before you rappel!) is to double your rope through a loop of webbing securely tied to the anchors.

A rope doubled over an anchored loop of webbing

Important: *don't use old, worn webbing for this connection!* You are guaranteed to run across anchors that still have webbing tied to them, left from the last climbers' rappel. Don't use this webbing unless it is in good condition (see pg. 299). Webbing quickly loses its strength in the sun; it may take only a few weeks of intense exposure before the loop is too weak to use (although webbing will often survive intact for several months). You will be able to approximate the webbing's status by examining it carefully: experience helps here, but it's fairly obvious when the webbing is really worn (it's very faded and stiff).

Once your rope is looped through the webbing, connect your descender to both of the rope's sides. You will rappel as though on two ropes: really it is the two halves of one rope. When you reach the **belay station** below, clip into the anchor (with **runners** tied to your harness), then disengage your descender from the rope. When the the last climber in your party has reach the belay station and anchored himself, pull one side of the rope down. This will send the other side of the rope up the cliff and through the anchor's webbing, whence it will fall back down to you.

A descending ring

The Descending Ring

SMC makes a descending ring. This one-piece aluminum ring is not a descender. Rather, it is designed to increase your safety when you rappel.

To use the descending ring, thread the anchor's webbing through the ring and tie the webbing securely. Now loop your rope through the ring, as though you were looping it through the webbing. The key difference is that your rope is now connected to the anchor via a metal ring, instead of pulling on nylon, which will quickly abrade.

Of course, you must leave the descending ring behind when you descend. But it's cheap, and other climbers will be able to use it. It's a good idea to carry a few descending rings with you when you are climbing a route from which you will need to rappel down.

You will climb some routes from which you must rappel to get back down. On these climbs you must retrace your route: rappel down to each belay station, secure yourself, and wait for your partner to follow. Remember to always test the rope before you rappel on it: the first climber down should pull on it to make sure that it easily slides through the anchor. If the rope gets stuck the climber nearest the anchors must adjust the rig until the rope is free.

If both you and your partner have descended a rope, and it gets caught somewhere, (even after you have tested it) you are in bad straights. Continue tugging on it, trying from different angles. If it refuses to budge, either you or your partner must climb back up the pitch and free it. This is a situation in which many accidents occur. Hopefully you brought along another rope so that one of you can reclimb the pitch safely, placing **protection** as you go. However, if not, your only option is to solo climb the pitch (unless you've reached the ground, in which case you can go find another rope with which to lead the pitch). You can attach a couple of Prusik knots (see pg. 76) between you and the stuck end of the rope, but this isn't a guarantee of safety. If you fall the rope may decide to come undone, in which case you are lost.

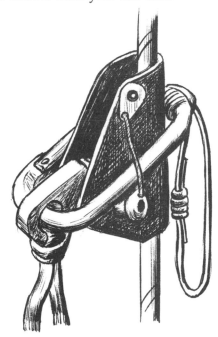

The Spelean Shunt

Using Backup

When you rappel you can use an **ascender** (see pg. 75) as a backup safety device. Clip the ascender to your rope, above your rappel device, and then to your harness. To descend you must keep one hand on your ascender, guiding it and keeping it from locking. This is awkward, and makes it very slow and laborious to rappel.

Climbers developed the **Spelean Shunt** as a way to easily protect their rappels without the awkwardness of using an ascender. The Spelean Shunt is simply a modified, springless **Gibbs ascender** (see pg. 79). The springless Gibbs will only grip your rope when you tug its cam down. This means that you can rappel quickly, trailing the shunt, and don't have to hassle with it on your descent.

All you need to rig the Spelean Shunt is a springless Gibbs, an **oval carabiner**, and a **sling**. Clip the carabiner into the ascender's cam and around its shell. Tie the sling to the far end of the carabiner (outside the shell) with a Girth Hitch (see pg. 46), which will keep the sling from sliding around.

When you pull the carabiner the Gibb's cam rotates down and locks onto your rope, stopping your descent. To unlock the shunt, pull the other side of the handle.

You can also buy a commercially-made shunt bar, the American Rescue Gibbs Shunt Bar. This bar works with the springless Gibbs, and is faster to rig than the Spelean Shunt.

There are also commercial shunts available, such as Petzl's. The Petzl Shunt consists of a toothed cam surrounding by a shell, with a handle. Although you can ascend with the Petzl Shunt, it was designed as a safety device, so use it as such. The Petzl Shunt is ready to go: simply attach it to your rope and harness.

The commercial shunt is the easiest to use, but it is an extra item to buy. It is also more specialized than the Spelean Shunt, which you can also use both as your main ascender and as a pulley ratchet (see Pulleys, pg. 259). And, if you don't have much money to spend, the Spelean Shunt is the cheaper option.

Alternative Ways To Descend

Using a descender is the safest and easiest way to rappel. However, you may not always have a descender with you when you need to rappel. Therefore, you should know several alternative rappelling techniques.

Dulfer Rappel

The Dulfer (Dulfersitz) is the classic body rappel technique. It allows you to descend a cliff using only a rope wrapped around your body. To rig the

The Spelean Shunt rigged with a shunt bar

Dulfer, thread the rope between your legs, diagonally over your chest, then diagonally down your back.

You have rigged the Dulfer correctly when the

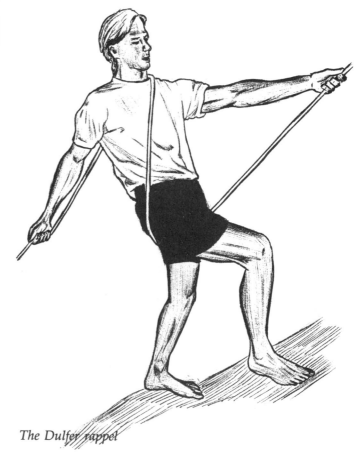

The Dulfer rappel

rope wraps around the outside of your hip on your braking hand side.

The Dulfer has the advantage of requiring no special equipment beyond a rope. It is easy and quick to set up, although it is also easy to rig incorrectly. Practice with the Dulfer on small boulders before you try it on higher cliffs.

Don't use the Dulfer on free rappels (a rappel in which you can't touch the rock). In such a rappel the rope will twist your body around, unwrapping itself. Actually, the rope tries to unwrap whenever you use the Dulfer, so descend slowly. Keep the leg with the rope around it below your other leg as you descend. This helps keep the rope from unwrapping.

Rope burns are a problem when you use the Dulfer. You will be forced to descend slowly due to the intense heat that develops from the rope sliding around you. Wearing tough clothes when you use the Dulfer is your best protection against burns.

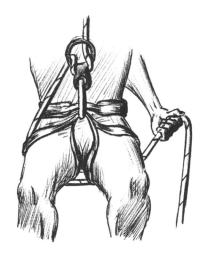

A rope fed through a descender and then under a climber's legs.

Using Your Body For Extra Friction

By wrapping your rope around your body you can increase any descender's holding power. One such arrangement is to wrap the rope under your legs before you begin to rappel.

Another way to slow your descent is to twist your rope two or three times around one leg.

This method works best on a free rappel. It also provides a quick way to stop your descent, so use it if you have trouble with your descender. It also offers a convenient way to lock off your rope, allowing you free use of your hands.

Carabiner Brake Rappel

You can always rig a series of carabiners to act as a descending device. You need only your rope, your harness, a locking carabiner, and at least four oval carabiners.

First, clip two oval carabiners, with their gates opposed (see pg. 130), into your locking carabiner. Now push a bight of rope through the ovals. Clip the remaining two ovals (under the rope) to the middle of the previous two.

A carabiner brake rappel rig

When you lean back on your rope it will tighten through the carabiner rig, allowing you to descend. Use your brake arm to control the speed of your rappel as you would with any descender.

If you want more friction, add another set of carabiners onto the first.

There are two advantages to using a carabiner brake rappel rig. Your rope will run straight and easily, with no twist, and you don't need to bring along an extra piece of gear, namely the descender, when you climb.

The only problems with the carabiner brake rappel rig are that, if you were tired, you might rig it incorrectly. Also, the rope abrasion will weaken the carabiners. And finally, the rig is not totally safe: if you don't keep an eye on your rope it might find a way out of the rig (unlikely, but possible).

Carabiner Brake Bar

You can use a brake bar rigged across a carabiner as a descender. Some manufacturers sell brake bars specifically for this purpose. These brake bars have a hole in one side (to slide over one side of the carabiner) and a slot on the other side (which fits over the other side of the carabiner).

Important: be sure to rig your rope so that it pushes the brake bar against the carabiner. If you rig it the other way the rope will simply lift the brake bar off the carabiner. This will leave you hanging from your hands!

In a pinch you can use various tools as improvised brake bars, such as a hammer or a piton.

Caution! The carabiner brake bar is a dangerous rig! This is because the brake bar pushes on the carabiner's gate, which is the worst place to load a carabiner (see pg. 128). Don't use a carabiner brake bar rig if you can possibly avoid it!

A carabiner brake bar

Pulling The Rope

You can slow another rappeller's descent, if you are below him, by pulling his rope taut. This action slows him by increasing the friction between the rope and his descender. Make sure he knows what you're doing before you go and tug on his rope!

Specifications

Strength

The strength of descenders varies from 3000 to 13,000 lbs. You can use the weakest descenders; the stronger ones are designed for the heavy loads that rescuers must deal with. However, you do need safety, and 3000 lbs. is your minimum.

A descender's strength rating decreases as you use the device. This is due to your rope, which slowly abrades the metal. The weaker descenders wear faster than the stronger rescue models: you're

compromising weight for strength and durability. Your choice.

Weight

Descenders weigh anywhere from 3 to 26 ounces. Like the rest of your climbing equipment, you want light weight. But lightweight means low strength and durability, as I mentioned above. If you are an alpinist, you may want to buy one of the lighter descenders. A rock climber (who will abuse the descender more than the alpinist) should go for a medium-range weight, while a rescuer needs the heaviest model.

Materials

Descenders, more than any other piece of gear, must be able to resist abrasion. With your rope running through the device at high speed, the metal under the rope quickly becomes worn.

Figure-eights and some rappel rack brake bars are made of aluminum alloys. These metals wear faster than harder metals, such as steel. However, they are lighter and rougher, offering more friction. To increase aluminum's durability manufacturers cover it with an anodized finish. This finish makes a big difference in wear, so much difference that when your aluminum descender's finish wears off the device won't last long.

There are two types of figure-eight finishes: hard and soft. Hard finishes last longer, and are more abrasion-resistant. But they wear unevenly, and if they wear through to the metal beneath, the edge of the finish becomes sharp, and can cut your rope. Soft finishes avoid these edges but wear faster.

Bobbins are made from a combination of aluminum alloy and steel parts. The bobbin's sideplates and wheels are aluminum alloy, while the rest of it (the smaller parts, the nuts and bolts) is steel. The only parts that suffer much wear are the aluminum alloy wheels. You can buy replacement wheels however, so this isn't a problem. Your bobbin should last you a long time.

If your descender is made of steel (the Seilbremse and some rappel rack brake bars) it is very abrasion-resistant. However, steel doesn't offer as much friction as aluminum, and it is heavier (although the device's weight depends on its size as well). You don't need to worry about the device's finish wearing off: steel will last long after its finish is gone.

General Safety Guidelines

Check And Double Check!

Many rappelling accidents are caused by careless climbers. These people don't check their equipment to make sure everything is properly connected. *Always double check your gear after you rig it, but before you use it!*

Check that your rope is securely anchored. Make sure it reaches to the bottom of the cliff, or to the next set of anchors. Make sure your rope is properly rigged to your descender. And check that your descender is attached to your harness with a *locked* carabiner, or two carabiners with their gates opposed. And examine your harness: it must be properly tied (if it has a buckle the webbing should be doubled back - see pg. 198).

Don't Carry Or Use A Knife When You Rappel!

Sometimes your clothing or hair gets stuck in your descender. *Don't use a knife to cut yourself free!* More than likely you will cut your rope: nylon cuts like butter when it is taut!

If your clothing or hair becomes caught in a descender, you must get your weight off the descender to free it. There are two ways to do this, with a Prusik knot or by hand, as I describe on pg. 76.

Know Where The End Of Your Rope Is!

Before you begin to rappel, know where the end of your rope is. One of the most common rappelling accidents occurs from descending right off the end of the rope! Don't let this happen to you! If it isn't likely to snag on the cliff when you throw your rope down, tie a knot at the end of the rope. Make the knot large enough to jam your rappel device, should you reach it.

Use A Secure Anchor!

Often when you rappel you must pull your rope down behind you. The only way you can do this, without leaving a lot of gear behind, is to use just one anchor. Make sure this anchor is totally bombproof! It must not break. It is the only thing between you and a sudden fall to the bottom of the cliff!

Care

Undoubtedly your descenders will regularly suffer abuse, because you, like most climbers, will find it very convenient to keep the device clipped to the front of your waist harnesses. In this position the descender gets knocked and scraped on the rock as you climb, and quickly collects nicks and scratches.

You cannot let sharp edges develop on any part of your descender. They will make small cuts in your rope when you rappel! And these cuts will weaken the rope, maybe even cut through the sheath. If any edges appear, sand them flat before you use the descender again. If you are at the cliffs without sandpaper, use a grainy rock to flatten the edges. Even a dull metal edge can cut through nylon amazingly easily: as if it were butter!

Note: try not to sand the metal surrounding a nick. You could sand your device's finish off, which would make it far less durable.

When To Retire Your Descender

Retire your descender if you find any cracks in it. Try not to drop the device because it may fracture. Such cracks can be impossible to see but very weakening. Drop-forged aluminum is the most likely to suffer from such an accident: you should retire it once this occurs. Steel is more durable and can survive small drops far better. However, inspect *any* descender whenever you drop it - if there's any sign of weakness, or you even suspect a crack, retire the device.

Retire your aluminum descender (such as a figure-eight or Seilbremse) when its finish wears through. Your rope will wear grooves in the finish. When these grooves begin to develop it is time to retire your descender.

Steel descenders (the figure-eight also comes in steel; the Seilbremse is only made of steel) are useful long after their finish is worn off. Therefore, it is harder to determine just when to retire a steel descender: the area under the rope gradually becomes thinner. And as this area gets thinner it becomes weaker, and overheats faster, both of which makes it more dangerous to use. Retire your steel descender when it loses a quarter of its original size (compare it to a new descender at a climbing shop).

Bobbins can last many years because you can replace their wheels. But if the device cracks or is bent, retire it.

Regarding Stop bobbins: the stop handle wears out from use. Its gripping ability will gradually decrease until it won't grip at all. You can track its status by letting go of its handle (locking it) and hanging on it. See how much you creep down the rope. With a new Stop you won't creep at all, but with an old one, needing replacement, you will slowly continue down the rope. You can buy a replacement handle. Regardless of whether or not you buy a new handle you can continue using the Stop as if it were a normal bobbin.

Accessories

Sandpaper
Use medium grade sandpaper, such as 320 grade, to flatten any edges or nicks that develop on your rappel device.

Bobbin Parts
You can replace most of the bobbin's parts. Petzl sells replacement parts for both their standard bobbin and the Stop.

Some Descender Manufacturers
Allp, Cassin, Chouinard, Clog, CMI, DMM, Petzl, SMC, and Wild Country manufacture descenders. See pg. 353 for manufacturers' addresses.

Etriers (Aiders)

A hard etrier

What Is An Etrier?

An etrier (pronounced a-tree-a) is a 4 to 6-step rope ladder - with each step wide enough to accommodate only one foot. Climbers use etriers when **aid climbing.** In fact, aid climbing without etriers is at best very difficult: usually it is impossible. Therefore, etriers are essential aid climbing tools.

An etrier provides secure footholds where otherwise the climber would have none. These footholds are vital: they provide a platform from which to place the next **piece of aid,** a place to rest when tired, and a ladder that allows the climber to make progress up the rock.

Types

There are two different types of etriers on the market: hard and soft. These names are arbitrary, but appropriate.

Hard Etriers

Hard etriers have either wood (not used much anymore) or aluminum rungs threaded onto cord or cable. They are difficult to find these days since most manufacturers sell only soft etriers. You may run across a used pair in a garage sale, swap meet, or for sale in the parking lot at a climbing area. If you buy such a pair you should examine the cord or cable holding the rungs. If it looks worn, replace it.

Hard etriers are easy to step into because of their stiff rungs. They are also comfortable to use because they give your foot stiff support without cutting into it.

Hard etriers have some disadvantages. First of all, they are bulky. This makes them difficult to pack and awkward to carry. Also, as you climb, a hard etrier's stiff rungs can catch on the rock, especially in cracks. When you are high up a cliff, the last thing you need to worry about is extracting your etrier from a crack! In contrast to wooden-runged etriers, those with aluminum rungs are also noisy: they clank and ring when they hit the rock.

Soft Etriers

A soft etrier is made entirely of **webbing.** It has 4-6 steps that are formed by loops in the webbing. These steps are often reinforced with additional pieces of webbing that help them stay open. Some soft etriers also have sub-steps in the first and second rungs (the top two). These sub-steps are designed to give you a little extra height, which can be invaluable in placing protection.

The soft etrier offers several advantages over the hard etrier. It won't jam as easily into cracks. Its rungs, being soft, wrap securely around your feet when you step into them. Soft etriers can also double as foot slings for ascending a rope because they keep your foot very stable. In a pinch you can even use a soft etrier as a **runner,** looped around rock flakes and knobs. All this adds up to greater versatility: the hard etrier just can't perform as many jobs.

A soft etrier

A soft etrier does have its share of problems. You'll find that it's more difficult to place your foot into the soft etrier's rungs because the flexible steps tend to fold in. Manufacturers have dealt with this problem by adding extra webbing to stiffen the rungs. Also, the soft etrier's rungs dig into the sides of your foot. You can solve this problem by buying etriers made of wide, 2-inch webbing (but they are heavier and bulkier). It also helps to wear **big wall boots** (see pg. 116) or light hiking boots. These types of boots are stiff enough to keep the webbing from digging into your feet.

Sub-Aiders

Some climbers like to add sub-aiders to their etriers. Sub-aiders are a subset of two rungs that connect to the top of each etrier.

The sub-aider allows you to stand with both of your feet equally supported, one in the sub-aider, the other in the etrier. Such stability is important when you're climbing, especially when you need to temporarily remove your foot from your second etrier in order to clip that etrier to the next piece of aid located above you.

Make Your Own Etriers

It is easy to make your own etriers. They will cost you less than $10 for the materials and take about 20 minutes of your time.

To make two etriers you will need two lengths of flat, one-inch webbing: one 20 feet long and one 17 feet long (I explain just why one etrier should be longer than the other under Technique). You should use **flat webbing** because **tubular webbing** is not stiff enough to keep the rungs open. The webbing should be double ply, rather than single ply, which is thinner and weaker by half (you can see the double webbing's two plies: one lays on top of the other). The width of webbing you use will depend on your needs, but note that one-inch is the minimum width that will provide support and yet keep the weight and bulk low. Two-inch webbing is more comfortable, but heavier and bulkier. For a really long aid climb where comfort is important I recommend you use two-inch webbing.

Tie your 20-foot piece of webbing into a loop with a Frost knot (see the illustrations). Before you do this, make sure there are no twists in the loop.

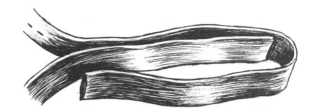

Beginning the Frost knot

Finishing the Frost knot

An etrier with a sub-aider attached

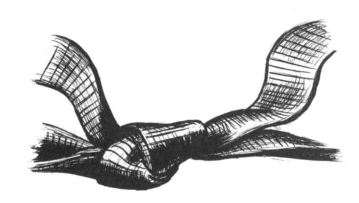

Making an etrier's loops with an Overhand knot

You are now ready to make the loop into a series of rungs. Make the first rung just large enough to easily accept your boot (put a boot on and try it to be sure). Such a small loop will give you the most height when you're standing in the top of your etriers, trying to reach the next piece of aid. You'll have to estimate the size of the other rungs; make them larger than the first. Your rungs are too large if you can't get five steps out of your etrier, which means you'll either have to settle for a four-step etrier or retie the rungs.

To make each rung stay open you must pull one side of the webbing up more than the other side, as shown in the illustration above right. Tie the webbing into a loop with an Overhand knot.

Repeat this process with your 17-foot piece of webbing. This time, however, tie only four steps into the loop. Remember to adjust the webbing so that the rungs will stay open, as demonstrated in the illustration.

You may want a third or fourth etrier as well, especially if you are planning a long, multi-day climb. Make these etriers out of shorter, thinner webbing, such as 1/2-inch webbing 10 to 12-feet long, and with only two or three steps, to save weight and bulk.

Make Your Own Sub-Aiders

Once you've made your etriers you have the option of adding sub-aiders to them. You should add sub-aiders to only two of your etriers; leave any others without them (to save unnecessary weight and bulk).

To rig your sub-aider you will need a 7-foot long piece of flat webbing. The webbing can be thinner than the one-inch material you used to make your etriers: 1/2 or 9/16 of an inch width will do.

Loop the webbing through your etrier's Frost knot. Tie it with a Ring Bend knot (see pg. 293). Now tie an Overhand knot in the loop, forming two steps.

Your sub-aider's rungs should be about the same size as the rungs in your etrier.

Grab Loops

You can loop a small, 30-inch piece of 1/2-inch tubular webbing through your etrier's Frost knot.

This is a grab loop. A grab loop gives you something to hold onto while you're climbing up your etriers, making the process much easier. Attach a grab loop to each etrier.

Technique

Climbing with etriers is a sequential process. Once you learn the correct sequence you can develop a rhythm that will let you progress rapidly up the cliff.

You need at least two etriers to aid climb. However, you can also use two sets of etriers, each set consisting of two etriers connected by a **carabiner.** This rig is heavier and bulkier than the first, but is easier to use. (Carry whichever etrier or set of etriers that you aren't using clipped to your harness or gear sling.)

To begin aid climbing you must place the first piece of aid. Now clip both of your etriers (with individual carabiners), or one set of etriers, to this first piece. Also connect your daisy chain (or a **cow's tail**) to the aid, with a carabiner. (This serves two functions. One, it keeps you connected to the aid, which, assuming the aid holds, means that you are secured from a fall, and two, if the piece pops out you won't lose it because it is attached to you.)

Test the security of your aid placement by tugging on the etrier, even gingerly stepping onto it. (But don't commit all your weight to it until you are confident the piece will hold.) Note: it's helpful to have one etrier longer than the other. Always clip the longer one to the new piece of aid first, and you'll find it easy to test your new protection by stepping into the extra (lowest) rung, which hangs down lower for just this purpose.

An aid climber using etriers to test a placement

When you are confident that the piece of aid will hold, walk up your etrier until the aid is at your waist level. Connect your **rope** and the **Fifi hook** that is on the end of a short cow's tail (a runner, daisy chain, or chain of carabiners) to the aid. The cow's tail should be attached to your harness; using it like this allows you to hang from the aid and rest. (Note: once you have attached your rope to the aid you can disconnect your daisy chain, and then reconnect a shorter length of the daisy chain to the aid. If you do this you won't need the Fifi hook/cow's tail combination. Try both ways and see which one you prefer.

Walk as far as you can up your etriers. Climbing on low-angle, even near vertical, rock you should be able to stand in either the top or the second-to-the-top step of each etrier. While climbing overhanging rock you won't be able to stand as high because you will lose your balance (it helps to connect

A climber standing in etriers with the aid at waist level

then your rope, and then walking up your etriers to place the next piece of aid, until you reach the top of your climb.

A climber placing aid from the top rung of his etriers

a short section of your daisy chain to the aid; this will keep you close to the rock).

When you are standing as high as possible in your etriers, reach up and place your next piece of aid.

Putting your weight on one etrier, unclip the other one and clip it to the new piece (or, if you have them, simply connect your other set of double etriers). Also connect your daisy chain to this new aid (but before you do, make sure your rope is still attached to the previous placement!).

Carefully test this newly-placed protection as you did the previous one. When you are satisfied that it is secure, transfer your weight onto it. Now unclip your lower etrier and connect it into the new aid. Walk up both etriers - one foot in each - until the new piece is at waist level. Hook your cow's tail to the aid and clip in your rope.

Continue this 6-step process of placing your aid, connecting your etriers and daisy chain to it, testing it, transferring your weight to the new piece,

As you have undoubtedly realized, aid climbing is complex. You will find it very absorbing. You must pay attention to many things, including your stability, the security of your aid placements, maintaining the correct sequence of actions, and attending to all the small details that will inevitably come up as you climb. You must also find a way to rest your legs. They must last the length of the **pitch** (the distance between belay stations), which can sometimes take a few hours to climb.

A climber standing in 2 etriers: one clipped to the new piece of aid and one clipped to the previous piece.

How To Rest Your Legs

A good way to rest your legs, in a manner that is both stable and comfortable, is to tuck one of them, in its etrier, underneath you. You will have to experiment a little with this leg's position to find the most stable and comfortable stance, but most climbers find that the best setup is to twist their foot under them, as illustrated right. To keep yourself stable, place your other foot, in its etrier, against the rock.

Cleaning The Pitch

After you or your climbing partner has led the pitch, and placed the aid, the other climber must follow the pitch and retrieve all the gear that the leader has just placed. This process is called **cleaning the pitch.**

There are two ways to clean the pitch. The first is slower: you actually repeat the aid climb, clipping

to each piece and removing the previous one. The second method is much faster, and is therefore more popular, especially on big wall routes. It involves using ascenders to ascend a second rope, not the one clipped to the aid, that the leader anchors to his belay station.

Resting in etriers

Using the first method of cleaning the pitch requires you to carry out a series of activities. At first these activities will seem complex, but as you practice doing them (on actual climbs) they will flow together naturally in your mind until they become automatic. Read the next paragraph slowly, visualizing each step. This will help you grasp the process as a whole.

To begin cleaning the pitch, unclip your rope from the first (lowest) piece of aid. Next clip your shorter etrier to this piece, and climb up its steps until you are standing in both the etrier and sub-etrier, one foot in each. When you are in a stable position, reach up and unclip your rope from the next higher piece of aid. Connect your long etrier to this aid. Transfer your weight onto this long etrier and remove all the gear, including any carabiners, runners, and the shorter etrier, from the previous piece of aid. (Note: when you stand in the long etrier the previous piece of aid is not too low to reach.)

Cleaning the pitch: a climber reaching down to remove the previous piece of aid

The final step is to remove the aid, being careful not to drop it. Some pieces of aid are easier to remove than others: chocks are the easiest, pitons can be hard (I discuss removing pitons on pg. 248), **copperheads** are often difficult (I discuss removing copperheads on pg. 151), and bolts are impossible, so don't try!

Continue this sequence until you reach the belay ledge, which is the end of the pitch, where you will rejoin your partner.

The other method of cleaning the pitch, by ascending a second rope, is much easier. Once your partner has anchored the second rope to his belay station, you can attach your ascenders to it and begin ascending (see pg. 81). As you ascend, remove the pieces of aid when you come to them.

When you reach the top of the pitch, you are done. Amazingly simple!

Care

Your etriers will gradually wear out from the elements and from abrasion. You should check them often: before and after each climb as well as during a long climb. If the nylon is severely worn (more than 50%) then you should retire the etrier.

If you are using commercially-made etriers, you will need to check the loop connections periodically. These connections are sewn, and the threads will gradually wear out from rock abrasion and weathering. If they appear worn you can either resew them or discard the etrier.

If you have made your own etriers you may have to adjust the knots occasionally. They move around with use, making some steps larger than others.

Key Point

"You should not need to free a chock very often. If you think carefully about each chock's placement . . . you will avoid jamming (it) in the first place."
See page 182

Extractors (Nut Keys; Nut Tools)

An extractor

What Is An Extractor?

Sometimes a **chock** becomes stuck in a crack. An extractor is a hooked length of thin metal that enables a climber to retrieve the chock. An extractor often has many holes drilled along its length. These holes decrease its weight and allow you to clip or tie your extractor to your **rack.**

Although not a vital piece of equipment, extractors can be very helpful. You never know when you will be faced with a chock that is stuck tight in a crack. Or with an **active camming chock** that has walked itself deep between two slabs of rock. Extractors can free both. They are also helpful for threading **slings** and **runners** through rock tunnels and behind natural **chockstones.**

In addition, you can use an extractor to clean dirt from a crack. You'll only need to do this if you're one of the first climbers up the crack.

It's Easy To Drop!

Extractors are easy to drop. The best way to avoid dropping your extractor is to loop a thin cord through one of its holes. Before you unclip the extractor from your rack, put the loop around your wrist. This is not a foolproof connection, but it will stay out of your way until you need it, and it is fairly secure.

A bulkier but more secure connection is to tie a five foot length of cord to your extractor. Tie the other end of the cord to your gear sling. The length of the cord allows you to use the extractor while it is connected to your sling.

Using the hole of an extractor to retrieve a stuck active camming chock.

The Extractor's Design

I think the best extractor design is one which narrows from its handle to its hook. This means that the widest part of the extractor is in your hand. This design is the easiest to hold.

Some kind of a hook on the extractor's end is imperative. The hook can leverage around rocks and into crannies that are too small for your fingers.

The DMM Nutter has two perpendicular hooks on its handle in addition to its end hook. These two hooks allow you to retract an active camming chock's trigger bar.

Other extractors have holes for the same purpose. By sliding the hole over the trigger bar, you can retract the active camming chock.

The hole of an extractor can't fit every kind of active camming chock. These holes are designed mainly for Friends (a type of active camming chock made by Wild Country) or similiar chocks which also have a metal rod trigger. They can't pull back the trigger of a Hugh Banner Quadcam (another type of active camming chock), for instance, because it has no metal rod to hook the hole over. The DMM Nutter's two hooks allow you to retract the trigger of both a Friend and a Hugh Banner, and most other active camming units.

Yet these same two hooks can be problematic. They prevent you from easily gripping the extractor; they dig into your hand. You can work around the hooks, but it can be frustrating.

> ## A Cable Extractor
>
> A cable extractor is a short length of cable with two loops swaged onto one end.
>
> The cable extractor is excellent for retrieving Friends, because you can slip the two loops over the device's trigger, then tie the extractor to a sling, and yank. You achieve a stronger pull with the consequent leverage.

A cable extractor

Avoid Needing To Use Your Extractor

You should not need to free a chock very often. If you think carefully about each chock's placement, and consider whether or not the chock will be easy to remove, you will avoid jamming the chock in the first place.

When you test a chock which you have just placed (see Give A Tug, pg. 329), give it a light tug. A hard tug is usually unnecessary, although notable exceptions are heavy **passive camming chocks**, such as the largest Hexcentrics and Tri-cams. You must give these chocks a hard tug or their own weight may dislodge them.

Materials and Size

Most extractors are made from chrome molybdenum steel (Chrome-moly). Chrome-moly provides good strength and durability.

The length of manufactured extractors varies between 6 and 8 inches. They tend to weigh around 50 grams (about 1.5 ounces).

Make Your Own Extractor

You can make some aluminum shelf supports into extractors. They will not last as long as a manufactured extractor, but they do the job.

You will need to modify the shelf support slightly. A hacksaw, some 220 grade sandpaper, and an electric drill with a 3/4 inch (and maybe a 1/2 inch) drill bit are all the tools you need.

An aluminum shelf support which you can make into an extractor

Saw the clips off the handle end of the shelf support. Smooth the cut edges with sandpaper. You need to drill a hole in the handle to tie some cord through so you can carry the extractor. Drill the hole toward the edge of the metal; this way you can

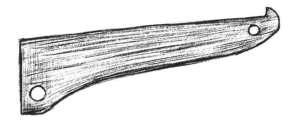

A modified aluminum shelf support

Some Extractor Manufacturers
Chouinard, DMM, Wild Country, and Salewa manufacture extractors. See pg. 353 for manufacturers' addresses.

clip it to a **carabiner** if you want to. Use the 3/4 inch drill bit for this hole.

To retrieve active camming chocks you can also drill a 1/2 inch hole in the hooking end of the shelf support. The only drawback is that this hole will weaken the already thin aluminum. Try this out; if your homemade extractor breaks, simply make a new one without the hole.

Key Point

"Strength can be important in a gear sling. If you are out of runners you may have to improvise, using your gear sling as a runner. Your sling must be strong enough for this use."

See page 187

Gear Slings

A gear sling on a climber

What is a Gear Sling?

A gear sling is a bandolier-like loop with which you carry your **chocks**. This collection of chocks, **carabiners**, and other pieces of gear on your gear sling is called a **rack**.

Types

There are four types of gear slings: **single, adjustable single, double,** and **tiered**.

Single Gear Sling

The single gear sling is very basic. It may be merely an improvised looped **runner** thrown over your shoulder. Or you may prefer a more sophisticated commercial version, one that has padding for comfort.

The single gear sling is the simplest and lightest of all the slings. It has no extra straps or buckles to get in your way. It is usually runner strength, so you can use it as a runner if necessary (before you use it as a runner, make sure it is strong enough!).

You cannot adjust the size of your single gear sling. This is important because it effects the posi-

A single gear sling

tion of your gear. Your chocks may hang either too high or too low for you to comfortably climb with. Check the size of your gear sling at the store, before you buy it!

Some single gear slings are uncomfortable because they have no shoulder pad. This is only a problem if you intend to carry a heavy rack. Any wide shoulder strap (at least 1.5 inches) will ease your discomfort, while padding will add more comfort.

Adjustable Single Gear Sling

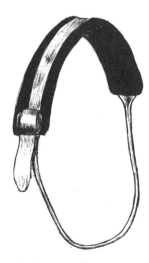

An adjustable single gear sling

The adjustable single gear sling has a metal buckle which allows you to alter its loop size. It always comes with a shoulder pad, so you don't have to worry about the buckle being uncomfortable.

The adjustable gear sling is versatile. You can adjust its loop size to fit many layers of clothes or none at all. This makes it useful for climbing in both the winter and the summer.

Before you climb, make sure you thread the sling's webbing back through its buckle, just as you would with your **harness.** This will ensure that the sling doesn't come apart half-way up the cliff. It will also allow you to use the gear sling as a runner, if you want to. (Again, check your gear sling's strength before you buy it!)

Double Gear Sling

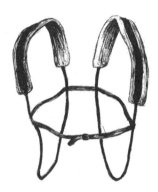

A double gear sling

A double gear sling is two single slings used together, one on each shoulder. It is held in place with a horizontal loop of **webbing** which encircles your chest.

The double gear sling is more comfortable than single slings. It also stays in place on your body, rather than shifting around as you climb. Obviously, the double sling allows you to carry more gear than you could with just a single sling.

A problem with the double gear sling is that it is heavier than a single sling. It also does not lend itself to being used as a runner.

Tiered Gear Sling

A tiered gear sling has two loops, one above the other, to clip your gear to. This is most useful for carrying **big wall racks** (where you are carrying lots of gear).

All tiered slings are sold as doubles and are adjustable. Like all double gear slings, tiered slings have a loop of webbing which encircles your chest. A5 (a manufacturer) makes their Big-Wall sling (which is tiered) so it can be separated into two

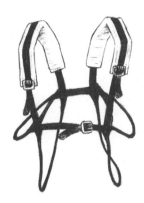

A tiered gear sling

single slings, making it more versatile than other tiered slings on the market.

Tiered slings obviously allow you to carry a lot of gear. They are also quite comfortable, distributing the weight of your rack over both your shoulders while keeping it close to your body.

They are slightly heavier than the others gear slings. Like double gear slings, they are awkward to use as runners. However, you aren't likely to run out of runners when you are using a tiered sling, because you only need a sling this large on trips in which you carry everything with you.

The Rack Belt™

Mountain Tools makes a gear sling in the form of a belt which clips around your waist. If you like your chocks positioned low, this may be the gear sling for you. It fits over your waist harness with room to spare. The belt holds your chocks with **gear loops,** similar to those of a harness. You can quickly and easily unclip the belt when you are changing leads. And just in case you drop it, the Rack Belt™ has a tie-in loop to keep it attached to your rope.

The main problem with the belt design is that your chocks will hang low. You may have trouble keeping your gear out of the way of your knees and feet.

A Rack Belt

Specifications

Size

The size of the sling is important. The gear sling must position your chocks in just the right place: easy for you to get to but out of your way.

Some people like their chocks very high on their chest, while others prefer tham at waist level. (If you like them really low, you may prefer to use your harness's gear loops. Or use the Rack Belt made by Mountain Tools that I just discussed.)

Strength

Strength can be important in a gear sling. If you are out of runners you may have to improvise, using your gear sling as a runner. Your sling must be strong enough for this use. Manufacturers will tell you in their catalogs if a gear sling is suitable as a runner. Its strength should be rated to at least 2000 pounds.

Materials

Gear slings are built around a base loop of webbing. Some manufacturers use **flat webbing,** others **tubular,** and still others use **supertape.** Flat webbing is not quite as strong, but it is cheaper.

Onto this webbing base manufacturers may attach some sort of padding, usually either foam, PolarPlus, or Synchilla. Adjustable slings have metal buckles. Manufacturers use high quality alloy metals for these buckles, which are very strong.

Construction

The gear sling's shape is important. This is particularly true in the area of the sling where you clip your chocks. This area is available in three different designs: flat, rolled, and individual loops. The loop design affects how easily you can clip and unclip your carabiners, and where these biners sit on your sling.

Flat Construction

By flat construction I mean that the webbing (whether it is tubular or flat) is not sewn into a roll. This means that it is soft and sometimes wide, which makes it awkward to clip. When you try to clip or unclip a carabiner it often snags the webbing in its gate notch.

Another problem with a flat gear loop is that your gear will slide together. This makes it slightly more difficult to find just the chock you are looking for. However, climbers have been using runners as gear slings for many years with few problems.

Using a runner as a gear sling has its benefits too. It is cheap, costing only the price of any runner you might buy. And it is versatile; you can use it as a regular runner any time you want.

Rolled Webbing

Some gear slings are sewn into rolls to hold your gear. Others use 5.5 millimeter nylon cord (which is usually encased in surgical tubing.) (While just as easy to clip, this cord is not as strong as webbing.) Both are easy to clip into. They are stiff and won't easily catch in a carabiner's gate notch.

Being a continuous loop, just like the unrolled webbing gear slings, the rolled slings allowed your chocks to slide together. As I mentioned before, this is only an inconvenience, and never a big problem.

Gear slings which are sewn rolled are the most popular type of sling available. They are simple, fairly versatile (they work as runners), cheap, and lightweight.

Individual Gear Loops

Mountain Tools make their gear slings with individual gear loops, as part of their MT Fastrack™ system. These loops are like the racking loops on your harness: nylon cord encased in surgical tubing.

Chocks clipped to individual gear loops

The gear loops are stiff, and you will find them easy to clip into. Their big advantage, however, is that they separate your gear. You can organize your **wedging chocks** apart from your **passive camming chocks,** for instance, and not worry about them jumbling together.

> ## Velcro Tabs
>
> Some gear slings have some small velcro loops attached to them. Each tab is designed to hold a chock. To use the chock, simply rip it out of the velcro, and you're ready to go. This speedy access to your protection can save the day when you are really stressed and need to place a chock without wasting time.

General Safety Guidelines

As A Runner!

Don't use your gear sling as a runner unless you are *sure* it is strong enough. It must be rated to at least 2000 pounds strength. Remember that this rating reflects the sling at its strongest; as it ages it will become weaker.

Double the Webbing Back through the Buckle!

When using adjustable gear slings, always thread the webbing back through the buckle! If you don't, the webbing may slip out, opening the loop. See Harnesses, pg. 195.

The webbing probably won't slip through the buckle when you are merely carrying a basic amount of gear. However, there is a chance that it might, and the resulting loss of your chocks would spell disaster. You cannot afford to take chances!

If you are using the gear sling as a runner, you must thread the webbing back through the buckle! If you don't, and the sling supports any length of fall, it will pull out.

Care

Treat the gear sling like your other webbing. Avoid excessive sunlight (ultraviolet light damages nylon) and rock abrasion. Keep it away from acids (including battery acid), solvents, and bleaches.

When to Retire Your Gear Sling

If the webbing on your gear sling is heavily worn you must retire the sling. You don't want your chocks tumbling to the rocks below because your sling broke! This is especially true if you intend to use your gear sling as a runner.

Your gear slings's strength will gradually diminish over time; abrasion, sunlight, and supporting a load all weaken the sling.

When your gear sling becomes faded and worn looking you should retire it. If you keep using it, you may be forced to employ it as a runner, which you must not do. You don't want to have to rely on worn out webbing for protection!

Modifications and Tune-Ups

A gear sling is so basic and inexpensive that it is not really worth trying to repair. You will find it much more economical to buy a new one. If your gear sling needs major work you should retire it anyway; it is not safe to climb with.

Despite all this, it is fairly easy to fix small, non-critical sewing problems. For instance, the padding may start coming off the webbing, or a sewn roll of webbing may start coming undone.

You need a needle and thread, and a pair of scissors. Double your thread to get maximum strength. There is no particular stitch that you need to do, as the stitches don't have to be very strong. If you want added strength, sew it twice.

The actual repair is very simple. Simply knot the thread, sew, knot it again, cut it, and you are done.

Accessories

Three items can help you perform the minimal repairs you can make on a gear sling: a needle, thread, and scissors. You probably already have these things lying around your house. If not, head over to your nearest fabric store and buy them.

Some Gear Sling Manufacturers

A5, Chouinard, Climb High, Gramicci, Fish, Misty Mountain Threadworks, Mountain Tools, Wild Country, and Yates manufacture gear slings. For manufacturers' addresses, see pg. 353.

Gloves

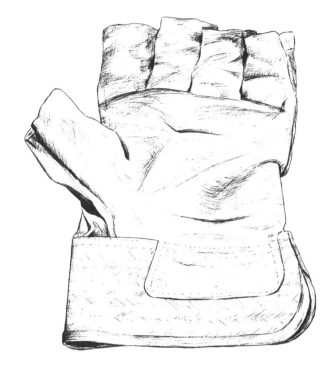

A fingerless glove

What Kind Of Gloves?

I am not talking about warm, comfortable gloves here. Rather, I'm referring to tough, leather (preferably goatskin), fingerless gloves that can take a beating. Gloves with fingers are awkward to climb with and leather fingers make it practically impossible to manage your equipment.

There are many types of fingerless leather gloves on the market. You want a pair that has tough, double leather palms, not just a soft suede palm. Ideally, the back panel should be made of mesh to keep your hands cool. And the gloves should have an adjustable strap to tighten them (Velcro straps are ideal).

Where To Buy Gloves

Not all climbing stores carry gloves suitable for rock climbing. However, check with the one near you to see what they do have. You may be lucky and find a good pair of gloves like Saranac's Wall Gloves. They cost around $20.

You can also check at a sporting goods store for weightlifting gloves. These gloves are tough, designed for grasping metal bars, and cost about the same as the Saranacs (however, sporting goods stores often have sales: check around).

If you can't find any gloves in either of these two places, go to a hardware store. Hardware store's sell leather fingered gloves, which you will have to modify by cutting the fingers off. The only problem with doing this is that the stitching at the fingers will gradually come out. The solution is to sew thread several times through the seams at the ends of the fingers. This sewing job takes 1-2 hours to accomplish.

Why Use Gloves?

You don't need gloves to have a pleasant day climbing at your local crags. Not, that is, unless you use a **waist belay,** or similar body-belay technique. Or if you enjoy fast **rappels.** Or your local crags are 1000 foot high **big walls** and you plan to make an extended journey up them.

Gloves save the skin on your palms from being burned off by a speeding rope. This rope burn is most likely to occur when you are belaying with a body belay technique, such as the waist belay. Body belay techniques don't have the stopping power of a belay device, and the rope will be pulled around your waist and through your hands while gradually stopping the falling climber. (For more on belaying, see Belay Devices, pg. 87.)

If you enjoy **sport rappelling,** you should buy a pair of gloves. Sport rappels are fast and build up heat quickly. Your protected hands will be able to handle both the heat and the abrasion from the rope. (For more on rappelling, see Descenders, pg. 157.)

Gloves are vital on big wall climbs. You will be handling rope and **webbing** and hammering **pitons** all day long, for several days. The gloves will save your palms from painful blisters and peeling skin.

Key Point
"If you want to try out aid climbing, or practice placing bolts . . . you can use a carpenter's hammer."
See page 192

Hammers

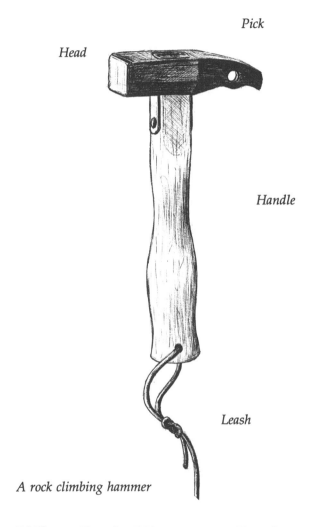

A rock climbing hammer

Head

Pick

Handle

Leash

What Is A Hammer For?

A hammer is very useful to a rock climber. It is a must for pounding in **pitons,** pulling out pitons, testing old fixed pitons, placing **copperheads,** or placing **bolts.** A climbing hammer has a pick on one end which is helpful for cleaning dirt and removing chocks that are stuck in cracks.

The Hammer's Design

Climbing hammers must have a flat head for pounding and a pick for retrieving. The pick must be slightly blunt, because you must also be able to hammer with it. For example, you can use it to

place a copperhead (see pg. 149). The pick should have a hole in it that allows you to clip a **carabiner** to the hammer. A carabiner is very useful for retrieving pitons and copperheads, among other things. You can attach a chain of carabiners to both your hammer and piton, for instance, and then yank the chain, dislodging the piton (this is only necessary with the most obstinate pitons).

Removing a piton with a hammer and a chain of carabiners

The hammer's handle must be securely connected to its head. With a wood handle, the connection must have a piece of metal protecting each side of the handle. Besides strengthening the connection, this design protects the wood in case you miss your mark and hit the rock.

The handle's connection to the head

Nylon and steel handles are riveted and epoxied in place. They don't need the protective metal strips because the nylon won't suffer from a blow.

Climbing hammers are sold with a leash. You should tie the leash to your gear sling with either a figure eight or a bowline knot. If you drop your hammer, the leash will keep it from bouncing down the rock and possibly hitting your partner below. (The chapter Your Rack discusses how to avoid dropping your gear. See pg. 47.) The leash must be long enough to allow you to hammer with your arm fully extended. Five feet should be enough.

A climber using a hammer with a leash

Weight

Swinging a hammer while you are climbing up a rock can be exhausting. The hammer will start to feel much heavier than it did on the ground. Consequently, you should buy a hammer that is light enough to easily swing, even after you have pounded in a hundred pitons. Yet the hammer cannot be too light: it needs weight to give it enough force. Light-weight climbers find a good hammer head weight is 17-20 ounces. The handle should add no more than 8 ounces. Bigger climbers may want a more substantial hammer: 24-26 ounce hammer head will be heavy enough.

If you are bringing a hammer for occasional use, bring a lightweight one. This will keep the weight of your **rack** down; the 17-20 ounce hammer will work fine.

You can change the hammer's swing weight by moving your hand along the handle. To rest your tired hand you can hold the hammer near its head. For good, powerful swings, grasp the end of the handle.

Using a Carpenter's Hammer

If you want to try out **aid climbing**, or practice placing bolts (in a small rock far away from any climbing areas!) you can use a carpenter's hammer. You probably have one around the house that will work fine.

But if you intend to do more extensive aid climbing, or place a number of bolts, a carpenter's hammer just won't work. It doesn't have the features of a hammer made for climbing. A carpenter's hammer has two claws instead of a solid pick; you can't hammer anything with the claws. It doesn't have a hole for clipping carabiners. And there is the problem of the handle. If you buy a metal-handled carpenter's hammer your arm will be vibrating after each blow. If you buy a wood-handled carpenter's hammer, it will soon be destroyed because it doesn't have the two protective metal strips near the head.

In the short term, a carpenter's hammer is much cheaper than a climbing hammer. However, a climbing hammer will last much longer and be more efficient than the carpenter's. A climbing hammer is a good investment if you intend to aid climb regularly.

Materials

The Head

The hammer's head must be tough enough to withstand repeated pounding. A5 uses forged chrome-moly steel, while the other manufacturers use investment-cast stainless steel. All of these hammers are very strong, but the forging process traditionally produces a tougher metal.

The Handle

A climber's hammer must have a handle which is both strong and able to damp the vibration from a blow. Hickory wood does both very well. The wood must be vertically grained, that is, its grain must run in the direction of the handle. This will give it the most strength. Salewa makes a nylon shaft which is also effective. Edelrid and Brenta both make steel-shafted handles wrapped in a neoprene grip. The neoprene helps dampen the blow's vibration.

If you buy a hammer with a wooden handle, make sure the wood has a tough finish on it. The finish must be able to protect the handle from all kinds of weather, and give you a good grip.

The Leash

Your hammer's leash can be made of either cord or **webbing.** Cord is more durable but since you can replace a worn leash, it doesn't need to last forever.

Care

Rock climbing hammers are designed to take abuse. They are tough tools and should last you many years.

There are two main climbing hammer manufacturers in the U.S.: A5 and Chouinard. Both manufacturers will replace, for a fee, customer's broken hammer handle.

Accessories

Holster

You need a holster for your hammer. Stiff nylon or neoprene hammer holsters both work well. The holster must stay open so you can quickly and easily stow your hammer. A plastic ring holster, such as the PLJ made by Wild Country, will work also. It is really a matter of personal preference: which one suits you?

Leash

You can replace your climbing hammer's leash as necessary. Accessory cord and webbing both work as hammer leashes (they are strong enough to repeatedly stop a falling hammer). Your leash should be about 5 feet long.

Some Climbing Hammer Manufacturers

A5, Brenta, Chouinard, Edelrid, and Salewa manufacture hammers for climbing. See pg. 353 for manufacturers' addresses.

Key Point
"You need to know how to improvise a harness. This is an important skill."
See page 201

Harnesses

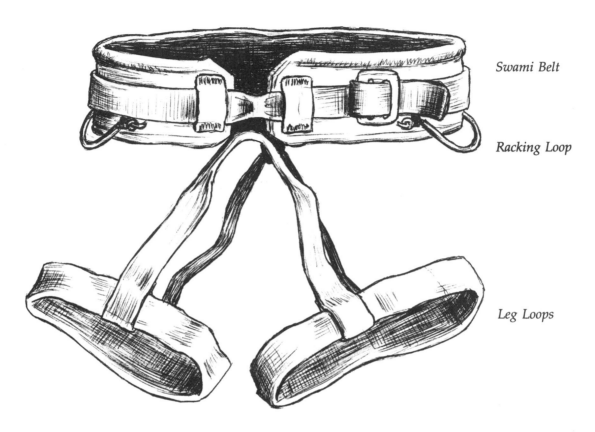

Swami Belt

Racking Loop

Leg Loops

A harness

What Is A Harness?

A harness is a system of **webbing** that securely wraps around your body. It attaches to your **rope,** which is a vital job. If you fall, your rope will catch your harness, which will catch you.

Your harness also plays an important role in the dissipation of your fall's energy. It must spread this energy evenly over your body, and keep you from being severely shocked or injured.

Types

There are two types of harnesses available: the waist harness and the full-body harness.

The Waist Harness

The waist harness is the most popular type of rock climbing harness. It consists of a **swami belt,** which wraps around your waist, and leg loops, which encircle your legs. The waist harness provides a comfortable seat by supporting most of your weight on the backs of your thighs.

In the past, climbers used the swami belt alone, without the leg loops. The advantage of this was simplicity. However, the disadvantage was pain. If you were to fall, your swami belt, being only one band around your waist, concentrated the force of your fall onto your waist and rib cage. Broken ribs were not unheard of. Since the purpose of your harness is protection, *don't climb with just the swami belt!*

The waist harness is ideal for most rock climbing. It is lightweight and has low bulk. It is easy and simple to put on. It is also easy to climb with because it doesn't restrict your movement.

The waist harness does have a few negative points. It is not certified by the **UIAA,** unless it is used in conjunction with a chest harness (see Full-Body Harness, below). However, this is one unusual case in which most climbers, myself included, have decided not to take the UIAA's recommendation. We feel that the advantages of using a waist harness without a chest harness outweigh its disadvantages.

The waist harness

It is true that a waist harness confines the force of your fall to a smaller area of your body (your waist and legs) than does a full-body harness. However, with many climbers taking countless falls over the years, the waist harness has proved that it is more than adequate for safely stopping even long falls.

There are two types of waist harnesses: the one-piece and the two-piece. The leg loops and swami belt of the one-piece are connected, whereas with the two-piece, or swami belt/leg loop combination, they are separate.

The one-piece waist harness is simple and easy to use because all the parts are connected. It is easier to put on than a two-piece waist harness.

The two-piece waist harness provides an individual fit. Because the swami belt is separate from the leg loops you can buy each in a different size. This makes the two-piece ideal if you can't fit your legs into a harness whose swami belt fits perfectly.

A Harness For Each Situation

Harnesses are very specialized these days. You will need different features from your harness depending on the kind of climbing you are doing. The following descriptions are summaries of the features you will need for some common types of climbing.

For The Beginning Climber

When you are learning how to climb rocks, harness comfort and simplicity are your main concerns. You need a comfortable harness so that you can enjoy yourself and you not have to waste your energy trying to adjust the harness while climbing. A simple harness is one that you can understand, that you can put on quickly and easily. You don't need anything fancy.

You do need a harness with a basic racking system. A few racking loops will do. I discuss racking systems later in this chapter, on pg. 199. You might also want a belay/rappel loop (see pg. 199), although this isn't imperative.

For The Intermediate Climber

As an intermediate climber you will be trying many different types of climbs. Your harness needs to work for all of them. This means that, although it shouldn't be really heavy, it should be padded for comfort. You may want it to be adjustable so you can climb in the winter as well as the summer. You will appreciate a racking system consisting of racking loops and maybe a quick-release Velcro tab. You might also want the convenience of a belay/rappel loop (see pg. 199) and a rear anchor loop (see pg. 199).

For The Advanced Climber

If you are climbing extremely difficult rock climbs, you need a harness that will let you perform at your best. To save weight you can dispense with extensive comfort, settling instead for light swami belt padding. Your harness should allow you to make a wide range of motions. You will also want a good racking system, including gear loops and a few quick-release Velcro tabs.

For The Big Wall Climber

Big walls take a long time to climb. You may be in your harness for four or five days. A comfortable harness is imperative.

A well-padded waist harness with a wide swami belt and wide leg loops will keep you comfortable. You can afford the extra weight resulting from this design.

You may also want a chest harness, or even go with the one-piece full-body harness. The upper support will help you remain upright, which is helpful when you are carrying a large big wall **rack**, and when you are ascending a rope.

Naturally you will want some racking loops. Quick-release tabs aren't necessary.

For The Alpine Climber

When you are climbing alpine terrain (mixed rock, snow, and ice), you need an appropriate harness. A lightweight harness is ideal, because the lighter you travel the easier it is. But your harness must also be strong.

The best combination is a basic waist harness with no webbing and no frills. It should be adjustable so that you can put it on over both thin and thick layers of clothing. You must also be able to put it on while you are wearing crampons and boots. Make sure you can drop the leg loops so that you will be able to go to the bathroom while remaining tied to your rope! You will need some racking loops and holsters for your ice axes on the harness as well.

The Full-Body Harness

The full-body harness is the safest type of harness to use. This is because it wraps around your legs, waist, and upper torso. The force of your fall is spread evenly over your body, which reduces the impact on any one spot.

The full-body harness is recommended by the UIAA. This is because it returns you to an upright position after you fall, even if you fall head first. If you were to become injured during a fall, returning to an upright position would be safer for you, and easier for others to help you as well.

A full-body harness is very useful if you are climbing with a heavy pack. If you fall, the pack will flip you over, but your harness will return you to an upright position. This is also true for big wall climbing, when you must carry a heavy rack.

Ascending a rope (see Ascenders, pg. 75) is much easier if you are connected to it with a full-body harness. The harness will keep your body vertical, which is the most efficient position in which to ascend.

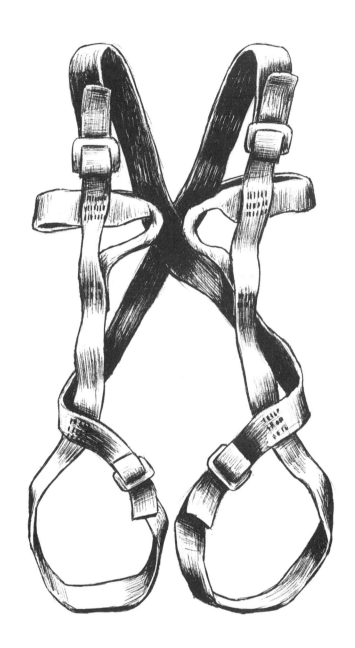

The full-body harness

With all these advantages, why is the full-body harness so unpopular? It is complicated, heavy, and bulky. It is hard to put on and take off. And it restricts your movements, which hinders your ability to climb.

Like the waist harness, the full-body harness is available in two types: the one-piece and the two-piece models. Unlike the one-piece waist harness, the one-piece full-body harness is more difficult to put on than the two-piece version.

The two-piece full-body harness consists of a waist harness and a chest harness. You must buy each separately.

Note: *you should not use a chest harness alone!* The entire impact of your fall will go directly to your chest (and maybe break a rib!), instead of being spread over your abdomen and legs as well.

Tying Your Harness

Both the waist harness and the full-body harness are tied at the waist, or swami belt, although the full-body harness may also be tied at the chest. Full-body harnesses utilize buckles, while waist harnesses may be tied in one of two different ways: with a loop of webbing or with a buckle.

A loop of webbing provides a very strong, almost fail-safe connection for your swami belt. However, it is not as popular as the buckled connection because it takes more time and is more of a hassle to tie.

Use a Ring Bend knot to tie the loop of webbing. This is the same knot you use to tie your runners. (To learn how to tie the Ring Bend, turn to pg. 293.)

Fitting a harness that is connected with a loop of webbing is different than fitting a buckled harness. The swami belt should have a 2" gap between its end loops.

These days, most harnesses are tied with a buckle. A buckle, while not quite as safe as a loop of webbing, is much more convenient. To tie the buckle, simply thread the end of your swami belt through the buckle, and then back again. This double pass is very important, because if you don't do it your swami belt can easily come undone.

Doubling the swami belt webbing back through the buckle

Some harnesses utilize double buckles. The idea is that they are safer (because they are easier to tie correctly) but they do not necessarily make a stronger connection. They also increase your harness' weight. If you feel safer with doubled buckles,

by all means buy a harness that uses them.

Fitting a buckled harness is easy. Just make sure there is a 2" tail of webbing left over, after you have doubled the webbing back through the buckle. Any less than this and the webbing may slip through the buckle. This rule also applies to your leg loop buckles.

Fitting Your Harness

To get the most comfort and security, your harness must fit you well. If it's too big, it will slip around your body, be a nuisance, and, if you fall upside-down, could let you slip out of it! A harness that is too small is just as bad: it is very constricting and is awkward to move in. Also, a small harness has the problem of not leaving a long enough tail of webbing through the buckle (I shall elaborate on this below).

Don't buy your harness in a size you hope to be in the future! I say this seriously. Salespeople have had customers who bought a small harness in the belief that they would lose enough weight by climbing to fit it! If you think you will be losing weight, or, more importantly from a climbing viewpoint, if you intend to use your harness in the winter, buy an adjustable harness instead.

Finding a well-fitting waist harness is easy if you follow two guidelines when trying on the harness. One, you should be able to just squeeze your hand between your thigh and the leg loops. And two, you should be able to put both your index and middle fingers between your waist and the swami belt (providing the swami belt connection is right, as discussed previously). Don't suck in your waist before trying this!

A chest harness should fit tight, but not too tight. You don't want to inhibit your breathing or your movements, yet you also don't want the harness shifting around your chest. The chest harness' tie-in loops should sit about an inch apart.

There is one last thing to consider when you are trying on harnesses in the store. Where is your center of gravity? If you have a short upper torso then your center of gravity will be fairly low, whereas if you have a long upper torso it will be high. Different harnesses have different tie-in points: some are high and some low. If you have a long upper torso you need a harness with high attachment points; the opposite is true if you have a short upper torso. If you had a long upper torso and you wore a harness with a low tie-in point, you would be top heavy and have an increased chance of flipping upside-down.

Any harness fits every climber differently. Take the time to find the one that fits you just right.

Harness Options

Some harnesses come with options, such as a racking system, a belay/rappel loop, and a rear anchor loop.

Racking System

A harness racking system consists of loops that are designed to hold your carabiners. Some harnesses have so many racking loops that you can carry all your gear on the harness, without using a separate **gear sling** (see Gear Slings pg. 185).

A good harness racking system gives you versatility. You may not like carrying your gear on your harness, but there may be some situations in which you need to. Many climbers use a combination of their harness racking loops and gear sling. You should keep your options open.

Racking loops are made of loops of cord covered in plastic, or loops entirely of plastic, that hang from your swami belt.

The loops should not hang very low, because that will put your chocks down around your knees. Upturned loops are preferable because they keep your chocks high and out of your way.

Some harnesses come with quick-release Velcro tabs. These tabs are ideal for those times when you need to quickly clip into a piece of gear. To use the tab, put a **quickdraw** into it (see Leading, pg. 49). When you need to clip into your **protection**, simply grab the quickdraw from the Velcro, which will quickly rip free.

A Belay/Rappel Loop

A belay/rappel loop is a sewn loop of webbing. It is very strong and encircles your harness' front leg loop and swami belt. Its function is to provide a quick and convenient place for you to clip your **locking carabiner** when you are either **belaying** or **rappelling.**

Never tie your rope to just your belay/rappel loop! Tie your rope through both your swami belt and leg loops as well. This gives you a backup: if one loop fails, the other will hold. Tying into just the belay/rappel loop neglects this backup, and is very dangerous.

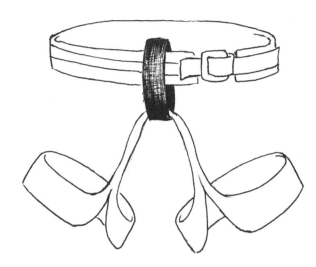

A belay/rappel loop

A Rear Anchor Loop

A rear anchor loop is similar to a belay/rappel loop, only it is positioned on the rear of your swami belt. Its function is to give you a convenient way to connect your harness to your **anchor** when you need to face away from this anchor.

The rear anchor loop has the same problem as the belay/rappel loop. It has no backup. If it fails, down you go! This simply means that your rear anchor loop must *never* be your only connection to your anchors.

Technique

Tying-In

You must secure your climbing rope to your harness (tie-in) in the strongest way possible. In the past climbers used the Bowline Knot (see pg. 202) for this connection, but the Figure-Eight knot is stronger and is now the most popular.

How To Tie The Figure-Eight Knot

The Figure-Eight is a fundamental climbing knot. Every climber should know how to tie it. It is a strong knot, it rarely slips, and doesn't weaken the rope as much as other knots do.

To tie the Figure-Eight, you need about 3 feet of rope. At 1.5 feet from one end, bend the rope and cross it over itself.

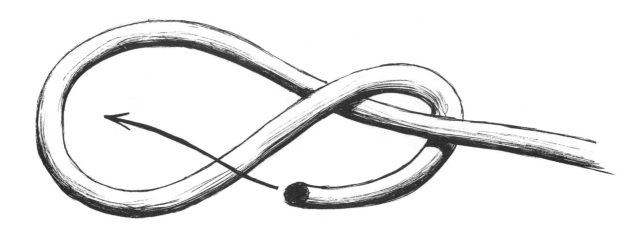

The first step to tying a Figure-Eight Knot

Harness

The second step to tying a Figure-Eight Knot

Harness

The final step to tying the Figure-Eight Knot

Loop the free end back the other way, but this time under the rope. Now thread it through, from above, the loop that you have formed. This will give you a figure-eight shape.

Pull some rope through this loop, until you have around 1.5 feet extending from the loop. (If you are tying-in to your rope, thread the rope's end through your harness.) Now thread the rope back out, along the same path that it went in. Make sure that you don't cross the strands along the way, as this will weaken the knot.

The Figure-Eight-On-A-Bight

Once you know the standard Figure-Eight knot, you can easily tie the Figure-Eight-On-A-Bight. A bight is a loop of rope; you tie this knot when you are in the middle of the rope, with no ends to thread through. Tying this knot is easier than tying the standard Figure-Eight, because you don't need to rethread the rope back through the knot.

Finishing the Figure-Eight-On-A-Bight

Improvised Harnesses

You need to know how to improvise a harness. This is an important skill. There will be times when you forget to bring your harness to the cliffs, or times when you arrive at the cliffs and find that your harness is worn through (rare though they may be), or even times when you must make a harness for a hiker who is way off the trail!

I will show you two ways to improvise a waist harness, and one way to make a chest harness. The first waist harness is called a Bowline-On-A-Coil, the second is the Dulfer Seat. The chest harness is called the Parisian Baudrier.

Bowline-On-A-Coil

The Bowline-On-A-Coil is very simple. You need nothing except your rope and the ability to tie a Bowline knot.

The Bowline-On-A-Coil has a big drawback: it is painful to hang from. The problem is that when you hang from the coil of rope one or two strands become tighter than the rest and dig into your torso.

Beginning the Figure-Eight-On-A-Bight

A Bowline-On-A-Coil

How To Tie The Bowline Knot
The Bowline is excellent for tying things onto a rope's end.

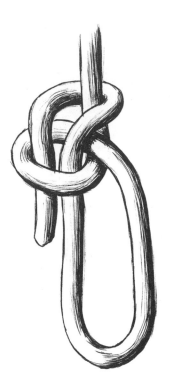

Finishing the Bowline

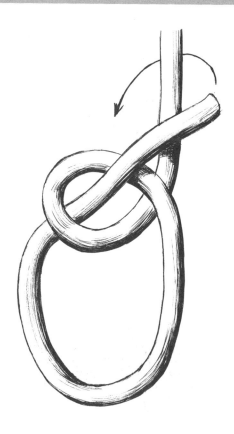

Beginning the Bowline

Important note: *You can die from hanging from a swami belt or coil of rope!* It takes only fifteen or twenty minutes of hanging for your diaphragm to stop functioning from the intense pressure on it.

Fortunately, there is a way to save yourself if you are stuck hanging from your coil of rope. It is known as the Baboon Hang.

Take a loop of webbing (a **runner**) large enough to fit over both your legs and flip upside down. Swing your legs over your head, with one leg on each side of your rope, and slide the runner over your feet and up your legs to your thighs. When you flip back over, the runner will catch your rope, putting most of your weight onto the back of your thighs, and relieving the pressure on your diaphragm.

Dulfer Seat
The Dulfer Seat, or Diaper Seat, is a good harness. All you need to fashion this harness is your rope, locking carabiner, and a 9-11 ft. length of **tubular webbing.** (If you don't have a runner this long, tie several together, until you reach the desired length.) The webbing's length depends on your

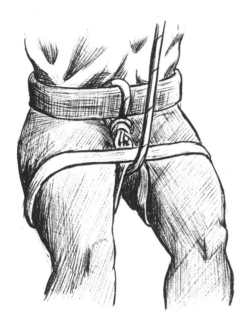

The Baboon Hang

body size. I recommend that you buy a twelve ft. length of webbing and measure how much you need when you make the Dulfer. If it's too long, cut the webbing down and use the short piece as a runner.

To construct the Dulfer Seat: tie your webbing into a loop, as you would with any runner (see Slings and Runners, pg. 291). Pass the loop around your back, at waist level. Clip the two loop ends to a locking carabiner. Reach down between your legs, grab one side of the webbing loop, and pull it through. Clip it to your carabiner.

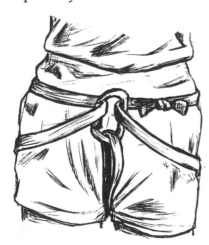

The Dulfer Seat

Now tie your rope through the lower loop and the two side loops. You are ready to climb.

If you have problems with the webbing falling down as you climb, you need a smaller loop. Or you can clip your Dulfer to another length of webbing tied around your waist, which will also act as a swami belt.

Parisian Baudrier

The Parisian Baudrier is a useful chest harness. It is easy to tie and stays in position. All you need to tie it is a runner made of an 8 ft. length of webbing.

First drape the loop over one of your shoulders. Then, with your opposite hand, reach back and grab the loop and tuck it under the arm pit of this same hand.

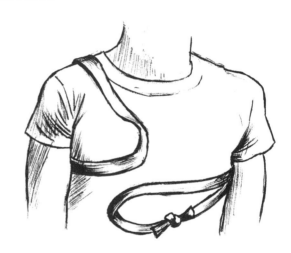

Beginning the Parisian Baudrier

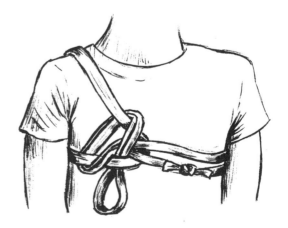

Finishing the Parisian Baudrier

Now tie the ends of the loop together with a sheet bend, and you are done.

Used in conjunction with the Dulfer Seat, the Parisian Baudrier makes a good full-body harness.

Materials

A harness' materials and construction determine its strength, comfort, and overall usefulness.

Webbing

A harness is made almost entirely of webbing. Webbing gives the harness both strength and comfort. The wider the webbing, the stronger and more comfortable the harness.

The webbing's strength is vital. You depend on your webbing to keep you connected to your rope. Your harness should be rated to hold at least 4000 lbs.

Most harnesses are made out of **flat webbing**. On a waist harness the widths of this webbing vary but the swami belt is usually wider than the leg loops. A common size uses a 3-inch swami belt and 2-inch leg loops. This provides enough comfort for most people, but if you are a large person you may want wider webbing. A full-body harness often uses only one size of webbing, which runs through the entire thing. Comfort is not sacrificed because the webbing distributes the load over your body.

Some manufacturers make their swami belts out of tubular webbing. It is stronger than the flat, but it is also thinner, and thin webbing is uncomfortable. If you buy a harness whose swami belt is made of tubular webbing, make sure that it is well padded.

Buckle

The weak point of a harness is its buckle. Manufacturers recognize this, and make their harness buckles from very strong aluminum alloy. When you buy a buckled harness, find out the buckle's rated strength. It should be greater than 3500 lbs.

Padding

A padded swami belt is very comfortable. Not all harnesses have padding, because it does increase the harness' weight. Alpine harnesses, which are designed to be light, never have padding. You should invest in a padded harness if you intend to do much **technical rock climbing**. The padding will keep you comfortable even when you are on the rock all day.

Manufacturers use different materials to pad their harnesses. Synchilla, Polar Fleece, Polarplus, and foam are all commonly used. These are all fairly similar, and offer good comfort. One note about foam: it makes you sweat.

General Safety Guidelines

Double The Webbing Back Through The Buckle!

Check your buckle to make sure the webbing is doubled back through it! If it's not doubled back, the webbing can slip through the buckle very easily. It has happened more than once before, with fatal results. Don't let it happen to you!

Tie Your Rope To Both Your Swami Belt And Your Leg Loops!

Always tie your rope through both your swami belt and your leg loops! Never tie it only to one or the other, or only to your belay/rappel loop, or rear anchor loop! By tying your rope through both your swami belt and your leg loops you have a two-part connection. This connection is redundant; if one fails the other is there to hold you.

Before You Belay Or Rappel, Check Your Buckle!

Some harnesses, specifically the single-buckled Chouinard models, but possibly others, can come undone when you use a large locking carabiner to rappel or belay. If the carabiner is large enough, and positioned next to the buckle, it can leverage the buckle open which allows the webbing to slip out. This happens only when you twist your body so the carabiner presses up against the buckle.

So far, no climber has been injured as a result of this happening. However, tests have been done which show that this is a potential problem.

The solution is to keep your rope tied between your locking carabiner and your harness' buckle. The rope prevents the carabiner from pressing against the buckle.

Care

Your harness, being made of nylon webbing, suffers from the same wear as other nylon products. Sunlight weakens it, as does abrasion. Nylon rubbing nylon wears quickly. Falls, by shock loading your harness, weaken it. Your harness will probably last through more falls than your rope, but you should consider retiring it after a severe fall, just as you should do with your rope.

Check your entire harness after every climbing trip. Look for worn threads. If any area is worn through you should retire the harness. This is particularly important with the tie-in point in the front of your swami belt and leg loops. Your rope will rub it, and nylon on nylon abrades quickly.

One way to save your harness from excessive wear is to alternate between two harnesses. Use your old, worn (but not too worn) harness for top-roping short climbs. Save your better harness for lead climbing. This will put less wear on your better harness, prolonging its life.

Accessories

Racking Kit
Some harness manufacturers sell racking kits for their harnesses. These kits are useful for replacing your harness' worn racking system, or for adding to a harness that is sold without a racking system, but can accept it.

Racking kits won't always work with the harnesses of other manufacturers, so check that the kit will work with your harness before you buy it. You can get racking kits from many climbing stores. If you can't find a particular racking kit you may have to order it directly from the manufacturer.

Belay/Rappel Loop
Many climbing stores sell belay/rappel loops. They cost around $5.

Some Harness Manufacturers
Chouinard, Climb High, CMI, Fish, Forrest, JRat, Misty Mountain Threadworks, Petzl, REI, Troll, Wild Country, Wild Things, and Yates manufacture harnesses. See pg. 353 for the manufacturers' addresses.

Key Point

"A haulbag's seams are its weakest points . . . (watching your clothes float to the ground 2000 feet below is a strangely frustrating yet spectacular sight!)."

See page 210

Haulbags (Haulsacks; Pigs)

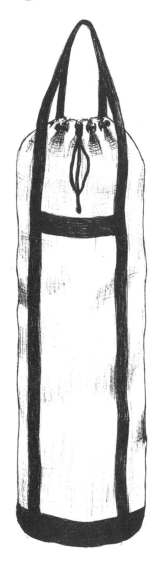

A large haulbag

What Is A Haulbag?

Some cliffs, called **big walls,** are so high that they take several days to climb. And, if the climbing is difficult, it may take even longer for you to reach the top. To survive such a long time on a cliff you need personal provisions, in addition to your climbing gear. These provisions include food, water, a sleeping bag, a **portaledge,** and clothes. But big walls are so strenuous that you would quickly be exhausted if you tried carrying all this stuff up the wall on your back. The solution is to haul your gear up after you, at the end of each **pitch.** However, to do this you will need a special hauling bag. If you were to haul a normal pack (one that has straps attached) up the cliff, it would repeatedly snag on the rock and suffer extreme wear from abrasion. It might even burst before you could reach the top of your climb.

To solve these problems, manufacturers design and make special haulbags - which look like duffel bags turned on their ends. A haulbag has removable straps and a streamlined exterior of smooth but tough cloth. This design is very durable. It also slides easily along the rock, making it an excellent bag to haul your gear in.

Types

There are two basic types of haulbags: large ones and small ones. Large haulbags offer plenty of interior space: from 6500 to 10000 cubic inches. Small haulbags offer only 1600 to 2500 cubic inches of space.

Large Haulbags

Large haulbags are ideal for really long, multi-day climbs. Although you may need more than one bag on such an adventure, bring as little gear as possible. Each additional haulbag requires a separate haul, and each haul slows you down. How much gear you bring depends on the season, and your appetite. For instance, you need more clothing in the winter and more water in the summer (around a gallon a day, as compared to half a gallon a day in the other seasons). What you eat, and how much of it, is a very personal thing. Remember that you will be burning lots of calories on a big wall, so you'll eat more than usual (for a discussion of food, see pg. 337).

How To Pack Your Haulbag

Store your seldom-used gear (possibly rainwear) on the bottom of the haulbag. Line the outside of the bag with tough items that will withstand abuse, such as your portaledge and other bivouac equipment (sleeping bag, cooking equipment, etc.). Place delicate items, such as your water bottles and then your food, in the center of the bag, where they will be protected by the surrounding items. On top of the food place any items you might need quickly, such as a first aid kit, guidebook, or your lunch. This is also a good place for any climbing gear that you don't need immediately.

Small Haulbags

A small haulbag

Small haulbags are designed for one-day climbs. If you are intending to climb a route that has enough pitches to keep you on the rock all day, the small haulbag will carry the food and water you need, extra clothing to keep you warm, and some of the climbing gear that you aren't using.

The Haulbag's Design

Why is a haulbag shaped like a duffelbag, but without the handles? There are two reasons: one, the duffelbag design is smooth, allowing it to slide up the rock without snagging, and, two, a large duffelbag can carry a lot of gear. On multi-day climbs a lot of gear is exactly what you need.

Two unfortunate problems with the haulbag's basic duffelbag-like design are: first, it's difficult to carry the bag on horizontal ground, and second, it's hard to get to the equipment you need, which invariably works its way down to the bottom of the bag.

To help solve the first problem, manufacturers have added removable shoulder and waist straps. On large haulbags the straps are comfortably padded, while on the small haulbags they are merely 1 to 2-inch wide webbing strips. These straps must be removable, so that when you are ready to haul the bag up the cliff they won't snag on the rock. Manufacturers connect shoulder straps to their haulbags with buckles; to disconnect the straps simply unthread the strap from the buckle. The waist belts of the large haulbags slide through a tunnel-like piece of cloth (made of the same material as the entire pack). The waist belts of the small haulbags connect to the bags like the shoulder straps: with buckles.

The second problem, that of accessing your gear, is not so easy to solve. The duffelbag shape simply doesn't lend itself to easy packing, or unpacking, without a zipper on the side. Yet a haulbag would be far too weak with a zipper: the zipper would quickly burst under stress. The only solution is to buy a large haulbag having a short, wide shape, as compared to a tall, thin shape.

A nice feature on some haulbags is a hideaway pocket made for storing the straps. You access such a pocket from outside the bag. This makes it easy to stow the straps, even if your haulbag is full (because you don't have to open your already over-stuffed bag and make room for the straps).

Some haulbags, particularly the small ones, come with closed-cell foam sewn along the inside where the straps are. This foam protects both your back and the haulbag's fabric from any protruding sharp objects you might be carrying inside. Some of these foam panels continue from the haulbag's backside down to its base, and provide the bag with added protection.

A haulbag must have a low-profile closure that won't snag the rock yet will repel water. Some of the large haulbags close with a drawstring that runs through several grommets in the top of the bag and pulls tightly over a flap that covers the gear.

Other large haulbags close with a heavy duty zipper under the drawstring. This design provides very good protection from rain.

For additional rain protection, you can buy many large haulbags with a collar (also called a skirt). The collar is a poncho-like piece of cloth (from the same tough material as the haulbag) that you drape over the top of the bag. The collar increases the bag's resistance to water and helps it slide along the rock.

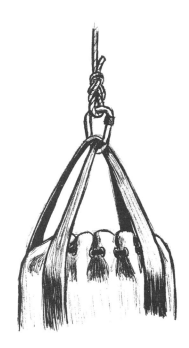

A large haulbag's 4-point haul line connection

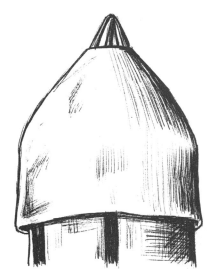

A large haulbag with a collar

Small haulbags have top flaps (with pockets) that buckle closed. These flaps are streamlined so they won't snag the rock. They cover all zippers and buckles with a smooth surface.

Some large haulbags have a separate, zippered pocket sewn into their sides or onto their top flaps. These pockets are ideal for carrying small items that would be otherwise easy to lose, or for holding your lunch or guidebook.

Haulbags have one more important feature: a connecting rig allowing you to easily, and securely, attach your haul line. Large haulbags use a different rig than the small ones.

Large haulbags have a sophisticated four-point connection consisting of four lengths of **webbing** that are sewn along the bag's entire vertical length. These pieces of webbing form two loops about a foot above the top of the haulbag's body.

Because the loops of webbing are sewn along the entire bag, they are very securely connected to it. This connection is very important because if they break, your haulbag will fall down the cliff!

You should attach your large haulbag to the haul line with a locking carabiner. Tie a **Figure-Eight-**

On-A-Bight (see pg. 201) on the end of your haul line and clip this to the locking carabiner.

Small haulbags have only three connecting points. There are usually two points on the front of the bag, consisting of **daisy chains** sewn along the bag's length, and a third (a loop of webbing) attached to the back.

Because these three connecting points don't form a loop, to attach them to your haul line you must rig them with additional webbing. Rigging this is easy: thread one **runner** through the top loops of both daisy chains. Now double a second runner through the single back loop and then thread it under the first runner. Connect your locking carabiner and haul line to this second runner.

Materials

Haulbags must withstand the tremendous abuse that comes from bumping and scraping over thousands of feet of rock. To provide adequate protection, manufacturers make their large haulbags out of a tough material such as heavy nylon Ballistic cloth, or vinyl-coated nylon. Both materials are smooth, but the vinyl-coated nylon has a glossier look (from the vinyl, which is a form of plastic). Manufacturers usually make their small haulbags

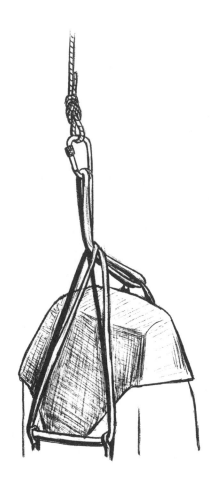

A haul line attached to a small haulbag with a locking carabiner and a Figure-Eight-On-A-Bight

Emergency Haulbag Repair

When you're on the cliffs, use duct tape to repair any holes or tears that develop in your haulbag. Seal the hole tightly, and then encircle the haulbag with the tape, thereby strengthening the patch.

How well this repair holds depends on how much rock abrasion it must survive. On a low-angle climb you may have to re-patch the hole several times a day, while on a vertical to over-hanging climb one repair might do the job.

Where To Buy Haulbags

Some climbing stores and mail-order catalogs sell haulbags. Several manufacturers who currently make haulbags are: A5, Chouinard, Fish, JRat, Mountain Tools, and Wild Country. See pg. 353 for manufacturers' addresses.

from thick Cordura nylon or a lighter form of Ballistics cloth.

A haulbag's seams are its weakest points. If a bag bursts, the problem probably started in the seams (watching your clothes float to the ground 2000 feet below is a strangely frustrating yet spectacular sight!). To reduce the number of potential weak points, manufacturers make their haulbags with only two seams: one down the side and one connecting the bag's bottom section to its sides. Each seam is stitched several times, and then taped (the tape protects the stitches from wear).

Manufacturers use nylon webbing to reinforce any critical connection points, such as the haul line loops. They sew the webbing along the entire length of the bag, which makes each connection very strong.

Headlamps

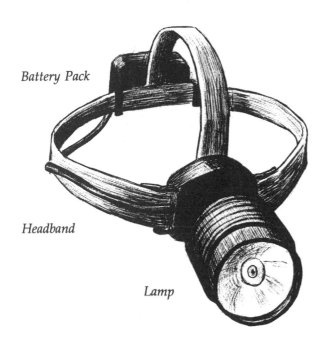

Battery Pack

Headband

Lamp

An electric headlamp

What Is A Headlamp?

A headlamp is a battery or gas-powered light that you wear strapped to your head. This design frees your hands for useful night-time activities such as: climbing, gathering firewood, cooking, reading, or any of the myriads of other things that you'll need to do while camping. Carrying a headlamp up the cliff in a small pack guarantees that you will have light when you need it. Many climbers have been caught high up the rock without a light, and have scary stories to tell about their near-blind descents. Consider a headlamp an essential piece of gear for any multi-day climb.

There are two basic types of headlamps on the market: electric and carbide. In this chapter I discuss only electric headlamps in detail, because carbide headlamps are unsuitable for rock climbing. I do briefly describe them on pg. 215.

The Electric Headlamp's Design

The electric headlamp consists of a bulb, a reflec-

tor, a housing that encloses the bulb and reflector, a battery pack, a wire connecting the reflector housing to the battery pack, and a mounting rig to carry it on your head. All these parts are required to make a useable headlamp, but how bright its light is and how long it lasts will depend on the bulb and battery combination you use.

In order that you can intelligently decide which bulb/battery combination you need, I will briefly discuss the principles that govern these two essential headlamp parts.

First of all, electric headlamps are powered by batteries. Batteries produce electricity; their power is measured as voltage. For instance, a common battery type is rated at 1.5 volts. To light a headlamp, the electricity produced by the batteries travels through a wire to the bulb. Bulbs always require a specified amount of power, or number of volts, to light up. Example: you would need two 1.5-volt batteries to power a common 3-volt bulb. The more volts you need to light up the bulb, the more batteries, or the larger a battery, you must have. Because weight is important in headlamps you will want to use a minimum number of batteries, each being as physically small as possible. The bottom line is: use headlamp bulbs that are designed to provide adequate light from very few volts.

However, to complicate things, not all bulbs are alike. Bulbs that require the same number of volts to light up may still produce different intensities of light. For instance, some 3-volt bulbs produce a more intense light than others. The reason for this is that every bulb's light intensity is measured in amperage, or amps. A bulb with a high-amp rating gives off more light than a bulb with a low-amp rating. In addition, a high-amp bulb drains power from the batteries faster than a low-amp bulb. So, if you use a high-amp bulb you will see a brighter light, but the batteries won't last as long as they would if you used a low-amp bulb.

You can buy two types of bulbs. Gas bulbs such as halogen, krypton, or xenon burn brighter than the other type, the vacuum bulb. However, gas bulbs draw more power from the batteries, just like a high-amp bulb. Even though they aren't so high tech, vacuum bulbs actually work better in climbing headlamps because they last longer. Besides, if you want a brighter light, just buy a vacuum bulb (which is cheaper than a gas bulb) with a higher amp rating.

With this basic knowledge, you can buy a headlamp to suit your varying needs. For example, cavers often need a light source that will reliably last for many hours; if it dies they must find their way out of the cave in absolute darkness, an impossible feat! So, on a long trip, a caver using an electric light will have a low-amp bulb and long-lasting batteries, plus lots of spares. As a rock climber your lighting needs will probably vary: perhaps you want a headlamp for use around camp, or to carry with you in case you are still on the cliffs at sunset. But, when you are on a multi-day big wall climb or an all-night trek over a mountain, you will need a reliable, long-lasting headlamp, just like the caver's.

Buy a headlamp that's versatile enough to cover all your needs. Many headlamps accept adapters for different-sized batteries; all of them accept bulbs of varying amperages. On some trips you may occasionally need a bright light, meaning that you temporarily replace your low-amp bulb with a high-amp one. If this is the case, bring along a spare high-amp bulb, and use it whenever necessary. REI sells a headlamp that comes with two bulbs, high-amp and low-amp, already in place. To change the headlamp's intensity, you simply flip a switch.

Batteries

There are two basic types of batteries available: the wet-cell and the dry-cell. A wet-cell battery is full of fluids: car batteries are wet-cell. Wet-cell batteries are not suitable for rock climbing because they are dangerous to carry around. It's easy to spill their acidic contents, and sometimes they explode (dry-cell batteries may also explode, but the chances are much less)! Dry-cell batteries are filled with solid paste compounds, resulting in a safer and tougher battery. You should use dry-cell batteries to power your headlamp.

There are many different types of dry-cell batteries on the market, but I will only discuss the three that are commonly used in headlamps (however, I also discuss the carbon-zinc, which is old technology, for clarification). The three types are: the alkaline, the lithium, and the nicad (rechargeable) battery. Their names descibe the primary chemical agent that powers them. Note that you can attach any kind of battery, even a wet-cell, to your headlamp, regardless of its original source of power, so long as the voltages match. Simply attach the wires coming from your headlamp's bulb to the new battery, which you carry either attached to your waist or to your head. I don't recommend that you take this option, unless you know exactly why you are doing it; otherwise you may end up with a battery that is less efficient than the original one.

Carbon-Zinc

Carbon-zinc batteries used to be the most common battery around, but have lately been replaced by alkaline batteries. Carbon-zinc batteries were available in many sizes, from AAA (the smallest) to the largest (6-volt) sizes.

Carbon-zinc batteries have several disadvantages. They provide power for only short periods and they have a short shelf life. They corrode easily and don't work well in cold weather.

On the positive side, carbon-zinc batteries do put out a uniform charge, which in turn produces a reliable light. And they lose their charge gradually: a nice feature that gives you plenty of warning before you must replace them.

Alkaline

Alkaline batteries have replaced the carbon-zinc as the most common battery currently on the market. Their power ratings and measurements are identical to carbon-zinc batteries. However, they last longer than carbon-zinc batteries, and are less corrosive. Also, they have a shelf life that is at least 3 times longer than the carbon-zinc's. This means that you are less likely to buy a "dead" battery. In addition, alkaline batteries will slightly recharge themselves after you turn them off.

Try to use your alkaline batteries at a constant amperage. If you change bulbs to alter your light's intensity the batteries will suffer a definite power loss.

Lithium

Lithium batteries are very popular in climbing headlamps. They are available in many different sizes, from the small disc batteries that power watches to the large "D" versions.

Lithium batteries perform better than all other batteries in cold weather. Most batteries have a shorter life, often by half, in freezing weather, but Lithium batteries actually last longer than they do in warmer temperatures. Lithium batteries also have a long shelf life: some models are guaranteed to last 10 years on the shelf!

Unfortunately, Lithium batteries are expensive. However, if you will need to use your headlamp in extreme cold, use Lithium batteries, regardless of the cost. They're more than worth it!

Nicads

Nickel-cadmium batteries (commonly known as Nicads) are rechargeable batteries. Although expensive, once you have bought a recharger (which is also expensive) you can reuse your Nicads many times before they die.

Unfortunately, few headlamps come rigged with Nicads. If you wish to use this type of battery you'll need to buy an adapter (you can get it at the same place you buy the Nicad) and wire it into the headlamp.

Nicads provide a steady, reliable source of power. However, when the power dies, it dies suddenly, without warning. So if you are on a cliff, far from your recharger (which must be plugged into a 120-volt outlet), you will be left without a light!

Summed up: use the alkaline battery for recreational use in moderate weather. Use the Lithium for the same purposes in cold weather. And use a Nicad if you don't mind the initial expense.

Brief History

It's impossible to say when the first headlamps were developed. Of course we know why they were developed: to aid in underground exploration. And since man has been exploring and living in caves since his earliest days, headlamps must have come along many years ago. Of course, they were probably nothing more than a candle strapped to a hat, or even tied to a headband. But they worked, and allowed people to search out hidden caverns.

But it was with industrial mining that the headlamp came into its own. This is when miners began using early versions of the carbide lamp.

As you know, Benjamin Franklin was one of the first to experiment with electricity. These experiments brought forth the new technology, and with it the battery. Early batteries were large, terribly inefficient devices. But experimenters gradually refined them, until they became small but powerful, and were able to charge a headlamp.

A climber in the 1860s

It is only in the last 20 years that battery technology has changed enough to radically affect headlamps. Now we have rechargeable batteries (Nicads) that are small enough to fit on a headlamp, and Lithium batteries which will keep it powered through the cold. And this says nothing of the technology that makes it possible to develop bright bulbs and small, durable reflector housings.

The headlamp of today is about the size of the original candle, but a bit heavier, and a lot more reliable.

Reflector Housing

Reflector housing is the name for the case that contains the bulb, reflector, and lens. It should be made of tough plastic, a strong, durable yet lightweight material.

The lens should be made from shatterproof, scratch resistant plastic. You will probably never see a headlamp with a glass lens, but if you do, don't buy it! Glass is the last thing you want to bring with you on a cliff!

Some headlamps allow you to adjust their beam's focus from spot to flood. This adjustment is made by rotating the lens. The spot setting focuses the light to throw a longer, narrower beam while the flood setting widens the beam to cover a larger area. This is a handy feature: when you are rappelling you need to see a wide area, but when you're reading a book or cooking you need light focused in one spot.

Most headlamps provide room for you to carry a spare bulb behind the reflector. This is handy because you should always carry an extra bulb (in case the first one breaks), and without the separate storage area you might lose or break the small, delicate bulb.

A separate battery storage container, at the rear of the headband

A spare bulb stored behind the reflector

You may want the spare bulb to be of a different amperage, so you can change light intensity. However, if you are sure you only need one intensity, bring two bulbs with identical amperage.

Battery Case

The battery case on a headlamp holds the batteries. Sometimes it sits behind the reflector housing. This arrangement is convenient because it confines bulb, reflector, lens, and batteries to one case. This means that you don't need to worry about snagging the wires, which are inside the housing. However, because this rig puts everything on your forehead, the headlamp may slip down your forehead. So before you buy such a light, try it on to make sure it doesn't slip.

Another common design locates the batteries in a separate reflector housing, at the rear of the headband.

In this design the batteries sit at the back of your head. Now the batteries balance the headlamp,

keeping it from falling down your forehead. However, the problem with this design is that there must be a wire running between the batteries at the back and the bulb up front. This wire can snag when you move along the rock, or through head-high brush, which is very irritating! If you do buy such a rig, make sure that the wire is housed in a durable sheath. Lightly tug on it; it shouldn't show any signs of separating from either the battery pack or the reflector housing.

A third popular location for carrying batteries is at your waist.

Use this rig when you need to carry large batteries (such as a 6-volt) that are too heavy to put on your head. You won't need a 6-volt battery for normal rock climbing, but I will briefly discuss this arrangement for your future information.

There are three problems with carrying your batteries on your waist. First, the location of the batteries can interfere with your rack and harness. Second, should the batteries leak, they will spill onto your harness, which may be eaten completely through, and will definitely become weakened. And third, the wire that connects the batteries to the bulb must be very long, which makes it likely to snag on everything that you pass by.

The Headband

The headlamp's headband keeps the entire rig attached to your head. Obviously, this is a very important job. The headband must be very secure, keeping the lamp in place, even when you are upside-down, or in the process of falling from a cliff.

Headbands are made either from elastic or rubber. The elastic model is more comfortable on your

A headlamp's headband

bare head than the rubber, but rubber grips a helmet better than elastic. Petzl makes metal clips which are designed to keep an elastic headband in place on your helmet, thereby solving this problem.

An elastic headband on a helmet with metal clips

No matter the materials, your headband should be adjustable, since it must fit both your bare head and your larger helmet. It must also be stiff enough to keep the heavy headlamp from falling down onto your forehead as you move around.

Before you buy a headlamp, try it on. Make sure the headband is comfortable and that it keeps the lamp in position. Swing your head back and forth, up and down. The lamp will move, but should maintain its basic position. If you already have a

helmet (see Helmets, pg. 219), bring it to the store. Attach the headlamp to it. The headlamp should stay securely in position, even when you knock your helmeted-head around.

Carbide Headlamps

Carbide headlamps are not good for rock climbing. This is because their light source is a small fire: an open flame instead of a light bulb. This flame can burn your gear (particularly nylon **ropes**, **webbing**, and **harnesses**), or be blown out by the winds that constantly sweep by many cliffs. However, I am briefly describing the carbide lamp here because I think it's an interesting piece of gear, and, who knows, you may decide to try it out some time.

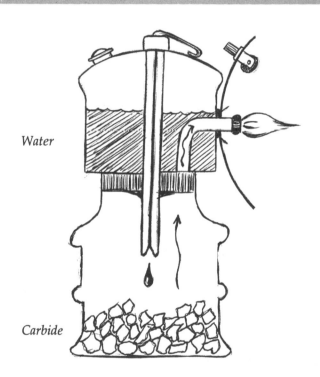

An X-ray view of the carbide headlamp

A carbide headlamp is a smaller version of a welding torch. Both of them are powered by acetylene gas. However, with a carbide headlamp the flame is many times weaker. But the design is the same.

Confining acetylene gas would be dangerous: it could explode. Carbide headlamps are made with safety in mind, so the gas is produced just before it is burned. This means that there is never enough gas to be a concern.

The gas is produced by mixing calcium carbide and water. These two substances are stored in a container that sits below the headlamp's reflector. The container itself is separated into two smaller chambers. The lower chamber holds calcium carbide, while the upper chamber is full of water.

To control the rate at which the gas is produced, the headlamp has a small adjustment valve. In the "off" position this valve prevents any water from mixing with the calcium carbide. But when you turn the valve "on", a drip tube opens and drops of water spill onto the calcium carbide. The result is the acetylene gas which rises up and out of the jet tube.

To light a carbide lamp, turn the water adjustment valve on and cup your hand over the reflector. After a few seconds acetylene gas will form a pool in the reflector which you can easily light once you remove your hand. You can make the flame brighter by opening the adjustment valve wider. This lets more water enter the calcium carbide chamber, which makes more gas.

Carbide headlamps have many advantages. They last only an hour or two, but they are quick and easy to re-charge. All you need to do is fill the container with calcium carbide and water, both of which you should carry along is separate plastic bottles. You must carry the used calcium carbide back home with you (dispose of it as you would motor oil) in another plastic bottle. A carbide headamp is very rugged, and if it does have a problem you can quickly and easily take it apart to repair it. In addition, carbide lamps provide heat, which can save your life in cold weather (prevent hypothermia).

I mentioned two of the carbide headlamp's main disadvantages before: it can burn your gear and blow out, leaving you without a light. Either of these problems should preclude you from using a carbide lamp for rock climbing.

Specifications

Usually a manufacturer will tell you how long his particular headlamp will last using certain batteries and bulbs. (Note that batteries are rarely included with the headlamp, but that usually you'll receive two bulbs with it.) This is useful information, be-

cause it gives you a reference point for comparing headlamps.

Weight

Your headlamp should be lightweight, because, if it isn't, your neck will quickly become fatigued. If you dread wearing the headlamp because it's uncomfortable, you may be caught in the dark without it! An acceptable headlamp weight is 6-10 ounces, including battery weight.

Sample Headlamp Specifications

Headlamp	Batteries	Bulb Amps	Battery Life	Intensity
REI Hi-Lo	2 6-volt	.15	17 hrs.	6
		.3	8.5 hrs.	3.4
Lithium Lamp	1.5-volt Lithium	.15	19.3 hrs.	6.1
			20 hrs at 0 degrees	
Petzl Zoom	3 1.5-v	.22	8 hrs.	7

General Safety Guidelines

Be Careful With Your Batteries!

Batteries can explode! You shouldn't have any problems as long as you follow the directions that come with the battery. In addition, here are some basic battery safety guidelines:

- Don't use different types of batteries together (example: an alkaline with a Lithium).
- Don't try to recharge any battery except a Nicad.
- Don't ever put your batteries in a fire - they will explode!
- Don't carry batteries loose in your purse or pocket (keep them wrapped in a bag).
- Do check your batteries occasionally for corrosion; if you see any, discard the batteries.

Care

Moisture causes corrosion, which, when it builds up, will prevent your headlamp from operating. Corrosion is simple to combat: keep the headlamp's electrical connections clean. These connections include: the bulb's contact base (unscrew the bulb and examine it), the battery connections (take out the batteries) and the wires (examine them to make sure they are connected securely).

Note: either store your batteries separately from your headlamp, or reverse them in their case. You don't want the headlamp to switch on in your pack and kill the battery!

Bulbs

You should always carry a spare bulb with you (having the amperage you will need). Most headlamps allow you to store the bulb behind the reflector (as I described earlier). In addition, you should carry some spare batteries. The best way to transport them is in an insulated container, such as a thick pouch. Don't allow the batteries to move around inside, as they may explode. Keep them bound together with a rubber band, or wound together tightly inside a plastic bag, which you then put in the pouch.

Batteries

No matter what kind of dry-cell batteries you use, you can prolong their shelf life by storing them in a cool environment, such as a refrigerator. This cool atmosphere helps to keep them fully charged. Before you use the batteries, however, warm them to about 70 degrees F. (room temperature). Lithium batteries are exceptions to this rule. If the weather is cold, carry your alkaline or Nicad batteries next to your body as you hike to the climb. This will warm them up.

When To Retire Your Headlamp

The great thing about a headlamp is that you can replace most of its parts. If something breaks, it's easy to get it fixed (talk to the manufacturer about this). Consequently, there is no limit to how long your headlamp can last, so long as you keep fixing it!

Accessories

Some manufacturers sell each part of their headlamps individually. However these parts - the reflector, its case, the lens, the battery case, and the headband, aren't sold in most stores, so you must contact the manufacturer directly. You can buy bulbs and batteries easily, since they are sold in most recreational, hardware, electrical, and appliance stores.

Key Point

"Before you buy a helmet, make sure it fits. A well-fitting helmet is almost comfortable, so you are more likely to wear it."

See page 221

Helmets

Shell

Foam Spacers

Inner Suspension System

Ventilation holes

Chin strap

A helmet, half of it an X-ray view

When To Use A Helmet

Cliffs, and rocks in general, are in a constant state of erosion. On most cliffs this erosion takes the form of falling rock (the exceptions include some types of limestone and sandstone, in moderate climates, that wash away gradually, without much rock fall).

Some cliffs have more falling rocks than others. Cliffs that endure frequent changes in temperature and other weather variations (dry to wet), suffer from erosion more than other cliffs, and have much more falling rock. One sure way to tell how much rockfall danger you will be in (before you climb) is to see how much rock is piled at the base of the cliff. If there are quite a few rocks, you need to be careful!

As a rock climber, you will need protection from this very serious danger. Unfortunately there is no way to entirely protect yourself. It would, for instance, be impractical to wear a full suit of armor up the cliff! But you can protect your fragile head by wearing a helmet. A rock climbing helmet is designed to protect your head from two things: fall-

ing rock and hitting your head on the rock if you fall.

If you are a beginner you are more at risk of being injured by rock fall. Advanced climbers are usually able to judge the rock's condition. They know when they should wear a helmet. The only way you can develop this judgment is to climb, and as you climb to observe the rock around you. Learn to spot shifting and loose rock, to pay attention to this subtle aspect of the sport.

A beginning climber is also more likely to hit his head on the rock if he falls. As a beginner you will usually be climbing low-angle slabs where, if you fall, you may tumble down, spinning end over end. Without a helmet your head may quickly be smashed on the rock. But even with a helmet this is dangerous, so, if you do fall on a slab, try to keep your balance by running backwards down the cliff until your rope catches you. More advanced climbers usually don't climb these low-angle slabs; they are more likely to be on vertical or overhanging rock where, if they fall, they will drop harmlessly out into space. For more information on how to fall safely, see pg. 61.

Helmets are vital for winter climbing. Rock becomes very brittle in the cold weather, and chunks easily break off. You will also need to watch for falling ice, which is just as potentially dangerous as falling rock.

Helmets are also mandatory on **big wall** climbs. Big walls constantly shed rock and, if you are injured while on such a large cliff, it will be very difficult for others to lower you down, or get help.

Despite the dangers, most rock climbers don't wear helmets. Helmets are uncomfortable, and comfort is important when you climb. Helmets are heavy, become hot, and make your head sweat. And, even though they are made with very small brims (if any) climbing helmets restrict your vision. On top of all these real problems, many climbers won't wear a helmet merely because it isn't stylish. But it isn't stylish to get injured and have to be rescued either, so if you think that there might be a danger of rockfall, wear a helmet!

Note: even if the cliffs appear solid you may still be in danger from falling rocks. These rocks may come down from other climbers above you. So try not to climb beneath another party, but if you must, wear a helmet. And if you ever hear the shout: "ROCK!" look out for dangerous projectiles! (The same is true for you: if you dislodge a rock, immediately yell "ROCK!" to warn anyone below you.)

The chances of your getting nailed by a rock are fairly small; the chance that this rock will hit you in the head is even smaller. But there is a chance, and this possibility has become a reality for many unfortunate climbers. Whether you wear a helmet or not is entirely up to you, but remember that if you get injured, you put your climbing partner, and possibly a rescue team, into the dangerous position of having to get you off the cliff.

General Features To Look For

Climbing helmets have some general features that distinguish them from other helmets, such as bicycle, football, or skateboarding helmets, which are not suitable for rock climbing. For one thing, climbing helmets are sold in climbing shops. They have very small brims, if any. They have headbands and chin straps, the latter being connected to the helmet at four points, producing fore and aft stability. And climbing helmets always have some sort of padding and suspension system inside. The padding is made of foam and lies along the inside of the helmet's shell. The suspension system is made of strips of webbing or nylon mesh which cover your head like a net, securing it inside the helmet and providing added shock absorption.

When a rock hits your helmet it is (hopefully) deflected by the shell. But the force from the rock must also be dealt with. If this force went straight to your head, even without the rock, you would end up with quite a headache! So your helmet must also absorb the force of the falling rock. Your helmet's shell dissipates most of this force evenly over its surface. What remains is reduced even further by the foam padding on the inside of the helmet. And any force that is left over is further diminished by traveling through your helmet's suspension system. When the blow finally reaches your head it should be so slight that you will hardly feel it.

Types

There are three types of helmets on the market: light, medium, and heavy-duty. The light helmet offers the least amount of protection but is the most comfortable to wear. Medium helmets compromise between good protection and light weight. Heavy-duty helmets offer the best protection but are fairly heavy to climb with. For helmet weights, see Specifications, pg. 222.

The Light-Duty Helmet

A light-duty helmet has a thin shell surrounding very thin foam spacers (if there are any at all) and a suspension system of either nylon mesh or webbing. To reduce this weight further, some light-duty helmets have hard plastic chin straps instead of the usual metal ones.

The light-duty helmet is the most comfortable type of climbing helmet to wear. It is very lightweight, often has good ventilation (from ventilation holes drilled through the shell), and has very little foam (foam is hot and uncomfortable).

Unfortunately, light-duty helmets do have some negative points. They are far weaker than the other two types of helmets. The light-duty helmet can easily withstand soft, spread out blows, but heavy, pointed rocks may penetrate. Another problem with light-duty helmets is that you may find the weight of your headlamp (see pg. 211) easily unbalances the helmet. The four-point chin strap helps with this problem, but you will still notice the headlamp's weight on the helmet, which may shift around as you climb.

The light-duty helmet is excellent for those times when you want protection but don't want the weight of a heavier helmet. This might include some light alpine climbing where speed is essential and any climbing in areas that suffer from little rockfall. Note that most light-duty helmets have passed the UIAA's tests (see below).

The Medium-Duty Helmet

Medium-duty helmets have a thicker shell than light-duty helmets. Medium-duty helmets have small foam spacers that are located at the helmet's sides, and also a suspension system.

The medium-duty helmet's shell is stronger than the shell of light-duty helmets. The foam spacers protect your head from blows to both the top and the sides, while still keeping the helmet's weight low. Some medium-duty helmets have ventilation holes. Medium-duty helmets offer a good compromise between light weight, comfort, and solid protection. Because they are in such a compromise position, they have no serious drawbacks.

The Heavy-Duty Helmet

A heavy-duty helmet is made with a thick shell and a full foam liner, as well as a suspension system. Some heavy-duty helmets have shells that also cover the climber's ears.

Heavy-duty helmets offer more protection than any other type of rock climbing helmet. Manufacturers are so confident in their heavy-duty helmets that most of them offer to replace the helmet free if it ever becomes damaged in a climbing accident.

Heavy-duty helmets have some negative characteristics. They are uncomfortable, having poor ventilation and too much foam. The foam makes your head sweat, which increases your discomfort. You will have a hard time forgetting that you are wearing a heavy-duty helmet, which means that you are less likely to want to wear it on the next climb.

But if you can bear its inherent discomfort, the heavy-duty helmet is the one to buy, because it is the safest on the market.

The UIAA's Helmet Tests

The UIAA independently tests climbing helmets. A helmet that passes these tests meets, and may exceed, all the minimum UIAA safety requirements. Although you don't really need to know more than that your helmet has the UIAA's stamp of approval, I am providing the following test descriptions in case you are interested.

There are five parts to the helmet test. The first two measure impact resistance from the top, the third impact resistance from the front, the fourth penetration from the top, and the fifth measures chin strap stretch.

The first impact resistance from the top test is measured by dropping a 5 kg. weight onto a helmet from 2 meters up. The weight is rounded, with no sharp edges. The helmet sits on an artificial head which is connected to instruments that measure the force inflicted by the weight. This force must be less than or equal to 10 kilo Newtons. (A Newton is a distance, mass, and time measurement used by physicists; a kilo is a thousand grams, equal to 2205 pounds.)

The second impact resistance from the top test is similar to the first, but with the 5 kilogram weight dropped from only one meter up. The measured force must be less than or equal to 6 kilo Newtons.

Impact resistance from the front is measured by tilting the artificial, helmet-covered head up and dropping a flat 5 kilogram weight from a height of half a meter onto it. As with the first test, the resulting force must be less than or equal to 10 kilo Newtons.

The penetration test is conducted by dropping a sharp, 1.5 kilogram weight 1.5 meters onto the top of the helmet. The weight must not reach the artificial head.

The chin strap stretch test measures how much the strap stretches when force is applied to it. Testers load the chin strap with 500 Newtons (half a kilo Newton). It must not stretch more than 25 millimeters under this weight.

Getting A Good Fit

Before you buy a helmet, make sure it fits. A well-fitting helmet is almost comfortable, so you are more likely to wear it.

Put the helmet on and tighten the headband (if it's adjustable) and the chin strap. Look in a mirror. Make sure the helmet covers your entire head. It's too small if it only covers the top of your head, and too large if it covers your eyes, ears, and neck.

Once you have tightened the chin strap, check to see whether the helmet slides forward and backward along your head when you look up and down. Test this by tugging first the helmet's front, then its back. If it moves easily, this is not the right helmet for you. Make sure the helmet is also secure from any sideways motion by pulling on the sides. Again, the helmet shouldn't move much.

A helmet that's just right

Now test the helmet for comfort. First, kneel on the floor, as if you were going to pray. Now hit your helmeted head a few times on the floor (make sure the floor is covered by a rug so you don't scratch the helmet). Also hit the helmet from the sides with your palms, first one, then the other. How does it feel? You shouldn't feel any pain, just a soft sensing of the blows.

Next, do a headstand. Have the salesperson help you so you don't crash into the clothing racks. Now bounce on your head. (If you aren't able to do a headstand you'll have to rely on the other tests.) Again, does the helmet feel comfortable in this position? It should; if it doesn't, don't buy it.

Once you have found a helmet that passes these tests, see if its suspension system is adjustable. If you want to do any winter climbing you will need the adjustability to accommodate a wool cap. The climbing store should have a few of these caps. Try

one on, then adjust the helmet and put it over the cap. The helmet should still fit well.

Another thing you should check are the helmet's available colors. Lighter colors (like white and yellow) reflect the sun better, keep you cooler, are more visible, and last longer than darker helmets.

If all these tests check out to your satisfaction, wear the helmet around the store for at least 30 minutes while you browse other gear. This is the ultimate test: is the helmet comfortable enough that you will actually be willing to wear it for hours on a climb? If you still like the helmet after the 30 minutes are up, buy it.

Specifications

Weight

A helmet's weight depends on how thick its shell is, how much foam padding it has, and the weight of its suspension system. And of course these factors also determine what type of helmet it is - whether it is heavy, medium, or light-duty. Heavy duty helmets weigh from 18-27 ounces; medium-duty helmets weigh from 16-18 ounces; light-duty helmets weigh anywhere from 13 to 16 ounces.

Regardless of how heavy your new helmet is, it will take some getting used to. When you first wear it on a climb your neck will feel tired, because your neck needs time to adjust to the heavier load it must now support. But after only a few days of climbing your neck will adjust; you should have no further problems with it.

Sample Helmet Specifications		
	Wt. (ounces)	Comments
Heavy-Duty **Joe Brown Super**	27	Offers excellent protection
Medium-Duty **Face Nord**	18	Good ventilation
Light-Duty **Petzl Vertical**	14.1	Very comfortable

Materials

Climbing helmets are made to be lightweight and strong. Reaching a good compromise between these two characteristics is hard to do: an extremely strong helmet, such as one made of metal, is heavy, and a heavy helmet is too uncomfortable for climbing. While searching for the optimum strength versus weight compromise, manufacturers must consider a helmet's shell, padding, and suspension system.

Manufacturers have found that rigid fiberglass, fiberglass combinations (fiberglass strengthened with various other substances, such as carbon fiber) and a material called Lexon are very strong and relatively lightweight shell materials. A lighter material, one that isn't quite as strong as fiberglass, is derived from polyamides. Polyamides have the benefit of flexing upon impact, which allows them to absorb more stress than if they were rigid.

Foam is the preferred padding because it is moderately lightweight and provides good cushioning. A fully-padded helmet is heavy but has excellent shock absorbing abilities. To reduce weight manufacturers usually decrease the amount of foam they put into the helmet, going from a full lining to small foam spacers. Some helmets have no padding at all - but these provide only minimum protection.

Unfortunately, foam doesn't absorb sweat. This is because it isn't breathable; it doesn't allow moisture to disperse through it. The result is discomfort: it's hard to concentrate on the climb when streams of sweat are trickling down your scalp! To alleviate this problem, manufacturers sometimes drill small ventilation holes in a helmet's shell. *Don't add ventilation holes if your helmet doesn't have any!* You will reduce the strength of the helmet, and may render it too weak to stop the smallest rock from penetrating to your precious skull.

Another way manufacturers try to reduce the amount your head sweats is to provide suspension systems inside the helmet, between your head and the foam padding. Climbing helmet suspension systems are made of nylon mesh, strips of webbing, or a combination of the two, with the occasional addition of plastic supports. The plastic supports usually wrap around the back of your head, and serve to keep the helmet stable.

Suspension systems provide a comfortable netting-like structure which separates your head from the rest of the helmet, including the foam. In lifting the foam off your head the suspension system improves the ventilation within the shell, which decreases the amount you sweat. More importantly, the suspension system also adds to the helmet's cushioning ability and its comfort.

At the base of the suspension system is a headband. This encircles your head, keeping the helmet

in place. Headbands are made of leather or webbing, and should be adjustable (so you can wear a hat if you want).

A plastic support on the back of the helmet helps keep it stable

The climbing helmet's chin strap is usually made of webbing. It connects to the helmet at four points, two on each side. This double connection adds stability to the helmet; with a four-point chin strap design your helmet won't slide up or down after it has been hit by a rock. The four-point chin strap also keeps your helmet from sliding forward when you attach a headlamp to the helmet.

Some chin straps are adjustable along each of their four points. This design allows you to alter your helmet's fore-aft position (for example, you can make the helmet sit higher on your forehead to accommodate the extra weight of a headlamp).

General Safety Guidelines

Use The Chinstrap!

When you wear your helmet, make sure that you tighten its chinstrap. The helmet won't do you any good if it goes flying off your head the minute you bump into something!

Care

Helmets are made to withstand falling rocks, but they are still vulnerable to damage. Solvents, particularly those with an acetone base, will eat through a helmet's fibers. Paint, especially oil-base paint, also damages helmets, so don't paint your helmet (although you can mark it with a felt-tip pen). Glue can eat through your helmet's shell so don't glue something to it. Above all, don't cut your helmet! Any cut is likely to weaken the shell, which relies on the integrity of its shape to maintain strength.

When To Retire Your Helmet

Generally speaking, your climbing helmet will last for years. However, if your helmet suffers a hard hit from a rock you should replace it. Such a blow will severely weaken the helmet, which might not be able to withstand another hit. As I mentioned before, most heavy-duty helmets have a free replacement policy if the helmet has suffered a hard hit. Medium and light-duty helmets don't offer this insurance; you will need to buy a new one.

Sunlight damages helmets, so store yours in the closet, or some other dark, dry place. When your helmet becomes faded and worn-looking (you will be able to tell), retire it.

Retire your helmet if it develops cracks, cuts, holes (other than those you made to mount your headlamp - see below), or becomes severely abraded. Helmet manufacturers can make small repairs, so before you retire the helmet, contact the manufacturer. Maybe there's a way to save yours.

Modifications And Tune-Ups

Mounting A Headlamp

Electric headlamps come with their own mounting system (see pg. 214). There are two basic types of mounting systems: the first is an elastic headband-like apparatus and the second is a bolt-on mounting bracket. I discuss each type in more detail in the chapter Headlamps, pg. 211. However, here I will cover some basics that you need to know for placing the headlamp on your helmet.

If you have a headlamp with an elastic headband mount, you don't need to drill any holes. Simply place the headband, with the headlamp attached, over your helmet. You can leave it like this, especially if it is made of stretchable, sticky rubber.

However, if the headband is made of elastic cloth (such as the Petzl mounting system) I recommend that you connect four metal clips (made by Petzl) to the brim of your helmet and to the headband, as illustrated above.

A headlamp-mounting headband made of elastic cloth

Note that some helmets have an elastic cord attached to the shell. This cord is designed to keep the headlamp in position, so if your helmet has the cord you won't need the metal clips. The cord is configured in two triangles, one in the front, the other in the back. To attach your headlamp (to the front triangle), unhook the top corner of the cord from its metal clip, put the headlamp on, and then replace the cord.

A headlamp-mounting headband under a triangle of cord

If you have the second type of headlamp mounting system, the one that requires you to bolt it on, you must drill some small holes into the helmet for the bolts. The size of hole you drill depends on the size of the bolts you use; try to keep the holes as small as you can while still being able to accommodate the bolts.

But before you do any drilling, first prepare for the job. You will need a felt-tip pen, two rubber washers for each bolt, the drill and drill bit (sized just larger than the bolts), all the bolts and nuts that come with the mounting bracket, the mounting bracket itself, and a wrench or pair of pliers to tighten the bolts.

Hold the headlamp mounting bracket against your helmet in the position you desire, and use the felt-tip pen to mark the locations of the bolt holes. These marks show where you need to drill. Before you drill, if possible remove the padding and suspension system from the inside of your helmet. If you can't do this easily, consider buying a headlamp that has an elastic mounting system (it will be easier to deal with). If it's too late and you already have your headlamp, drill carefully. Try to avoid damaging the padding and suspension system.

Once you have drilled your holes, push the bolts (with a rubber washer on each) through the helmet, *from the inside out*. This is very important: if you pushed the bolts from the outside in they will be pointing towards your head. Then the first time you bump your helmeted head your skull will be pierced by a bolt!

Now slide a rubber washer on each bolt end and position the headlamp mounting bracket over these. Tighten the bracket onto your helmet with the nuts, but be careful not to tighten the bolts too much or you may damage the shell. Tighten the bolts hand tight, no more. That's all: you're done!

Accessories

Drill And Drill Bits

You can buy these tools at any hardware store, and some department stores. I strongly recommend an electric drill with a full complement of bits. If you don't want to spend the money, see if you can borrow one from a friend or neighbor.

Wrench

Buy an adjustable wrench. It's a good investment which you will use for other important climbing gear modifications later.

Felt Tip Pen

Felt tip pens are available at stationary stores, department stores, and supermarkets everywhere.

Some Helmet Manufacturers

Edelrid, Joe Brown, Mountain Safety Research, Petzl, Romer Messner, and Salewa manufacture climbing helmets. See pg. 353 for manufacturers' addresses.

Key Point

"A file is useful for sharpening the edges of your . . . hooks. You can buy a fine metal file at any hardware store."

See page 230

Hooks (Sky Hook; Fifi Hook)

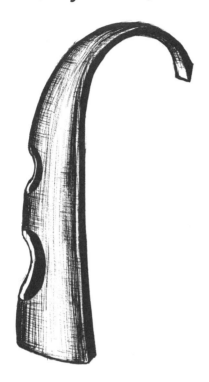

A hook

Different models of sky hooks

What Are Hooks Used For?

Some cliffs are so featureless that you must use aid to climb them. Using aid is using a tool, other than your body and climbing boots, to make progress up the rock. In essence, when you aid climb you use various pieces of your gear to build a ladder up the side of the cliff. Aid climbers use hooks to suspend themselves from minute edges and flakes, thin **seams,** and from **carabiners.**

Types

There are three basic types of hooks in use: the sky hook, the fifi hook, and the seam hook. Each one has a different purpose.

Sky Hook

A sky hook has a thin curved end which hooks onto small edges and flakes on the rock. Sky hooks come in many shapes and sizes, from small triangular shapes with sharp points, to others with flat points, to ring-angle hooks with large curves.

There is even a hook (the Peregrine Talon Hook) which has three prongs radiating from the center.

Each hook has a different use. The small triangular hooks with sharp points work extremely well for "bat-hooking." Bat- hooking is placing the tip of a hook into a small pre-drilled hole in the rock. (There are many such holes on some big walls, including El Capitan; the holes usually have a 1/4-inch diameter.) Flat-tipped triangular hooks are excellent for grabbing thin rock edges. The large, ring-angle hooks grab well on ledges and on two-inch-wide flakes.

The most stable sky hook design has a tripod which provides three points of contact. Two points at the hook's base keep the third point, the actual hook, from rotating out of position.

There are two ways to **sling** your sky hooks with **tubular webbing.** The first is to let the webbing hang from the inside of the hook, as demonstrated on the next page.

This method works best when you are hooking a small rock edge, and the hook allows the webbing to hang free. Different models of sky hooks achieve this in different ways. The most common way is to curve the two base points inward, keeping the body of the hook, and the sling, away from the

The bend in the sky hook allows the sling to lie free. Notice how the sling comes from the inside of the hook

This method of rigging your hook works best on large ledges and flakes. Notice how the sling hangs down the outside of the hook

rock. This allows the sling to lie between the base points, without disrupting the hook's stability.

The second way to sling a hook is to rig the webbing so that it hangs from outside of the hook. This method works best on larger ledges and flakes because the webbing actually keeps the hook in a more secure position.

Fifi Hook

Fifi hooks are very different from sky hooks. They are flat and have a broad curving shape.

Although fifi hooks aren't designed for hooking small edges and flakes, they are very useful for aid climbing. You can use them with a rig called a **"cow's tail"**: a sling, **daisy chain** (see pg. 153), or chain of carabiners attached to your **waist harness** and to your piece of aid (**piton, copperhead, chock,** etc.). The fifi hook connects the cow's tail to the aid, and allows you to quickly attach yourself to and then disconnect from your protection, which

A fifi hook

can be helpful on steep or overhanging walls.

The cow's tail keeps your body on tension, close to the rock. This allows you to reach up and place your next piece of aid, then attach your etriers and daisy chain to it, all the while hanging comfortably from your cow's tail. Normally you would hang from your rope, but this leads to problems when you try to clip the rope to the piece of aid above (you can no longer rest on the rope; you must balance yourself with your **etriers,** which is very difficult on steep or overhanging rock!).

Using a fifi hook instead of a carabiner with a cow's tail is advantageous because you can quickly and easily hook or unhook from your connection. You save both time and effort.

You can also use a fifi hook in conjunction with your etriers (ladder-like loops of webbing used in aid climbing). Tie the hook to the top of your etriers, in place of a carabiner.

With this rig you receive the same advantages as from the fifi hook with a cow's tail: you save time and effort.

Seam Hook

The name "seam hook" is arbitrary. I have used it because there is no generic name for this type of hook. Currently A5 is the only company selling seam hooks (the A5 Birdbeak). Chouinard used to sell the Crack-N-Up, which was a similar type of hook.

A seam hook

A seam hook in a thin crack

The seam hook is shaped like an anchor. It is very thin so that it can fit into narrow seams and cracks.

The seam hook is useful on many aid routes, especially the more popular ones that see a lot of traffic. This is because you can quickly place or hammer the hook into an empty piton slot, without needing to widen the slot and further damage the rock with a new piton. The seam hook is also easy to remove.

Seam hooks are particularly helpful when you are trying to aid climb a route using a "clean" style (you don't hammer anything into the rock). Again, it is the hook's ability to hold (without hammering) in old piton slots that makes this possible. If necessary you can hammer the hook into the rock, which will make for a secure fit.

The problem with using seam hooks is that they are not terribly strong and won't hold a hard fall. You should intersperse your seam hook placements with solid pieces of protection, such as a secure piton, at regular intervals, if you can.

Specifications

Strength

All three types of hooks are designed to support your body weight. However, fifi hooks and most sky hooks won't hold a fall. Fifi hooks aren't strong enough and sky hooks will often be pulled off the rock by your rope if you climb above them. Seam hooks may hold your fall, but they may not. This depends on how well the hook is placed and how much force it must withstand.

Weight

Hooks weigh anywhere from 1 to 5 ounces. This light weight stems from their small size, not from their materials (steel alloy is heavier than aluminum alloy).

Materials

Sky and seam hooks are made from strong steel alloys. This metal is heavy so, to keep the weight down, most manufacturers make the hooks small. Many hooks have a hard finish applied to increase their durability.

Fifi hooks are made from lightweight aluminum alloy. This metal is not as strong as steel, but the fifi hook doesn't need to be especially strong. It is also less durable; aluminum doesn't withstand abuse as well as steel.

Care

Hooks don't need much care. Occasionally you may find that the thin edge of your sky or seam hook needs sharpening, because it has become nicked in such a way that it won't fit on tiny edges or in thin seams. You can file the hook sharp with a fine metal file. It doesn't require much filing, just enough to thin the hook's edge.

Retire your hook when it bends or cracks, and is therefore no longer able to support your weight.

Accessories

File

A file is useful for sharpening the edges of your sky and seam hooks. You can buy a fine metal file at any hardware store.

Sling

You will need a sling for each of your sky and seam hooks. Tubular webbing is the best. Don't use cord because it is too wide; it will cause the hook to rotate. Different models of hooks have different size holes, but usually the widest webbing you will need is half-inch.

You probably need only a short sling, so buy 3 feet of the correct width (up to a half inch) of tubular webbing. This will make a loop that is approximately 12 inches long.

If you want more strength than tubular webbing can offer (although it is strong enough for most purposes), you can use **Spectra** webbing. Spectra is more expensive, but it is stronger and will last longer than tubular webbing.

Some Hook Manufacturers

Camp, Chouinard, Fish, Leeper, Petzl, Salewa, and Stubai are some hook manufacturers. See pg. 353 for manufacturers' addresses.

Kneepads

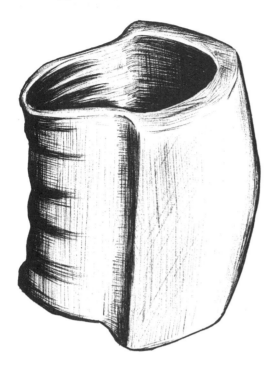

A kneepad

A climber using kneepads in a squeeze crack

When Should You Use Kneepads?

Your knees are complex and fragile joints. They are made up of interlocking muscles and tendons that help give your legs an incredibly wide range of motion. This range of motion is essential for climbing. But the rock you climb can wear your knees down: repeated scraping and wear can cause tendonitis or bursitis. Both conditions are very painful, and both will keep you from climbing.

Naturally, most of the climbing you will do won't involve scraping your knees over the rock. Using your knees is considered poor technique. However, there are specific situations when you will use your knees. These include free climbing a **squeeze chimney** (see above), **aid climbing** (see pg. 176), or while ascending a **fixed rope** see pg. 81). A squeeze chimney is a crack that is just wide enough to fit your body. To make upward progress you must push your feet, knees, back, and arms against opposite sides of the crack.

You will also use your knees when you aid climb with **etriers** and when you ascend a rope that lies on a rock slab. You will do both of these things, many times, on **big wall** climbs.

In these knee-abusing situations climbers use kneepads. Kneepads are designed to protect your fragile knees from getting damaged on the rock.

Types

There are two types of kneepads on the market. The first is a simple rectangular foam pad built into a wide loop of cloth (soccer style) that encircles your leg. The second has metal or hard plastic caps over its pads (you have probably seen skateboarders wearing these). There are many variations to these two basic types. Buy the one that you like best. Here are some guidelines.

Choose a pad which will protect you but won't impede your movement. A simple, soccer-style kneepad can do this. It's cheap, lightweight, offers reasonable protection, and has minimum bulk.

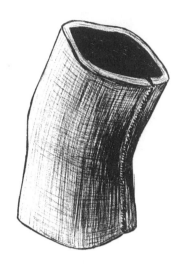

Soft foam kneepads

Skater's pads

Unfortunately these simple kneepads are not very durable; the rock will quickly rip up the foam. You can increase a pad's durability by wrapping it with a layer of duct tape before you climb. The tape protects the foam from rock abrasion, thereby extending its life, and adds another protective layer between your knees and the rock.

Foam kneepads provide enough friction to work well in squeeze chimneys. However, you must be sure that they fit tight, or they will slip. The foam pads allow you to bend your knees, more so than the skater's pads, and so work for aid climbing, where you rest by tucking one leg, in its etrier, under you (see pg. 178). They wear out quickly when you use them while ascending a rope that is lying on the rock.

A kneepad with metal or hard plastic caps - the skater's pad - offers both durability and protection.

Metal and plastic caps last a long time and protect your knees from sharp rocks that might quickly penetrate foam. The drawbacks to this type of kneepad include price, weight, and bulk. They don't grip the rock well, so climbing a squeeze chimney, where you must partly rely on the grip provided by your knees, is difficult. Skater's pads also impede your ability to bend your knees. This makes them undesirable for aid climbing with etriers because, as I explained previously, you must bend one leg under you to rest. To offset this problem you can push the kneepad down onto your calf when you want to rest in etriers. This allows you to get the durability of the hard cap and,

with a little more trouble, still be able to flex your legs. However, skater's pads work best for ascending fixed ropes.

The conclusion is that if you are going to do a lot of ascending on a rope lying against the rock, wear skater's pads. But for other types of climbing, use the more comfortable foam pads.

Care

Your kneepads' durability depends on its type. Simple foam pads are the least durable while skater's pads will last much longer.

If your kneepads become cut or worn, wrap them with duct tape. You can keep adding the tape as necessary, but eventually all the padding will disintegrate beneath it. Retire your kneepads when they no longer offer adequate comfort and protection.

Where To Buy Kneepads

Some climbing stores carry the simple foam kneepads. Sporting goods stores carry the widest selection of kneepads, including different varieties of foam pads and occasionally skater's pads. If you want skater's pads but can't find them at the sporting goods store, visit your local skateboarding shop.

Passive Camming Chocks

wedging chocks, pg. 325), while an **active camming chock** mainly uses a camming action (see active camming chocks, pg. 65). In this chapter, I will only discuss passive camming chocks.

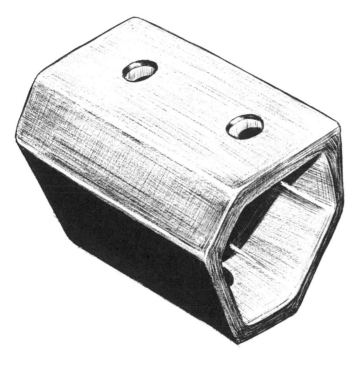

A passive camming chock

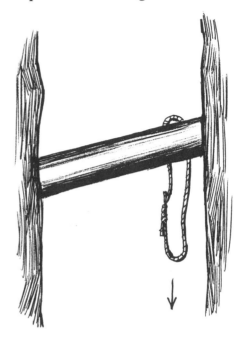

How a passive camming chock cams in a crack

What Is A Passive Camming Chock?

As you climb a crack, you place **chocks** into it. When you are sure that these metal devices are anchored in the crack, you clip your **rope** to them with a **carabiner.** Then, if you fall, your chocks keep you from falling too far. This is how you use chocks to protect yourself while **free climbing** (climbing without using your equipment for progress). If you were **aid climbing,** you would place a chock and then use it to pull yourself up the rock. In this way you would use your chocks to build a ladder up the cliff as you progressed.

A chock can use either a wedging action, a camming (rotating) action, or a combination of the two to hold it in a crack. Depending on how you place it, a passive camming chock will use any one of these methods to keep itself secure. By contrast, a **wedging chock** mostly uses a wedging action (see

A passive camming chock has no active parts. It consists of just two pieces: the head and the sling. Its camming action stems from the natural motion of the head as it positions itself in the crack. This natural motion is what makes the chock passive. In contrast, an active camming chock is pushed into position by its springs.

In the past few years, climbers have started to rely more on active camming chocks than passive ones. This is understandable, since active cams are much quicker to place and can provide protection where passive cams can't. However, this does not mean that passive cams don't have their place on your rack. They are lighter than active cams, and much cheaper. And their construction is very basic. This means that they are reliable. Passive camming chocks do not have little parts which can easily break, and you don't have to oil them.

Note: In the next few pages I will demonstrate different ways to place passive camming chocks. However, all chocks, including passive cams, are directional. This means that *the chock will only hold if it is secured against the direction of force that might pull on it.* A properly-placed chock must usually support both a downward and an outward pull. I explain this in more detail on pg. 329.

Generally, once placed, passive camming chocks are easy to remove. Simply push them in the opposite direction to the way they are cammed and they will come free. The notable exception is the Tri-Cam, which, after it has held a fall, can be very difficult to remove.

Types

There are currently two types of passive camming chocks on the market: the hexagonal chock and Lowe's Tri-Cam. Other manufacturers make hexagonal chocks, but the name Hexentric, the trade name for Chouinard's hexagonal chocks, is the name most climbers use when refering to a hexagonal chock. For clarity, I do the same.

Hexentric

The Hexentric passive cam has six sides. These sides are not equal; the chock is not hexagonally-shaped. It was originally (hence its name), but Chouinard realized that the Hexentric would hold better if it was eccentricly shaped - that is, if its sides were of unequal length.

The eccentric design not only holds better, it also has a wider size range. Instead of offering only two sizes it offers three. Each Hexentric has two width sizes and one length size (the distance between the endwalls). The two widths cam into position, while the length wedges in.

Most Hexentrics are sold without slings. You must add your own slings before you can use these chocks (to learn how, see Slings and Runners, pg.

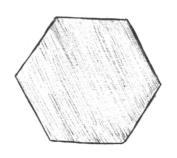
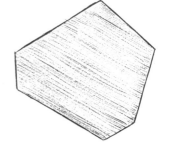

The hexagonal shape   *The eccentric shape*

291). In the past, climbers used the widest nylon cord that could fit because width meant strength. Since the advent of high-strength cord (**Spectra** and **Kevlar**) the holes in Hexentrics are drilled 5.5 mm wide to fit it. These small holes are very advantageous because they give the Hexentric more strength than if the holes were larger.

You can also buy the three smallest Hexentrics (#1, #2, and #3) pre-slung with wire. The advantage of wire is that it is stiff and enables you to reach above your head, or deep in a crack, to place the chock. However, it has the disadvantage of increasing the leverage on a placed chock; if you use a wire-slung hexentric, clip a **runner** to it (see pg. 51).

The smallest Hexentric, the #1, is so small that its holes can be drilled to only a 5 mm diameter. This means that if you buy it without wire you must use 5 mm nylon cord, which is much weaker than the 5.5 high strength Spectra or Kevlar cord the larger Hexentrics are slung with. To get the strongest connection, buy the #1 pre-slung with wire, since wire is stronger than the thin 5 mm nylon.

The Hexentric's small width   *The Hexentric's large width*   *The Hexentric's length*

Hexentrics offer secure protection in a variety of cracks. Naturally, they fit perfectly in wedging positions.

They also cam in **parallel cracks.** Note: the Hexentric will hold better when placed with its sling crossing it, as demonstrated below.

A Hexentric camming in a parallel crack. Notice how the sling crosses the Hex, tightening it.

Hexentrics are not always easy to place. Sometimes they slip into position immediately, but on smoother cracks you can waste valuable time placing them securely. However, the more you practice placing your Hexentrics, the easier it will become to use them.

Hexentrics are available in a wide range of sizes. They start at just under a half an inch and progress all the way to 3 inches. Chouinard used to make even larger sizes, but, unfortunately, they no longer do. You may run across some used ones, though, and if you like climbing wide cracks, buy these. They work well, but you must make sure that they are securely placed. If not, the Hexentric's own weight could pull it out of position.

Another important point about Hexentrics: they are cheap. They usually cost just a few dollars more than most wedging chocks (remember that you must buy cord to sling each Hex). You can ready yourself to climb a wide variety of cracks by buying a complete set of Hexentrics.

A Spring-Loaded Passive Camming Chock

The BigBro (manufactured by Mountain Hardware) is a spring-loaded passive camming chock. It is a two-piece aluminum alloy tube; one piece slides into the other. A spring is wound inside the larger tube, and, at the push of a release button, the smaller tube pops out. To lock the BigBro open, spin its collar against the larger tube.

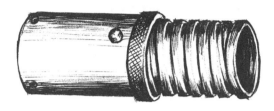

A BigBro

To release the BigBro, unspin the collar and push the smaller tube into the larger one.

BigBros are designed to protect parallel-sided offwidth cracks. The set of four BigBros has a size range of 3.2 to 12 inches.

A BigBro anchors in a crack by passive camming. When you place the chock, make sure its sling (which attaches to one side) is positioned slightly higher than the other side. This ensures that the chock will rotate tighter if it must hold a fall.

On the negative side, BigBros don't work in flaring cracks. They take time to place, and require practice both at placing and **cleaning.**

The Tri-Cam

The Tri-Cam has a very unique shape. This shape gives it versatility; it can fit a wide range of crack shapes and sizes. The Tri-Cam also offers very secure placements: as you pull down on it, it cams tighter.

Lowe sling's their Tri-Cams with sewn **webbing.** Each size of Tri-Cam has a different color of webbing; once you become familiar with these chocks, you can look at your rack and quickly identify the one you need.

A set of Tri-Cams covers a wide range of sizes. They begin at 5/8 of an inch and continue up to 5 1/ 2 inches. The larger sizes are excellent for wide crack protection. If you are using a large Tri-Cam, give it a sharp tug before you load it to be sure it is

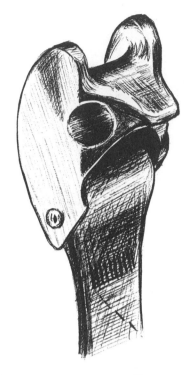

The Tri-Cam

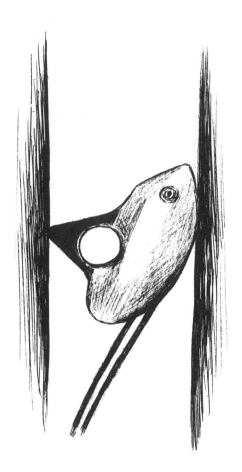

A Tri-Cam camming in a parallel crack

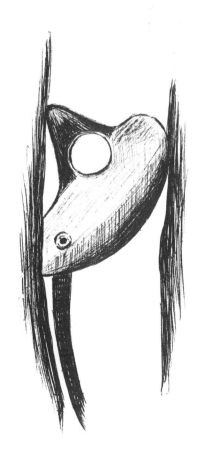

A Tri-Cam camming in a thin crack

securely placed. If it isn't, its own weight could cause it to fall out.

There are three ways to place a Tri-Cam. To utilize its camming action completely, you must run the webbing along the groove behind the chock. Used this way, the Tri-Cam can hold in both parallel and some **flaring cracks.**

For a combination of camming and wedging action (the second way to place a Tri-Cam), let its webbing hang naturally. This gives less of a camming action, and only works when the chock fits exactly into the crack.

The final way to use the Tri-Cam is simply as a wedge. Because of its three-pronged shape, you can successfully wedge a Tri-Cam into some pocket-shaped cracks.

Tri-Cams have a disadvantage: they can be very hard to remove after holding a fall. When you fall, much of the force of your fall is concentrated on the

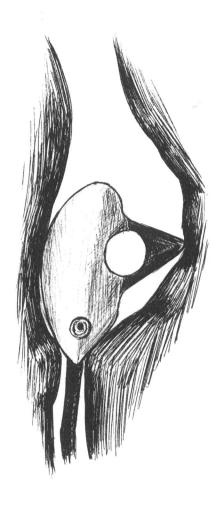

The Tri-Cam wedged in a pocket-shaped crack

Tri-Cam's main prong. With the force of your fall concentrated on it, this prong digs deep into the rock. When this happens it becomes very hard to remove.

The Tri-Cam's rock-breaking ability presents another problem. If you are using a Tri-Cam in weak rock, it could break so much rock that it wouldn't be able to protect you. So be careful where you use your Tri-Cams; they work best in strong granite.

You should practice placing your Tri-Cams before you try to use them on any leads that might stretch your limits. At first, you will find it hard to place Tri-Cams with one hand. And you may have difficulty spotting potential placements. But once you have learned how to use them, Tri-Cams are fairly quick to place, and offer good placement versatility.

Passive Camming Chocks That Aren't Made Anymore

The following passive camming chocks aren't manufactured anymore, but you may find some used ones. For some important information on buying used gear, see pg. 30.

Titons

At one time Forrest manufactured Titons, which are "T" shaped chocks. They were available in 17 different sizes, from 7/16 inch to 7 inches long.

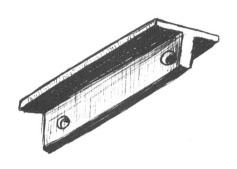

A Titon

You can sling your Titons through the holes on the stem of the "T". Cord and webbing both work with Titons, but Spectra webbing is your best bet, being both stronger and lighter than nylon cord.

For maximum security you must tie the sling to different places on your Titon, depending on how you are going to use it. In the following placement illustrations, take particular notice of how the sling is tied to the chock.

There are a variety of ways to place Titons. The larger ones placed lengthwise work well for wide crack protection. For it to hold, you must tie the sling to the upper end of the Titon. When you apply a load, the sling will pull the Titon, camming it tightly.

You can also place Titons in horizontal cracks. Here you should loop the sling through *two* holes. If you don't, it will get caught between the edge of the Titon and the rock, and could be cut while stopping a fall.

You should practice placing Titons to become efficient with them. They are similar to Tri-Cams in this sense. As they are placed differently than

A Titon in a wide crack

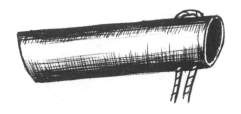

A tube chock

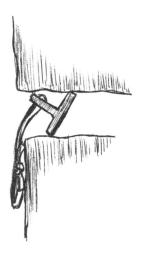

A Titon in a horizontal crack

other chocks, you must become familiar with their use before you rely on them.

Rack your Titons vertically. The longer ones may bang your knees, but by hanging them vertically you leave room on your gear sling for other chocks.

Tube Chocks

A few years ago, Chouinard manufactured a set of tube chocks. These were simply various lengths of extruded aluminum tubing. Each tube had holes for a sling, and tapered ends to securely fit the sides of a crack.

A tube chock provides secure protection in vertical wide cracks. Use it like a Titon: tie the sling in one end, and place this end above the other.

Tube chocks don't work well in other placements. They rotate in horizontal cracks; use them horizontally only in very secure positions, such as in **slots** (but a wedging chock will probably work better!).

Rack your tube chocks like the Titons: sling them vertically to conserve space on your gear sling.

Specifications

Passive camming chock specifications are straightforward. They include only size, strength, and weight. Before you buy a passive cam you should make sure that its specifications fit your needs.

Size Range Or Dimensions

The size range or dimensions of a passive camming chock tell you the size of crack it will fit. Each Tri-Cam has a size range, because its size is variable: it rotates either smaller or larger. A Hexentric has size dimensions, including width and length, which aren't variable (they tell you exactly how large a crack the chock will fit).

Determine the size of chocks you need from the size of the cracks in your area, or the cracks that you like to climb. There is no point in buying, or carrying, wide crack protection if there aren't any wide cracks where you climb!

Strength

A passive camming chock's strength is mainly dependent on the strength of its sling. The metal heads of the chocks are solid and without moving parts, which means they are very strong. So the stronger the sling you use, the stronger your chock will be.

The bend in your sling as it loops through the chock can weaken it. If it is too tight, the fibers on the inside of the bend will stretch less than those on the outside. This uneven stretching damages your sling.

Manufacturers know this now, but some of them might not have realized it a few years ago. This is important if you are thinking of buying a used passive camming chock. The distance between the holes should be at least twice as long as the width of the sling. If they aren't, be aware that your sling will be slightly weaker than it would be otherwise. (See page 271.)

Weight

Although designed to fit most of the same type of cracks as an active camming chock, most passive cams are lighter. On a long climb these lighter chocks will be a relief. Passive cams weigh anywhere from 1 to 10 ounces (their larger sizes present little to no weight advantage over active cams). Remember that you must add a sling to most Hexentrics, so in practice they will be slightly heavier than their listed weight.

Sample Passive Camming Chock Specifications

Type	Strength	Weight	Expansion Range
Hexentric	2425.5 lbs.	2.2-5 ounces	.437-3 inches
Tri-Cam	1810-5200 lbs.	1-9.4 ounces	.62-5.5 inches
BigBro	3200 lbs.	5.4-32.7 ounces	3.2-12 inches

Materials

Manufacturers' use strong, lightweight aluminum alloys in their passive camming chocks. These metals are durable: you can expect your passive cams to be around for many years.

One General Safety Guideline

Placement Is Everything!

Any chock will hold only if you have placed it correctly. A well-placed chock is very secure, whereas the same chock in a bad placement won't support a feather. So to be safe, practice placing your chocks *before* you climb.

Care

A passive camming chock does not require much care. Its one-piece design makes it very tough. Despite this hardiness, you should examine your passive camming chocks occasionally, as you do with all your equipment.

Look For Problems

The rock will scratch up the surface of your chock, but this is normal and won't weaken it. Also keep an eye open for cracks in the chock, although these are unlikely. *If you find any cracks, no matter how small, retire the chock!*

Check The Sling

Keep an eye on your passive cam's sling. It will suffer wear from rock abrasion, dirt, and sunlight (ultraviolet damage), in addition to stress from holding your falls. Check the sling's knot; it can gradually work itself loose. When you retie the knot, remember to leave the ends of the cord at least 2 inches long. This is important because, when you fall on a sling, some of it slips through the knot. These 2 inches will keep the knot tied, even after it slips a bit.

When To Retire Your Passive Camming Chock

Passive camming chocks often last many years. This is because they are made of a single heavy-duty piece of metal. You won't need to retire the chock unless it bends severely or cracks, both unlikely, although they may occur under severe loading (a high fall factor, see pg. 269). You will have to replace the passive camming chock's sling occasionally (see Slings and Runners, pg. 291).

Modifications and Tune-Ups

You will have to replace your passive chock's sling when it gets old. Webbing wears quicker than cord, and will have to be replaced first. Replace webbing when any part of it is cut through, or when it has become faded and stiff. Replace the cord when its sheath wears through or it is cut in some way.

Plastic Tubing

If you have any old style Hexentrics, their sling holes will be too large for Spectra, Genesis, or Kevlar cord. The Hex's holes are 8 or 9 millimeters, depending on its age and size, and the cord is 5.5 millimeters. If you want to sling your Hexentrics with this high-strength cord and keep them from sliding around, you will need to buy some plastic tubing. The tubing fits over the cord and fills the holes in the Hex.

Using plastic tubing on a Hexentric

Accessories

Sling

You must sling most Hexentrics, all Titons, and all tube chocks. You can use either webbing or cord; I recommend cord because it is stronger and will last longer. Use either Spectra, Gemini, or Kevlar cord, because they are very strong.

Plastic Tubing

You can buy plastic tubing at any climbing store: it is quite cheap. It comes in two sizes so to get the best fit take your chocks with you.

Pitons (Pin; Peg)

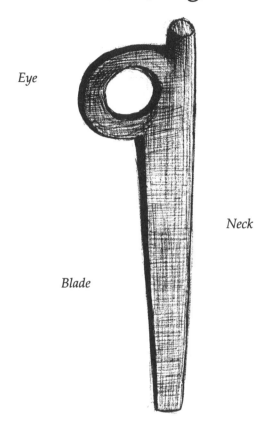

Eye

Neck

Blade

A vertical piton

What Is A Piton?

Pitons are metal wedges designed for use in **aid climbing.** To use a piton you must hammer it into a crack until it wedges securely. When the piton is anchored you can attach your etriers (see pg. 173) to it, climb up them as high as you can, and insert another piton, farther up. In this way you can progress up otherwise impassable sections of rock.

Pitons provide multi-directional **anchors.** This means that, when you hammer a piton into a crack, it will anchor a load that comes from any direction. This is a big advantage over chocks, which are uni-directional anchors: chocks will stop a load only if it comes from the correct direction.

Types

There are several different types of pitons to fit the wide variety of cracks found on most climbs.

Vertical

Vertical pitons are not manufactured anymore because they presented climbers with too many problems. However, I am going to discuss them anyway because you should know their problems and because you need to be able to recognize them if you see any at garage sales or swap meets.

Vertical pitons are made with the eye and the blade along the same plane. Manufacturers don't make vertical pitons anymore because they are not as versatile as horizontals. For example, a vertical piton is useless in a corner crack because the eye sits flush against one side of the corner: there isn't enough room to clip in a **carabiner.**

A vertical piton in a corner crack

A vertical piton does not hold well in vertical cracks that have parallel sides. When you load the piton the only thing keeping it in place is the pressure it exerts against the sides of the crack. Although this pressure may support your body weight, you can't rely on it to hold a fall. Instead, you should hammer the vertical piton into a slot that has solid rock below it; the rock will provide more holding power.

Horizontal

The Lost Arrow - a type of horizontal piton

A horizontal piton has its eye set perpendicularly to the blade. This design allows you to use the horizontal in corner cracks, horizontal cracks, and vertical cracks. In corner cracks, the horizontal's perpendicular eye guarantees that you will be able to clip your carabiner to it.

A horizontal piton in a corner crack

Horizontal cracks are the most secure places in which to hammer a piton. When placing the hori-

zontal piton into a horizontal crack, *remember to hammer the piton with its eye down.* This is the strongest position for the piton in this type of crack.

A horizontal piton in a horizontal crack

The horizontal piton has good holding power in vertical cracks as well. This comes not only from the pressure between the piton and rock, but also from the horizontal's natural rotation (camming action) into the sides of the crack.

A horizontal piton in a vertical crack

There are currently two types of horizontal pitons available: Lost Arrows and Knife Blades/Bugaboos.

Lost Arrows

Lost Arrow pitons were originally designed by John Salathé back in the 1940's. The Chouinard factory has since refined this design and created an excellent version of the original.

Lost Arrows are exceptionally well-designed horizontals. They taper on two planes, along both their depth and their width. The taper along the width allows you to use the Lost Arrow in place of a standard Angle piton (3/4 inch) if necessary. The Lost Arrow is a very durable, forged piton that you can re-use hundreds of times.

Knifeblades/Bugaboos

Knifeblades and Bugaboos both have the same overall shape, but Knifeblades are smaller. Both pitons have very thin blades, thinner than those of Lost Arrows.

A Bugaboo piton

Knifeblades and Bugaboos come drilled with two holes. *Don't clip your carabiner to the hole in the piton's blade:* that hole is there only to reduce the piton's weight. Instead, clip your carabiner to the hole in the angled part of the piton. Clip to this hole in both vertical and horizontal crack placements.

Angles

Angle pitons have a "V"-shaped cross-section. They are designed to fit into wide cracks.

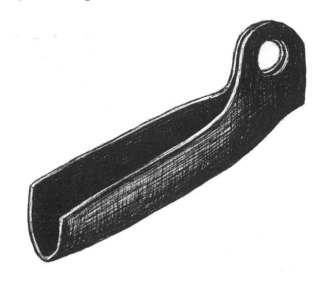

An Angle piton

Angles are very stable pitons. This stability comes from the three-point contact of the Angle's spine and its two edges against both of the crack's sides.

In a horizontal crack place your Angle with its edges down and its spine up. This position provides the most stability and strength against the downward pull of the load.

If you were to place the Angle in the reverse position, with its spine down, it would be much weaker.

In a vertical crack place your Angle so that its edges are on one side of the crack and its spine is on the other.

Bongs

Bongs are larger versions of Angle pitons. To reduce the Bong's weight manufacturers make them out of aluminum and punch holes through their blades at regular intervals.

Aluminum is a fragile metal, and therefore Bongs are fragile. However, if you are careful not to drop them, your Bongs should last a long time.

Although you will usually hammer a Bong into position, occasionally you can slot it as if it were a **wedging chock.** Find a place in the crack that constricts but will still allow the Bong to fit and push

An Angle in a horizontal crack

An Angle in a vertical crack

Stacked Angles

A Bong

the piton into position. Now tug on the Bong to make sure that it will hold. Note: when you wedge a Bong into a crack it becomes a chock. As a chock, the Bong is uni-directional and will stop your fall only if it is positioned in the correct way (that is, if you have properly anticipated the direction of the load make sure the Bong is secure against a pull from that direction).

You cannot always connect a carabiner to your bong after you place it because the rock is in the way. Instead, you must tie a **sling,** or **runner,** through the Bong's holes and then clip your carabiner to the sling. Tie the sling through the holes in the Bong that are closest to the rock, be-

cause these will give your placement the strongest position.

RURP

The short acronym RURP stands for a longer name: the Realized Ultimate Reality Piton. This piton is sold by Chouinard, but Clog sells a similar one called the Micro Razor. Clog's is a little longer than Chouinard's, but not long enough to qualify as a Knifeblade. For convenience I am going to refer to them both by the trade name RURP.

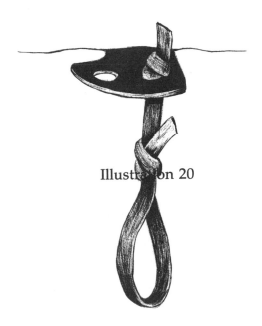

A RURP

A RURP in a horizontal crack

RURPs are very small, hatchet shaped, almost razor-thin pitons. They were designed by Yvon Chouinard for insertion into thin seams that wouldn't permit even a thin Knifeblade to enter.

Even though they are very thin, RURPs are designed to support your body weight. However, a RURP often won't have enough holding power to stop a fall, so you need to be very careful when you use them! You don't need to hammer RURPs very far before they hold, so practice placing your new RURPs before you use them on a climb.

RURPs come drilled with two holes that are designed to take thin **webbing.** You cannot connect a carabiner through these holes because they are too small. After you insert the RURP in a horizontal crack, thread the webbing through the hole in its body. Tie the webbing with an **Overhand knot** (see pg. 175). Clip your carabiner to the webbing.

When you place a RURP in a vertical crack, loop your webbing through the outside (lower) hole. Tie the loop with either a **Ring Bend** (see pg. 293) or a **Double Fisherman's knot** (see pg. 292) and then clip a carabiner to the loop.

Note: Clog sells two models of Micro Razors, one that is similar to Chouinard's, the other which is bent like a Knifeblade. This bent piton has additional holding power in vertical cracks because it rotates, just like a Horizontal piton.

A RURP in a vertical crack

Leeper Z

Ed Leeper designed the Leeper pitons. They have a "Z"-shaped cross-section which provides excellent holding power.

A Leeper Z stacked with angles

Although Leeper Zs provide strong anchors by themselves, they also work well for stacking Angles (see below, pg. 247). You can "nest" the Angles along the Leeper Z's folds. Stacking Angles is useful because it allows you to increase the security of a placement. Where only one piton might easily slide out, several stacked pitons wedge against each other, and tighten against the sides of the crack.

You don't need to hammer the Leeper Z far into a crack for it to become secure. But if you don't drive it all the way to its eye, remember to tie it off with a **hero loop** (see pg. 295).

Technique

Placing pitons is an art. It takes lots of practice to become good at nailing (placing pitons). A good nailer knows just how far he needs to drive a piton for it to hold. And he doesn't overdrive the piton because this makes it hard to remove.

Placing

You need a hammer (see pg. 191) to drive pitons into cracks. Whenever possible, try to hammer your pitons into horizontal cracks. Horizontal cracks are much more secure than vertical ones. When inserting a piton into a horizontal crack, always position it with its eye down. This is the strongest position.

For maximum security you need to use the correct type and size of piton in a crack. The piton you use is determined by the crack's size and shape. Unless the crack is shallow you should be able to insert the piton 2/3 of the way with your hand. Now hammer it in the rest of the way, right up to its eye.

Sometimes you must place a piton in a crack that's too shallow to accept it's entire length. The best technique to use in this situation depends on the crack. In a shallow vertical crack you can sometimes combine a wedging chock or copperhead with a piton. Choose a piton which will barely fit the beginning of the crack, or is even slightly too large, and a likely chock (or **copperhead**). Hammer the piton in until you can just slide the chock between it and the bottom of the crack. Position the chock so that its metal head is above the piton, with its sling hanging below. Now hammer the piton until the chock's head catches securely on it. Clip your rope to the chock.

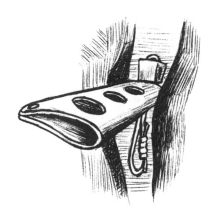

Using a chock with a piton

Often you will not want to use both a chock and a piton at once. The best thing you can do is to find the appropriate piton (one that just fits the crack) and hammer it in until it is almost at the bottom of the crack. Be careful not to pound the piton into the bottom, or bottom out, because with one blow the piton will bounce out of place. You will lose all your security; the placement will be worthless! When the piton is in position, tie a hero loop to it. What's a hero loop?

Hero Loop: A hero loop is a small loop made from 20 inches of 1/2 inch webbing.

Tie the hero loop to your piton with either a **Girth Hitch** or an Overhand Knot (see pg. 175). The Girth Hitch (pg. 46) is the quickest way to attach the loop, but the Overhand Knot is more secure. Slide the hero loop as close as you can to the rock. This will reduce the leverage on the piton.

In shallow cracks you can also stack pitons. Stacking pitons is a method of placing them next to each other so that they help each other push against the sides of a crack. Stacked pitons often provide a more resilient anchor than a single piton can: they have enough flexibility to absorb some of the load. You can stack Horizontal pitons, Angles, Bongs, and Leeper Zs.

Stacked pitons can also be effective in some wide cracks, especially if you have used up your larger Bongs or Angles. (You can stack Bongs, but their security is decreased because they are so large - they have more leverage acting on them.)

When you stack pitons, be sure to thread a sling through each piton's eye. This will keep them attached to each other if they fall out of the crack.

As I noted before, Leeper Z pitons are excellent for stacking with Angles. You can put an Angle along each of the Leeper Z's folds.

If you don't have a Leeper Z, the most secure way to stack Angles is with their spines against the sides of the crack and their edges together.

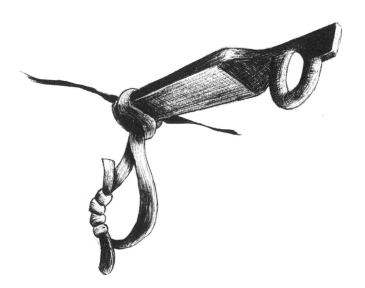

A piton tied-off with a hero loop

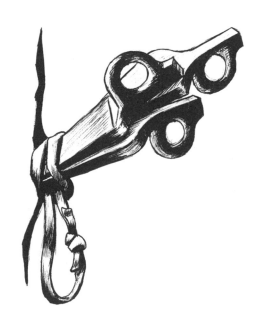

Stacked Lost Arrows

Using Pitons On Expanding Flakes

Expanding flakes are pieces of rock that have separated from the main cliff and remain connected on only one side. They are often very fragile: if you lightly tug one it will vibrate back and forth. It is difficult to place a piton behind an expanding flake. You must be very careful to keep the flake from expanding as you place each piton. If you place too large a piton the crack will widen and the pitons below you may fall out!

Many climbers use chocks instead of pitons as **pieces of aid** behind expanding flakes. Any of the three types of chocks may be necessary, including **active camming, passive camming,** or wedging. If, for some reason, you are out of chocks you can combine a piton with a wire **rivet hanger,** or even a sling (although the latter is very weak). Insert a piton (of a size that just fits behind the flake) with your hand and place the wire above and to the side of it. Attach a runner to the wire.

Combining a piton and a rivet hanger behind an expanding flake

Note that, when you are aid climbing an expanding flake, you should connect yourself, with a daisy chain, to the piece of aid that you are placing. This way if the aid that you are standing on pops out, you might not fall (the daisy chain will keep you connected to the just-placed piece of aid - hopefully this piece will hold!).

Testing

Once you have placed your piton you should test it to make sure that it is secure. Actually, you can often tell how secure the placement will be as you hammer it. Listen to the noise the piton emits as you strike the last few hammer blows. Not always,

but often, a secure piton will give a rising ringing noise. Another way to test the piton is to lightly strike its eye. Your hammer will seem to spring back from a properly-placed piton.

Unfortunately these tests are not always reliable. Experience will help teach you which pitons are well-placed and which ones will pop out with the slightest pull. However, pitons are surprising tools. Many expert nailers have had what they thought were secure pitons pop out on them. (Remember, that, while pitons can be surprising, if it's well-placed the piton can be as strong as a bolt.)

Removing

Removing a piton is a very important job. You must retrieve your metal wedge, but at the same time not lose it to gravity, and also avoid wasting your energy with unnecessary motions. Pitons are much easier to remove when your partner, the one who placed them, has not over-placed them. **Cleaning** your own **pitch** (removing the pitons that you have placed) will teach you a lot about placing them properly. Practice placing and removing pitons before you stake your life on them.

The best way to remove a piton is to hit it (on its head) back and forth, along the direction of the crack. Hit it as far as it will go in each direction before hitting it the other way. The piton will gradually work its way loose, and you can eventually pull it out, either with your hammer's pick or with your hand.

Once you have removed a piton, be careful not to drop it. Sometimes pitons pop out suddenly, and you must catch them before they fall. The best solution is to attach either a sling or a carabiner (which is quicker to connect) to the piton just before the last few blows remove it. But be sure not to hit your carabiner!

If you have trouble removing a piton you can attach a **cow's tail** (a length of sling, **daisy chain,** or chain of carabiners) to it and to your hammer. Yank the cow's tail out quickly in the piton's weakest direction.

Removing a piton from behind an expanding flake can be awkward. You must be careful not to pry the flake off the rock. Take a large piton, one that just fits, and hammer it slightly into the gap. This should open the flake enough to loosen the other, smaller piton. When you have removed this one you should be able to hit the large piton free with just a few taps.

In large cracks, where you might use a Bong, you

can sometimes reach behind the piton. From this position you can easily remove it by hitting it out.

Be sure to tie a sling between it and your rack to catch the piton if it suddenly comes flying out.

Brief History

A climber in the 1860s

No one knows exactly how long climbers have been using pitons. Around 1880 Emil Zsigmondy, a Viennese climber, discussed pitons in his book, *Die Gefahren Der Alpen* (The Dangers of the Alps). So we know that climbers were using pitons before that date.

Before World War Two climbers used soft iron and steel pitons. These early pitons caused numerous problems, the principle one being that they could rarely be reused. This made it very difficult to climb long routes, for it was almost impossible to bring enough pitons to protect the climb.

This situation changed after the Second World War. The change began with a Swiss-born American named John Salathé. He was a skilled blacksmith who used his talent to forge the original Lost Arrow pitons from the axle of a Ford. These axles were made of a hard steel that was far lighter and more durable than the soft metals previously used. Salathé's piton design was revolutionary: it was the father of the Chouinard Lost Arrow that is still sold today.

The other pitons that are in use today were developed in the 1950's and early '60's. First Charles Wilts designed the Knifeblade. His original models were thinner than those that are sold now, but still very durable. In 1957 Jerry Galwas manufactured a set of hard steel pitons, including some large 1 1/4 inch Angles. These were the first successful large pitons. Finally, in 1960, Yvon Chouinard developed the RURP. He designed this piton "specifically for the first ascent of the West Face of Kat Pinnacle in Yosemite."[1]

These newly-designed pitons allowed climbers to ascend the massive granite cliffs of Yosemite. Rock walls that were previously unthinkable were suddenly open for exploration. It was with these pitons that climbers were, and still are, able to succeed on extreme aid climbs.

In recent years climbers have begun using pitons less and less. This is due to two factors. First, pitons destroy the rock they are placed in. Rock destruction has become a major issue in the popular climbing areas, such as Yosemite, where so many climbers climb a particular route that the rock becomes totally altered from its original form. Second, the advent of new equipment (chocks) has made pitons unnecessary in many placements. This is true for wide cracks, slots, thin seams, grooves, and flakes. In many cases, such as flakes, new chocks (such as active camming chocks) make a difficult piton section far easier. The new chocks are designed to work with the rock, to anchor themselves successfully without breaking the rock apart.

However, with fewer climbers using pitons there are fewer knowledgeable people to teach the skill of placing and removing pitons. Some climbers fear placing pitons is becoming a lost art. Others think that this skill isn't disappearing fast enough. But regardless of the controversy, many **big wall** climbs still require pitons. In order to ascend these cliffs you must be able to use pitons well, and this ability only comes through practice.

[1]From the 1989 Chouinard Catalog

Specifications

Size

Of course you cannot adjust a piton's size. So it is very important for you to carry a wide range of pitons, to cover all the potential cracks you may come across on your climb.

The thinnest pitons are the RURPs. RURPs come in one size: nearly razorblade thin. Their blade length varies with the manufacturer, but is around 1/2 an inch.

Knife Blades are 1/8 of an inch thick and are available in two lengths: 3 and 3 1/2 inches. Bugaboos, at 5/32 to 3/16 of an inch, are thicker than Knife Blades. Their lengths vary from 3 1/2 to 4 7/8 inches.

Lost Arrows come in 8 sizes, beginning at 5/32 and continuing to 9/32 of an inch. Their lengths start at 1 3/4 and go to 4 5/8 inches as their widths increase.

Angles begin at 1/2 by 4 inches and progress up to 1 1/2 by 6 inches. The Standard Angle is 3/4 by 5 5/8 inches.

Bongs take over where Angles leave off. They vary from 2 to 4 inches wide and are 6 inches long.

Finally, there are 7 sizes of Leeper Z pitons. They come in four standard sizes, ranging from 1/4 by 2 inches to 9/16 by 3 1/2 inches. The last three standard sizes are available in shorter versions with a length of 1 1/2 to 1 3/4 inches.

Weight

Weight is a very important factor in choosing aid climbing gear. If you're not careful, you can easily find yourself lugging over 40 lbs. of gear up a cliff, plus your **haulbag**-full of equipment! The only way to reduce this weight is to bring along just the gear that is absolutely necessary. Naturally this is very hard to predict beforehand! Only experience will teach you how much gear to bring on any particular climb.

For general reference, pitons weigh between half an ounce (a RURP) and over 7 ounces (a large Angle).

Materials

Most modern pitons are made from chrome-moly (molebdenum) steel. This material is very hard, strong, and lightweight. A chrome-moly piton can be re-used many times before it wears out. This incredible durability more than offsets the chrome-moly piton's high cost.

In general, hard metals, such as steel, are very strong but brittle, especially in cold weather. Chrome-moly is an alloy metal with the strength of steel but the flexibility of alloy.

Soft metal pitons, such as soft iron and steel, were popular in the past and are still made by some European manufacturers. They are cheap and provide good permanent anchors (fixed pitons). However, when you use them you will find that they have several problems. They don't survive repeated pounding for very long; often insertion or removal from a crack will force them to bend. And because they anchor so well they are very hard to remove; this characteristic can make them hard to re-use on a climb. The soft metal's anchoring ability comes from its habit of meshing into a crack, following its curves and blending with the rock. In addition, soft metal is heavy, much heavier than chrome-moly.

Quality pitons made today are either stamped or forged. Manufacturers use a tool called a die to stamp (cut) pitons out of thin metal sheets. Forged pitons are made by heating and forming the metal into its final shape.

Note: don't use cast pitons. Manufacturers cast pitons only when the metal is of such bad quality that they cannot stamp or forge it. If you suspect that a manufacturer may be selling cast pitons, call and ask him. No reliable manufacturers (including Chouinard, SMC, and Clog, and others) use casting to manufacture their pitons.

General Safety Guidelines

Always Use More Than One Piton!

Never trust your life to one piton! Use at least three securely-placed pitons for an anchor (see pg. 53). Place your pitons as securely as you can - if one fails you must trust the next one below to catch your fall.

Care

Pitons are made to be pounded. However, this doesn't mean you should drop them at every opportunity! Be particularly careful with any aluminum pitons you might carry (such as Bongs); they are much more fragile than your others.

When To Retire Your Piton

A modern chrome-moly piton is designed and manufactured for durability. Manufacturers recognize the need for a reusable piton, and chrome-moly is their answer. Such a piton can last many years, but its lifetime depends on how frequently you use it, and in what kind of rock. Chrome-moly pitons will become harder and more brittle each time you use them, until eventually they will crack.

Examine your pitons before and after every climb. Retire a piton when you discover any cracks, no matter how small. A crack seriously weakens the piton. Look for cracks around the eye of horizontal pitons; on Angles cracks tend to occur on the back (the bottom of the V).

Key Point

"A portaledge is not a totally safe, stable ledge. ... Your portaledge may become unbalanced and suddenly flip sideways ... if you weren't connected to your (separately) anchored rope you could wake up while falling through the air!"

See page 257

Portaledges

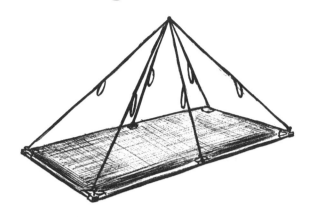

A portaledge

What Is A Portaledge?

The portaledge is one of the great achievements of hi-tech rock climbing gear. It is in fact a portable ledge which you haul with you up the cliff! It is made with a metal frame that supports a cloth bed, and a suspension system that connects the entire apparatus to the rock. Once you have securely attached your portaledge to the cliff, you can sit on it, sleep on it, or have lunch on it, and all of this in comfort!

When Do Climbers Use Portaledges?

Big wall climbs are so high that they often take several days to complete. Consequently, you, the big wall climber, must find places to sleep as you journey up the cliff. But big walls usually have sheer faces with few ledges. And these ledges are rarely very large: some may be two feet wide, others not more than a few inches. So finding a ledge to sleep on is very difficult. If you do find one, you will be lucky to find it at the right time. More than likely you will come across the ledge in the morning, when you still have a full day of climbing in front of you. In other words, the ledge, when it exists, will often be useless for sleeping on.

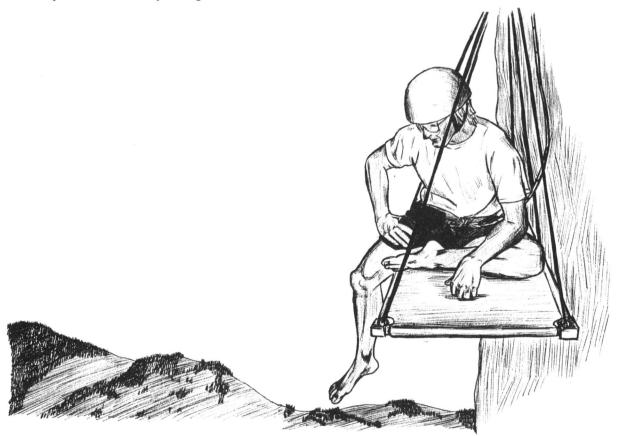

A climber using a portaledge

A portaledge is the hi-tech solution to this problem. Instead of relying on the rock to provide you with a place to sleep, bring your bed with you! A portaledge has one additional advantage over a rock ledge: it comes with a waterproof rainfly to protect you from big wall storms. So bring a portaledge on any multi-day climb you make, whether it is up the tallest rock cliff in the world, or a mere 1000-footer!

Brief History

A climber in the 1860s

Climbers first began to sleep on the cliffs when they started climbing big walls, back in the late 1800's. At first it was easy to find wide ledges because the routes were not very difficult (climbers weren't as skilled as they are now). But as climbers grew more skilled and their routes got harder, they had more trouble finding a comfortable ledge upon which to set their blankets. So they began bringing their hammocks up the cliffs with them. By anchoring each end of the hammock in a crack, these early adventurers could sleep in comfort, even on vertical rock.

Gradually climbers altered their hammock's design to suit their needs. They made the hammock wide in the chest area, so it would be more comfortable, and they added a flap to protect them from the rain. The more advanced hammocks had a length of cord connected from one end to the other to keep the flap up, off the climber's head. And the open side of the flap zippered closed, for total weather protection.

Unfortunately, hammocks are not very comfortable for sleeping in. They force your back into a bowed position. Maintaining this position through a long storm, or even over several nights on the cliff, can be quite painful. And, to rig a hammock you need to find two cracks, or **bolts,** that are the correct distance apart to support its ends. Finding these properly-spaced cracks can be difficult, especially when there are two or more climbers, each having a hammock! Despite all these problems, until quite recently big wall climbers had no workable alternative to using their hammocks.

In the early 60's Warren Harding designed the Bat Tent. The Bat Tent was an innovative hammock design that hung from only one point.

The bat tent was easy to set up. However, it was too uncomfortable: it forced the climber into

A Bat Tent

a tight position that didn't allow easy movement - a terrible problem if you're restless. Also, it wasn't totally rainproof because water could get into the hole formed at its connection point.

Then Greg Lowe came up with the Lurp tent, which was the prototype design for the modern portaledge. The Lurp tent had an aluminum frame and flat bedding. It hung from one point at the top of its rainfly.

The Lurp tent's design was excellent for waiting out a storm: it was rainproof, comfortable, and allowed the climber to sit up and move around. It is these features that have made the basic Lurp tent design (the modern portaledge) the only really functional bed on the market for a climber.

Portaledge Design

The portaledge gets its structural stability from the integration of its frame, bed, and suspension system. The metal frame provides a strong but flexible structure. The cloth bed stabilizes the frame by tightly wrapping around it. And finally the suspension system supports the frame in several locations: at each corner and in the middle of each side. There shouldn't be more than six such locations, because so many suspension straps would be inhibiting. Some portaledges allow you to adjust the tension of the cloth by tightening their built-in tensioning straps.

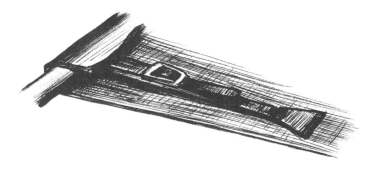

Bed tensioning system

Every commercial portaledge comes with a rainfly, which is very important because storms are common on big walls. You will naturally want to be protected from them; a cold, wet storm can be very dangerous, perhaps causing frostbite or hypothermia.

Portaledges are easy to assemble and disassemble. You can carry one disassembled in your haulbag, then assemble it whenever you want to bivouac (set up camp). Practice rigging your portaledge before you take it on a climb; you must be able to quickly and easily assemble or disassemble it, while hanging from the rock.

You may decide to pre-assemble your portaledge and haul it up the cliff, outside of your **haulbag.** This allows you to quickly set the portaledge up at every **belay station,** which means you can sit on it and **belay** your partner in comfort as he **leads** the next **pitch.** In addition, hauling the pre-assembled portaledge saves you from the time-consuming tasks of setting it up every sunset and taking it down every sunrise.

However, if you haul the assembled portaledge up the rock, it must endure severe abrasion, and you must keep it from snagging on small flakes and ledges. I recommend that on low-angle big walls you carry your dis-assembled portaledge in your haulbag, while on vertical rock you haul it separately, pre-assembled.

Improvise A Portaledge

Commercial portaledges, at approximately $300, are outrageously expensive. And, while this is understandable, since portaleges are extremely hi-tech pieces of gear, the high price is too much for most climbers. But there is an answer to this problem: improvise! You can bring practically anything up a cliff, given the time and determination, so coming up with a cheap, workable portaledge shouldn't be much trouble.

The best portaledges are stable, durable, lightweight, waterproof, and cheap. An improvised portaledge is usually able to meet at least two of these requirements. For example, a 6-foot by 3-foot 1/2-inch plywood board is very stable, and very cheap. Although it isn't extremely durable, it should be able to survive one big wall. Unfortunately, the plywood is quite heavy, and comes without a rainfly, although with a little ingenuity you could rig it with a plastic tarp.

An even better do-it-yourself portaledge is the typical lawnchair (use the long, lie-down version). This not-so-hi-tech device actually meets three of the five requirements: it is stable, lightweight, and cheap! However, it isn't very durable - if you take it up a big wall, tape its edges thoroughly with duct tape (and bring another role of tape for mid-route repairs). It isn't rain-proof either, and is very drafty (while you could protect yourself from the rain with a tarp, cold wind will easily slice up through the lawn chair's netting). The lawn chair works best during the summer!

Technique

Anchoring A Portaledge

Anchoring a portaledge means connecting it securely to the cliff. To do this you need several secure points of **protection** which will act as your **anchor**. Wherever you have such protection you can hang a portaledge, whether this is on a small ledge or even against a sheer rock face. Note: I don't recommend rigging a portaledge so that it hangs free beneath an overhang, because your anchors won't be as secure and the portaledge will be very unstable, since it has no vertical wall to support it.

Anchoring a portaledge properly is very important, because if the anchors fail you could lose your bed! Note that you should always remain tied to a **rope** that is connected to separate anchors so that, if your portaledge falls, you don't. I discuss anchoring thoroughly, beginning on pg. 53. Before

you try any leading (or definitely before you attempt to climb a big wall!) you should read, understand, and practice setting up anchors until you know how to set a strong, safe anchor quickly in any situation.

Any secure anchor consists of a number of separate points of protection. Two, well-placed bolts are generally considered secure, as are 3 or 4 well-placed **chocks** or **pitons**. To connect your portaledge to the anchor, you will need several **carabiners** and runners. Attach a carabiner to each point of protection, and then a **runner** to each carabiner. The runners must meet, and be under equal tension, at one point. Here you attach a **locking carabiner** (or two carabiners with their gates opposed - see pg. 130). Connect your portaledge's suspension system to the locking carabiner. This setup divides the portaledge's weight equally among the protection points, which reduces the load any one point must support.

Anchor Yourself Separately

Always remain tied to an anchored rope when you are on a big wall! And always anchor this rope to a different set of anchors than those you use for your portaledge! This is very important! You need the security of backup anchors, in case your portaledge's anchors fail, or the portaledge breaks, or you roll over in your sleep and fall off the ledge!

Specifications

There are only two specifications you must consider before you buy a portaledge: its size and its weight. Size is important, especially if you are a tall person or you want to sleep two people on one ledge (in which case you need a double). And minimal weight is mandatory in a portaledge, which you haul up long climbs that demand a lot of other heavy gear.

Here are the portaledge specifications from two manufacturers, A5 and Fish.

A5's single portaledge is described as measuring 2 feet, 3 inches wide by 6 feet, 9 inches long. It weighs 9.5 pounds, although with the rainfly it weighs 12 pounds. Fish's single portaledge is 2 feet, 8 inches wide by 6 feet, 5 inches long. It weighs 8 pounds - 11 pounds with the rainfly.

A5 makes two types of double portaledge. The first is called the Double Ledge (double), the second is called the Wall Condo (condo). The double

A portaledge's suspension straps connected to its anchors

is 3.5 feet wide by 6 feet long. It weighs 11 pounds - 14 pounds with the rainfly. The condo is the same size as the single, but has the addition of a hammock attached underneath it. It weighs 10.5 pounds - 13 pounds with the rainfly.

Unfortunately, Fish doesn't sell a double portaledge.

Materials

A portaledge must be strong enough to support the weight of you and your gear, yet survive buffeting from storms, and abuse from rock abrasion. It must also be lightweight, and its rainfly rainproof. So the materials that manufacturers use for their portaledges are important, since they must meet these requirements with as little compromise as possible.

Manufacturers make their portaledge frames out of aluminum alloy or Chromoly (Chrome Molebdenum) tubing. Both of these metals work well: aluminum alloy is lighter and more flexible than Chromoly, but it is also weaker. Manufacturers use aluminum alloy for the frame's corners. These corners are often square (so they don't roll along the rock), but sometimes round, and are machined to fit the frame's tubing exactly.

The bedding material used should be strong, and unlikely to rip. Manufacturers use tough pack cloth material: it is both very strong and durable. Note that one side of the bedding (along the length) should have scuffguards (extra heavy-duty cloth, such as thick vinyl-coated nylon). This is the side that sits against the rock when you set the portaledge up, and it must be durable enough to survive rock abrasion.

The rainfly must be wind and rain-proof. Manufacturers have found that 200 denier Oxford cloth works very well (the denier number indicates the thickness of the fabric). The rainfly also needs scuffguards on one side and its two corners (the side that lies against the rock). It should also have some method of closing securely: two common ways are with either a zipper or a drawcord.

The portaledge's suspension system should be made of nylon **webbing.** It needs to be adjustable, so you can make the portaledge horizontal no matter where you are. The webbing should have attachment points built in, such as **daisy chains** or individual loops. These attachment points are great for organizing your gear: you can clip different

An attachment point on a webbing suspension strap

bundles of equipment up and out of the way until you are ready to sort them.

The hauling bag that holds the portaledge is also important. Some manufacturers offer thin hauling bags that won't survive abrasion from the rock, so watch out for this. These bags seem designed more for carrying the portaledge when you're on the ground than when you're hauling it up the cliff (if you have such a bag, consider dismantling your portaledge and putting it into your haulbag). A good, strong hauling bag (such as one made of vinyl-coated nylon - on the rock side anyway) is ideal, because it encloses the portaledge, providing a smooth surface that won't snag the rock as you climb.

General Safety Guidelines

When Using Your Portaledge, Don't Unclip From Your Rope!

A portaledge is not a totally safe, stable ledge. It is designed to provide a place to eat, sleep, or relax. However, it doesn't offer enough security for you to unclip from your rope! Your portaledge may become unbalanced and suddenly flip sideways. It can even rip down the middle (unlikely, but possible). In either situation, if you weren't connected to your anchored rope you could wake up while falling through the air!

Care

A portaledge is designed to last many years of big wall climbing. Since it is not a life-supporting piece of gear, it doesn't need to remain as strong as your rope does, for instance. In other words, you can use your portaledge until it is ready to break - and that should be a long way off.

There is not much you can do to care for your portaledge while climbing. The rock will scrape it, the rain will cover it (hopefully only the rainfly - if you set it up in time!), and the sun will damage it. But this is the kind of abuse that portaledges are designed to withstand. It is contact with other things, such as battery acid, solvents, and knives, that can really damage a portaledge. Try to keep your portaledge away from such substances; store it in a clean, dry, dark place, preferably the same place you store your rope (see pg. 284).

When To Retire Your Portaledge

I have already mentioned that your portaledge should last you many years, perhaps your entire climbing career. But this depends on the events that go on during these years. For instance, if your portaledge somehow falls 2000 feet to the ground, it will be nothing but a useless pile of cloth and metal!

You can usually repair any part of your portaledge. If the bedding rips, you can buy new bedding. If you accidentally cut a strap on the suspension system, you can replace it. You can even replace a broken frame. But the real question is, is it worth saving and repairing your portaledge, or will it be cheaper in the end to simply buy a new one? To make this decision, figure out what parts need to be replaced, and call the manufacturer. Describe the damage to him; he will in turn give you his opinion about what to do.

Pulleys

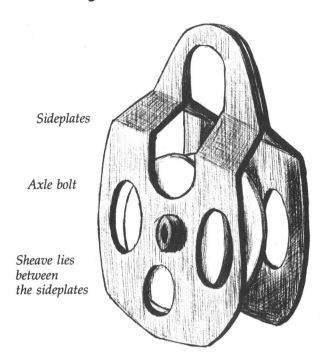

Sideplates

Axle bolt

*Sheave lies
between
the sideplates*

A pulley

What Is a Pulley?

A pulley is a wheel, or sheave, mounted to spin around an axle. Many lubricated bushings or ball bearings keep the sheave's spin around the axle even and smooth. Two sideplates encircle the sheave, connected to it at the two ends of the axle. The sideplates meet above the wheel, where there is a hole for you to connect the pulley (with a carabiner) to an anchor.

What Do Climbers Do With Pulleys?

Pulleys are essential on long, overnight climbs. On such climbs you must take along a lot of personal gear packed into a **haulbag** (see Haulbag, pg. 207), gear such as food, water, cooking equipment, a **portaledge** (see pg. 253), and a sleeping bag. Hauling this gear up the rock after you is hard work. Pulleys make the job easier.

When you use a pulley to haul, it becomes part of a hauling system. The other parts of the system include your **rope, carabiners, ascenders,** and **anchors** (see pg. 53). Of course there is also the load you must haul, and you, the person who must expend the energy to haul it.

For a pulley to work effectively in a hauling system, its design must meet certain requirements. First, its sheave must be large enough (in diameter) so that it won't stress your rope. A sound rule of thumb: the sheave's diameter should be 4 times larger than the width of your rope. This means, for example, that you need a 2-inch sheave for an 11-millimeter rope.

Then you need to decide whether you want to use a single-sheaved pulley or one with double sheaves. For use in hauling systems you will need only a single sheave. A double sheave is needed in complex setups (such as some rescue operations) where you must pass a rope through the same pulley twice, or when you are hauling with two ropes.

A double-sheaved pulley has a middle plate, called a becket. The becket rotates, so you can connect it to the two sideplates or leave it at the bottom of the pulley.

The pulley's sideplates must extend beyond the sheave. This design keeps your rope running freely, even when the pulley lies against the rock.

Extended sideplates allow the rope to run freely

The pulley's sideplates should be able to swing. A swinging sideplate spins freely around the axle, which allows you to connect the pulley to the middle of your rope.

A fixed sideplate is very awkward to connect to a rope, especially when you're on a cliff: you must thread the rope through the pulley, beginning at one end of the rope and continuing until the pulley is in the proper position. So avoid pulleys with fixed sideplates.

The sideplates must contain carabiner holes.

These holes should be large enough to accept all carabiner sizes: 3/4 inch holes work well. Some pulleys even have holes that are large enough to accept two carabiners. If you want a very strong connection, two carabiners will provide it.

The next thing you must consider is whether you want a pulley mounted on a bearing or on a bushing. Not all manufacturers give you this option: SMC/Russ Anderson and Climb High are two manufacturers that do.

The bearing design contains many ball bearings that are sealed in a hub. This seal is permanent, which means that if there are any problems, such as the sheave won't spin, you cannot break the seal to fix them. However, the seal also keeps dirt and grit from fouling up the bearings. In addition, sealed bearings spin smoother than bushings, but are more expensive.

A pulley's bushings

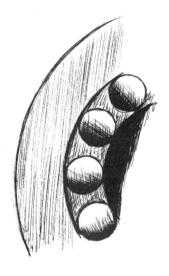

A pulley's bearings

Bushings are lubricated metal sleeves. Pulleys with bushings are not sealed, and are therefore subject to being fouled by dirt, which ruins their spin. However, because the bushings aren't sealed you can disassemble, clean, and re-grease them when they become dirty.

To summarize: a pulley with bushings is cheaper, requires more maintenance, but works fine if the cliff doesn't have much loose dirt or grit. If you have the money, and especially if you plan on using the pulley in dirty terrain, buy one with bearings.

Note: you will come across some pulleys that have neither bearings nor bushings. They have nylon sheaves that spin on a simple bolt, without either bearings or bushings. These pulleys are inexpensive and lightweight, but don't spin well when loaded with more than 10 pounds. However, they are cheap, so if you are intending to haul only lightweight loads, they will work.

Alternative Pulley Designs

There are two pulley designs that are distinct from a standard pulley. The first is the knot-passing pulley, while the second is the edge roller.

A Knot-Passing Pulley

Russ Anderson manufacturers a knot-passing pulley. Its sideplates are made with enough room above the sheave to allow a knot tied in a 1/2 inch rope (maximum size) to pass through.

You won't need this pulley in most of your climbing adventures. It is designed for times when you need to tie two ropes together, which you won't have to do except in very unusual circumstances, such as a rescue or for a long haul (longer than your single length of rope).

Rollers

While not strictly a member of the pulley family, rollers are similar devices. They feature a rolling cylinder which you place on the sharp edge of a

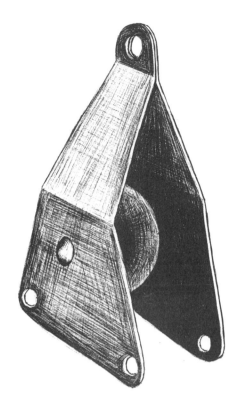

A Russ Anderson knot-passing pulley

A one-piece roller

cliff or building. The roller allows your rope to pass freely over this edge, without suffering abrasion.

There are two types of rollers on the market: one-piece rollers and a two-piece rollers. The one-piece version works well for mounting on squared-off edges, such as those at the tops of buildings.

The two-piece roller offers rope protection from edges of varying angles. You must buy two small **oval screw links** (see pg. 136) to connect a two-piece roller together.

A roller is an extra piece of gear that you won't need for rock climbing. However, you might consider buying one if you plan on participating in some rescues, or perhaps doing some **bouldering** or caving.

Hauling Systems

A hauling system is a configuration of gear that helps you haul a load. Different hauling systems offer different mechanical advantages, which determines how much work you must do to raise the load. For example, a 2:1 mechanical advantage means that, for a given pull, you must lift only half the weight of the load. So, if you were hauling a 200 lb. load, and you had a perfect 2:1 advantage, it would take a mere 100 lbs. pull to raise the load. A good mechanical advantage allows one person to haul a load far heavier than he would otherwise be able to lift.

Unfortunately, a mechanical advantage only makes each individual lift easier. To haul the load up the cliff, you must still expend as much energy as if you had no mechanical advantage at all. This is due to the nature of mechanical advantages: the distance you must haul the load increases as the load decreases. So, with a 2:1 advantage, hauling a 200 lb. load up 100 ft. would be the same as hauling a 100 lb. load up 200 ft. However, since human bodies are built for endurance, climbers find it easier to spend less energy over a longer period of time. Thus, they rig a hauling system (with a good mechanical advantage) whenever they must haul a load.

Since rigging a hauling system takes time, you should carefully decide which situation calls for a mechanical advantage. For example, if you need to make one short haul in the entire day, and it is a light load, you probably won't want to set up a hauling system. If, on the other hand, you need to make several hauls during a day you will probably want a mechanical advantage to help you, unless the load is extremely lightweight.

Hauling systems use block and tackle to create their mechanical advantages. Tackle is another name for a rope, while a block is a pulley or similar device that bends the rope and allows it to run through the bend. Each bend in the rope changes the mechanical advantage, and makes the hauling easier. However, each bend also creates friction between the block and tackle. A pulley reduces this friction to a minimum, while some substitute device, such as a carabiner, increases the friction. The more friction, the harder it is to pull the rope. So, although in a pinch you can substitute your carabiners for pulleys, they will make you work much harder.

Note that you will also spend more energy than necessary whenever you pull away from the line of the load you are hauling. This might be unavoidable if you had to place a directional pulley over a cliff edge to avoid abrading your rope.

Ascenders (see pg. 75) are critical components in any cliff-side hauling system. Ascenders act as ratchets: they allow you to pull the rope up but prevent it from sliding back down when you let go. Handleless ascenders work very well, although handled ascenders are easier to move along the rope because you can grip them easily. If you don't have any ascenders, use a **Prusik knot** (see pg. 176). You will need to weight certain ascenders for them to ratchet properly: I will tell you which ones when necessary. Use whatever is easily available to you as a weight (for example, a **rack** full of gear works well), and clip it to the ascender with a carabiner.

You can use standard carabiners to connect your hauling system together, but **locking carabiners** are safer.

Your Anchors Must Be Strong

You will be rigging your hauling system at the end of every **pitch**, at the **belay station**. The belay station may be a ledge, but often you won't be so lucky: it will consist of several anchors to which you connect yourself and your hauling system. It's difficult to work in such conditions, so take your time and be efficient (to save valuable climbing and hauling energy).

The anchors supporting your hauling system must be able to support twice the load you are hauling. (To learn how to rig an anchor, see pg. 53). The reason is simple: on one side the anchor must hold the load you're hauling, while on the other side it must support the load you exert while pulling the load up.

I discuss three different hauling systems below: the Yosemite Lift, the Traveling Pulley, and the Z Rig. They provide 1:1, 2:1, and 3:1 mechanical advantages respectively. I then demonstrate a 4:1 system, the Piggyback. The first three are systems you should learn, while the fourth gives you the ability to haul really heavy loads, if necessary. You can rig many other hauling systems: with enough gear and anchors, you could create a 32:1 mechanical advantage, or higher. However, this would be useless for rock climbing, because it's far too slow and complex to set up.

Note: describing a hauling system makes it sound far more complex than it actually is. I think the illustration at the end of each description will help you understand what I am trying to say.

You should practice rigging any hauling system (rig it on a tree branch, a rafter, or a pull-up bar) before you use it on the cliffs. Once you have rigged a system a few times, setting it up on a cliff will not be such a challenge.

The Yosemite Lift (1:1)

The Yosemite Lift is simple to set up but gives no mechanical advantage. It is a 1:1 system, which means that you will lift one pound of load for every pound of force you exert. However, the Yosemite Lift does direct your rope downward so that you can use your body weight, and particularly your legs, to haul. This will give your hands and arms as much of a rest as possible so that you will have their strength to climb the next pitch.

To rig the Yosemite Lift, you will need 2 secure anchors (although in a pinch you can get away with a single - **bombproof** - one), one pulley, and 2 ascenders. Attach your rope to the pulley, and the pulley to the anchor (with a carabiner). Now connect an upside-down, weighted, and anchored ascender to the loaded side of the rope. Clip (with a carabiner) an **etrier** (see pg. 173) or a **runner** (shorter than your leg, about half its length) to a second ascender, which you connect to the free end of your rope, near the pulley. The Yosemite Lift is illustrated on the next page.

Hauling with the Yosemite Lift is simple. Place

length of rope. Clip an upside-down ascender to the pulley and attach it to the long section of rope. Clip your second ascender, weighted and upside-down, to the lower anchor (the third one) and attach it, below the first ascender, to the long section of rope.

The last step is to tie a Figure-Eight-On-A-Bight onto the free side of the short length of rope. The resulting loop gives you a handhold with which to pull. The Traveling Pulley system looks like this.

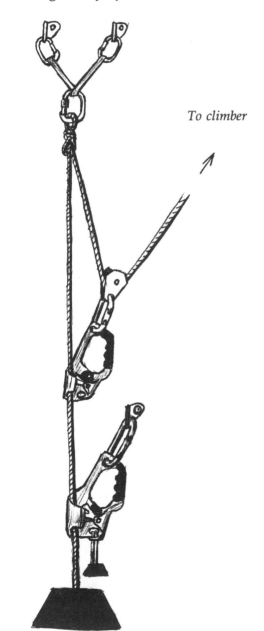

To climber

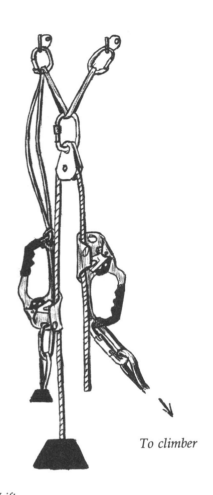

The Yosemite Lift

your foot into the etrier and push down. The load will rise. (On heavier loads you will have to push down with your entire body.) When your foot is fully extended, slide the attached ascender back up to the pulley. The other ascender, the one that's anchored, prevents the load from slipping back down when you reposition your foot.

The Traveling Pulley (2:1)

The Traveling Pulley system provides a 2:1 mechanical advantage. To set up this rig you need 2 anchors, 1 pulley, and 2 ascenders.

Clip a locking carabiner to the upper anchor. Then tie your haul rope to this carabiner with a **Figure-Eight-On-A-Bight** knot (see pg. 201). Leave just enough rope on the short end to haul with. How much rope this should be depends on how long a pull (fetch) you want to make (8 feet is adequate).

Now place a pulley halfway along this short

To climber

The Traveling Pulley

To haul, pull the rope up. When you have pulled as far as you can, reach over and slide the hauling ascender back down the long side of the rope. The lower ascender will keep the load from sliding back down while you do this. Repeat the pulling motion until you are done.

Unfortunately, the Traveling Pulley system will fatigue your arms quickly. This disadvantage makes the system useful only for short, light hauls. If you have heavier hauling to do, use the Z-Rig.

The Z Rig (3:1)

The Z Rig hauling system gives you a 3:1 mechanical advantage for hauling. It requires 3 anchors, 2 pulleys, and 2 ascenders. The Z Rig is similar to the Traveling Pulley system; it simply adds another pulley, thereby creating a 3:1 system.

Tie your rope to the upper anchor lying farthest from you with a Figure-Eight-On-A-Bight. Leave at least 12 feet between the knot and the rope's end. Clip a weighted, upside-down ascender to an anchor that is at least three feet below the two upper anchors. Attach this ascender to the loaded side of the rope. Attach a second upside-down ascender to this rope, just above the other ascender. Connect a pulley to the free end of the rope and the upper ascender. Now run the rope through the second pulley and attach this pulley to the second upper anchor. Finally, tie a loop into the free end of the rope (with an overhand knot), and clip your etrier or foot sling to it.

To haul, step down on your etrier or foot sling. This will pull the lower pulley and its ascender up to the upper pulley, hauling the rope with it. When the lower pulley prevents you from hauling any further, slide it back down to its starting position. The lower ascender will keep the load from slipping back while you do this.

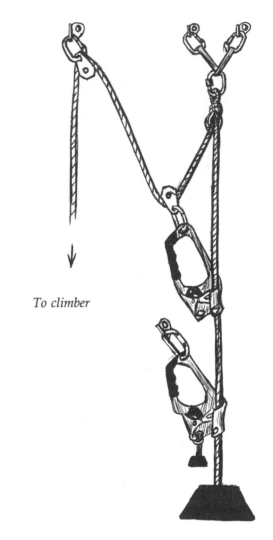

To climber

The Z rig

The Piggyback Hauling System

The Piggyback hauling system, or "Pig", provides a 4:1 mechanical advantage. Although it allows you to haul heavy loads, it is not very useful for most rock climbing situations. For one thing, you won't need the 4:1 advantage for the loads you will be hauling up the rock; they just won't be that heavy (if they are you better reconsider your equipment list!). The Pig is a slow hauling system: it takes four times as many pulls to complete the haul as a 1:1 system. This is a big disadvantage on a big wall where speed is an essential ingredient for success.

The Piggyback rig is complex to set up. Although it only needs the same number of pulleys (3), anchors (3), and ascenders (2) as the Z rig, the Pig requires 3 sections of rope. This extra rope is heavy, bulky, and takes time to sort, all of which make it a hassle to bring on a big wall where equipment management is already a problem.

The Piggyback hauling system looks like this:

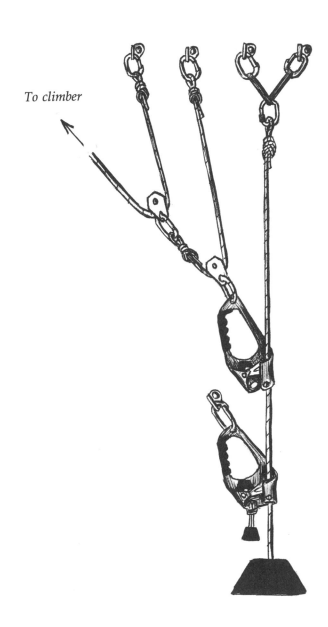

To climber

The Piggyback

heavy duty. Light-duty pulleys accept up to a 1/2-inch rope whereas heavy-duty pulleys accept a maximum 5/8-inch rope. For standard hauling while rock climbing you will need only the light-duty pulley.

Pulley sheave sizes range from 2-4 inches in diameter. It is important to maintain the proper safety ratio between sheave diameter and rope width: it must be at least 4:1. This ration insures that the pulley doesn't bend the rope too much, thereby weakening it. For example, a 1/2-inch rope is the largest rope you can use with a 2-inch pulley sheave; any larger and the ratio would be broken. A 5/8-inch rope works with a 2.5-inch pulley sheave. However, larger sheaves are even better; the big bends in your rope are, in addition to not weakening the rope, easier to pull. Of course, a large sheave also weighs more and is bulkier than a small one. For most of the hauling you will be doing a 2 to 2.5-inch sheave will work fine.

Strength

Rock climbing pulleys are very strong. Standard-duty models are rated from 4100-6000 lbs. Heavy-duty models are much stronger: they range from 9000-13000 lbs.

Unless you are involved in rescue work or similar heavy hauling you won't need a heavy-duty pulley. Standard-duty pulleys will easily withstand the stress of basic equipment hauling. However, remember that any directional pulley must withstand a force equal to twice the load that you are hauling.

Weight

Pulleys can be very heavy. They start off at a reasonable 3 ounces for a 2-inch nylon-sheaved pulley and go all the way to over 3 lbs. for a 4-inch heavy duty model. A good, standard duty 3-inch aluminum-sheaved pulley weighs around 13 ounces. This is about the heaviest pulley you will need to bring up a cliff with you, unless you are involved in rescue operations or similar ventures.

Materials

Pulley manufacturers use materials that offer various compromises between light weight and high strength. For common hauling, manufacturers make lightweight and minimum strength (still strong) standard-duty pulleys; for heavier loads

Specifications

Size

When you are buying a pulley you need to make two size-related decisions: how thick a rope will the pulley have to accept and how large is the pulley sheave's diameter.

The maximum width of rope a pulley will accept depends on whether the pulley is made for light or they offer heavier but very strong heavy-duty pulleys.

For standard-duty pulley sheaves, manufacturers use lightweight materials such as nylon, Celcon, and aluminum alloy. These materials vary in durability, with nylon being the least durable, followed by Celcon, and then aluminum. Standard-duty pulleys all use aluminum on their sideplates, because it provides good strength and is lightweight.

Heavy-duty pulleys are made with either aluminum or stainless steel sheaves. Stainless steel offers the best corrosion resistance, which you may want if you need to haul gear up sea cliffs. Heavy-duty pulleys come with steel or alloy steel sideplates. Steel sideplates are often found on single pulleys, whereas the alloy steel, being lighter, is preferred on double pulleys.

You can buy both standard and heavy-duty pulleys with either bushings or bearings. Bushings don't spin as well as bearings, but they are stronger. Manufacturers seal the bearings into the pulley and permanently lubricate them. This means that they stay free of mud and grit, but if they break you have to buy a new pulley. You can clean and re-lubricate pulleys that have bushings.

Some manufacturers sell light-duty pulleys that feature a sheave spinning on a single bolt with no lubrication. Such a simple pulley has an uneven, stiff spin and isn't very durable. However, it is very cheap and lightweight, so you might want to buy one to keep for emergencies.

General Safety Guidelines

Strong Anchors!
A pulley's anchor must be very strong. Your entire load of gear depends on this anchor to keep it from crashing to the ground below. If you have doubts about the security of an anchor, place another, or maybe two. The equipment you are hauling is your key to success on a big wall: you cannot afford to lose it.

Note: if you are hauling a climber, rather than gear, your anchors must be even more secure. *Never use dubious anchors to haul a climber!* You should use at least three secure anchors, just as you would to belay a climber.

Care

Pulleys are durable pieces of equipment that, with a little care, can last many years. Keep your pulley out of the dirt, mud, and general grime. Be careful that you don't bend a sideplate, as this can leverage the axle bolt and make the sheave rotate poorly.

The sideplates are weaker when they are separate from each other; storing them with a carabiner through the hole will keep them together.

When To Retire Your Pulley
Retire your pulley when it either doesn't rotate smoothly or has sustained major structural damage (such as developing cracks). This damage can occur to any part of the pulley, including sideplates, sheave, axle bolt, end fittings, and bushings or bearings. Although you can't examine sealed bearings, you'll know they have problems if the sheave doesn't rotate smoothly. The strength of any pulley ultimately depends on its axle bolt, so you should unscrew the bolt occasionally (before you leave for a **big wall climb**!) and examine it for weaknesses (such as nicks, cracks, or bends). For dis-assembly instructions, read the first part of Cleaning and Lubricating Bushings, below.

Modifications And Tune-Ups

Manufacturers don't sell parts for their pulleys, so the only repair you can make is to clean and re-lubricate the bushings. (You can't do this with bearings, because they are sealed.)

Cleaning And Lubricating Bushings
Because bushings aren't sealed they attract dirt and other grit. This interferes with their smooth operation and necessitates a cleaning and re-lubricating job. You can feel when the bushings need cleaning: the pulley sheave won't spin evenly.

The first thing you must do to clean a bushing is determine whether you need an allen wrench or a regular wrench to undo the end fitting from the axle bolt. You need an allen wrench if the fitting looks like this:

An allen wrench end fitting

A regular wrench works if the fitting looks like this:

A standard wrench end fitting

Obtain the appropriate type of wrench and some other tools, including: a rag, solvent, open can to hold the solvent, and grease. Now you are ready to clean and re-lubricate the pulley.

Begin the job by taking the end fitting off the axle bolt. This will release the sideplates, exposing the bushings. Push the bushings out and into your can of solvent. Rub them with your fingers until all the grease and dirt is gone, and then wipe them dry with your rag. Wipe off the solvent before you start the next step. Now coat the bushings with grease (put on too much rather than too little). Push the bushings back into the sheave and clean off any excess grease. Slide the axle bolt back in, then put on the sideplates (make sure they face the right direction), and finally fasten the end fittings onto the axle bolt. The sheave should turn smoothly and easily, just like new.

Accessories

Allen Wrench

Allen wrenches are inexpensive tools sold at most hardware stores and even some supermarkets. They usually come in a set of several sizes: be sure to get a set within the range of the bolt on your pulley.

Grease

If you are re-lubricating your pulley's bushings, you need some grease. Automotive wheel bearing grease works the best. You can find a can of it in any automotive shop.

Solvent

Use kerosene or some other type of solvent to clean the old grease off your pulley's bushings. Hardware and paint stores, as well as some supermarkets, sell solvents.

Wrench

Buy an adjustable wrench; you will be able to use it for many things other than pulleys. Hardware stores and some supermarkets sell adjustable wrenches. Maybe you already have one in your tool kit.

Some Pulley Manufacturers

CMI, Petzl, SMC/Russ Anderson are some well-known pulley manufacturers. See pg. 353 for manufacturers' addresses.

Key Point

"A rope is made much stronger than the load it is intended to support. This is to allow for outside influences that can weaken the rope. The common weakening influences, the ones that will probably occur while you are climbing, include: sharp bends, knots, and water."

See page 271

Ropes

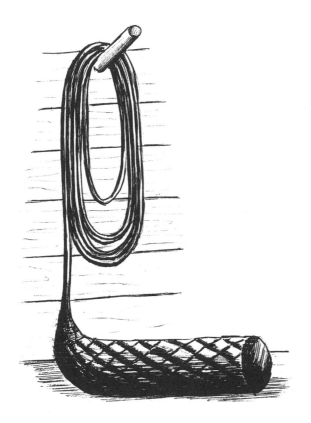

A rope

What Do Climbers Use Ropes For?

Your climbing rope is the critical safety link that connects you to the rock. If you use a rope properly by anchoring it to various points of **protection** along the **route,** and you fall, your climbing rope will safely stop your fall.

In addition to stopping falls, ropes are used to quickly ascend (with **Ascenders,** see pg. 75) or descend (see **Descenders,** pg. 157) a cliff, and to haul up bags of gear (see Pulleys, pg. 259). A rope is a fundamental tool of the modern climber.

Modern climbing ropes are multi-colored lengths of nylon fiber, with a **dynamic kernmantle** design. There are many reasons that climbers use this type of rope. To really understand these reasons, you need to understand the stresses that a climbing rope in use undergoes. These stresses dictate the climbing rope's design.

The Climbing Rope's Design

Climbing ropes must support dynamic loads. A dynamic load is a moving weight, such as a falling climber. Dynamic loads differ from **static loads,** in which the rope supports a stationary weight, such as a pack that you haul up off the ground.

Loading a rope dynamically puts much more stress on it than loading it statically. When a rope stops a falling climber, it must absorb a sudden load, a load which, for a few moments, is much higher than the climber's actual weight. For example, you might be able to lift a 50-pound bag of cement off the ground. But if this bag fell on you from the top of your house, you would certainly not be able to catch it! The same is true for most ropes. A static (non-stretchable) rope that had a tensile strength (ultimate strength) of 100 pounds would quickly snap if it had to stop a 50-pound weight that fell from 10 feet above the rope. This is because the rope is not designed to withstand sudden, or dynamic, loading. Dynamic loading puts too much energy on the rope too quickly, and the rope's fibers are overloaded by this sudden stress.

Fall Factors

Climbers use fall factors to determine the severity of a dynamic load. The most severe load possible has a fall factor of 2; such a fall puts the maximum strain on your rope. A fall factor of one is moderate, and a fall factor of less than one is light. But all three fall factors are for dynamic loading, and all three put more strain on your rope than a simple static load (fall factor 0) would.

It's easy to determine a fall factor: divide the distance you will fall by the length of rope between you and your **belayer.** For example, if you climb 10 feet above your belayer, and don't place any protection, you will fall 20 feet even though there is only 10 feet of rope from you to your belayer. This ratio equals a fall factor of 2, and is very hard on your rope, your belayer, and his belay **anchors.**

If, however, you climb 10 feet above your belayer and place an anchor halfway between you, at 5 feet up, you will fall only 10 feet on 10 feet of rope. This ratio will give a fall factor of one, which is much less damaging to everyone involved.

A **toprope** anchor always gives a fall factor of less than one, even if there is slack in the system and you fall some distance. Example: say you are toproped and climbing a boulder. Now your belayer forgets to pull up slack. Because of all the slack in

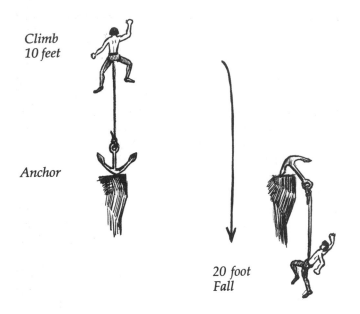

Climb
10 feet

Anchor

20 foot
Fall

A fall factor of 2

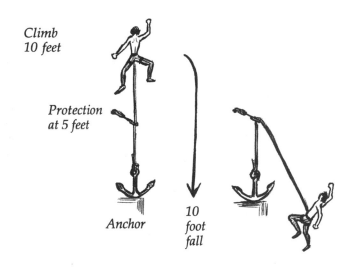

Climb
10 feet

Protection
at 5 feet

Anchor

10
foot
fall

A fall factor of 1

the system, you fall 5 feet before the rope catches you. But the boulder is 20 feet high, and there is 20 feet of rope from your belayer to the anchor (which is above you), and then an additional 10 feet of rope from the anchor to you. This totals 30 feet of rope between you and your belayer. Divide this into the 5 feet you fell, and you have a fall factor of a mere .166!

So the basic principle is: the more rope you have between you and your belayer, and the shorter your fall, the weaker the force of your fall: the weaker the **impact force**.

Stretch

The only way a rope can absorb the sudden stress of stopping a falling climber is to stretch. Stretching allows a rope to gradually absorb a fall's force, slowly bringing the climber to a stop, without over-stressing the rope's fibers. A new climbing rope will stretch to about 40% beyond its original length before it breaks! Basically, you can fall any distance on a modern, new climbing rope without breaking it (assuming it doesn't cut over a rock edge).

A rope that stretches is called a dynamic rope. A static rope has no stretch (or very little). *Dynamic ropes are the only ropes suitable for rock climbing!*

Bridge jumpers use bungi ropes, ropes that are made of elastic strands and have incredible stretch. These ropes work great for jumping into free space. As long as you start high enough off the ground you can bounce up and down, without fear of hitting anything. But in rock climbing, you don't have this luxury. You are rarely far enough away from the rock that you can fall without fear of hitting a ledge, or even the ground (if you're low enough). You need to be able to stop as quickly as possible.

In addition, your climbing rope must not stretch much under your body weight. If you were trying to ascend a stretchy rope (with some ascenders), you might not be able to actually get off the ground until you had climbed perhaps 20 feet of rope! Likewise, if you were **rappelling**, or being lowered, and you wanted to stop somewhere along the cliff, you would have to stop a few feet above your desired position to account for the rope stretch, or creep.

A stretchy rope has the additional problem of being more likely to cut over a rock edge. As the rope stops your fall it bounces up and down. This creates a sawing action against the rock, which quickly abrades a rope.

Impact Force

Impact force is another factor dictating that your climbing rope must stretch. Impact force is the amount of force transmitted to you and your **protection system** (anchors, **carabiners, harness,** and **runners**) from your rope as it stops your fall.

Climbing ropes are designed to *safely* stop falling

climbers. This means that the rope must do more than just stop your fall, it must stop your fall *and* absorb the force generated from your fall (the impact force) so that this force does not reach, and injure, you. For example, if you were to fall while attached to a steel cable (which is very static), it would stop your fall abruptly, and transmit most of the impact force directly to you, perhaps snapping your back! A dynamic rope will bring you to a gentle stop, no matter how severe the fall. Climbing ropes are designed to break before imparting too large an impact force: you are guaranteed a gentle tug from your rope at fall's end.

A rope with a low impact force is not only more gentle to you, but also saves your equipment. If you were to fall on a rope that had a high impact force (a static rope), your protection would suffer serious stress, possibly enough to dislodge most of it. A low impact force increases the chances of your protection remaining anchored in the rock.

A rope with a low impact force is also less likely to cut over a rock's edge. In the event of a fall, the rope won't pull on the edge as hard as it might if it had a high impact force.

So rope manufacturers are left with a problem. How do they make their ropes with low impact force *and* low stretch? They are able to do so only by careful compromise. First of all, they make sure a rope has a low enough impact force that it won't damage a fallen climber. Then they try to reduce the rope's stretch, but still keep the impact force low. This is difficult to do.

Abrasion Resistance

Your climbing rope needs to have high abrasion resistance. It will be running over rough rock, around sharp corners, and through thin cracks. All of this will put your rope's sheath (the covering) through tremendous abuse.

A kernmantle rope has good abrasion resistance. The rope's design means that an inner core supports most of the load (about 70%) leaving the outer core much more slack, and therefore able to be manufactured with more abrasion resistance. The sheath is braided because braid makes a tight, abrasion resistant surface. It also makes the rope's surface smooth so that it easily slides along the rock, or through carabiners. This reduces **rope drag,** which is good because rope drag makes climbing very difficult. Tight sheaths also keep dirt and grit away from the rope's core. This lessens the

chance of the core fibers being abraded or cut through.

A tightly-braided sheath has the additional advantage of gripping the core securely. If the sheath is cut through, it is much less likely to slip than if it was made of loose braid. And tight braid is ideal because it protects the soft inner core much better. Note that *you must retire a rope whose sheath is cut* (or at least cut out the bad section, leaving two shorter pieces of rope)!

Handling

Your rope must also be easy to handle. This means that it shouldn't kink or twist; such problems are difficult and time consuming to get rid of. Your rope should also hold a knot well: you should be able to easily tighten the knot, and it should stay tight. In addition, you need to be able to coil and uncoil your rope quickly and easily, with little hassle.

Good handling is possible only with a loosely-braided sheath. This brings up a problem for manufacturers, as they must compromise between a tight braid for abrasion resistance and a loose braid for handling. Both qualities are equally necessary in a climbing rope, but reaching a balance between the two is difficult. As a result, manufacturers usually make their ropes with an emphasis on either one or the other. For example, Beal makes ropes that handle well, but abrade rapidly (their sheath fuzzes up). Edelweiss ropes do the opposite, since they emphasize abrasion resistance. You must try several ropes to see which qualities you prefer; climbers often take several years to settle on a certain rope, if they ever do.

Rope-Weakening Factors

A rope is made much stronger than the load it is intended to support. This is to allow for outside influences that can weaken the rope. The common weakening influences, the ones that will probably occur while you are climbing, include: sharp bends, knots, and water.

A sharp bend in a rope severely reduces the strength of the rope. If you wrap your rope 180 degrees around a bar that has a diameter less than or equal to the rope's diameter, your rope will lose half its strength. (Note that if the rope wraps 180 degrees around a bar ten times its own diameter or more, it won't loose much strength.) Both carabiners and knots put sharp bends in a rope, so both weaken it.

Nylon becomes 10-15% weaker when it is wet, so a wet climbing rope is weaker than a dry one. Remember this when you are caught in the rain while climbing. Your rope should still hold your falls, but it won't hold as much weight as it would if it were dry.

Brief History

A climber in the 1860s

The first ropes climbers used were made with **laid construction.** Laid rope has three strands, each containing many twisted fibers. The strands are themselves tightly twisted around each other to form the rope.

Laid construction has several positive aspects: you can easily inspect the rope's interior for damage by untwisting the rope and looking at its core. It handles abrasion well because the outer fibers fuzz up and protect the other fibers. It is also an inexpensive rope to manufacture and to buy.

However, the laid rope does have some problems. It stretches too much under body weight (low load) and not enough under high load (such as a fall). So it transmits a high impact force to the fallen climber. It also spins (untwists) under a free load, such as a climber ascending a rope hanging out in space. It has a lot of rope drag; this makes it difficult to climb with. Laid rope also kinks easily, which makes it difficult to handle. And above all, laid rope in the past was made of natural fibers, such as hemp, manila, cotton, and sisal. These fibers are weak, have low energy absorption capacity, and rot quickly.

Nylon was first introduced into rope construction during World War Two. This synthetic fiber demonstrated much higher strength than natural fibers, resistance to rot, good energy absorption, low stretch under body weight (low load) and high stretch under heavy load, which means that it has a small impact force.

There weren't many active climbers after the second World War, so the rope market was small. This didn't give rope manufacturers any incentive to design a specialized climbing rope, which left climbers using the only nylon ropes then available, those made for marine use, called Goldline. Goldline ropes were good, but they didn't have enough abrasion resistance to be really useful for rock climbing. Climbers finally convinced the rope manufacturers to make a rope with better abrasion resistance. This one was called the Mountain Lay Goldline. It became *the* climbing rope for many years.

The transformation of rope construction from laid to kernmantle took several evolutions. The first was the solid braid rope.

Laid construction

Solid braid construction

The solid braid rope was easily abraded, which made it too weak to be useful for rock climbing.

Next came the Samson 2-in-1. This rope had a braided core inside a braided sheath.

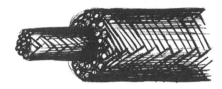

Samson 2-in-1 construction

The Samson 2-in-1 was a stronger rope, but it had too much stretch under low load. Another problem was that its sheath provided half of its strength. When the sheath became damaged (through abrasion) the rope was weakened.

The final step in climbing rope development was the kernmantle. The kernmantle rope has a braided sheath surrounding a core of continuous fibers.

Kernmantle ropes were first used by European climbers. By the early 1970's they had become the standard climbing ropes everywhere, having excellent handling qualities, abrasion resistance, high strength, low impact force, and low stretch under body weight.

Specifications

When you look through a manufacturer's catalog for ropes, you will see the following specifications: diameter, length, number of UIAA falls, working elongation percentage, and weight. I will briefly discuss each spec so that you will be able to more accurately evaluate a rope.

Diameter

Climbing ropes come in different diameters. Each diameter is intended for a different purpose.

Most climbers will need just one rope. This rope should be 11-millimeters (7/16-inch) wide. The 11-mm. rope is thick enough to survive sharp rock edges, so it isn't likely to get cut. It is also very durable, and will survive many leader falls. The 11-mm. rope is known as the climber's "workhorse" rope. Buy this rope for all around climbing use.

The 10 and the 10.5-mm. ropes are also intended for climbers using a single rope. However, these ropes (particularly the 10-mm.) are more specialized, being designed for ascents where light weight is more important than high strength. Use the 10.5 when you want a lighter leading rope but still need enough durability to take a few falls. The 10-mm. rope is not as durable, and is meant for climbers who are intending to make a fast ascent without many falls.

It is easier to climb some routes with two ropes. Two ropes are stronger than one, and, if you use two ropes you will always have enough rope to rappel down afterward. Two ropes are also ideal for cliffs with many sharp edges because two ropes must be cut instead of just one. There are two methods of using two ropes: the first is called **double rope technique** and the second **twin rope technique.**

Double rope technique occurs when you clip each rope into alternate points of protection. This technique helps you avoid rope drag problems, such as when you are climbing routes that zigzag, have a large overhang, or have several overhangs. Double ropes are also called **half ropes,** and range in diameter from 8.6 to 9.8 mm. Note: *use a rope for double rope technique only if the manufacturer recommends his rope for this!*

Twin rope technique is where you use two ropes as if they were one. In other words, you clip *both* ropes to every point of protection. Once you get high up the cliff, with many points of protection between you and your belayer, and you have a small fall factor, you can clip your twin ropes alternately. However, I don't recommend this unless you are certain that you have the knowledge to judge the situation accurately! Twin rope diameters range from 8 to 8.8 mm.

Length

The length of rock climbing ropes has changed over the years, reflecting a general increase in the standard length of a **pitch.** This length was originally 120 feet, then it grew to 150 feet, while now it is usually 165 feet, although many 150-foot ropes are still sold. Climbing ropes have become longer because the standard length of a pitch (the distance from one **belay station** to the next) has gotten longer. You can climb many modern routes with a 150-foot rope, but, if you prefer the security of knowing your rope is long enough, get a 165-foot rope. If you want to combine two pitches into one, you can usually get by with a 180-foot rope (although you have to be careful about doing this, because you won't always reach your goal).

Number Of UIAA Falls Sustained

This spec reports the number of UIAA test falls a particular model of rope was able to withstand before it broke (I describe the UIAA's rope tests below). The number varies: with 11-mm. ropes it is from 6 to 11, with 10.5 to 10-mm. ropes it is from 5 to 10, and with 8 to 9-mm. ropes it is from 4 to 12.

Most beginning climbers think this is the most important specification to consider. However, knowledgeable climbers have conflicting views: many consider impact force and working elongation much more important. But the other side says any rope that can withstand a high number of test falls is more durable, and less likely to cut over a rock edge.

There is truth to both viewpoints. I recommend that you try to buy a rope that can survive many test falls, but also has a low impact force and working elongation.

Sample Rope Specifications

Manufacturer	Size (mm)	Weight	# UIAA Falls Sustained	Impact Force	Working Elongation
Beal	11	79 g/m (8.8 lbs)	11	880 kg.	6 %
	10	63 g/m (7.03 lbs)	5	800 kg.	8 %
	8.8	49 g/m (5.4 lbs)	7	500 kg.	7.5%
Bluewater	11	79 g/m	10	890 kg.	5.2%
	10	64 g/m (7.1 lbs)	6	940 kg.	8.4%
	9	53 g/m (5.9 lbs)	11	600 kg.	10 %
Chouinard	11	79 g/m	11	940 kg.	5.5%
	10.5	70 g/m	7	880 kg.	6 %
Edelrid	11	73 g/m (8.2 lbs)	8	1090 kg.	7.6%
	10.5	69 g/m (7.7 lbs)	8	980 kg.	7 %
	9	53 g/m	12	720 kg.	7.3%

Impact Force

The impact force rating gives the maximum amount of impact force a rope will transmit to the climber. This is a very important specification, as it tells you how hard a tug you and your protection will receive from your rope as it stops your fall: the lower the impact force the better.

Impact force ratings for 10 to 11-mm. ropes range from 1,789 to 2,225 pounds. With 8 to 9-mm. ropes they range from 1,119 to 1,586 pounds.

Working Elongation Percentage

The working elongation percentage is the percentage that a rope lengthens while holding a 176 pound (80 kg.) weight. The lower this rating the better.

Working elongation % ratings for 10 to 11-mm. ropes range from 8% down to 3%. The ratings for 8 to 9-mm. ropes range from 12% down to 4%.

Weight

A rope is the heaviest single piece of gear that you will have to carry up the cliff. However, unless you want to solo (climb without a rope!) you can't avoid this. Manufacturers usually list the weight of their ropes by the meter. Rope weights range from 37 to 82 grams per meter. For a 165-foot rope this works out to around 4.1-8.9 pounds. However, remember that you need two of the lighter ropes, and their combined weight will often equal more than the weight of a single, heavier rope.

The UIAA's Rope Tests

The UIAA (see pg. 351) conducts independent rope tests. A manufacturer's rope that has passed these tests gain the UIAA's mark of approval, for two years. After two years the rope must be tested again.

I will briefly discuss how three important rope tests are conducted.

The UIAA's approval of a rope is very important to a manufacturer. Many climbers won't buy a rope that isn't approved, and so the manufacturer's sales drop. There is a recent trend away from this, however, as some manufacturers are selling ropes that aren't UIAA approved, and climbers are buying them. Probably the reason is that manufacturers still provide their specifications, so the climber is able to make an informed decision about the rope.

The Drop Test

In a climber's eyes the drop test is the most critical test that could be made. This test is designed to simulate a leader fall. The UIAA measures both the rope's impact force and the number of falls a rope can withstand.

To conduct the test, the UIAA anchors one end of a 2.8-meter length of some manufacturer's new rope, which they then run through a carabiner-like device. Next they load its free end with either an 80 kg. load (if they're testing a single rope), or a 55 kilogram load (for one double or twin rope). They also test two double and twin ropes at a time, dropping the 80 kg. weight.

The anchored end is .3 meters away from the carabiner-like device, so the actual length of slack rope is 2.5 meters. The load is dropped from this height, and ends up falling a bit more than 5 meters, due to the rope's stretch. The result is a fall factor of 1.78.

In order to pass the test, a single rope must have an impact force of less than 12 kilo newtons, which equals approximately 2,646 lbs., and withstand at least 5 falls before it breaks. A double or twin rope must register an impact force of less than 8 kilo newtons, which is equal to about 1,654 pounds, and withstand at least 5 falls.

The Working Elongation Test

The working elongation test measures a rope's stretch under load. This is a very important test, since climbers need a rope that has low stretch.

The UIAA testers place an 80 kg. load on a length of rope. They let the load hang for 10 minutes, and then remove the load for ten more minutes. They then replace the 80 kg. load with one that weighs only 5 kg. They measure 100 centimeters of the rope. Then they replace the 80 kg. load and remeasure the 100 cm. length. The UIAA gives resulting stretch, or working elongation, expressed as a percentage. This percentage must not be more than 8 percent on a single rope and 10 percent on double or twin ropes.

Be aware that a manufacturer may give the rope's *impact force* elongation instead of working elongation. The impact force elongation is the percentage that the rope stretches when it reaches its maximum impact force. This test has been discontinued because it is only approximate.

Knotability Test

The UIAA's knotability test makes sure a rope will hold a knot well. The smaller the knot's interior diameter, the better the knot will hold. Most manufacturers do not list this result, because if the rope has been UIAA approved, you know it will hold a knot.

The UIAA tests a rope's knotability by tying an overhand knot into a length of the rope and placing a load on it. The tester then attempts to insert a thin, conical rod into the knot. If he succeeds, the rope does not pass.

The UIAA also tests ropes for their diameter, length, static strength, and sheath slippage. Although it is nice to know the results of these tests, it is not vital: you just need to be sure that your rope has passed.

Materials

Climbing ropes are made out of nylon, a synthetic material composed of a group of polyamides, which are chemically similar resins.

There are two basic types of nylons used for ropes: type 6 (also called Perlon) and type 6.6. Type 6.6 is tougher than type 6; it handles abrasion, heat, and all-around wear better. Unfortunately, many climbing ropes are still made of type 6 nylon.

Nylon has many qualities which make it excellent for use in climbing ropes. It is very strong, lightweight, and has good energy absorption ability. It also has a high abrasion resistance, and its melting point is fairly high (around 480 degrees Fahrenheit). Nylon molecules have the ability to hold together, which means that manufacturers can make the fibers extremely long. Fishing line is an example of a long, single (monofilament) strand of nylon. If you have ever caught a fish, you know how strong this fiber is. Climbing ropes are made from many individual nylon fibers, wrapped around each other, which makes the rope very strong.

On the negative side, nylon does absorb water easily. When it is saturated, the fiber becomes 30% heavier and 10-15% weaker. Nylon also suffers damage from ultraviolet light (sunlight). So try to keep your rope out of direct sunlight as much as you can. Another problem with nylon is that in cold weather it freezes, which makes it difficult to handle. However, you can partly alleviate this problem by scraping the rope with your **extractor,** or a brush.

To reduce the water saturation problem, manufacturers offer dry treatments with some of their ropes. The treatment consists of impregnating the nylon fibers, either before or after construction, with silicon, teflon, or paraffin. So far, none of these substances have shown themselves to be clearly better than any other. There are also varying reports about the methods used to impregnate a rope. Impregnating it before construction may weaken the rope, while treatment that is put on after construction wears off more quickly.

Other Rope Fibers

Rope manufacturers use many different fibers to make their ropes. Ropes made for ordinary, around the house or office, non-life-supporting uses, or utility purposes, are often made of natural fibers. Manila, hemp, sisal, cotton, and many other natural fibers provide good material for these ropes. However, natural fibers are useless for rock climbing ropes, as they are much too weak, can't support the dynamic loads, and deteriorate quickly in the outdoors.

Nylon is not the only synthetic fiber used in ropes: polyester and polyolefin are two others.

The most common form of polyester found in ropes is terylene. Terylene is not as strong as nylon, which makes it unsuitable for rock climbing. However, it does have excellent water resistance, and it loses little strength when wet, which makes it ideal for utility use in wet climates and marine situations.

Polyolefin doesn't work for rock climbing because it can't resist abrasion and it has a low melting point. However, polyolefin is very strong. It also floats, which makes it ideal for water rescue, water skiing, and similar activities. Polypropylene and polyethylene are two types of polyolefin fiber. Popular polypropylene ropes are Ulstron and Tenstron. Courlene is an example of a polyethylene rope.

Construction

Climbing ropes (dynamic ropes) have a kernmantle construction. Kernmantle is a German word that means core/sheath. The kernmantle construction is exactly that: a core of continuous fibers surrounded by a sheath of braided fibers. The core is made up of fibers that are twisted into strands. These twists give the rope some of its dynamic (stretching) quality. But to prevent the rope from spinning when you are dangling free from a rock, manufacturers lay the strands parallel to each other.

Kernmantle construction

The braided sheath of a kernmantle rope provides excellent protection for its core fibers. Manufacturers braid the fibers tightly to keep out dirt and to make the rope run smoothly over rock (even the "soft" ropes, with good handling characteristics, have tight sheaths - relative to other ropes). The sheaths of climbing ropes are usually dyed several colors: this makes them easy to identify.

Technique

As I already mentioned briefly, there are two different ways you can climb with a rope. Single rope technique works like this: clip either a single rope or twin ropes into every point of protection along your route. Double rope technique means that you use two ropes and clip each one to alternate points of protection as you climb.

Flaking Out Your Rope

Before you can use your rope, you must uncoil it. And you must do this uncoiling properly, or the rope will tangle. Climbers refer to this important uncoiling of their ropes as "flaking the rope out."

To flake your rope out, hold it (coiled) in one hand and, with the other hand, remove every coil, one by one. Toss each coil on the ground (preferably on a rock or jacket to keep the rope clean), one on top of the other. You should form a loose pile of rope which will have a definite top and bottom.

When you have flaked out your entire rope, use the top-end first. For example, if you are leading a climb, tie yourself to the top-end of the rope. This way the rope will easily follow you up the rock, without tangling on itself.

Single Rope Technique

Single rope technique, in which you clip your rope (or twin ropes) into every point of protection, is the technique most climbers use, particularly non-Europe climbers. You can use either one thick (10-11 mm.) rope or two thinner (8-8.8 mm.) ropes, also called twin ropes. The advantage of using a thicker rope is that you only have one rope to manage, which makes it easy. You also have less weight and bulk to haul around. Twin ropes provide more security because you are trusting your life to two ropes: if one breaks the other is there to catch you. Twin ropes also allow you to rappel the entire rope's length, whereas with the single rope you can rappel only half that (you must double the rope through your anchor). Twin ropes have potential abrasion problems that single ropes do not: if you fall, the ropes will rub on each other: nylon abrades nylon very quickly. One solution is to use a separate carabiner for each rope.

Single rope technique works best when you are climbing straight routes. If a route meanders you will find yourself pulling yourself up against a lot of rope drag, which is very awkward. You can avoid most rope drag problems by paying attention to where you clip your rope, and how long a runner you need at each piece of protection. If possible, don't clip your rope to a point of protection that will induce a sharp bend. Example: if you must traverse to the side before returning to your route, don't clip your rope into any protection on the traverse. Instead, make the traverse and then, when you return to the original line of your route, clip your tope into a piece of protection there.

Sometimes you won't feel comfortable making such a traverse without clipping your rope in. If this is the case, use your runners to keep the rope straight. The farther your rope is from a straight line, the longer a runner you should use.

This is also true when you climb overhangs.

Double Rope Technique

Double rope technique involves alternately clipping each of two ropes (of from 8.6-9.8 mm. in diameter) to your protection. Europeans invented this practice, and they still favor it more than the rest of the world, although, with more climbers everywhere using double rope technique, this is changing.

There are many advantages to using double

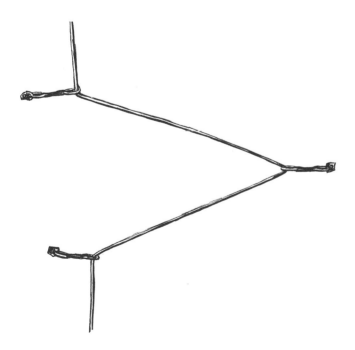

Clipping your rope to a piece of protection on a traverse increases rope drag. Instead, climbing through the traverse and then clipping in your rope is better.

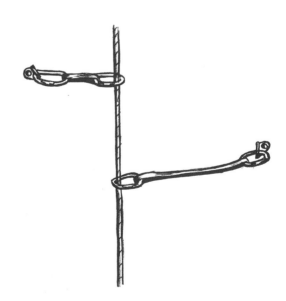

Using runners to keep the rope straight

ropes. Like twin ropes, they give you enough rope for a long rappel, and, if one rope is cut by the rock, you still have the other to hold you. In addition, double ropes allow you to reduce rope drag, which is especially important on routes that zigzag.

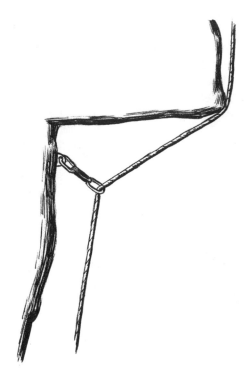

Too short a runner on an overhang

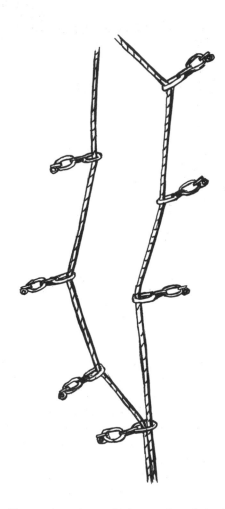

Using double ropes on a meandering route; minimal rope drag.

Double ropes also make it easier to climb overhangs.

On traverses, double ropes provide the second climber (the one cleaning the pitch) with more protection.

Important: after you climb a long **runout** (a length of rock with no protection possibilities), you should clip both ropes into the first piece of protection you reach.

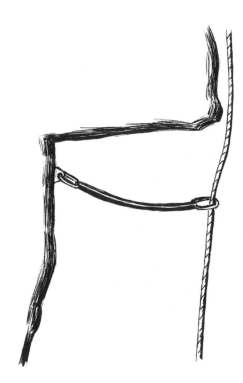

A good, long runner on an overhang

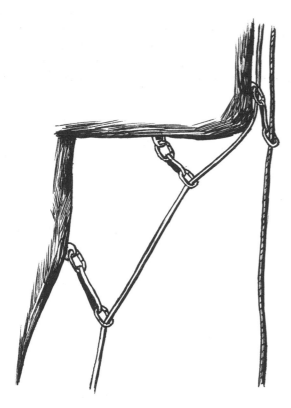

Using double ropes on an overhang

Double ropes protecting the second climber on a traverse.

Using double ropes is a more complex operation than climbing with a single rope. You must clip each rope alternately to the points of protection, but you must do this without crossing the ropes. If you cross your ropes you will have serious rope drag problems. In addition, your belayer must not cross the ropes; it is easier to use a **belay device** that separates the ropes (such as a Sticht Plate).

If you want to use a double rope technique, buy each rope in a distinct color, such as one red and the other blue. This will allow you to quickly and easily identify a rope, which is helpful when you are trying to communicate with your belayer. For instance, you can tell him that you need slack on the red one, or tension on the blue one.

Some manufacturers sell a single, 300-foot rope that has two colors, one on either end of the rope. Such a rope works well for double rope technique (providing it is the correct diameter), because you only have to coil and carry one rope, although it's a bulky one.

Toproping And Your Rope

When you toprope a climb you anchor your rope from above the climber. The belayer may sit either at the bottom or at the top of the climb. Because of this set up, there is no possibility that the you, the climber, could fall any distance (your belayer takes in rope as you ascend the rock). And since you know this, you feel secure enough to attempt routes that you would not otherwise consider. And on these harder routes you fall a lot. The result of these constant falls is rope damage.

To save your beautiful new dynamic climbing rope from the destruction inherent in toproping, you might consider using a cheaper static rope for the job. An 8 millimeter static rope provides ample strength (3300 pounds) for protecting a toproped climber. And, at approximately $.60 per foot, such a rope is quite cheap.

Important: you can only use a static rope for toproping, rappelling, or hauling. *Don't use a static rope for leading!*

Coiling Your Rope

When you are done using your rope you need to coil it so that you can carry it down from the cliff. You should also store your rope coiled.

I will show you two basic ways to coil your rope. They are both simple, easy to do, and quick to complete, and you should learn them both. Over time you will probably develop a preference for one or the other. Use whichever way works best for you, and the situation you are in.

However you coil a rope, you should always let the coils twist whichever way they want to. You may end up with some crossed coils, but this is fine. If you force your rope into neat coils, you may torque the fibers against their natural direction, which will damage them.

While you coil a rope, feel it for soft spots and look for sheath abrasion. For more discussion on both problems, see Care, on pg. 283.

The Mountain Coil

You can make the mountain coil by holding the rope about a foot from one end and pulling up loops of rope with your free hand. Pile these loops into your holding hand until you have around 10 feet of rope left.

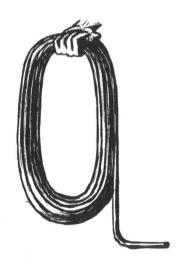

Looping the Mountain Coil

Take a foot of this free length of rope and double it back on itself, as illustrated below.

Wrap the remaining rope around the coils, starting from the bottom of the doubled-back piece and

Beginning the Mountain Coil's end-wrap

working your way up. When there is only a foot or two of rope left, and you have at least 5 wraps, thread the remaining rope through the doubled rope beneath it.

Finishing the Mountain Coil's end-wrap

Tighten the doubled bit of rope by pulling its free end. This will cinch the wrap tight.

You can lay your rope around your neck as you coil it. This allows you to save the energy in your already tired hands. Let the coils hang to about waist level.

You can also wrap the coils around your feet and knees, although I don't recommend this. It forces your rope into neat coils, even if the rope objects, which, as I've already discussed, isn't good for it.

The Butterfly Coil

Start the Butterfly Coil the same as you did the Mountain Coil, with the rope in your holding hand, about one foot from its end. But instead of forming one large loop below your holding hand, you make two loops, one on either side of your hand.

Lay the loops back and forth, as illustrated.

Laying the loops back and forth

Try to make the loops equally long, so that they balance each other. When you have around 10 feet of rope left, wrap the rope around the two coils, pulling them together, with your holding hand in the middle.

Beginning the Butterfly Coil's end-wrap

When you have around 3 feet of rope left, and you've made 4 or 5 wraps, thread a loop of the rope through the middle of the coil - the place your hand is holding the rope.

Push the free end of your rope through the loop, and pull it tight.

You can rig the Butterfly Coil twice as fast as the Mountain Coil, if you know where the middle of your rope is (mark the middle if you haven't al-

ready). Start from the middle, and coil the rope exactly as you did before. When you finish the coil (in half the number of loops) you will have both rope ends coming through the coil.

Finishing the Butterfly Coil's end-wrap

The Backpacker's Coil

If you want to carry your rope as if it were a backpack, rig the Butterfly Coil doubled, but leave the last 15-20 feet of each end free. Place the coil on your back and pull the free ends over your shoulders, one on each side.

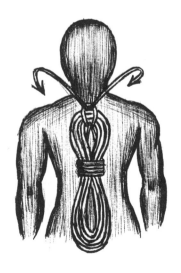

Step one to the Backpacker's Coil

Cross the rope ends over your chest, and wrap them back, around the rope.

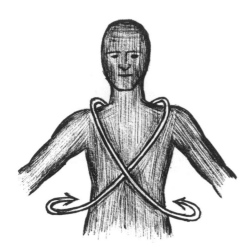

Step two to the Backpacker's Coil

Step three to the Backpacker's Coil

Pull the free ends around your waist, and tie them together with a Square Knot (see below).

How To Tie A Square Knot
A square knot is quick and easy to tie. Simply follow the illustrations below.

Beginning a Square Knot   *Finishing a Square Knot*

Coiling Your Rope At The Belay
When you have climbed the first pitch, and are belaying your partner as he climbs up to you, be careful where you coil your rope. On some climbs (such as overhanging cliffs) you can let the rope hang beneath you, but on others the hanging rope can get in your partner's way, or snag on the rock. To avoid these problems lay the rope in Butterfly Coils over your horizontal leg, as illustrated below.

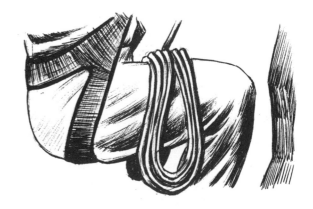

A climber coiling the rope over his leg at a belay station

The Rope Bag

A rope bag is a portable bag that holds your rope. There are several different rope bag designs available. The more traditional design has a drawcord top that opens onto a bucket-like bag.

Modern rope bag designs often have a zipper down the entire length, which widens the bag, making it easier to insert your rope.

Some rope bags are just large enough to hold your tightly-coiled rope. These bags protect your rope from the sun, dirt, and other harmful substances. But the best rope bags do all this and also allow you to easily pull the rope from the bag. This means that you can belay directly from the rope bag, or tie the bag to you and rappel with it. The rope will easily feed out.

To rig your rope bag for this, tie one end of your rope to the tie-off loop in the bag's bottom.

Now feed your rope into the bag, letting the coils pile onto each other. Occasionally shake the rope bag to settle the coils.

A **daisy chain** is a useful addition to a rope bag. Connected to the outside of the bag, the daisy chain's many loops allow you to easily connect the rope bag to your harness or belay station. You can carry a rope bag on a climb,

A modern rope bag design

and, if both you and your partner have one, you will never have any slack rope hanging down from the belay station.

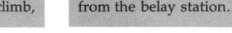

General Safety Guidelines

Don't Step On Anyone's Rope!

Don't ever, ever stop on any climber's rope! If you do, expect to get yelled at. Stepping on a rope crushes the rope's core fibers, severely weakening it. Climbers go through all kinds of contortions to avoid trampling a rope, and you are expected to do the same!

Don't Run Your Rope Over A Rock Edge!

Never allow your rope to run over a rock edge! If you are setting up a toprope, lay runners from the anchor, over any rock edges, to the vertical face.

Under tension, a nylon rope cuts like butter. If your rope lays on an edge you are running the risk of cutting it.

Care

Your rope demands more care than any other piece of rock climbing equipment. You must keep a constant eye on your rope, making sure that it isn't suffering any abuse. Many things can harm your rope, but it won't take you long before protecting your rope becomes second nature.

Sunlight (ultraviolet light) damages nylon, so keep your rope out of the sun as much as possible. When you're belaying you will have a pile of rope lying next to you; try to keep this in the shade, or under a shirt. If it is impossible to do this, don't worry too much because your rope won't be in the sun enough (in normal use) to be damaged.

Dirt, glass, and other grit will damage your rope. Try to keep your rope on a clean rock, on a jacket, or in a rope bag. If your rope becomes extremely dirty, wash it before you climb with it again. This will remove any damaging grit that may have penetrated to the rope's core.

Keep your rope away from any heat sources, such as fire. Nylon melts at around 480 degrees Fahrenheit, and weakens at slightly cooler temperatures. Don't dry your wet rope in front of the campfire! Also, try not to let your rope lay inert on hot metal, such as your just-used descender.

Nylon running over nylon quickly abrades and melts the inert material. Avoid rigging your rope directly to a piece of nylon, such as a runner. Instead, use a carabiner between the two. There is one common exception to this: rappelling. When you rappel you may need to loop your rope directly onto a runner that is connected to the anchor. This part is fine, because neither the rope nor the runner are moving. However, when you pull your rope down, it runs quickly over the runner, burning and abrading it. Such an abused runner is much weaker than it was originally, and you should *not* use it again. Instead, tie a new runner into the anchor. Experienced climbers fudge this rule a bit, often re-using an obviously-used runner (it will have black friction burns). They have the judgement to determine how badly damaged a runner is; until you have the same knowledge, don't re-use the runner!

Keep your rope away from acids (like battery acid), solvents, oils, grease, hydrogen peroxide, bleaches, chlorine, cresol (some disinfectants are made of cresol), and phenol (phenol is present in some resins, marker pens, and, diluted, in carbolic acid, which is an antiseptic).

Storing

Store your rope in a clean, cool, dark, and dry place. This could be a closet, or basement (not a musty one), or perhaps your well-insulated, waterproof garage. Store your rope in its rope bag, if you have one.

Cleaning Your Rope

You will need to clean your rope periodically. This is important because water and soap will lift the dirt out of a rope's core, which in turn increases the rope's life span.

Don't clean a brand new rope! New ropes are slightly oily, which keeps the rope supple. The oil will soak in after you use the rope a few times, particularly after you rappel or lead with it. Once you have used your rope a few times you should clean it, because a cleaning will shrink and tighten the fibers, making them more resistant to dirt.

You can give your rope a quick, but thorough, rinse with a rope washer. Rope washers are made to fit onto a garden hose and allow you to pull your rope through the device. The water pressure in the confined space will clean your rope well. However, if your rope is really dirty, you should wash it with soap in a washing machine.

Yes, you can wash your rope in a washing machine! Use a front-loading machine, one with a glass door (not plastic). You can find such washing machines at many laundromats. Top-loading machines have central agitators, and your rope will tightly wrap around these, causing both rope abrasion and possible damage to the agitator.

Wash your rope at the "cool" setting, use "warm" if it's really dirty. *Never wash your rope in hot water!* Hot water will weaken the nylon fibers. Use soap, or *mild* detergent, if your rope is really dirty. The soap actually lifts the grit out of the water (which removed the grit in the first place) and suspends it, preventing it from floating back into the core.

The best way to dry your rope is naturally, in the air. However, if you are in a hurry you can use a

Helping Your Rope Recover From A Fall

After your rope has stopped your fall, you should lower it to the ground (if possible), untie it, and let your rope recover. When the rope stops your fall its fibers stretch and suffer structural deformation. Unless you allow the rope to recover, this stretch and deformation will compound slightly when you take another fall. After many falls this compounded damage will leave your rope with little energy-absorption capacity.

When you are toproping a climb you have more of a chance to let your rope recover from a fall than if you were leading. After a climber falls, completely untie the knot that connected him to the rope. Let the rope hang straight for at least 10 minutes before you use it again.

Periodically (such as once every month or two) you should hang your rope, weighted with a couple of pounds, from a cliff. Try to rig the rope so it hangs free from the rock. The idea is to let the rope unwind, or spin out its twists and kinks. Leave your rope hanging for around 10-20 minutes.

tumble dryer, but be sure that the heat setting is on "low!" If you air-dry your rope, keep it out of the sun. Hang it loosely across something, such as a closet clothes rack. It will take 2-3 days to dry completely.

When To Retire Your Rope

Rope retirement is a contestable issue. Some people say 5 years, some 2, some say even less. But everyone agrees that this depends on how much you use the rope, how many falls it has taken, and how well you have cared for it.

Regardless of any other factors, if your rope has survived a long, severe fall, retire it. Chris Gore says (in the August, 1988 issue of *Climbing*) that "in an old quarry, they simulated the UIAA test fall, using a fall factor of 1.78, but increased the drop to 30 meters (98.4 feet) rather than the standard 5 meters (16.4 feet). The results were horrifying: of all the 10.5 mm and 11 mm ropes tested, not one held more than a single fall." He is speaking about rope tests conducted by Arovo-Mammut (a rope manufacturer) which were designed to determine the amount of damage a rope receives from a long fall. Obviously, the results were not good.

Constant low fall factor (under FF 1) falls also damage ropes. If you put your rope through such use (using it 6 days a week), retire it before a year is up.

If you use your rope less frequently, say only on weekends, and it doesn't suffer any major falls, you should be able to use it for around 2 years. If you use your rope only occasionally, such as on holidays, don't use it longer than 5 years.

Additionally: if your rope's sheath wears through at some point retire the rope (or, if the rest of the rope is fine, you can cut this section out and have two shorter ropes). If you feel a soft spot in the rope's core, retire the rope (or, as before, cut it into two parts). A soft spot means that the rope's inner fibers are severely damaged; note that the sheath around the damaged core may look fine.

Note: when you retire a rope, cut it into many small pieces! If you throw the un-cut rope into the garbage, or even leave it in your garage, someone may come along and use it.

Log Book

A log book is a written account of your rope's history. Keeping a log book will help you determine when you should retire your rope. You should re-cord the rope's manufacturer, the date you bought it, the date of each entry, the type of climbing (leading, hangdogging, etc.) done, the number, and length of falls, if any, and any other comments you think are important.

Sample Log Book Entry

Layne Gerrard's Rope Log
Manufacturer: Edelrid
Type: Classic MD
Size: 11 mm.
Length: 50 m.
Color: green/yellow/black
Date bought: 1/18/89

Date	Description of Use	# Falls	Estimated Fall Factor
2/19/89	Toprope (TR)	N/A	
4/09/89	Leading	None	
4/19/89	Leading	One 8 ft. fall	1
4/28/89	Toprope	N/A	
4/29/89	Leading and TR	None	
5/16/89	Leading	2 12 ft. falls	.6
5/20/89	Leading	None	

Modifications and Tune-Ups

Cutting

If you need to cut your rope, for any reason, you should do it properly so that the ends won't come undone. There are several ways to do this. The simplest method is to use a commercially-sold rope-cutting gun, a device that is designed specifically for cutting nylon ropes. A rope-cutter is expensive, but if you plan on cutting a lot of ropes you may want to invest in one. Using the rope-cutter is easy. All you need to do is turn it on, wait until the blade gets hot, and slice the rope. The hot blade automatically melts (and seals) the rope ends so that they won't unravel.

Make sure that the end fibers are thoroughly melted together. If they aren't they may unravel, which would make your rope difficult to use.

A cheaper, but effective, way to cut your rope is to use a hot knife. Take a knife and put its blade in a fire, or other heat source. Wait until it is extremely hot (glowing). Then cut your rope, as if you were using a heat gun.

You can also use tape, a cold, but sharp, knife, and a heat source (such as a stove burner or flame) to cut your rope. First, tightly tape the section of rope you intend to cut. Then cut through the middle of the tape.

Cutting a rope with a cold knife requires tape

Finally, melt the rope's fibers by applying the heat source.

Melting the rope's end-fibers

When all the fibers are melted together, remove the tape.

There are two other, commercially-available, ways to finish the ends of your rope. One is a plastic tube that you fit over the rope end, and then heat. The tube melts, and shrinks onto the rope, wrapping it securely in a protective sheath.

The shrinking plastic tube stiffens the ends of your rope, which can make them awkward for some situations, such as tying knots.

The other is a rope-end protector called a whip-end dip. It is a liquid vinyl substance into which you dip your rope's end. You must wait for the coat to dry, and then apply two more coats for your rope to be fully protected.

Whip-end dip increases the diameter of your rope's ends slightly, which can make your rope more difficult to use. Like the shrinking tube, this substance also stiffens the rope's ends. However, try to apply it only to a small area, to limit the problem. Whip-end dip comes either clear or in several different colors, which allows you to mark your rope if you want to.

Identification Marks

Climbing ropes come in many different colors. However, this color assortment is limited, and you may partner up with someone who has a rope that looks just like yours. If this is the case, consider applying some sort of identifying marks to your rope.

You can buy commercial rope identification tags. These are strips of plastic tape that have a section on which you can write your name and perhaps the date you bought your rope. Then you apply the clear tape to the rope.

You can also mark your rope with a marker pen (be sure not to use a phenol-based marker!). Use different colored bands on the rope's ends, or the middle, to make your mark.

Middle Mark

You should mark the middle of your rope. You will need to quickly find your rope's middle when you are rappelling, and it when you are setting up a long toprope, or when you are using the Butterfly Coil.

Some ropes come with their middles already marked. However, if yours doesn't you can apply one with a marker pen or tape (the athletic tape you use on your hands is fine). I don't recommend dying the rope unless you know a lot about this, because some dyes damage nylon fibers.

Accessories

Whip-End Dip

Whip-End Dip comes in 4-ounce cans. You can buy it in some climbing shops or rope stores (such as marine supply stores), or through climbing and rescue mail order companies.

Rope Bag

Several companies make rope bags, including A5, Mountain Tools, Outdoor Research, and PMI. You can buy rope bags at some climbing shops and through most climbing equipment mail order companies.

Identity Markers

Identity markers come in books of 60. They are sold in climbing shops and by climbing and mail order companies.

Hot Knives

You can buy hot knives at some hardware stores and climbing shops (particularly the ones specializing in rescue). You can also get them through the mail order companies. They are expensive, costing from $40-80.

Rope Washer

You can buy various rope washing devices through mail order companies. SMC makes an inexpensive rope washer that is available in some climbing stores.

End Tubes (Shrinking Tubes)

This clear tubing is sold by the foot through various climbing and rescue mail order companies, as well as some climbing stores.

Rope Manufacturers

Beal, Blue Water, Chouinard (Beal makes their ropes), Cousin, Edelrid, Edelweiss, Mammut, Maxim, New England Ropes. See pg. 353 for manufacturers' addresses.

Key Point

"A sit bag is not a harness. You must always wear your harness when you use a sit bag! ... Do not trust your life to a sit bag; it is not strong enough!"

See page 289

Sit Bags
(Belay Seat; Butt Bag)

A climber using a two-point sit bag

What Is a Sit Bag?

A sit bag is a lightweight cloth chair. It is designed to give you a comfortable seat when you are **belaying** from a **hanging belay.** It can also support you on overhanging **aid climbs** and **Tyrolean traverses,** although it is an extra piece of gear to worry about and can become more of a hassle than it's worth.

Not A Harness!

A sit bag is not a **harness.** *You must always wear your harness when you use a sit bag!* The sit bag is designed to add comfort to your situation, not to keep you on the cliff. Do not trust your life to a sit bag; it is not strong enough!

Types

There are two types of sit bags, the two-point and the three-point.

Two-Point

The two-point sit bag is connected to the rock by only two points, one on each side. This means that although the bag is lightweight, it is unstable. You may slip out of it. But this should be only a minor inconvenience because your harness will support you.

Three-Point

The three-point sit bag has three points of connection: one on each side and one below the crotch.

This design gives good stability. It is slightly heavier than the two-point bag (by around .4 ounces), but it is a much more comfortable design.

Note: the shape of the seat also affects the sit bag's stability. The wider the seat, the more stable it will be. However, a wide seat is heavier than a thin one.

Fold-Away Sit Bag

Some manufacturers, such as Misty Mountain Threadworks, make sit bags that fold into a pouch. This pouch has a strap that you tie around your waist: you carry the sit bag as if it were a fanny pack. When you are ready to use the sit bag, simply open the pouch and pull it free.

Not Essential, But Comfortable

The sit bag is strictly a luxury item. But on a multi-pitch climb, a **waist harness** won't provide enough comfort at hanging belays. If you know you are going to be hanging out in space a lot, as you would on a **big wall,** I recommend that you invest in a sit bag.

A three-point sit bag

Slings And Runners
(Static Accessory Cord; Webbing; Supertape; Tape)

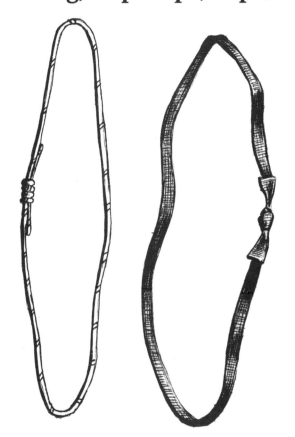

A sling and a runner

What Are Slings And Runners?

Slings and runners are technically two different pieces of gear. Slings are loops of static accessory cord (it looks like a thin climbing **rope**), while runners are loops of **webbing** (flat strips of woven nylon). It's only the construction of the two nylon loops that make the difference. However, you can use either a sling or a runner in place of the other, which is why I have included both of them in one chapter. In addition, climbers interchange the two names, sometimes calling a sling a runner, and vice-versa. But this doesn't really matter, as both slings and runners (different though they are) fulfill the same functions.

What Do Climbers Use Slings And Runners For?

Slings and runners serve many very important functions in rock climbing. They are necessary for slinging **chocks**, setting **anchors**, as **rappel loops**, and as **quickdraws.** You can also use them to make **harnesses, Prusik loops, daisy chains, cow's tails,** and **etriers.** Slings work better than runners, and vice-versa, for some of these jobs, and in some situations. I discuss the jobs best suited to slings, and those to runners, below.

Note: climbers usually refer to the cord that they rig their chocks with as slings; when they say runners they usually mean the webbing loops that they use to connect their rope to their protection.

Common Uses For Slings

Slings are loops of rope-like static cord. They come in many diameters, from 3-9 millimeters. Most of their uses require medium-sized cord.

Climbers use slings to rig their un-wired **wedging** and **passive camming chocks.**

A wedging chock rigged with a sling

The sling's cord usually works better than the runner's webbing for this job, because it provides excellent strength, energy absorption, and abrasion resistance. In addition, cord is slightly stiffer than webbing, and will stand vertically on its own, which allows you to reach up and place a cord-slung chock over your head. A runner is so flexible that it won't give you any extra reach.

Using Webbing For Slings

If you climb many thin cracks, consider slinging a few (one or two) of your chocks with webbing (runner material). If a crack you are climbing widens as it gets deeper, you might be able to set a chock in it. But the front of the crack may be too thin to allow cord to fit through. Webbing, however, can fit this situation perfectly.

A chock slung with webbing fits some thin-but-widening cracks

The sling's cord is also ideal for making Prusik knots. With this knot the cord grips the rope much better than webbing, and is easier to loosen and slide upward, which you must do frequently (see Ascending, pg. 75).

Use a **Double Fisherman's Knot** to rig a sling from cord. This knot is strong and has low bulk, so it won't get in your way while on your rack. The knot itself requires 16 inches of cord (if you're using the common 5.5 millimeter cord), 8 inches from each end, so you will need a minimum cord of 3 feet for most slings (this allows for a large enough loop). Some climbers and manufacturers recommend that you use a **Triple Fisherman's Knot** if you are using **Spectra** or **Gemini** cord. However, the Triple Fisherman's knot takes around 10.5 inches (32 inches per side) for the knot itself, and ends up a bit bulkier than the Double. As long as you check it frequently, making sure that the cord doesn't un-knot, the Double Fisherman should do the job. But use whichever knot you have the most confidence in.

The Double Fisherman's Knot

The Double Fisherman's knot is easy to tie. Loop 11 inches of one cord end around the other end.

The first step to a Double Fisherman's Knot

Now loop the cord around again.

The second step to a Double Fisherman's Knot

Finally, thread the cord's end under these two loops, and pull tight. Leave a tail of at least 2 inches on either end of the knot (when under load, the knot will slip slightly; the 2-inch tail allows for this).

The third step to a Double Fisherman's Knot

Repeat this procedure with the other cord end. When you are done, pull the two knots together, making any necessary length adjustments. Your knot should look like this:

The finished Double Fisherman's Knot

The Triple Fisherman's Knot
You begin the Triple Fisherman's knot just like the double version, but you add another wrap around the cord before threading the end under. The finished knot looks like this:

The Triple Fisherman's Knot

Common Uses For Runners
When you loop and tie webbing it becomes a runner. To make a runner you must loop the webbing with a **Ring Bend Knot** (also called the **Water Knot**).

The Ring Bend Knot
To tie the Ring Bend Knot, make an **Overhand Knot** on one end of the length of webbing. Make sure you don't twist the webbing; it must lie flat for maximum strength!

The first step to a Ring Bend knot

Now get rid of any twists in the rest of the webbing, and thread the other end back through the Overhand Knot (follow the knot in reverse).

The second step to a Ring Bend knot

Tighten the knot, making sure to leave a tail of at least 2 inches.

Runners have many important functions, including use as quickdraws, tie-off loops, and simple runners. You'll use them primarily as runners: to keep your rope in a straight line while you climb, preventing rope drag on you and your protection. To use a runner like this, place it between two **carabiners,** one attached to your piece of protection, the other to your rope.

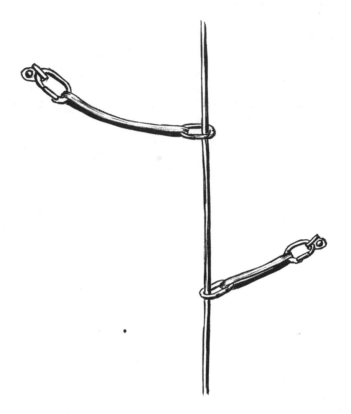

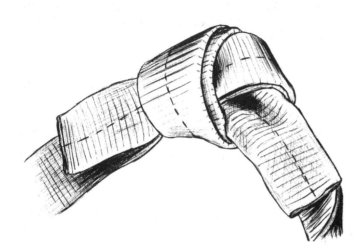

The finished Ring Bend knot

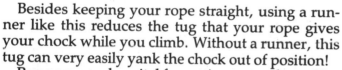

Using runners to reduce rope drag

Besides keeping your rope straight, using a runner like this reduces the tug that your rope gives your chock while you climb. Without a runner, this tug can very easily yank the chock out of position!

Runners are also vital for setting up anchors. Use them to connect your individual chocks into one solid anchor. For more on anchors, see pg. 53.

It's best to carry your large runners over your shoulder like a bandolier. But put them on *after* you put on your **gear sling** so you can get them off again!

Quickdraws

A quickdraw is a runner that is pre-rigged with 2 carabiners. This rig allows you to quickly connect your rope to your chock: instead of having to first connect a carabiner to the chock, then take off a runner and connect it to the carabiner, fit a second carabiner to the runner, and finally connect your rope to this carabiner, you can simply clip the quickdraw to the chock and then attach your rope.

A climber carrying a runner over his shoulder

Sewn Runners

You can buy commercial runners that are made specifically to be used as quickdraws. They are sewn together with bar tack stitches, eliminating the bulky knot and providing a stronger connection than the knot!

Bar tacks on a sewn runner

The only problem with a sewn runner is that its stitches gradually wear out from dirt and abrasion. You can prevent this problem by wrapping the stitches with tape (use cloth athletic tape, not duct tape).

Tape over a sewn runner's stitches

Some sewn runners are sewn in the middle of their loops, dividing them into two loops, for attaching carabiners at either end.

A runner with its loops sewn together

This design keeps the carabiners from sliding around and stiffens the sling, which makes it easier to make long reaches up to place your protection. However, the use of a stiffer sling puts increased leverage on a chock.

An interesting variation on this type of sewn sling has one of the loops turned perpendicular to the other. This loop is meant for your rope-connecting carabiner; it keeps the carabiner's gate out, away from the rock, which makes it less likely to open accidentally.

Tie-off Loops

Aid climbers use small runners as tie-off loops (also called **hero loops**). A tie-off loop is ideal for connecting several pieces of gear together, and for tying-off a **piton** (see pg. 247). The standard length for a tie-off loop is 20-24 inches, which forms a loop of 4 or 5 inches.

Load Limiters

A load limiter is a commercially sewn runner. However, unlike an ordinary sewn runner, it has many more stitches that form it into two wing-like sections.

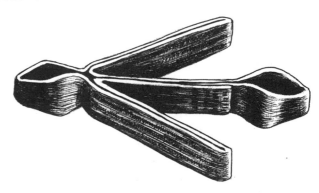

A load limiter, without its sheath

The "wings" are covered by a sheath of light material, such as Lycra, which keeps them from flapping around.

The idea behind the load limiter is that it will reduce the load placed on a piece of protection. This is useful when you are connected to a marginal, weak placement, one that looks like it will easily pull out. If you fall, and the force of your fall reaches 400-550 pounds, you will activate the load limiter. This means that you will rip its stitches open, pulling the wings apart. This reduces your fall's load without putting much stress on the weak piece of protection.

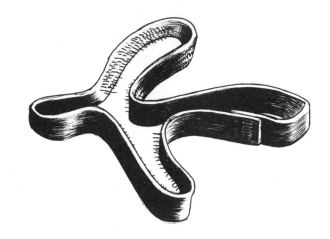

A used load limiter

A problem with most load limiters is that, when they rip apart, they vibrate so much that the gates of the connecting carabiners can vibrate open. This means that when you reach the end of your fall you have a good chance of being supported by a carabiner with an open gate, which provides a very tenuous connection! Example: a Chouinard Light D carabiner has a normal, gate-closed strength of 5060 pounds. Its gate-open strength is only 1320 pounds! A good solution to this problem is to use a **locking carabiner** whenever you use a load limiter.

Specifications

Strength

The strength of both slings and runners is important, because you will use both of them in your protection system. Therefore, both must be able to withstand the force of your fall.

Looped slings and runners are stronger than the cord or webbing they are made from. For example, while the rated strength of one-inch, **tubular webbing** is 4000 pounds, its loop strength is around 5000 pounds.

A good minimum loop strength for both slings and runners is 3500 pounds. Slings and runners must withstand more than the load of your fall, they must also withstand the braking power applied from your **belayer.** Since both slings and runners weaken over time through supporting high loads, weathering, and abrasion, they won't remain at 3500 pounds for long.

Slings

The strength of nylon slings varies with the diameter of the cord, or with the size of the webbing (see below). Three millimeter cord has a strength of around 500 pounds, 5 millimeter cord a strength of over 1000 pounds, and 7 millimeter cord a strength of 2500 pounds.

Kevlar cord has a strength of about 4000 pounds. However, it weakens to 3500 pounds when tied into a loop. Spectra's strength is slightly higher, and a knot doesn't weaken it significantly.

Runners

Sewn runners are stronger than knotted ones, **supertape** (a special tubular construction, see Materials, pg. 297) is stronger than normal webbing, and Spectra is stronger than nylon.

One-inch nylon webbing has a strength of around 4000 pounds, as does 11/16-inch supertape. An 11/16-inch sewn runner has a strength of 4500 pounds, and a Spectra runner is rated at 6000 pounds.

Diameter/Width

The diameter of a sling or runner is important, because it adds to the bulk of gear you must carry up the cliff.

Slings

Nylon static cord varies in width from 3-8 millimeters. Kevlar, Spectra, and Gemini all have a diameter of 5.5 millimeters.

Runners

There are a wide variety of runner widths available. Thinner runners are better not just because they cut down on bulk, but also because they put less strain on carabiners. Use runners with a maximum width of 11/16-inch.

Nylon supertape can be as narrow as 1/2 inch, while the standard width for nylon tubular webbing is one inch. Spectra comes only in 9/16-inch widths.

Length

Naturally, you can buy your slings and runners any length you please. However, certain lengths do work better than others.

Slings

Slinging your chocks takes a minimum of 3 feet of cord - each. You don't want your slings to be too short, because a short sling is more likely to leverage the chock out of position. Use longer slings for larger chocks, as they are heavier, and therefore more likely to fall out. Example: use 5 feet of cord for a large Hexentric (a type of passive camming chock).

Runners

A 5-foot length of webbing yields a tied loop of approximately 2 feet. This length is ideal for a basic runner. It fits easily as a bandolier if you are of medium to slight build. It may be a little too tight if you are heavily built. If so, try using a 5 1/2-foot length. You can double this runner back on itself to use it as a short quickdraw. Use 10 feet of webbing to make a double runner (a 4-foot loop), and 15 feet for a triple runner.

Quickdraws come in various lengths, from 4 to 12 inches. The 4 and 6-inch versions are ideal for either straight bolted routes or cracks. The 8 and 12-inch versions keep your rope straight when routes meander slightly.

Materials

Slings and runners are both two forms of rope. A sling is the traditional round rope, only smaller, while a runner is a "flat rope," having a wide but thin construction. In the past, slings and runners were both made of nylon. Now, however, slings may be made out of either nylon, Kevlar, Spectra, or Gemini. And while slings are still predominately made of nylon, some are made of Spectra.

Slings

A sling is a thin static **kernmantle** (a type of construction, see pg. 276) rope. A static rope has little stretch, and the kernmantle construction has a core of fibers surrounded by a sheath.

Nylon Cord

Nylon cord is the traditional sling material. Nylon cord comes in many sizes, which makes it versatile. This material has excellent flexing capacity, which means that you can tie and retie a knot many times without weakening the material. Its strength and energy absorption capacity (ability to absorb the force of a fall) increase with the diameter of the cord. Nylon is also easy to cut, and to melt, so as to keep the new ends from fraying.

There are two basic problems regarding using nylon as a sling. The first is that nylon has low abrasion resistance. This means that it won't last very long on the rocks. The second is that both its strength and its energy absorption capacity are size dependent. So you must use a wide sling diameter to get strength, but modern chocks have only 5.5 millimeter holes. And 5.5 millimeter nylon sling has a loop strength of under 2700 pounds, which is much too weak to use on a single, life-supporting sling. Note that older chocks (before the 1980s) have a variety of hole sizes: the larger the chock, the larger the hole. Manufacturers made them this way to fit as wide a nylon sling as possible (nylon was the only type of sling material available then). If you have such chocks you can use nylon cord with them, although it will be weaker than either Kevlar, Spectra, or Gemini. Use the largest cord you can fit through the holes.

Kevlar Cord

Kevlar cord is actually made with a nylon sheath and a core of kevlar. It comes in only one size: 5.5 millimeters.

The advantage of Kevlar is that it is very strong. This is why it can be made so thin: the 5.5 millimeter cord has low weight and bulk and still gives a maximum loop strength of over 4000 pounds. Kevlar is also stiff, which makes it easy to place a Kevlar-strung chock into a crack high above your head.

Kevlar has several problems, however. Because it is so stiff you can't knot the cord very many times without damaging its fibers. And it has low abrasion resistance, even less than nylon (remember that it does have a nylon sheath, however, which partially helps). Kevlar also has a low elongation at breaking point, which means that it doesn't absorb shock loading well (as from a fall). In addition, Kevlar loses a lot of strength when it's knotted: a Kevlar loop tied with a Double Fisherman's knot breaks at approximately 3500 pounds! And finally, it is difficult to finish the newly-cut ends of a Kevlar cord. This is because the Kevlar core has a lower melting point than its nylon sheath, so fusing the two together is impossible. However, there is a solution to this problem; I discuss it under Modifications and Tune-Ups, on pg. 300.

Spectra Cord

Spectra is another strong fiber, that, like Kevlar, also comes in only the 5.5 millimeter size, and has a nylon sheath.

Spectra is stronger than Kevlar! It has an maximum loop tensile strength of around 5000 pounds. It is also much more flexible than Kevlar, which means that you can safely tie it many times without weakening it (still not as often as nylon, however). Spectra also handles shock loading better than Kevlar, and has excellent abrasion resistance, higher than both nylon and Kevlar.

Because Spectra is so flexible, it is hard to make overhead placements with it. The Spectra sling bends under its own weight - a chock is just that much heavier! Spectra has the additional problem of not holding its knots well, which is why some manufacturers and climbers recommend using the Triple Fisherman's Knot. And, finally, Spectra has the same end-finishing problem as Kevlar.

Gemini Cord

Gemini fiber is a recent addition to the market made up of a combination of Kevlar and Spectra cord. It is designed to incorporate the best characteristics of both: their high strength, Spectra's abrasion resistance and load absorption, and a good mix of Spectra's flexibility and Kevlar's stiffness. This combination cord also comes only in a diameter of 5.5 millimeters.

Like Spectra, the Gemini fiber doesn't hold knots well. So, as when using Spectra, consider tying a Triple Fisherman's Knot, and check the knots frequently.

Runners

Runners are made of a static flat rope called tubular webbing. Manufacturers use one of two fibers, either nylon or Spectra, for runners.

Nylon Tubular Webbing

Nylon tubular webbing is the most common, and the cheapest, runner material available. As with nylon slings, the strength of nylon webbing is size dependent. However, it also depends on the nylon webbing's construction. Flat nylon construction is the weakest: *never use **flat webbing** in a life-supporting function!*

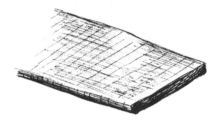

Flat webbing

Tubular nylon construction is much stronger: one-inch tubular nylon webbing has a maximum loop strength of approximately 5000 pounds. Climbers use tubular nylon webbing for runners.

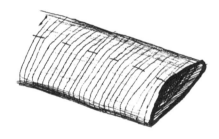

Tubular webbing

Manufacturers weave tubular webbing in two different ways, the spiral pattern and the chain. The spiral has continuous ribs that spiral down its length; it has no seams.

Tubular webbing with a spiral weave

The chain weave looks like the spiral weave, until you examine the sides, where you will see a seam. This seam is connected with thread (roll the webbing 90 degrees to find the seam).

Tubular webbing with a chain weave

The spiral weave design is much stronger than the chain weave. The thread connecting the chain weave may break due to abrasion, which will destroy the entire runner!

Another version of nylon webbing is called supertape. Supertape is tubular, but has a tighter weave than normal tubular webbing. This extra density gives the webbing more strength, so you can use it in thinner strips than the normal tubular material.

Nylon webbing has the same characteristics as nylon cord. It is flexible, handles repeated knotting well, and has good shock absorption capacity. On the negative side, it has low abrasion resistance, melts quickly when rubbed against other nylon, and is quickly damaged by sunlight.

Spectra Webbing

Spectra webbing is made out of a mix of nylon and Spectra fibers. Blue Water makes the webbing, and only in 9/16-inch widths. Spectra webbing has a tubular construction, and holds up to 6000 pounds! The webbing is only available in sewn runners, because Spectra webbing doesn't knot well. It has the other characteristics common to Spectra cord: good abrasion resistance, load absorption, and flexibility.

General Safety Guidelines

Slings Are Not Climbing Ropes!

Don't use your accessory cord as a climbing rope! Accessory cord is static, meaning that it won't stretch. Climbing ropes are **dynamic** (lots of stretch), which gives them the ability to absorb shock loading when you fall. Besides being static, accessory cord is also too weak to support a fall.

Leave Tails On Every Knot!

Leave a 2-inch tail of webbing on each side of a knot. When webbing supports a load some of it slips through the knot. The 2-inch tail will keep the webbing from sliding all the way through and coming undone.

Check The Knots!

Check the knots of your slings and runners frequently. They will gradually slip through, and eventually come undone. You should retie them whenever their "tails" are less than 2 inches long.

Care

Slings and runners are not as expensive as rope, so you can afford to replace them more often. This also means that you don't have to care for your slings and runners as carefully as your rope. In fact, both slings and runners are designed to withstand the abuse a rope usually goes through: in other words, they are designed to save the rope. So don't worry too much about your slings and runners. Instead, when they get old and worn, replace them.

When To Retire Your Slings And Runners

Your slings will last longer than your runners. Slings are thicker and more durable than runners, and you won't use them as frequently. You need runners for every climb (you don't need any slings for a **bolted route**), and to set up most anchors.

Retire your sling when its sheath is cut through, or it has become extremely faded and worn-looking. Also, retire it if you feel a soft spot in it: this means that the core fibers are broken.

Retire your runner when 50% of its fibers are worn through (your estimate). Also retire it when it looks faded and is stiff from weathering and sunlight. If it has severe burns, such as those created by friction, or is cut anywhere, retire it.

Modifications And Tune-Ups

Cutting Cord (Slings) And Webbing (Runners)

Cutting static cord, such as nylon or Spectra, is easy to do. An electric rope-cutter or a hot knife helps, but any sharp knife will do. If you are cutting nylon cord, you need to tape over the cut area first (masking tape works well). If you are cutting Kevlar, Spectra, or Gemini cord, you don't.

To cut nylon cord: tape the area you want to cut by tightly wrapping masking tape once or twice around. The tape keeps the fibers together until you can melt them. Then, cut through the center of the tape. Now you're ready to finish the ends.

Cutting Kevlar, Spectra, Gemini, and webbing is even easier. You don't need to use the tape, just your knife, and something to melt the end-fibers together after you make your cut.

Finishing Newly-Cut Ends

When you cut either static cord or webbing, you need to fuse the end-fibers together so they don't fray.

Nylon

Nylon is easy to work with, whether it's static cord or webbing. All you need is a heat source, such as an electric rope-cutter, a hot knife (heat it in a flame), or an open flame, and a paper towel.

With an electric rope-cutter or hot knife, simply apply the cord to the hot device and melt the cord's fibers until they are thoroughly fused. If you are using an open flame, apply it all around the end of the cord, again until the fibers fuse together.

Be sure to apply the heat evenly to the nylon end. If you are working with cord, wrap a paper towel tightly over the hot, melted end and pull the paper towel off, using a twisting or rotating motion. This will press the hot fibers together, forming a clean end. If you are working with webbing, apply the heat source evenly over the webbing. The fibers won't take long to melt together, and will cool in a few seconds.

Kevlar, Spectra, and Gemini

Since you won't need to cut Spectra runners (they come sewn), you will only be fusing the ends of Kevlar, Spectra, and Gemini cord. You need either an electric rope-cutter, hot knife, or a sharp knife, a heat source, and a paper towel.

Kevlar, Spectra, and Gemini fibers have a higher melting point than nylon. Since the three cords have a nylon sheath, fusing the core to the sheath is impossible. The solution is to melt only the nylon sheath, which will keep the inner cord in position.

After you have cut your sling, pull the sheath about a quarter-inch back from the end, exposing the core. Cut the exposed core at this place. Now slide the sheath back over the core; it should extend 1/4-inch beyond the core. Apply your heat source (the hot blade of the electric rope-cutter, the hot knife, or a flame) to the nylon sheath. When it fuses together, grasp it with the paper towel and, with a rotating motion, pull the towel off the cord. This will bind the nylon fibers together, and seal the end of the sling.

Accessories

Cloth Athletic Tape

Use 2-inch cloth athletic tape to cover the stitches of your sewn runners. You can buy the tape at any sporting goods or climbing shop, many pharmacies, and some supermarkets.

Electric Rope-Cutter

Electric rope-cutters are expensive, but they make cutting your slings and runners easier. You can buy them at some hardware stores, marine shops, and mail order climbing companies.

Knife

A thin-bladed, sharp knife is ideal for cutting both slings and runners. You can buy such a knife at hardware stores, sporting goods stores, and cutlery shops. Or you may already have one in the kitchen.

Masking Tape

Wrap your slings with masking tape before you cut them. The tape will prevent the fibers from fraying before you have a chance to melt them. You can buy masking tape at any stationary store or supermarket.

Paper Towel

You probably already have a roll of paper towels in your kitchen. If not, a rag will work fine.

Some Manufacturers of Slings And Runners

Beal, Blue Water, Cassin, Chouinard, Petzl, Wild Things, and Yates manufacture slings and runners. See pg. 353 for manufacturers' addresses.

Key Point

"Superglue is not healthy. It contains Cyanoacrylate, which is a powerful bonding chemical. . . ."
See page 303

Superglue

A container of superglue

Why Superglue?

Some rocks are brutally sharp and love to cut your unsuspecting fingers. For protection from these rocks you can coat your fingertips in superglue. When the glue dries it forms a tough, protective shell. As you climb this shell gradually wears off. If the rock is really rough you may need another coat after only one **pitch** (the distance between **belay stations**) of climbing.

Superglue is also an effective "finger band-aid." If you cut your fingers during a climb, and the pain and blood make it too difficult to continue, you can glue the wound shut. It's best not to get the glue in your blood stream because it isn't healthy. Instead, close your wound and apply the glue over it. This can be tricky, but if you first hold your wound closed and wait for the blood to congeal (it should only take a few seconds), then you can apply the glue with ease. The superglue will keep the skin closed and form a protective sheath at the same time.

Don't use superglue to protect your entire hand. It will take too long and use too much glue. **Tincture of Benzoin** (see pg. 307) is better for this purpose because it is easier to apply over the larger area, and is healthier for you. However, the Benzoin doesn't give the same strong protection as superglue, which is why the glue is better for your fingertips.

Is Superglue Healthy?

Superglue is not healthy. It contains Cyanoacrylate, which is a powerful bonding chemical and is unhealthy. There are clear warnings on the packets of glue stating that you should avoid skin contact. This is mainly because you can stick your fingers together, and they can be very difficult to pry apart. *Once you've applied the glue, keep your fingertips apart!* Also: *wait for the glue to dry before you touch the rock!* Superglue dries in about 30 seconds.

Superglue is incredible stuff; it really will glue your hand to the rock if you aren't careful. Of course, once the glue is dry, you can climb with no problems.

How To Remove Superglue

If you are using superglue on your uncut fingers, it will wear off as you climb. You won't need to clean your fingers later. However, if you have closed a cut with superglue, you must clean the wound after your climb. This could be painful, but the cut will heal quicker once it's free of glue.

Wash your hands in warm water and lather with soap. Gently rub the cut with soap, rinse, rub again, and rinse. Go through this process until the glue is gone. Acetone will dissolve superglue, but it is very unhealthy for you.

When you have cleaned the glue off, rinse your cut in cold water for at least 30 seconds. Put some disinfectant on the cut, then a bandage and you're done.

Where To Buy Superglue

Many stores sell superglue. Shop at a supermarket, hardware store, stationary store, or art store. Duro is one of the commonly available name brands. You can also buy Krazy glue. It isn't as strong but it is healthier. Both glues come in small tubes which cost around $2 each.

Key Point

"You may want to use a combination of both the finger and hand (tape) wraps. This will give you maximum protection from really rough cracks."

See page 306

Tape

Why Tape?

Climbers use athletic tape to protect their hands and fingers. This is useful for climbing rough cracks and for supporting injured joints. For example, if you suffer from a slight tendon pain in your elbow, you might find relief by wrapping tape two or three times around your forearm, just below your elbow.

The most common places you will need tape is around your fingers and hands.

What Kind Of Tape? What Size?

Cloth athletic tape is the best kind of tape to use. It has the advantages of being tough, sticking well, and providing fairly good **friction** to the rock.

I have found that the 1.5-inch wide tape works the best for my average size hands. This size is wide enough to easily cover my hands, yet if I rip the tape down the middle it is perfect for wrapping my fingers. If you have large hands you may want the two-inch size; the one-inch size works well for small hands.

How To Wrap The Tape

There are many ways to tape your hands and fingers. I will show you some ways I have found particularly effective.

Fingers

Tape around your fingers must allow your finger to flex but also must not slip off. The best way to achieve this is to wrap a figure-eight pattern around your joint.

If you want to tape both finger joints, wrap separate patterns around each one.

If your finger is recovering from an injury, such as tendonitis, it needs a lot of support. You must use two layers of tape. If you have a bandaged cut, just tape over it.

For the first layer, tape the figure-eight pattern I described above. The second layer is a little different. Bend your finger slightly and spiral the tape up the finger, from your hand out. Be careful not to wrap the tape too tightly.

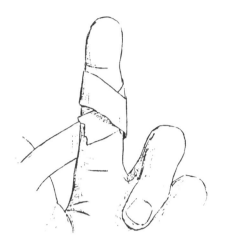

Beginning a figure-eight wrap around a finger

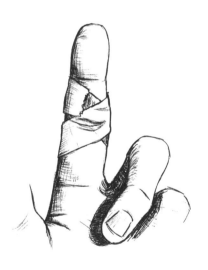

Finishing a figure-eight wrap around a finger

Hands

Taping your hands is vital to protect them from the rough edges of a **hand crack.**

The best wrap I have found is one which you can take off and use again. This is nice, because you save tape.

First lay one horizontal strip across the back of your hand. Then lay three strips perpendicular to this piece.

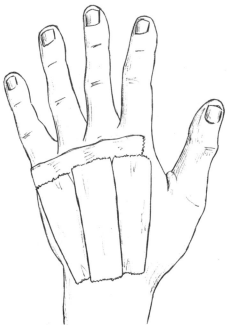

Step #1: lay one horizontal, then three vertical strips of tape on the back of your hand

Run a length of tape diagonally from the bottom of your hand, up around your index finger, then back to the starting point. Do the same with your pinky.

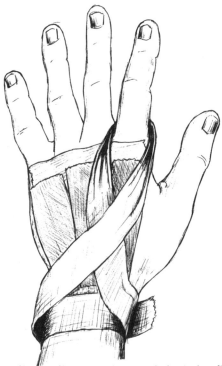

Step #2: tape diagonally up and around the index finger (remember to do the same with your pinky)

Finally, tape around your wrist. Make sure you don't wrap this too tightly; you don't want to cut off your circulation!

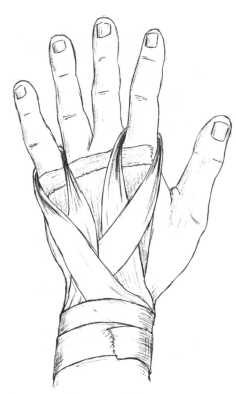

Step #3: tape around your wrist

To remove the wrap when you are finished climbing, simply cut it on the inside of your wrist. Pull the entire thing off your hand. This may hurt a bit (because the tape sticks to your hair), but it is worth saving the protective glove you have made.

To reuse the tape, simply slide it back over your index and pinky, and retape your wrist.

You may want to use a combination of both the finger and hand wraps. This will give you maximum protection from really rough cracks.

Market Opportunity: why doesn't somebody manufacturer a crack climbing glove to replace tape?

Where To Buy Tape

You can buy athletic tape at pharmacies, climbing shops, and some supermarkets. Johnson and Johnson sells tape which works well. Zonas makes tape specifically for climbers. Try them both; discover which one you like best.

Tincture Of Benzoin

A bottle of Tincture of Benzoin

What Is Tincture Of Benzoin?

A tincture is a solution containing amounts of water, alcohol, and a chemical substance having medicinal properties. Benzoin, a resin that is extracted from certain Asian trees, is the medicine. It has the ability to protect your skin from abrasion due to rough surfaces, such as rock.

How To Use Tincture Of Benzoin

Many climbers find Benzoin's protective ability very helpful. Just pour the tincture on your hands, fingers, or any other area you want to protect (maybe your elbows, if you are planning to climb a wide crack). When the tincture dries (about 30 seconds) your skin will be able to resist rock abrasion much more effectively than it could otherwise. You may notice this protective effect particularly on your fingers, because the skin won't peel so much.

Benzoin's skin-hardening process is not like superglue (see pg. 303), which provides a tough, protective shell. Rather, Benzoin soaks into your skin, and increases its resistance to abrasion.

You will probably need to apply the tincture only once, at the beginning of your climbing day. How often you use it depends on how much climbing you do, and how rough the rock is. You can pour more tincture on whenever you feel the need, because tincture of Benzoin is a healthy substance.

How To Carry Tincture Of Benzoin

Tincture of Benzoin is a liquid. It comes in a bottle. This bottle is made of amber glass, which protects the tincture from sunlight. Although the bottle is strong, I recommend that you put it inside a zip-lock plastic bag when you take it climbing. Should the bottle break, the plastic bag will keep the liquid from leaking all over your pack.

Where To Buy Tincture Of Benzoin

You can buy a bottle of tincture of Benzoin in most pharmacies. It will cost you approximately $6 for an 8-ounce bottle.

Key Point
"As a supplement to climbing-specific training, you can play other sports for variety and excitement, as well as derive their training benefits. Particularly consider activities that improve your sense of body . . . and those that increase your oxygen intake. . . ."
See page 322

Training Devices

The hangboard, a commercial training device

What Is A Training Device?

A training device is an apparatus designed to help improve your athletic ability. Each sport has its own training devices; for example, boxers use a wide variety of punching bags to improve their skills. Climbers use training devices too, devices that can strengthen the muscles they use while climbing. With stronger muscles a climber will be able to stay on the rock longer, and to grasp smaller holds.

Of course, strength training won't improve your climbing technique: you must climb frequently to develop this. But a regimen of regular climbing together with supplementary strength and endurance training will give you the ability to climb harder **routes.**

Note: you can injure yourself by overtraining or by using improper training technique. Remember to do every exercise in a controlled manner, and to emphasize form more than how much weight or how many repetitions you can do. Above all, *stop immediately if you feel sharp pain* (which is different from the dull burning of a healthy but sore muscle)!

Types

Although there are a number of training devices for climbers on the market, you can use almost anything as a training apparatus. If you use your imag-ination, you can improvise, which will save your money for actual climbing gear. In this section I will discuss both the improvised and the commercial training devices that many climbers currently use. This information will open your mind to the potentials, and show you how easy it is to start training.

Trees

Trees are excellent training devices. Many climbers have learned to **belay, rappel,** and **aid climb** on the trees in their backyards. But trees can be even more useful: with access to the right tree you have a potential training center at hand. If your tree is large enough, and has enough strong branches, you can lean ladders and climbing walls against it, hang ropes from it, put a pegboard on it, and practice free climbing along its branches. Of course, in a tall tree you must be careful not to fall!

Stairs

With the right set of stairs, you can workout at home two different ways. First, any staircase works fine for running, or walking, up to the top. This is an excellent exercise: it builds leg strength, endurance, and increases your cardiovascular capacity. And climbing stairs is easy on your knees. This is only true for ascending, however. Descending stairs can be damaging, because you may jar your knees with every step. Try to walk slowly and gently down the stairs after you ascend them.

The second method of using your stairs is unorthodox, and requires a certain type of stair. The idea is to climb the stairs from underneath, with your hands, as if you were climbing an overhang, with each stair being a hold. However, to be able to do this, you need stairs that don't have a solid base beneath them: metal fire-escape stairs work best.

Climbing up some overhanging stairs

Climbing like this can be dangerous: you're not roped-up, so don't fall! And, don't climb under a stair that is high off the ground; if you do, realize that you're responsible for your own life! The owner of the building probably won't want you to exercise like this, for liability reasons, so I recommend asking permission first, or climbing low, one-story stairs in an out-of-the-way location.

Also, watch out for people walking down the stairs. They may inadvertently step on your fingers!

Warmup Grips

A warmup grip is something that you hold in your hand and repeatedly squeeze. This could be a tennis ball, a racquet ball, a chunk of wax, a plastic-handled, spring-loaded grip, a rubber doughnut, or a Sorbothane (a putty-like substance) grip.

Although some grips are meant to strengthen your fingers, none of them provide enough resistance to do so. Instead, they all work well for warming up your fingers before you begin strengthening exercises or climbing. Warmed fingers are better prepared for the exertion of gripping small rock edges, and are less likely to become injured.

Some warmup grips

A Pull-Up Bar

A pull-up bar is anything that you can use to pull yourself up on by lifting your hanging body up to the bar, using only your arms. Thus, a tree branch, a ladder rung, a door jam, a piece of **webbing** hanging from a bar, or a commercially-sold pull-up bar will all work.

When you have the strength, you can get an added benefit from a pull-up bar by using certain shapes and sizes of handholds. For instance, the 1/2-inch edge of a doorjamb provides a climbing-specific pull-up bar; the thin edge exercises your fingers more than a round bar. However, you need to be strong to do pull-ups on such a thin edge without injury. Until you have enough strength to pull yourself up in a controlled manner, don't use a doorjamb! Instead, use a round, metal pull-up bar and wrap your fingers and thumb securely around it. Your fingers won't get as much of a workout, but your upper body and forearms will receive just as much benefit. And this will provide you with a base level of strength from which to improve.

Of course, you can use a round bar and make your workout harder. Don't encircle the bar with your fingers and thumb when you grip it. Instead, grasp it only from above, and only with your fingers. Or, use a bar that rotates around an axle (a simple design would be a pipe slipped over the bar). When you grasp the bar, it will rotate, which forces you to readjust your grip. This will give you a very punishing workout that will reward you later on the cliffs.

A Rope

A thick rope (1.5 to 2 inches in diameter) is a wonderful but simple climbing-specific training apparatus. Hang the rope from something, such as a tree branch, the rafters in your garage, or even from the chimney on top of your house (although it

A climber using a climbing rope

works better if the rope hangs free). Once you have securely anchored it, climb up the rope, hand over hand. Through practice, build up your strength to

the point that you don't need to use your feet when you climb. Simply climb the rope with your hands.

This exercise will give you the maximum arm-strengthening benefit: you gain from gripping the rope (finger and hand strength), pulling up on it with one arm (your entire arm and most of your upper body benefits), and locking off (holding your arm in position so that you can pull up with your other arm) Rope training mimics frequently-used climbing moves.

For this exercise, a long rope is better than a short one. However, you probably won't have anywhere to hang a really long rope (more than 20 feet), unless you have a suitable tree. Instead, you'll have to settle for something shorter, perhaps only 10 feet. But this is okay, you'll just have to climb it more frequently to receive the same benefit.

After you have developed the strength, two ropes will provide you with a more intense workout. Hang the ropes parallel to each other, shoulder-width apart. To climb them, grasp one rope in one hand, the other rope in your other hand. Slide one hand up the first rope, lock off, and then slide your other hand up the second rope. Lock this arm off, and go back to the first hand. Try not to swing sideways, because this will make it more difficult to climb.

An interesting variation to this exercise strengthens your abdominal muscles as well as your arms. You can do it on either one rope or two, although it's easier on one. Grasp the rope normally, and pull yourself up. Now lift your legs out, so they're perpendicular to your body. Keep your legs out as you climb the rope. This is a very strenuous exercise. To avoid injury you must be careful not to arch your back (make sure your abdominal muscles do the work).

To avoid injury, stay in control when you climb a rope. Stop climbing it when you must strain to simply hold on.

Just like running stairs, it is healthier to climb up a rope than to descend it. If you can, once you reach the top of your rope try to rig another way of getting down, such as by placing a solid ladder next to the rope which you can climb down. If this is impossible, wrap the rope around one of your legs and slide down. You'll still need to use your hands of course, but at least some of your weight will be supported by your legs.

A climber using 2 ropes

A Ladder

There are two kinds of ladders that can provide good training for rock climbing: rope ladders and wooden-runged ladders.

Both ladders have high injury potential. You shouldn't have any problems so long as you stay in control when you use a ladder, and don't overtrain with it (give your body a few days to recover between ladder workouts).

Rope Ladder (Bachar Ladder)

Climbers have developed narrow rope ladders meant specifically for training. These ladders are known as Bachar Ladders (after Chouinard's commercial version - which was itself named after climber John Bachar). They are narrower versions of the rope ladders at fairs that you try to walk along to reach the bell at the top, but which inevitably spin and dump you onto a pile of straw below. Remember those? The rungs of Bachar ladders are made of PVC piping, connected on either side by ropes. The ropes come together at each end of the

ladder, to form one strand (which makes the ladder inherently unstable).

To set up the Bachar Ladder, anchor the two ends with one higher than the other, the lower one starting anywhere from 5-7 feet above the ground (where you can reach it while standing). Angle the rope at least 30 degrees up from this point, more if you can, and then anchor the high end. The greater the angle, the harder the workout, but also the higher the other anchor must be placed. However, you don't want the ladder to be vertical, because you can do vertical pulling on your rope and pegboard (described later).

Using the Bachar Ladder is simple to describe, hard to do. Grasp the first rung with one arm, pull yourself up on it without letting the ladder rotate (it will be trying to), and reach for the next rung. The ladder tries to rotate because its ends are anchored to single strands. If the ladder rotates, you'll have a hard time hanging on!

The Bachar Ladder will increase your arm, forearm, and wrist strength, pulling strength, and lock-off ability. It provides very climbing-specific muscle and co-ordination training.

However, Bachar Ladders have a bad reputation. They are known for destroying climber's joints, especially elbow tendons. However, if you use a Bachar Ladder correctly, you probably won't become injured. First of all, make sure you angle the ladder upward. This will force you to climb up, and to pull up, which puts much less stress on your elbows than pulling horizontally would. Also, when you reach the top, don't climb back down the ladder! Instead, get off, whether by climbing down a tree, or a solid ladder, or even jumping to the ground, it doesn't matter. One solution is to rig the Bachar Ladder on a hill, so that you remain close to the ground even though still pulling up.

Also, don't run laps on the Bachar Ladder: that is, don't repeatedly climb it back and forth. Climb it just a few times, the exact number depending on your level of fitness. When you get tired, quit. You are most likely to get injured if you repeat a motion, especially when you are tired!

Chouinard stopped selling Bachar Ladders a few years ago, because of all the injury problems it induces. However, you may run across a used one (in a garage sale, or the parking lot below the cliffs). If so, check the cord for wear before you buy it.

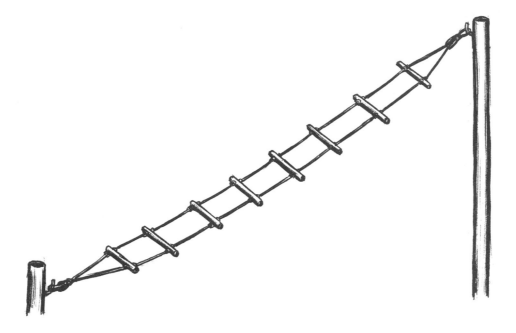

A Bachar Ladder

Make Your Own Bachar Ladder

You can also make your own Bachar Ladder. For a 10-rung ladder (about 20 feet long), all you need is 7 feet of one-inch PVC piping, approximately 50 feet of 5 millimeter accessory cord, a roll of tape, a saw to cut the PVC, and a drill with a 1/4-inch bit to make holes in the PVC for the cord.

Cut the PVC into 8-inch lengths for rungs. Drill 1/4-inch holes for the cord through either end of each rung. Double the cord and tie a **Figure-Eight-On-A-Bight** (see pg. 201) about 2 feet from the doubled end. This makes the loop from which you can hang one end of the ladder. About one foot down from your **Figure-Eight Knot,** tie an **Overhand Knot** (see pg. 175) on each cord. Now insert both cords through the holes in a rung and slide it down onto the Overhand Knots. Tie additional Overhand Knots (one on each length of cord) just past the rung. This will secure it in place.

Make Overhand Knots in both cords for the next rung about 2 feet down from the first. Thread the rung on both cords, push it down to the knots and tie new Overhands to lock that rung in place. Continue with this process until

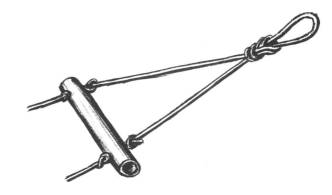

The starting end and first rung of a Bachar Ladder

you have secured all 10 rungs. You have two free ends of cord left. Tie them together with a **Double Fisherman's Knot** (see pg. 292). Pull the resulting loop taunt, and at its middle, tie a Figure-Eight-On-A-Bight. This is your second end loop. Now you just need somewhere to hang your ladder!

The finishing end of a Bachar Ladder

A Wooden Ladder

A wooden-runged, wooden-sided ladder of the type you can buy in paint or hardware stores is also a good training device. You don't want a free-standing folding ladder, but one that you must lean against a structure like your house or tree. When you have leaned the ladder against something, climb up the overhanging (underneath) side. Depending on the angle and the intensity of your training, you may want to use both your arms and feet to ascend, or just your arms (which is harder).

As your strength develops you can also climb by gripping the ladder's sides, in a pinch grip, although this is very strenuous.

A climber training on a wooden ladder

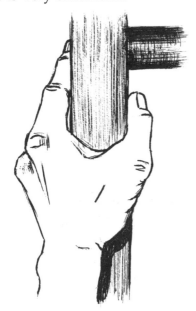

A climber pinch-gripping the sides of the wooden ladder

Before you use your ladder, anchor the top of it to the tree or whatever you're leaning it against. You don't want it to come sliding down while you're climbing! This is particularly important if you are climbing only one side of the ladder, as you might if you were pinch-gripping its sides, because you can easily unbalance it.

Pegboard

A pegboard is a vertically-positioned board with multiple holes drilled into it. The holes are large enough to accept a peg. To use the pegboard, you hold a peg in each hand, insert one into a hole, pull yourself up on it, then insert the other peg, pull up on that, and so on until you reach the top of the board.

Pegboards offer climbing-specific training because they simulate the arm movements you make while climbing. The constant pulling, locking off, then pulling with the other arm mimics the movements of an exaggerated climb - exaggerated because you don't use your feet. It's only on the hard climbs that you do not use your feet.

You must be careful when you work out on a pegboard, or you could injure yourself. Always warm up well before you use it. Never run laps on it (repeated up and down climbing)! Instead, rest between each ascent, and stop *immediately* if you feel an sharp pain in your shoulders or arms. In addition, it's healthier to climb up a pegboard than down it, so if you can, provide a way to walk down when you reach the top. Perhaps you can place a ladder next to your pegboard.

Gymnasts have used pegboards for many years, so if you want to buy a good, manufactured, training pegboard, look for a gymnastic equipment supply company near you. However, if you don't want to spend the money, you can easily make your own

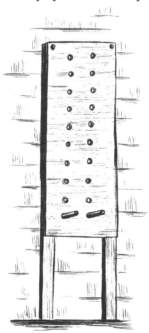

A pegboard

board. You will need a hardwood board, preferably kiln-dried (this process keeps the board from cracking), two hardwood dowels (one inch in diameter), a drill, one-inch drill bit, and mounting bolts. The board should be slightly wider than your shoulders so you can drill holes which are shoulder-distance apart. The taller you can make your pegboard the

better, up to 10 or 12 feet. Of course, the height you end up with depends on how much room you have. Don't mount your pegboard from the ground, rather, from about head height. This means that you will need a 10-20 foot high wall to support the pegboard.

After you drill the peg holes, apply 2-3 coats of varnish to the board, so that it can withstand weathering over time. Then mount it in any appropriate location; you can even bolt it to the side of your house.

Wrist Strengtheners

A wrist strengthener is a device that you use to strengthen your wrists and forearms. The simplest version of a wrist strengthener is a barbell, perhaps one with light weights on it, that you hold in your hands, while your hands are resting on your knees, palms down. Extend your hands slightly beyond your knees, so you can rotate them 90 degrees downward. As you do this, let the barbell gently roll down to your finger tips. Then use your fingers to pull the bar back up into your hands, then return your hands to a level position.

The wrist roller is a slightly more complex wrist strengthener. It consists of a weight tied to a 4-foot cord, which is itself anchored and wrapped around a short wooden bar. This bar is long enough to accommodate both your hands.

A wrist roller

To use this type of wrist strengthener, hold the bar in your hands, palms down, with the weight resting on the floor. Now begin rotating the bar so that the cord wraps around it and eventually lifts the weight up. When the weight reaches the bar, lower it back down in the same way.

There are several types of modern, commercially-available wrist strengtheners on the market. These consist of two metal handles, one on either side of an internal resistance mechanism. When you turn the handles, you are pushing against the load generated by this mechanism.

Climbing Machines

Recently the trendy exercise industry has come up with a new toy: a climbing machine. One of the most popular designs is the Versa Climber, but there are others that do the same thing. The idea behind the machine is to provide you with an endless climb. Instead of pulling yourself up the machine, and running out of room to climb (because of a low ceiling), you step on and pull its handles down to you.

A climbing machine

You can modify some climbing machines to make them more climbing specific. For example, with the Versa Climber you can actually climb on the overhanging side. In addition, if you have basic carpentry skills and the time (a few hours), you can attach wooden holds to the machine's handles. This smaller grip will give your fingers an excellent workout.

Climbing machines provide a good cardiovascular workout: it's just like climbing stairs, only at the same time you're also pulling with your arms. This means that you're using your entire body, and working both sides equally, as you would if you were actually climbing a rock.

Hangboard

A hangboard is a pull-up bar, developed a step further to make it climbing specific. Instead of having a simple round bar to hold onto, the hangboard is a flat board covered with various climbing holds. To do a pull-up you grab any two of the holds, one in each hand, then pull yourself up. The holds strengthen your fingers by putting them in positions similar to those used when you are climbing.

A hangboard

There are two basic ways to use a hangboard; most climbers combine the two. The first way is to do pull-ups with it, the second is to hang from it. The pull-ups will strengthen your upper body while the hangs specifically develop your finger strength. For a combination routine do 2 pull-ups, followed by a 10-second hang on one set of holds. Then, after taking a rest, grab two new holds. Do 3 pull-ups on them and then hang 30 seconds. By using such combinations you can accurately simulate the hand pulls you will be making on a climb. For example, if you must start a climb by grabbing two small edges, pulling up, then moving into finger pockets, you can do this on your hangboard, and so prepare yourself well for the climb.

Yes, you can injure yourself when you use a hangboard! Shoulder, elbow, and finger tendon injuries (the kinds of injuries that take time to heal!) are too common with these boards. To avoid injury, pay attention to your body. Don't try to push yourself too fast. If you feel a sharp pain (sharp pain is an indication of a joint injury), immediately stop working out and rest for a few days. You should also rest between every set of pull-ups and hangs, because when your muscles get tired they put more stress on your joints. Very importantly, when you hang from the board, keep your shoulders forward, head up. If you lean your head forward, your shoulders will rotate back and put most of your weight onto your shoulder tendons. One sure sign that you're in the wrong position is if you hear your shoulders click.

You can either buy a commercial hangboard, or make your own. Some commercial hangboards are made of a polyester resin mix, and are textured to give you a good grip. Others are made of wood. They all offer many different holds, including slopes, different-sized edges, pockets, and pinch grips. The type and number of holds varies with each model of hangboard.

Some commercial hangboards (such as the Hueco Board) have built-in **carabiner** clip-in points. This allows you to connect a series of carabiners to the bottom of your board and then, when you are actually hanging from it, unclip a carabiner then re-clip it to the top of the board. Such a strenuous workout will prepare you for the same motion on the rock, which you must use to place a chock and connect your rope to it.

Metolius used to sell their hangboards with bungi cords hanging beneath them. The idea was that, by stepping onto the bungi cord, you could do pull-ups and hangs at less than bodyweight, which means that you could hang longer. However, Metolius has since stopped selling the bungis, and has issued warnings to anyone using them, because they learned that a bungi could slip out from under your feet and hit your eyes!

It's cheaper to make your own hangboard, which will be just as effective as most commercial ones, but won't look as good. Besides saving money, by making your own hangboard you will be able to customize it to your needs: you can put on the exact size and shape of holds that you want to grab.

I am presenting a sample hangboard design. As with my other designs in this book, construct it if you want, or just use it to get ideas for your own design.

Before you design your own hangboard, you should decide where you are going to put it. It is important that you make your hangboard the right size; after all, you need a place large enough to use

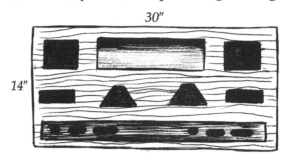

My sample hangboard design

it! Try to make the hangboard at least as wide as your shoulders, because doing pull-ups on holds that are shoulder-width apart is easier (your elbows will swing naturally to the sides of your chest, instead of into it).

When you bolt or screw the holds onto your hangboard, arrange them so that the large ones are at the top and the small ones are at the bottom. A large hold would jab into your forearm if you had positioned it below a smaller one.

Crack Machine

A crack machine is a simulated crack. You can buy a crack machine commercially, or make your own. The commercial versions consist of two bolt-on (or screw-on) sides which you attach to a wall. These sides are made of textured polyester resin, which, although it doesn't feel like rock, is durable, looks good, and provides some friction. It also has irregular sides, which makes a crack that is easier to climb than a parallel-sided one.

Crack machines come in short sections. If you have the space, and want a long crack, you can place one section above the other.

You can adjust the width of the crack by bolting the sides closer together or farther apart. However, commercially-available cracks work best for fist cracks or narrower. If you want to practice various offwidth (wide crack) techniques you will need a deeper crack machine. This is to accommodate your arm bars (inserting your entire arm) and leg jams (inserting your entire leg).

You can make a simple do-it-yourself crack machine out of wood. The advantage to making

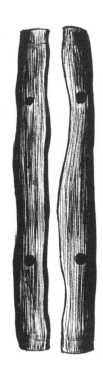

A commercial crack machine

A home-made crack machine

your own crack machine is that you can make it specifically to fit your needs. In addition, making your own crack machine is cheaper than buying a commercial version, providing you have the time to construct it.

An easy home-made crack machine consists of two 2 by 6-inch boards running alongside each other. They should be as long as possible, although this really depends on the amount of space available to you. The space between the two boards is the crack, so you should vary this distance according to the size of crack you want. Use medium-hard boards, because you don't want them to splinter, but you want them soft enough to provide you some friction.

You can connect the boards together with wooden spacers, made of 2x4-inch boards (their length depends on the crack's width). Put a spacer on each end of the crack machine and one or two in the middle, depending on how much support the boards need to maintain their stability (the longer they are, the more support they need). You don't want many spacers, however, because they get in the way when you're climbing.

To use this type of crack machine, anchor it securely to something, such as by bolting it to a vertical wall. Or, if you want to work on roof cracks, you can lay it horizontally across 2 tall (4 to 5-foot high) sawhorses.

The problem with this simple design is that you can't adjust it. However, you can solve this problem by making several different cracks, such as a finger-crack, a hand-crack, and an offwidth-sized one. Also, by cutting the spacers at angles, you can make a crack flare and narrow (don't flare it too much, or the smooth wood will make it almost impossible to use!).

A flaring home-made crack machine

Climbing Wall

A climbing wall is any large surface that you can climb on. It can be made of many substances, including cemented stones, plywood with attached holds, or more realistic looking pre-fabricated polyester resin.

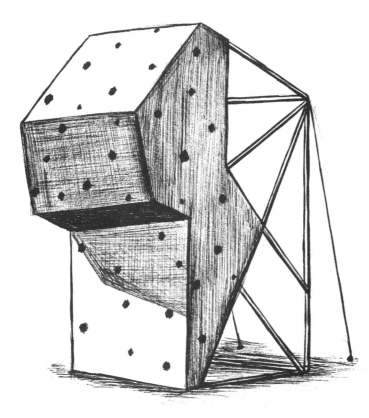

A commercial climbing wall

A climbing wall is a great training tool. Unlike most of the other training devices, with a climbing wall you can actually improve your climbing technique simply by climbing. You can learn how to keep most of your weight on your feet, how to rest in a vertical position, how to lieback or stem, how to heel or toe hook, how to lunge, how to mantle, and how to do most any other climbing move you can think of. (I describe the basics of these moves in the chapter Moving Over Rock, pg. 33). All you need to do is arrange the holds in the correct pattern to simulate the climb you want to practice. Also, if you don't live close to the rocks, a climbing wall will provide you with an easy-access climbing surface any time you want it.

Some climbing walls are located in public places, such as in some climbing shops, climbing-specific gyms, or even stone walls, but you can also have your own. Having your own wall gives you an individual workout station, an apparatus that you can modify to suit your needs. Besides its climbing surface, you can rig up a number of other training devices on the wall, such as a rope, a pull-up bar, a crack machine, and a pegboard.

If you want to make your own climbing wall, consider the problems. Do you have enough space? A climbing wall is a large structure (the larger the better). Not everyone actually has a place to put a climbing wall. Are you thinking of putting the wall outdoors? This is fine, if you have year-round warm weather. However, few people live in such an ideal place, and the rest of us find that our motivation to exercise outdoors decreases with the temperature! If you possibly can, erect your climbing wall inside. After all, one of the reasons for having a wall is that it gives you a place to climb when it's too cold and wet to climb on the real rocks. You might be able to put your wall in a garage, or even under a balcony (maybe you can put holds on the roof formed by the balcony!).

Also, if you build your climbing wall in your backyard, it may intrude upon the privacy of your neighbors. If you think this might be a problem, go talk to the neighbors; explain what you are doing. They'll probably be more understanding of your eccentricity if you inform them before you build.

Once you have decided to install a wall, you have several options. From the cheapest to the most expensive, these options are: make your own wall, from your own design, from my design or from a commercially-sold design. You can buy the pre-manufactured parts of a wall, usually of exotic, rock-like materials, and assemble it yourself. Or you can have climbing wall designers custom build a wall for you. We'd all like to have a fantastic wall, perhaps a piece of El Capitan herself, in our backyards! However, economic realities force most climbers to either visit a friend's climbing wall or build one for themselves, out of wood. Although not very exotic, a wooden climbing wall can provide you with all the training you need.

Climbing Wall Designs

First of all, what is the basic design concept of a wooden climbing wall? It consists of a flat surface, preferably vertical, but with an adjustable base, to which you attach holds. These holds may be home-made pieces of wood or commercially-available polyester resin holds. You can screw, bolt, or even glue these holds in place. However, bolting is best because it provides a strong connection. Also you can easily change a hold's location, and thereby alter your climb.

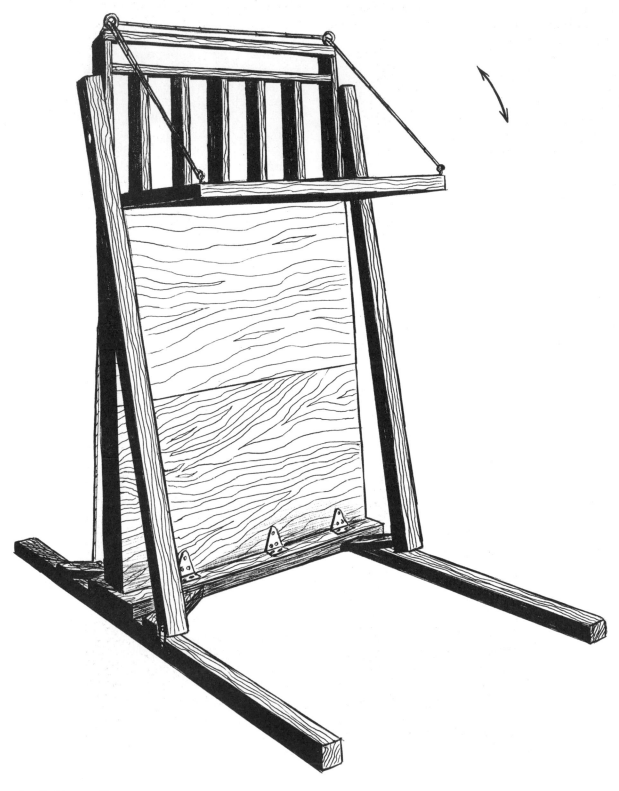

My sample climbing wall

I offer you the design of a wall I made. Use this design if you like it; perhaps it will give you some ideas for your own wall.

My wall is 8 feet wide by a little over 12 feet high. However, you can easily change these dimensions. Eight feet is a good minimum width: it stabilizes the structure and gives you room to move around. Don't make the wall higher than 12 feet, unless you are planning to use a rope, because you don't want to injure yourself by falling off! Consider the wall as a boulder problem: a short practice rock.

You can change the finished wall's angle from vertical to overhanging. You can modify it with panels on the back to make a slab (not shown). In addition, the overhanging panel is adjustable (vertical or horizontal), and gives you a roof to climb on. The overhang also gives you a place to do pull-ups, to mantle, to hang and lift yor legs out, perpendicular to your body (strengthening your abdomen), and to do finger traverses (traverse along the panel, using only your fingers to hang on).

Without its panels, the wall is simply a carpenter's stud wall. The structure is heavy, and takes at least two strong people to set up.

My sample climbing wall, without its panels

Climbing Wall Materials List (For An 8x12-Foot Wall)

Wood:
10	12-foot 2x4's
1	8-foot 4x6
2	12-foot 4x4's
2	10.5-foot 4x4's
3	4x8-foot sheets of 3/4-inch plywood
1	1/2-inch, 20-foot nylon static rope

Hardware:
1	5-pound bag of 3.5-inch screws
3	Heavy-duty steel hinges
3	Light-duty steel hinges
9	Large screws to fit heavy-duty hinges
9	Smaller screws to fit light-duty hinges
2	One-inch pulleys
2	Eyebolts
2	Small screw links (sized to connect pulleys to eyebolts)
2	1/2x4.5-inch bolts
2	1/2-inch nuts
4	1/2-inch washers
4	1/4x4.5-inch bolts
4	1/4-inch nuts
8	1/4-inch washers
2	3/4x6-inch mendplates

Tools:
1	Hand saw (electric saws are much faster!)
1	Electric drill, with bits from 1/16-inch to 1/2-inch
2	#2 screwdriver bits (so you can use your drill to place the screws - make sure you get the right head, either standard or phillips)
1	#1 screwdriver bit (to screw the large hinges in place)
1	#2 Screwdriver
2	Adjustable wrenches for bolts (up to 1/2-inch)

You also need enough bolts for the holds you are planning to use. If you make your own holds out of wood, you need 2 bolts per hold. Use 1/4x2-inch bolts with one washer and one wing nut per bolt. Commercial holds usually come with their own mounting hardware.

Alternative Ways To Train

Because climbing rocks is an athletic sport, anything you do to improve your overall athletic ability will help your climbing. As a supplement to climbing-specific training, you can play other sports for variety and excitement, as well as derive their training benefits. Particularly consider activities that improve your sense of body (balance, coordination, and kinetic sense), and those that increase your oxygen intake (cardiovascular activities). Tai Chi, gymnastics, and tumbling will improve your flexibility and overall body awareness. Aerobic sports such as running, swimming, biking, and rowing (good upper body workout) will increase your oxygen capacity, and thin you down.

Lifting weights is another important training supplement. With proper weight training you can strengthen climbing-specific muscles, such as those in your upper body, which will improve your ability to hang onto the rock.

However, if you want to lift weights, you will need access to the equipment. You can buy your own set, if you have the money and space. Or you may decide to join a gym (city recreational centers and Y's are cheap alternatives to expensive modern gyms). If you don't know how to weight train, I recommend that you work with someone who does. Using weights improperly can really hurt your body! One advantage to the large modern gyms is that they have a staff of trainers who will help you accomplish your goals.

Some Games To Play

Here are several fun games that will also improve your overall body skills.

Tightrope

Walking a tightrope is a good way to develop your sense of balance. You should begin with a stiff cable or a thin beam of wood (a 2x4 turned on edge), but with practice you will soon be jumping onto a thin rope with perfect balance.

Don't use your climbing rope for a tightrope! First, it is extremely thin and difficult to walk on. More importantly, you will weaken it if you walk on it. Instead, use a utility rope (it can be as thick or as thin as you want).

To rig a tightrope you need two strong trees or posts. They should be spaced 10-20 feet apart, although the greater the resistance the more slack you will have in your rope. And, although possible, it's harder to walk across a loose rope. Tie the rope

to a tree, about 2 feet off the ground, by wrapping it approximately 5 times around the trunk (you will need more wraps on a thinner tree), as illustrated below.

The wrap anchoring one end of the tightrope

Now, with the help of 3 or 4 people, pull the other end of the rope taut and wrap it around the other tree, securing it tightly with the same wrap that you used for the first side. That's all there is to it!

The Crane

I call this game the crane, because it involves balancing on one leg and picking things up with your teeth, much as the bird does. You can play it alone, or with friends.

You will need several small pieces of food, such as pieces of cookies, chocolate, or even apples. Put a piece of food on a rock or tree trunk at about waist height. Now each of the contestants must, one at a time, stand on one leg, bend over, and pick the food up with their teeth. They cannot use anything for support or balance. The contestants that succeed in picking up the food that lies at waist height get to compete in the next round, which involves retrieving food that is lying closer to the ground. Eventually, you try to pluck food directly from the ground.

Note that all the contestants should warm up before playing, because deep leg bends are strenuous.

A climber doing "the crane"

A sample board-walking course

Board-Walking

A game of balance; board-walking is just that: walking over boards. But these boards are not flat, wide, and stable. Instead, use thin boards, a 2x4 or even a 1/2x2, and stand them on their edges. Set several end to end, or side by side, forming an irregular course, and try to walk across them!

One way to play the game is to have each contestant start at one end of the course, try to reach the other end, then turn around and retrace his or her steps, all without touching the ground. You can make the course more difficult after every round by decreasing the board lengths and increasing the distance between them.

Footbag

Hitting a footbag, or hacky-sack, is a great way to warm up and loosen up before training. Although you can use practically anything (such as an orange, apple, or tennis ball), a commercially-available footbag works better. Such a footbag is made of leather and, filled with small plastic beads, is easier to hit around than the other items.

There are two rules to the basic footbag game: you must not let the bag hit the ground, and you can only hit it with your feet. These simple rules make for a lively and very interesting game!

Some Manufacturers Of Training Devices

Chouinard, Colorado Academy of Artistic Gymnastics, the Fitness Group, Heart Rate, Inc., International Mountain Equipment, Metolius, Sole Survivor, Treco, and Vertical Concepts. See pg. 353 for the addresses of these manufacturers.

Key Point

"You must position your wedging chock along the direction of potential force! This direction changes as you climb. . . ."

See page 331

Wedging Chocks
(Nuts)

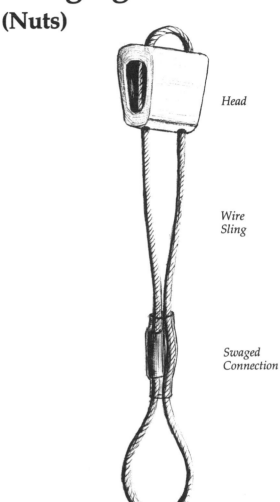

Head

Wire
Sling

Swaged
Connection

A wedging chock

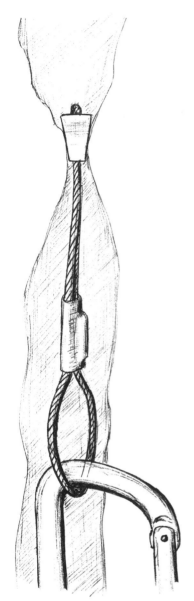

A wedging chock wedged in a crack

What is a Wedging Chock?

A **chock** is a device which securely locks in a crack splitting the rock that you are climbing. Climbers place these chocks in cracks and then connect their **ropes** to them, thereby anchoring themselves to the rock. A wedging chock is a type of chock which provides security by wedging into the crack.

There are no moving parts on a wedging chock; it consists only of a metal wedge-shaped head and a wire or cord **sling**. Using a chock to secure yourself against a fall is a natural way to protect a climb. After you use the chock you remove it and take it with you, leaving the rock unscarred.

There are three basic types of chocks, including **active camming** (see pg. 65), **passive camming** (see pg. 233), and wedging chocks. The wedging chock is the simplest. It is made in only two sizes, and the range of crack sizes it can fit is therefore limited. Wedging chocks are designed to fit narrow cracks; if you want to place protection into a wide crack you must use either a passive or an active camming chock.

Each wedging chock manufacturer offers his wedges either individually or as a set. A set usually contains from nine to 13 differently-sized chocks.

Brief History

Climber in the 1860s

No one is really sure when rock climbers began using chocks to protect themselves from falling. But by the 1940's, chocks were in common use.

The original chocks were small pebbles taken from riverbeds. A climber would place a pebble in a crack and tie a length of cord around it, then connect it to his rope. The term "chockstone" comes from this improvised use of these protective pebbles.

By the late 1950's climbers were using common nuts (the kind that screw on a bolt) as chocks. The nut had to be modified first: the threads were drilled out and any sharp edges filed down. Because these nuts had a ready-made hole, they were easy to thread with cord.

The first chocks machined specifically for climbing were made by John Brailsford in 1961. He began by making a strong resin-bonded chock which he called "Acorns." He later developed "Moacs" which were aluminum wedges with holes drilled to accept cord. Moacs provided the proto-type for modern-day wedging chocks.

Trevor Peck made the first wire-slung chocks in 1962. By 1966, two companies, Troll and Clog, were producing chocks in their factories.

Since then, manufacturers have designed more elaborate and versatile chocks. But nothing has replaced the fundamental wedging chock for its simplicity and the security it gives when placed correctly.

Types

There are two types of wedging chocks: small ones and large ones. Manufacturers give these chocks many names, including: Rocks, Stones, Stoppers, Nuts, and Offsets, among others.

Small Wedging Chocks

The first small wedges were designed by Roland Pauligk. He made them for the small, shallow cracks that are common on Mt. Arapiles, Australia. These small wedges were a great success, and are still made. They are called RP nuts.

Since then, many other types of small wedges have been manufactured. Some are modeled after Pauligk's original straight-edged, slightly tapering, trapezoidal design. Others have innovated slightly different shapes. For example, Hugh Banner Offsets have an asymmetrical trapezoidal shape (notice the teardrop-shaped cutout on the face; it is to avoid rock knobs). Wild Country Stones have extremely rounded sides.

A Hugh Banner Offset —
a type of small wedging chock

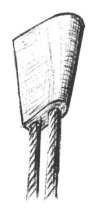

A Wild Country Stone —
a type of small wedging chock

Small wedging chocks are designed to fit small and awkwardly-shaped cracks. These otherwise hard-to-protect placements include shallow cracks, slots (often made by pitons that were removed), and pockets.

A small wedging chock in a pocket

A small wedging chock in a shallow crack

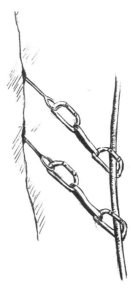

Two small wedging chocks placed close together for added security

A small wedging chock in a slot

The main problem with small wedging chocks is their low strength. This results from their small size and thin wire, and cannot be avoided. If you are climbing a thin crack where the only chock you can place is a very small wedging chock, you should try to place two of them instead of just one. This will give you extra security.

Small wedging chocks are always slung with wire; cord will not fit. This wire is soldered or otherwise placed into the head of the chock. *Be careful when you remove a small wedging chock from a crack — a sharp tug may damage the wire's connection.*

Large Wedging Chocks

Large wedging chocks are larger versions of small wedges. They are roughly based on the same trapezoidal shape, but with more variations, especially curves, than the small wedges. (A small wedge is not able to take advantage of a curved shape; for the curve to provide security it must be larger.) A curved shape gives the most stability to a large wedging chock; it provides stable three point contact with the rock.

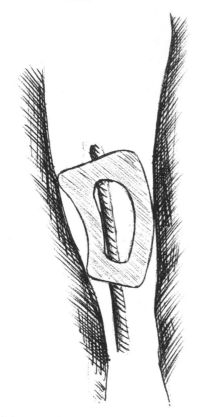

A large wedging chock demonstrating 3-point contact

Some large wedging chocks have scooped out grooves in their sidewalls (The DMM Wallnuts are good examples). This design enables the wedge to avoid small rock irregularities.

Many climbers find it easier to place and remove (clean) a straight-sided large wedge. However, the straight-sided wedge doesn't provide the same grip on the rock as a curved one. The edges of the wedge are also important. Rounded edges make it easier to remove the wedge; sharp edges tend to catch the rock.

The majority of large wedging chocks are slung with wire. However, with the largest wedges manufacturers usually offer you choice: you can buy them wired or loose. Loose means that you buy the head alone; then you must buy some cord to sling the chock. The best cord to use is **Spectra**, although **Kevlar** also works well. See Slings and Runners, pg. 291. The advantage to buying your chocks loose is that the cord is stronger than the wire the

chock would be connected to otherwise.

In the past, the holes in a large wedging chock were very big. This was so you could place as large a sling as possible (you had to use nylon cord, which gains strength as its size increases). Now, however, all the holes are drilled to 5.5mm in diameter, fitting the Spectra and Kevlar cord perfectly. Note: if you buy some old wedging chocks you may find that their holes are too large to fit Spectra. Climbing stores sell plastic tubing to fix this problem. See Modifications and Tune-Ups, pg. 332.

Large wedging chocks are much stronger than their smaller brothers. This is due to the difference in the width of the wire sling and the metal head. A larger head allows the holes to be drilled farther apart, which widens the bend in the sling. The wider the bend in the sling, the less it will be damaged under load. See the chapter called Rope, pg. 269, for more information.

Color Coding

A color-coded wedging chock is easy to identify. When you know your chocks, you can look at a crack and know just which chock will fit it. Color coding makes it easy to identify one chock out of all the others on your rack. It takes time to become this familiar with your chocks; the best way is to practice placing them.

Most manufacturers do color code their wedging chocks. They use colored plastic tubing, sometimes around the swaged connection (the wire loop is connected by a piece of metal bent tight around it), and sometimes around the end of the sling.

Technique

A placement is the position of a chock in a crack. A good placement is very trustworthy; a bad placement very untrustworthy. Generally speaking, the more rock surface in contact with your wedging chock, the more secure the placement. In other words, *don't trust a chock wedged between two small rock nubbins*; two large, solid sides of a crack are much more trustworthy.

There are an infinite number of ways to place a chock. You must use your imagination. The most common placement is in a vertical crack; in a horizontal crack you may have to use two wedging chocks opposed:

Wedging chocks opposed in a horizontal crack

Or you can stack them to fit a wide crack:

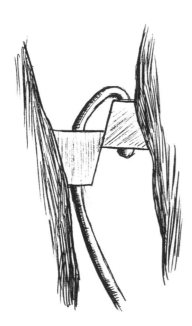

Wedging chocks stacked

There are many other variations to these basic placements. Placing chocks is a skill that some climbers turn into an art: every chock in perfect position, the climber has created a secure **protection system**.

A word of warning: *make sure that you place each wedging chock in the direction of the force that will act on it.* Usually this will be diagonally down and out. Once you place a second chock above the first, the force of a fall on the first chock will be more horizontal than vertical.

Test the Chock

After you place it, make sure your large wedging chock is secure from all the potential directions of

force by lightly tugging it in each direction. In most vertical cracks, this means tug it once down and then once out, away from the rock. Don't tug the chock too hard; this will make it difficult to remove. If you see any movement, you should definitely reposition the chock.

You may damage your small wedging chock if you try to test its position by tugging on it. Its wire connection is very fragile and you must not crack this connection. A very *light* tug will do, if you must tug at all.

Fallen Climber

The direction of force on a series of chocks

Specifications

Size

Every wedging chock has two size measurements, width and depth. These measurements are very important. They tell you the size of crack that a particular chock will fit. Because you cannot change the size of the wedging chock as you can with an active camming chock, for instance, you must buy a variety of wedging chocks to fit the range of crack sizes you are likely to encounter.

Some manufacturers make the width of one wedge roughly equal to the depth of the next larger wedge. This is particularly useful if you need two wedges of the same size, which, as I already mentioned, may happen if you want to place your wedging chocks close together for added security. Other manufacturers make the width of a wedge a size between its depth and the depth of the next larger wedge. This adds size variety to your set of wedges.

Strength

The strength of the wedging chock is usually determined by the strength of its sling. If it is slung with wire, its strength depends on how thick the wire is. The thicker the wire, the stronger the chock. The wire of a wedging chock will almost always break before the chock's head does.

Small wedging chocks have a wide variety of strength ratings (they increase as the chock gets larger). The smallest chocks have a strength rating of around 500 pounds. *These are meant to be used in* **aid climbing** *only; they are not designed to hold a fall!* In other words, they will support your weight but are not strong enough to support the force of your fall. The strength rating of small wedging chocks goes up to around 2000 pounds, more or less, for the largest sizes.

The strength rating of large wedging chocks also varies, but not as much. The smaller sizes tend to start at 1000-1500 pounds (notable exceptions are the 1 and 2 Chouinard Stoppers, rated at 770 pounds). The rest of the large wedges have a strength rating of between 2500-3300 pounds. The exact rating depends on the manufacturer, of course, but this should give you a rough idea of the strength rating of wedging chocks.

Weight

I must keep stressing the importance of equipment weight. Your rack can get very heavy when you carry a lot of wedging chocks, even though each alone is lightweight. One way to reduce this weight is to bring along only those chocks that you will actually need on a particular climb. This is a fine judgement call, however, because you must not be stuck half-way up a crack out of chocks! Experience helps develop this judgement.

Wire Size

The wire's diameter and length are important, because they affect the strength, durability, and stability of the wedging chock. Generally speaking, the thicker the wire, the stronger it is and the longer it will last. A long wire adds stability to the chock by being flexible. It absorbs some of the rope's jerking which occurs as you climb, and reduces the chance of the chock leveraging out of position.

Materials

How sharp a wedging chock's edges are makes a difference in its performance. Sharp edges cause two problems: they increase the chance of the chock shearing (breaking), and they are harder to remove from the rock. However, sharp edges can also be advantageous. They offer more bite; they grip the rock better than rounded edges. Manufacturers usually leave the edges of their small wedging chocks sharp while rounding the edges of their large wedging chocks. Small wedging chocks need as much bite as they can get because their small size reduces their contact with the rock, which in turn reduces the security of the placement.

The wedge's shape is also important: the more exaggerated its curve, the more likely it is that the wedge will shear under load. However, manufacturers know this and compensate for it. For example, the DMM Wallnuts are extremely curved, which increases their chance of shearing. DMM has solved this problem by putting each wedge through a special hardening process.

Many different types of metals are used to make wedging chocks, including brass, steel, and aluminum alloy. Some of these metals are stronger than the others. However, it is the construction process manufacturers use that really determines a chock's strength. *Rely on a wedging chock's strength specifications and your skill in placing the chock.*

Wedging chocks strung with wire are weaker than those slung with high strength cord (such as Spectra). Also, the smaller the wedge, the thinner (and weaker) the wire.

Although cord such as Spectra is stronger than wire, it has some basic disadvantages. Obviously, it cannot be used with most wedging chocks because it is too big to fit in them. It also does not have the stiffness of wire; this is both good and bad. A stiff wire makes it easier to place a wedge above your head. However, a stiff wire also leverages the wedging chock, meaning that the wedge is more likely to fall from the simple movement of your rope as it follows you up the rock. The longer the wire, the less it will leverage. *Always add a quickdraw to a wedging chock to reduce the leverage.* A quickdraw is a runner with two carabiners, one attached to the wedging chock and the other to your rope.

A wedging chock connected to a rope with a quickdraw

The Wire Connection

The way the wire is connected to a wedging chock is important. The stronger the connection, the stronger the chock. Small wedging chocks are so small that the wire must end in the wedge.

To connect the wire to the wedge, manufacturers either mold or solder the wire in place. With a molded wedging chock, the wire cable is inserted while the chock is still hot and soft. When the metal hardens, the wire becomes a part of it. Connection by soldering is more common however; holes are drilled in an already finished wedge, the wires are put in and soldered in place. When you look at a soldered wedge, make sure the soldering is neat. A clean soldering job shows that care and attention has been paid; the joint is probably very strong.

Large wedging chocks are big enough for the wire to loop through the wedge. This means that the two wire ends must be connected together by swaging. Swaging is the term used to describe a technique of pressing a metal clip around the ends of a loop of wire. Swaging is the strongest way to connect a wire loop, and therefore the most popular.

General Safety Guidelines

Correct Positioning!

You must position your wedging chock along the direction of potential force! This direction changes as you climb and place more protection. For example, in a vertical crack, each chock you put in must be ready for a downward tug. But if you fall, your taut rope will lift the previous chocks and pull them horizontally out from the rock. If you have not secured them from this outward direction of pull as well, chances are they will pop out, which will leave you with only one piece of **protection** (the last one placed).

Use a Runner!

Always connect a runner to your wedging chocks! A runner helps reduce the tug of your rope on the chocks. This means that a runner increases the security of your chock's position.

Care

If your wedging chock is slung with wire, try not to bend it; it may kink. A kink weakens the wire.

If you sling your wedging chock with a cord, try to keep the cord out of the dirt. Avoid excessive sunlight, acids, and bleaches. For more on caring for cords, see page 299.

When to Retire Your Wedging Chock

The head of a wedging chock lasts a long time, and so the wire or cord will wear out first. You can replace cord, but once wire wears out you must replace the chock. The wire will bend, kink, start to fray, and then break. Retire your wired wedging chock when its wire begins to fray or has a severe kink in it.

Modifications and Tune-Ups

You cannot fix any part of a wedging chock. If your chock is slung with cord which breaks, you can replace the cord. Replacing a wire sling is not a viable option because, in terms of time and money, it would be cheaper to buy a new chock.

Adding Plastic Tubing

If you are trying to sling some old wedging chocks with Spectra or Kevlar, you may find that the wedge's holes are too big. An easy solution to this problem is to buy some plastic tubing to put around the cord and fill the extra space. You can find this tubing at your local climbing store. Show the salesperson the chocks you want to sling, and try fitting the tubing over the cord to make sure it is the correct size.

When you get home, cut enough tubing to fit through the wedge's head and still have about a half inch extra on each end. Put your cord though this tube, then thread the entire thing through the wedge's holes.

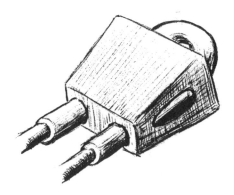

A wedging chock slung with cord and plastic tubing

Because the plastic tubing bends tightly as it loops through the wedge, it remains in position.

Accessories

Plastic Tubing

Plastic tubing is easy to find at a climbing store (just ask the salesperson). You need different lengths of tubing depending on the size of the chocks you want to sling. Approximate each size, then add a little to save yourself a trip back to the store.

Non-Technical Gear

Rocks and cliffs are rarely conveniently located. Usually they are at least a few miles out of town, often they are much further away. Some cliffs are so close to the road that you can touch them from your car; others are deep in the backcountry and require a multi-day hike to reach. The accessibility of a cliff determines how much gear, other than your technical climbing equipment, that you need to bring along. You will need essentials such as food, water, a pack, and different types of clothing. What kind and how much of these essentials you bring will change as you get further from society: you must plan accordingly.

And remember the weather! The weather plays a very important role in dictating the kind of clothes you bring, how much food and water, and any other special items (such as sunscreen) you will require.

I will briefly discuss the basic non-technical gear that you may need. Remember that these are just suggestions and that you should bring, wear, and eat whatever you want. Experiment with different foods and gear until you get the mix that you like the best. Just as you should attempt short climbs before the longer ones, take short hikes to the cliffs before attempting longer, more committed trips.

Clothing

A climber is a gymnast; his apparatus is the rock. To successfully ascend the rock the climber must be able to move smoothly, freely, and gracefully. His clothing should allow him to do this.

The most important piece of clothing for you, the climber, is the pant. Your pants should keep you warm, comfortable, and protected, but at the same time allow total freedom of hip and leg motion. The type of pant that works best depends on the weather and the type of climb you are making. In hot weather, on a climb where you won't need to use your knees, shorts are ideal. They provide lots of ventilation to keep you cool, and allow total freedom of movement. Shorts don't work well in wide cracks, however, because they don't protect your legs, especially your knees.

If you want to climb a wide crack, I recommend you wear a very tough pair of long pants. Some old jeans should work fine, although jeans usually re-

strict your leg motion. If this bothers you, try some karate-style pants (tough, thick cotton pants that are cut very loose: made for unrestricted movement). You can also wear sweatpants, although they aren't nearly as durable as the other two. Taping the knee areas with cloth athletic tape will help keep your sweatpants together.

If the weather is too cool for shorts, you have several options, some of which I just mentioned. Sweatpants are ideal. They are warm, allow total movement, don't catch easily on the rock, and are reasonably durable (but not in wide cracks!). They are also very comfortable, which makes them good for wearing around the camp, or for hiking.

As I mentioned before, karate-style pants are also an option. They are more durable than sweatpants and allow total motion. Unfortunately, they are so baggy that they sometimes catch on the rock, and often block your view of your feet, which can make it difficult to find your footholds. Also, karate-style pants are not as warm as sweatpants because they are so baggy (they permit too much ventilation).

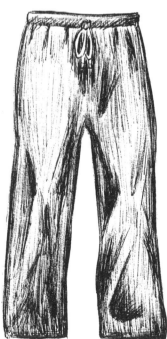

Karate-style pants

There are some pants on the market that are a cross between sweatpants and karate-style pants. Gramici and A5 are two manufacturers of these pants. The pants look like sweats: they are loose, have elastic bottoms and a gussetted crotch, all of which combine for excellent freedom of movement. But the pants, like karate-style pants, are made of tough cotton that is more durable and grips the rock better than sweatpants. And the bottoms are thinner than karate-style pants so they won't catch on the rock.

You can also climb in a jeans. In fact, jeans are the most durable pants you can climb in, and provide excellent protection from the rock. However, jeans restrict your leg movements, making them impractical and uncomfortable for most climbing.

You may want to wear tights. Tights, such as those made of spandex/nylon combinations, fit skin tight, support your muscles and still allow total freedom of movement. They don't catch on the rock, and will never block your view of your feet. They come in many fantastic colors, and are fashionable among most of the top rock climbers around the world.

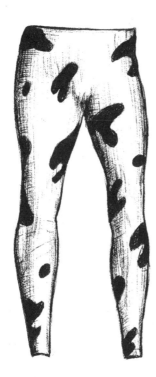

Tights

Tights do have some problems, however. They are not very warm, especially in the wind, which cuts right through them (you can buy thicker ver-

sions, however, which offer more protection). They have no durability; once a hole starts it quickly becomes massive, spreading out around the rest of the pant as though it were a run in a stocking. And tights are not always comfortable. They start off feeling fine, but as you climb in them they can become itchy, especially if you sweat a lot (the man-made fiber aggravates your sweaty skin).

Polypropylene tights are another option. These pants are made of thick polypropylene, which is a soft, warm material. They don't have the nylon tights' wild colors, nor do they fit skin tight, but they are tighter than sweats. They offer an excellent range of motion, and are very comfortable. They also work well as long underwear.

If the weather is too cold for just one pair of pants, try wearing some long underwear or a pair of tights underneath your pants. Tights under sweatpants makes a good combination. If the weather is even colder, you are entering the domain of alpine-climbing and mountaineering, and need to buy special clothing made for these situations. Such clothing requires experience way beyond this book: go to an outfitting store and talk with the knowledgeable salespeople you find there.

Likewise, I am not discussing rain gear, because rock becomes very slippery in the rain, and is usually too difficult to climb. On rainy days, climbing anything but overhangs (where the rock is dry) is very dangerous, so you should wait for the sky to clear.

An important note for men: I recommend that you wear underwear when you climb (unless you are wearing tights)! If you don't, and you fall, your genitals may become painfully, excruciatingly, caught under your **harness'** leg loops!

Socks are the next bit of clothing to consider. You may not want to wear socks at all while you are climbing. Many climbers don't. Socks interfere with your ability to feel the rock through your climbing boots. However, if your feet sweat a lot, wear socks anyway! Sweaty feet slide around inside boots. Even if your feet don't sweat much, on a hot day consider wearing socks.

But if you do wear socks, what kind of socks should they be? Thin liner socks, such as those made of polypropylene, absorb your sweat and still give you a close connection to the rock. Cotton athletic socks reduce your feel of the rock but keep your boots tight on your feet (and you won't have problems with sweat). Thin wool socks are durable, but warm. They don't get rid of your sweat, so your feel will feel as though they are in a Florida summer (very humid)! However, wool socks are ideal if you are climbing in cold weather.

Try these different socks until you find the ones you like the best. Or maybe you want to bring several types of socks along, so you'll be prepared for cold, moderate, or hot weather!

And now to the upper body. Naturally, the shirt you wear is dictated by the weather. If it's hot, wear a lightweight T-shirt or tanktop. If it's moderate, wear a long sleeve shirt. If it's cold, put on a sweatshirt or sweater over your long sleeve shirt which is over your T-shirt. If it's windy, wear a windbreaker. And if it's rainy, hide inside your tent, car, or stay at home! If it is really, really cold where you want to climb, you're into mountaineering again, so make a trip to your local outfitting store and talk to a knowledgeable salesperson.

Unless it is summer, and you're in an area which is very hot, bring a sweatshirt, sweater, or light jacket with you. When the sun sets it will probably get cold. And you may have to walk some distance to reach the warmth of your car.

Approach Shoes

An approach shoe is the shoe (or boot) that you wear while walking to the cliffs. You don't want to use your climbing boots for this job because they aren't made for it: they will wear out too fast. Instead, you need a pair of shoes that are comfortable enough to walk in, support your feet during steep hiking, and grip the rock well (you will often need to scramble up easy slabs and boulders).

The type of shoe that you use depends on the terrain you are planning to cover, and the length of your trip. If you are walking to an artificial wall just down the street, you really don't need any shoes. Tennis shoes are fine for a short hike up a good trail, while for long, multi-day expeditions in the high mountains you may want a serious hiking boot. Light, cloth hiking boots provide a good compromise, offering comfort and light weight while still providing good foot and ankle support and rugged durability. Many shoe manufacturers are producing these shoes, catering to the growing demand that is partly generated by rock climbers. Sample light hiking boots include Hi-Tec's Sierra Lights and Sierra Classics, Vasque's Clarion Boots and Shoes, and Nike's Lava High Boots.

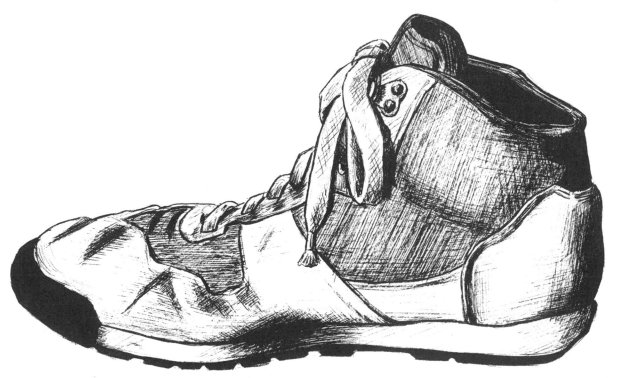

A light cloth hiking boot

Hat

Hats are useful while climbing. If it's hot, a hat can protect you from the sun. If it's cold, a hat will keep you warm.

In hot weather you will find a visored hat indispensable. This is especially true when you are halfway up the cliff, belaying your partner, and staring up into the bright sun. A light-colored hat with a visor works best. There are many suitable hats on the market, including baseball hats and hats with continuous brims.

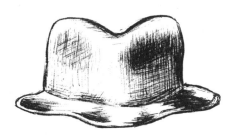

A hat with a continuous brim

One problem with a visored-hat is that the visor gets in your way when you climb. If you are wearing a baseball hat, reverse it so that the visor is behind you. A hat with a continuous brim is more awkward: it is nearly impossible to get the brim out of your way. Some of these brims are stiff enough to fold up and stay there, and some have snaps that will hold the brim up, but most don't. You may want to attach a length of cord to the hat so you can hang it from your neck, out of the way.

If the weather is cold you should wear a hat to keep you warm. It is well known that 25% of your body's heat escapes from your bare head, and that you feel cold first in your toes, then in your fingers. These extremities don't function well when they're cold, and you need them in top condition when you climb. So wear a hat in cold weather. It can help keep your all-important fingers and toes warm.

Wool hats work well. A simple cap will do, similar to that worn by many sailors.

You may want something more exotic, like an Inca-style hat with earflaps. These hats are very warm and functional. Mountain climbers often wear them.

A Balaclava will also work, but you will probably only need it in the extreme cold.

A sailor's cap

An Inca-style hat

A balaclava

Climbing With Glasses

Many climbers wear glasses, whether prescription glasses or sunglasses. Glasses rarely get in one's way; in fact, sunglasses are almost mandatory on some cliffs because of the glaring rock. Note that glare is exaggerated after a rain (any remaining water reflects the light).

If you climb with your glasses you will probably scratch the lens occasionally. Usually these scratches aren't too bad, but sometimes they can force you to buy a new pair. The best scratch prevention is awareness: be aware that you have glasses on, and be careful whenever you need to bring your head close to the rock.

Note: I recommend that you don't climb with glasses that contain glass lenses. If the glass hits, or is hit by, a rock, it may shatter, perhaps sending a sliver into your eye. Plastic lenses are much safer even though they scratch more easily.

If you do wear glasses while you climb, be sure to use a glasses strap. The strap guarantees that your glasses will remain on your head, even if you fall. Losing your glasses as you climb can be frustrating, expensive, and possibly dangerous (if you can't see without them!).

A pair of glasses with a strap

There are several different glasses straps on the market. They all work well so choose the one that you find most comfortable. You can find them in any climbing shop, outfitting store, sporting goods stores, many supermarkets, and some other general stores.

Food

What kind of food should you bring along when climbing? And how much of it? Your answers to these questions will be different from everyone else's. Everybody has different tastes and appetites. However, there are some basic principles that can guide you toward a diet that works for you.

First of all, there are two aspects to food: the food you normally eat (when you aren't climbing) and the food you bring with you on a climb.

Regarding the food you normally eat when not climbing, note that many of the best climbers study nutrition carefully and follow special food regimens. They normally eat very little - just enough to supply the proper amount of energy - because they are trying to keep their weight down (they often weigh at least 10 pounds less than the average weight for their height). Most top climbers don't eat meat because it is fatty (although they are careful to consume protein), and fat adds to your bodyweight without adding useable energy (top climbers have an average body fat of 5% fat for men and 12% for women - much lower than the general public). Such dedicated climbers stick to natural foods, particularly carbohydrates, eating only those foods their body can efficiently turn into energy. Basically, they just don't eat most of the foods that the rest of us consume every day.

But is this what you want to do? Probably not. Unless you are really focused on becoming an exceptional climber you don't need to follow a strict diet. You can continue to eat as you have always done, although you may find that your diet slowly and naturally changes as you pursue the sport. This isn't always the case, but many climbers begin to eat less and pay more attention to what they do eat as they become more and more focused on climbing. Do what you feel comfortable with; after time and practice you may find yourself climbing hard **routes** without changing your diet at all.

The food that you eat on the day you climb - both before and during the climb - is very important, because it directly affects your energy level. Climbers use a lot of energy. And when you begin you must have enough energy stored up that you can climb without becoming fatigued.

I am going to describe how I eat when I climb so that you can gain a few ideas about foods that might work for you. Remember, food choices are very personal. Everyone has different tastes as well as different nutritional needs. Listen to what your body is saying about food. If the food I describe is abhorrent to you, by all means, don't eat it! And if you have a craving for a particular food, eat whatever it is you crave! Cravings are your body's way of letting you know that it needs the benefits a particular food has to offer.

I don't like to eat a heavy meal on the day that I am climbing. It takes me a few hours to digest such a meal, and I am too sluggish to climb well while my body is digesting food. After eating a heavy meal it takes me 2-3 hours before I am able to climb well again, and feel good. Eating a large meal also takes time, and when I am on a long climb I don't have a lot of time to give.

To solve this problem I prefer to snack throughout the day. But in order that snacking will give me enough energy, I need to begin the day with a large breakfast. Breakfast gives me long-term energy; I am able to use it all day. For breakfast I usually eat grains, such as cereal, and fruit, because they are a good source of long-term energy (complex carbohydrates, which take longer for the body to break down but provide energy for a longer period of time. Simple sugars, such as those found in sweets, are easy to break down, but their energy doesn't last so long.)

During the day I eat a combination of short and long-term energy food. The short-term energy food gives me a quick burst of energy when I need it. Bananas are an excellent short-term energy food, as are other fruits, as well as cookies, chocolate, and sweets. The long-term energy food I eat helps keep my base energy high throughout the day, bolstering the energy I received at breakfast. Grains, such as those in bread, are an excellent long-term energy food: the body is able to break them down with little effort, certainly far less energy than is necessary with meat, for instance (although meat is also a long-term energy food). However, because the body must work harder to digest any long-term energy food, I eat less of it on a climb.

The actual menu that I usually end up with is: peanut butter and jelly sandwiches made with wheat bread, bananas or other fruit (bananas are ideal, although they rot quickly), and, if I'm feeling extravagant, cookies (oatmeal, because I get the long-term energy from the oats in addition to the short-term sugar energy).

Water

You certainly need water when you climb! Your body will need water not only to replace the water you lose (sweat) while climbing but also because of the adrenalin pump you receive from the excitement of being high on the cliff. Also, your tendons will weaken, dry out, and may easily become injured if you don't drink enough water! This is a very serious problem, especially in such a tendon-related sport as climbing.

However, don't drink too much water! Too much water will sit heavily in your stomach. It will make you feel sluggish, which will affect your climbing. Drink your water in small mouthfuls, with at least thirty seconds between each drink. Drinking slowly is even more important if you are dehydrated because in such a condition your body won't be able to accept the water quickly. It will just sit in your stomach, and make you feel nauseous.

How much water you need will vary according to conditions. I usually bring a full, 2 liter bottle (almost 2 quarts) with me. Sometimes I bring the bottle back nearly full while other times the bottle is empty at noon and I am desperately parched. It is sometimes hard to anticipate how much water you will need. However, if you study it, the weather will tell you a lot: if it's hot, bring more water than you think you will need. I have learned to bring along one of those full, plastic gallon-containers of water, which I leave in my car, wrapped in a blanket to keep cool.

Be sure to carry your water in tough plastic containers that will survive the hard, abrasive rock. You can buy these containers at most climbing and camping shops. Plastic 2-liter soda bottles are cheaper and work well, but you may want to wrap the bottle in duct tape first to strengthen it (this is especially important if you are climbing a big wall).

Concerning water for long climbs: on long, **multi-pitch** climbs you must bring water with you up the rock! Carry it in a daypack, or as a canteen on your belt. If you are on a **big wall** climb, you must also carry water in your **haulbag** (at least a half-gallon per person, per day).

Toilet Paper

Toilet paper is an item that you forget to bring on a climb only once. Now I never go climbing without bringing some along; in fact, I just leave a roll in my pack, all the time.

A full roll of toilet paper is too bulky to pack. Instead, wait until about half the roll in your bathroom is gone, then confiscate it! Be sure to loop a rubber band around the roll to keep it from unravelling in your pack or, when you reach the rocks, you will have a mess.

An important issue for anyone recreating in the outdoors is where, and how, to defecate. All to often these days I stumble upon rocks surrounded by white splashes of toilet paper, some half-buried, others blatantly flapping in the breeze. This ugly situation is bound to get worse as climbing becomes more popular. I urge you to act responsibly, bury your waste, then pack your toilet paper out. Most people bury their toilet paper with the rest of it. The problem with this is that the paper takes a long time to mix into the earth, and may come uncovered, then pollute the land. Carry a sealable plastic bag to accommodate your paper; you can throw the full bag away when you reach a suitable sanitary disposal site (such as an outhouse).

If you are on horizontal ground when you need to defecate, and there isn't a restroom or outhouse available, you will have to find a private place in the open. Stay at least 150 feet away from any sources of water! This is sometimes hard to do, especially in canyons, but try. Stay out of gullies and holes because water travels through these in a storm. Your best bet is to find some private high ground.

Once you have found your potential site, dig a hole. If you didn't bring a shovel, grab the nearest rock or stick to scoop the earth away. Dig 6-8 inches down, no more or less. Why? This is where the most powerful eroding agents in the soil lie. Be careful to keep the earth you have dug out close by so that you can throw it back into place when you are done. And when you have finished, pack the dirt down tightly, and make sure everything is well buried.

If you are on a multi-day route, defecation is a problem. Most climbers have resorted to simply leaning out, dropping their load, and watching it smear its way down the cliff. This is easy for the climber doing it, but is disgusting for those who come behind. Until the rains wash the cliffs, other climbers must climb past disgusting trails of feces. By the way, this is also a very good reason not to follow a party of climbers up the cliff, but to choose a less-traveled route.

A more sanitary method of defecating while on a climb is to bring along several tough, plastic ziplock bags for the purpose. They must be large enough to be easy to hit (a miss could be devastating!). Use the 8-inch by 8-inch variety, or larger. When you have finished, shut the bag and place it in a larger, sealable garbage bag, which you use only for this purpose.

How To Shit In The Woods, by Kathleen Meyer, also from Ten Speed Press, provides a more in-depth discussion of this often ignored, important but delicate subject.

First Aid Kit

You should always bring at least the rudiments of a first aid kit with you on a climb. Bring several bandages, gauze pads (you can apply these with your cloth athletic tape), disinfectant, and two aspirin. Naturally, if you have a particular medical condition, bring the necessary medical supplies.

Sunscreen

Rocks in the sun are very bright, especially after a rain. And because you will be facing the rock you climb, you may become sunburned from the reflected light. If you want protection from sunburn, apply sunscreen to your exposed areas, particularly your face, before you climb. Sunscreen is essential on any big wall climb.

Warmup Grip

Many climbers hike to a cliff and immediately begin to climb, without first warming up their limbs. They are asking for an injury: cold tendons tear easily. Your finger joints are vital to climbing and you should warm them carefully before you climb.

A good time to warm your fingers is during your hike to the base of the cliff. This is easy to do: repeatedly squeeze a warmup grip. There are many different warmup grips available (see pg. 310): some are rubber doughnuts, others are fist-shaped

Sorbothane devices, while the simplest are tennis balls and racquet balls.

You can actually warm up your fingers without a grip by bending them back and forth. The problem with this is that you may forget to do it - it's much easier to remember to warm up your fingers when you have something in your hand to remind you.

Sewing Kit

A sewing kit is useful on any multi-day climbing trip. With a few needles, 2 or 3 spools of thread (and perhaps a spool of thin fishing line), 2 large safety pins, two buttons, and a small pair of scissors (you can also use a pocketknife), you should be able to make basic sewing repairs. You also need a case, or small bag, to carry the kit in.

Daypacks

You will need some sort of pack to carry both your technical and your non-technical climbing gear to the cliffs. Daypacks work well because they are small (low bulk), lightweight, and inexpensive. A daypack holds enough equipment for a day's worth of climbing. You will need a larger pack if you intend to bring along any camping supplies. Likewise, daypacks can't carry all your gear on a big wall climb (you will need a haulbag - see pg. xxx). You can wear a daypack up the cliff, but only up easy routes because the pack makes balancing difficult.

The features you get with a daypack depend upon how much money you are willing to spend for it. Try to get a pack that has a top pocket which is separate from the rest of the pack. This pocket is ideal for small things such as toilet paper, sunscreen, guidebooks, wallets, and keys. The pocket should have at least one adjustable strap that connects it to the lower section of the pack. This design allows you to carry your **rope** outside of the pack, under this strap, between the top pocket and lower bag section.

A comfortable waist belt is also a big plus, as are padded shoulder straps. The waist belt is more important, because a good waist belt allows you to carry most of the pack's weight on your hips as you walk. This is far easier than carrying the weight on your shoulders, especially when you are climbing.

A daypack's carrying capacity is important. Most daypacks have a capacity that ranges from 1000 to 3000 cubic inches. The smaller ones work for carrying a small selection of gear, enough to do some **leading.** The larger ones give you enough room for a lot of gear, such as your **aid climbing** equipment. Choose the size that fits the type of climbing you want to do.

Accessory straps on the outside of the daypack are useful. They allow you to attach gear that won't fit inside the pack, such as extra water bottles, jackets, and shoes.

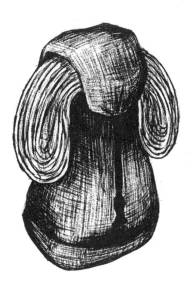

A rope held between the top pocket and main body of a daypack

You can spend anywhere from 50-200 dollars on a daypack. The more expensive models are more comfortable, have more accessory straps, and are usually more durable. The cheaper models are basic, have fewer accessory straps, and are less comfortable, but they work.

Packing Your Daypack

Packing your daypack can be a fine art. Throwing in a pair of **climbing boots,** some food, water, and a **chalkbag** is easy. But when you need to carry all your gear, and really fill the pack up, then it gets more complex.

You can take it as a given that you will have to pull almost everything out of your daypack whenever you need something, even if it is just one item. This is the way daypacks are designed: they load from the top and everything you want sits at the bottom.

So, granted that the order in which you pack your gear doesn't matter too much, the important issue is comfort. Daypacks don't have stiff frames or rigid sides that prevent their contents from jabbing your back. They are soft, and if an object is pointed the wrong way, you will feel it.

I try to layer all the soft gear along the bottom and back of my daypack. I put my heavy hardware (**chocks, carabiners, descender**) at the bottom of the pack, but on top of a bundle of **runners.** Then I put my sweatshirt (which I always pack as padding, even if it is 100 degrees at night) along the back of the pack. The next thing that goes in is my water bottle, which I put along one side, making sure that it sits vertically, its mouth aimed harmlessly towards space. I fill the inside gap with my harness, climbing boots (placed against the side of the pack that is farthest from my back - boots are notorious for piercing and jabbing), and any remaining odds and ends. Finally, my chalkbag sits at the top, although, if yours leaks, you may want to hang it from the outside of your pack. Then I close the flap and lay my rope over the top, and close the top pocket, which contains all the small pieces of gear, such as tape, toilet paper, plastic bag, food, keys, and sunscreen. And that's all there is to it, you are ready to climb!

Appendices

Rating Systems

Climbs vary in difficulty. Some are simple, easy walks up the cliff, while others require intricate, gymnastic moves to reach the top. And climbers themselves exhibit varying levels of skill: a move easy for one climber is impossible for another. So how do you, the climber, match your skill to the climb, and find a **route** (a path up the cliff) whose difficulty suits your needs, whether they are to warm up, climb a fun, moderate route, or push back the limits of your ability?

Climbing rating systems solve this problem. Climbers developed rating systems to quantify the difficulty of a climb. When a climber establishes a new route, he gives it a rating. He communicates the new route's rating, name, and location to other climbers through a guidebook which is compiled every few years by any climber willing to take on the task. You can contact a guidebook's editor through the address he leaves in the book. Most climbing areas have guidebooks (if yours doesn't you will have to learn the names and ratings of local routes from other climbers). A guidebook provides a detailed map and description of an area's climbs. You can buy an area's guidebook at its climbing store.

The rating that a climber gives his newly-established route reflects his subjective opinion of that climb's difficulty. Usually a climber establishing new routes has refined his skills for several years, and therefore has an accurate sense of a climb's difficulty: he compares it to the other rated climbs that he has made. If he has mis-rated a new route, the next few climbers up the route will reach a consensus and give it a more appropriate rating.

You are probably wondering why I have been saying rating systems, in the plural. After all, since the goal of a rating is to standardize the difficulty of a climb, using different rating systems will only confuse things! Despite this fact, there are currently 6 major rating systems in use, each belonging to a particular nation of climbers. Obviously, this is confusing, especially when you are in a foreign country trying to determine which route to climb. To help you with this problem, at the end of this discussion I have compiled a table of the 6 rating systems, compared against each other (I have also included a seventh system, the NCCS, which is an old system that is still used in a few parts of the U.S.).

The Yosemite Decimal System

The Yosemite Decimal System (YDS) is the standard U.S. rating system. I am going to discuss it in detail, which will help you understand how any rating system works.

The Classes

First, there are the classes:

Class 1: Walking uphill

Class 2: Using your hands occasionally to scramble up slopes

Class 3: Easy climbing constantly requiring your hands for support. You probably won't need a rope, but use one if you feel uncomfortable.

Class 4: More exposed climbing, so bring and use climbing equipment if you feel the need.

Class 5: Difficult **free climbing** up small holds and with lots of exposure. Requires climbing gear.

Class 6: **Aid climbing** (using tools other than your body to make progress up the rock). Requires even more equipment than class 5 climbing.

Currently, most rock climbers ascend class 5 routes. Class 6 climbing (aid climbing) isn't as popular because it damages the rock. Also, aid climbing isn't as necessary as it formerly was, because more climbers are able to free climb old aid routes, changing them from class 6 to class 5, and making aid obsolete on all but the hardest climbs.

Where Does A Beginner Start?

If you are a beginning climber, you may be wondering how hard a climb you should start on. Unfortunately, there is no clear answer. It depends on your natural athletic ability, your receptivity to new information, and your mental state. The only way to determine how difficult a rock you should start climbing on is to try to climb a few short routes. If the first one is too hard, try an easier route, and vice-versa. Some beginners start climbing 5.2 routes, while others are able to immediately climb 5.7. Don't become discouraged if you can't climb a certain route! Perseverance is the key to becoming a good climber, so stay after it. Let that route become your goal.

Because **technical rock climbing** (climbing with ropes and protection) is done in the fifth and sixth classes, both classes are divided into more specific levels of difficulty.

Class 5 is split from the easiest, 5.0 (pronounced "five zero"), to the current hardest, 5.14 ("five fourteen"). In addition, once you reach 5.10 ("five ten") - which is different from 5.1 ("five one") - the fifth class is further divided into letter grades. Thus you have: 5.10a, b, c, and d, and 5.11a, b, c, and d, and on to 5.14. Note that although 5.14d is the currently the hardest free climb rating, this will change. As climbers improve, the ratings continue to increase - undoubtedly we'll soon have 5.15 climbs.

Some climbs are rated without the letters. But they still differentiate between difficulty beyond the 5.9 level. They are rated as either hard or easy. For example, 5.10+ is a hard 5.10 climb (comparable to 5.10d), while 5.10- is an easy 5.10 (5.10a).

Class 6 is also called the A class (standing for aid). It is split into several different levels, the number depending on who you talk to. It definitely starts at A0, and everyone agrees it goes to at least A5. However, some climbers think it should keep going to A6, A7, etc., as the climbs are established. But other climbers feel that A5 connotes the hardest aid climbing possible, and that as harder routes are completed, the previous climbs should be down-graded accordingly. This is what has been done in the past, with an A4 route from 30 years ago now going at A0, or even free (5.13-14). As there is currently no consensus among climbers, I can't tell you what to expect for the future.

The Qualifying Rating

Often guidebooks will give climbs a qualifying rating as well as a difficulty rating. The qualifier may be a number of stars (the more the better), or an adjective such as "good," "great," etc. The qualifier is useful for modern climbers who, unlike their predecessors, are usually able to spend only the weekends at the cliffs. The qualifier allows you, the weekend climber, to quickly find the most aesthetic, or outrageous, route around, which means that more of your time will be spent on memorable cliffs than on unaesthetic lines that you'd rather forget.

This is the idea behind the qualifier, anyway. Actually, I have never climbed a route I didn't like. Some are certainly more exciting, or offer a better view, but climbing is so fantastic that any climb will do for me. Note: a highly-touted five star climb is more likely to have a line of climbers waiting to do the route. Climbs with fewer stars see fewer ascents. Some climbers posit from this that guidebook editors "hide" some of the best routes by giving them a poor qualifier rating!

The Grades

A climb's grade describes the level of commitment involved to reach the top. A grade may be given to any class of climb, even a walk, for it simply describes the average time required to complete a route.

Grade I: 2 hours.
Grade II: 4-6 hours.
Grade III: One day.
Grade IV: *At least* one long day.
Grade V: 1.5-2 days.
Grade VI: More than 2 days.

Note that grades are often given simply as a roman numeral, without the word "grade."

Incredibly, some advanced climbers are climbing Grade VI routes in one day, as if they were Grade III! But these aren't your average climbers, and the grades remain unchanged to provide guidelines for the rest of us.

The Final Rating

The final rating of a long route may contain the grade, the free climbing rating, and the aid climbing rating (if there is any aid climbing on the route). For instance, a Grade IV route that was of 5.6 difficulty and had a short section of easy aid climbing would look like this: "IV, 5.10, A0."

On the other hand, a short, one or two **pitch** route won't have a grade (it's length is obvious). Rather, it will simply say "5.10," or perhaps "A3."

Rating Differences

After you have been climbing for more than a few months, you may get the urge to travel to other climbing areas. By this time you will probably have learned about the local ratings from discussing them with other climbers and climbing the routes. From this experience, when you climb a route you may be able to estimate its rating. But when you visit another climbing area, you may be surprised to find that the routes there are either harder or easier than a similarly-rated climb back home. In general, moderate climbs (5.8-5.11) vary the most from place to place. The climbers that are able to make hard climbs (5.12 and up) often travel between climbing areas, and so they are more successful at maintaining standard ratings.

Ratings And Your Ego

We all want other climbers to think that we're something special, that we've got *the talent*. And since bragging about your skill, whether it's real or not, is considered poor style (in a sport where style is everything!), you are forced to either impress others simply by the way you climb (recommended), or to use some subtler means. Climbers have occasionally been known to lose control and resort to the latter method, in the form of altering ratings, or **"sandbagging,"** as it is called. For instance, Fred might sandbag Hilda by telling her that a climb is "only a 5.8," when actually it is a 5.10. The idea is that when Hilda, who is not a 5.10 climber, unsuccessfully attempts the climb, and then later finds out its real rating, she will come away impressed with Fred's apparent ability. "Geez, that guy's so good he thought the 5.10 was only a 5.8." Of course, this is just what Fred wants her to think!

Undoubtedly you're wondering why I'm rambling like a paranoid, but I have a serious reason. You can get other climbers into trouble by sandbagging them. If they decide to attempt a route on the basis of your inaccurate rating, they may become committed to something that's way beyond them. And this could lead to an accident. *If you don't know a climb's rating, simply tell other climbers exactly that!*

There is a discernable pattern to the variations in ratings around the U.S. Routes up boulders are usually technically harder than their ratings - this is to make up for their short length. The eastern U.S. is said to be harder than areas west, and climbs in Yosemite are well-known for being easy for their ratings. It's a good idea to climb some easier routes when you first arrive in a climbing area, to find out how the ratings compare to your previous experience before you get into something over your head!

The Ratings Chart

Rating Systems

YDS The Primary U.S. System	NCCS[1] (U.S.)	French	West German (UIAA)	Australian	East German	British	
5.4	F5	3	III				HS
5.5	F6	3	IV	12		4a	HS
5.6	F6	4	V	13			VS
5.7	F7	5a	V+	14	VIIa	4b	VS
5.8	F8	5b	VI−	15 / 16	VIIb	4c	HVS
5.9	F9	5c	VI	17		5a	HVS
5.10a	F10	6a	VI+	18	VIIc	5b	E1
5.10b	F10	6a	VII−	19	VIIIa	5b	E1
5.10c	F11	6b	VII	20	VIIIb	5c	E2
5.10d	F11	6b	VII	21	VIIIc	5c	E2
5.11a	F12	6c	VII+	22	IXa	5c	E3
5.11b	F12	6c	VIII−	23	IXa	5c	E3
5.11c	F13	7a	VIII	24	IXb	6a	E4
5.11d	F13	7a	VIII	25	IXc	6a	E4
5.12a	F14	7b	VIII+	26	Xa	6b	E5
5.12b	F14	7b	VIII+	26	Xa	6b	E5
5.12c	F15	7c	IX−	27	Xb	6b	E5
5.12d	F15	7c	IX	28	Xb	6c	E6
5.13a	F16	8a	IX+	29	Xc	6c	E6
5.13b	F16	8a	IX+	30	Xc	7a	E7
5.13c		8b	X−	30		7a	E7
5.13d		8b	X	31		7a	E7
5.14a		8c	X+	32		7b	E8
5.14b		8c	XI−			7b	E8
5.14c		8c	XI−	33		7c	E9
5.14d		9a	XI	33		7c	E9

[1]From Vogel, Randy. *Joshua Tree Rock Climbing Guide.* Denver: Chockstone Press, 1986.

Conversion Tables

About The Conversion Tables

You may think it odd to find weight and measurement conversion tables in a book on rock climbing. "Don't these tables belong in a cookbook?" Unfortunately, that's the problem: in a cookbook they don't do you any good. You need the conversion tables to help you find the best piece of rock climbing equipment, not the correct amount of rice!

Finding the best piece of gear usually involves comparing equipment specifications between many rock climbing gear catalogs. But when you look through your catalogs, you'll notice that each one presents gear specifications in either metric or U.S. units, but not both. And, unless you have both metric and U.S. units imprinted on your brain, comparing specifications is impossible without a conversion table!

To help you out, I've included the common weights and measurements that you'll run into when looking for gear. But if I have missed one, you'll find it easy to make the conversions. For instance, if you want to convert the weight of a carabiner from ounces to grams, multiply the number of ounces by the number of grams in one ounce. A 2-ounce carabiner weighs 56.7 grams (2 x 28.35). This formula holds true for both weights and measures.

Weight Conversion Table

Note: all pounds and ounces are avoirdupois (the standard)

Ounces to Grams		Pounds to Kilograms	
.0353	1	.5	.227
.177	5	1	.454
.353	10	1.5	.68
.5	14.175	2.205	1
.706	20	5	2.268
1	28.35	10	4.536
1.236	35	15	6.804
1.5	42.525	20	9.072
1.765	50	22.046	10
2	56.7	100	45.36
2.2	62.37	220.5	100
2.5	70.875	500	226.8
2.765	78.388	1000	453.6
3	85.05	2000	907.2
10	2.835	2646	1200
		3000	1360
		3307.5	1500
		4000	1814.4

Ounces to Grams		Pounds to Kilograms	
		4851	2200
		5000	2268
		6615	3000

1 pound = 16 ounces
1 pound = 453.6 grams

1 kilogram = 35.3 ounces
1 kilogram = 1000 grams

Measurement Conversion Table

% Inch	to	Fraction Inch	to	Millimeters
.039				1
.063		1/16		1.588
.118				3
.125		1/8		3.175
.158				4
.188		3/16		4.762
.197				5
.217				5.5
.236				6
.25		1/4		6.35
.276				7
.313		5/16		7.936
.315				8
.332				8.5
.354				9
.375		3/8		9.525
.394				10
.41				10.5
.433				11
.438		7/16		11.113
.472				12
.5		1/2		12.7
.563		9/16		14.288
.625		5/8		15.875
.686		11/16		17.463
.75		3/4		19
.813		13/16		20.64
.875		7/8		22.225
.938		15/16		23.813
1				25.4
2				50.8
3				76.2
4				101.6
6				127

Feet to		Meters	
.5		.152	
1		.305	
1.5		.457	
3.28		1	
100		30.48	
145		44.2	
164		50	
180		54.954	
200		60.95	

1 foot = 12 inches
1 foot = 304.8 millimeters

1 meter = 39 inches
1 meter = 1000 millimeters

The UIAA

Climbers are individuals, and come from a heritage that has always stressed independence and freedom. But this spirit of individuality has led to some problems in the past, including the marketing of poor-quality equipment. Since there was no independent testing of any manufacturers' gear, climbers actually knew very little about the equipment they used. And unfortunately manufacturers were unwilling to provide the necessary knowledge, so climbers usually bought gear on the manufacturer's reputation alone.

To solve this problem, a group of European climbers founded an international quality-control organization, an association that would conduct impartial and rigorous testing of climbing equipment throughout the world. Their organization was called the UIAA, or the Union Internationale des Associations d'Alpinisme.

Through its role as an impartial equipment testing organization, the UIAA has helped climbers tremendously. It opened the doors of communication between climbers and climbing gear manufacturers. The UIAA achieved this by making public the tests they conducted and the results of these tests. With this information in their possession, climbers became much more selective buyers. The manufacturers soon saw that the best way to increase their sales was to provide more information about their gear, to explain this information, and to make sure that their gear gained the UIAA's stamp of approval. The net result was that the quality of climbing gear increased tremendously.

The UIAA is based in Switzerland. It has evolved into something more than just a quality-control organization, to the point where it now oversees sport climbing competitions through a sub-organization called the Comite Internationale des Competitions d'Escalade (CICE). However, the UIAA's main function is still to test climbing equipment. Although they test many types of climbing gear, climbers attach the most value to the UIAA's stamp of approval when it's on ropes and helmets.

If you want more information about the UIAA, write to this address:

U.I.A.A.
P.O. Box 237
CH-1211
Grenevall
Switzerland

Manufacturers

Most climbing gear manufacturing companies started out as simple one-man operations. For example: while attempting the first ascent of some difficult cliff, a climber saw the need for a specific tool. So he made this tool, and when he had used it, and proved that it was effective, other climbers paid him to make them one. Soon the entrepreneurial climber had a small business going out of his car. And when the business became too large, the climber-turned-manufacturer opened up a shop. This shop grew to international proportions due to the increase in climbers. Suddenly the climber was the head of an enormous organization, a huge business interest.

Yvon Chouinard, who founded the current Great Pacific/Chouinard (an international climbing gear manufacturer) is a prime example:

"I started out my business as a blacksmith, hand-forging these climbing pitons, and I had all my work stuff portable so I could go up and down the coast and work out of my car."

— from *Surfer*, volume 31, March, 1990

The point is, since climbers founded and still work at the climbing manufacturing companies, the companies are very responsive to your concerns and suggestions. If you have any such comments, give them a call: you can be assured that they will be helpful and provide knowledgeable answers.

Returns

If you are unhappy with your purchase, haven't used the product, and have the receipt, you can return it to the place you bought it (unless there are certain conditions specifically preventing returns: perhaps you bought a sale item). Don't return the gear to the manufacturer unless you bought it directly from them. (Note: not all manufacturers sell gear to individuals — their catalogs will inform you of their policy.)

Repairs

Most manufacturers will repair their products. However, between shipping and repair charges, and the length of time it takes for you to receive your repaired gear (the manufacturer may need to send the gear to the home office, in another country), you might find that buying a new item is both cheaper and faster. If you have an item needing repair, call its manufacturer and find out what your options are (is it repairable, how much will the repair cost, how long will the repair take).

Defective Products

Although they have many quality-control tests, manufacturers occasionally let a defective product get to the stores. To avoid buying a defective product, carefully examine every piece of gear you intend to buy — before you part with your money.

But defects are not always obvious — if they were, the manufacturers would have found them! So if, after using it, a defect in your gear becomes apparent (it must be a manufacturing-related defect, not a problem arising from mis-use!), give the manufacturer a call. Explain the situation; more than likely he will want to check the product out himself. If he agrees that the product has a manufacturing defect, he will quickly replace it with a sound piece of gear.

Some Manufacturers' Addresses

I have listed the addresses of 62 climbing gear manufacturers below. They are located in the U.S.A, in Canada, and in Europe. I have tried to include phone numbers, but sometimes they weren't available. Bear in mind that these are just some of the many manufacturers in existence, and that their addresses may change.

A5 Adventures
1109 S. Plaza Way #286
Flagstaff, AZ 86001
(602) 779-5084

Adventure 16
4620 Alvarado Canyon Rd.
San Diego, CA 92120

Beal
2 rue Rabelais
38200, Vienne, Cedex
France
74 53 04 14

Black Diamond
P.O. Box 90
Ventura, CA 93002
(805) 653-5781

Blue Water
209 Lovvorn Road
Carrollton, GA 30117
(404) 834-7515

Brenco Enterprises
7877 South 180th Street,
Kent, WA, 98032

Camp S.P.A.
Via Roma, 23
22050 Premana
Italy

Canadian Alpine Manufacturing, Ltd.
1140 River Rd.
Richmond, B.C., V6X 1Z5
Canada

Claudius Simond and Fils
Les Bosson S 74400
Chamonix
France

Climb High
1861 Shelburne Rd.
Shelburne, VT, 05482
(802) 985-5056

Clogwyn Climbing Gear Ltd.
Clwy y Bont
Deiniolen, Gwynedd, N. Wales, LLSS 3DE
United Kingdom

Colorado Custom Hardware
P.O. Box 5353
Durango, CO, 81301
(303) 247-9385

D. Best Mountaineering
P.O. Box 177
Long Barn, CA, 95335

Dakota Bolt Works
1801 Centre St.
Rapid City, SD, 57701
(605) 348-9109

DMM International, Ltd
Llanberis, Gwynedd
United Kingdom
(0286) 872222

Dolt USA
2421 South 34th Place
Tucson, AZ, 85713
(602) 745-0024

Dudley Sac Mountain Gear
626 Elm St.
Leadville, CO, 80461

Edelweiss, USA
PO Box 110
Spencertown, NY, 12165
1-800-445-6664 and (518) 392-3363

Entre Prises
Z.I. St Vincent de Mercuze
38660 Le Touvet
France
76 08 53 76

5.10
P.O. Box 1390
Glendale, CA, 91209
(818) 768-3068

Faces
Olde Englishe Rd.
Matlock, Derbyshire, DE4 3LT
United Kingdom

Fish
Box 685
Sierra Madre, CA, 91025
(818) 355-8296

Fitness Group, The
P.O. Box 251
Edmonds, WA, 98020
(206) 771-6660

Forrest Mountaineering, Ltd.
840 Bannock St.
Denver, CO, 80204

Gibbs Products
202 Hampton Ave.
Salt Lake City, UT, 84111

Go-Pro, Inc.
P.O. Box 1357
Healdsburg, CA, 95448

Great Pacific/Chouinard
(see Black Diamond)

Heart Rate, Inc.
3186-G Airway Ave.
Costa Mesa, CA, 92626
(714) 850-9716

High Adventure Sports
P.O. Box 3756
Redding, CA, 96049

HME
360 Chestnut #5
Carlsbad, CA, 92008
(619) 434-6498

International Mountain Equipment
Box 494, Main St.
North Conway, NH 03860
(603) 356-7013

JRat
948 Pearl Sr.
Boulder, CO, 80302
(303) 444-2779

Jumar
Walter Marti
Apparatebau
CH 3713
Reichen Bach
Switzerland

Kong S.P.A.
24032
Calolziocorte (BG)
Italy

La Sportiva
Localita Piera, 5
38038 Tesero, Trento, Italy
(0462) 83052

Latok Mountain Gear
P.O. Box 380
Lyons, CO, 80540

Leeper, Ed
Salina Star Route
Boulder, CO, 80302

Liberty Mountain Sport Corp.
P.O. Box 306
Montrose, CA, 91020
(818) 248-0618

Lowe Alpine Systems
Box 189
Lafayette, CO, 80026

Mekan Boots
1400 Foothill Dr.
Salt Lake City, UT, 84108
(801) 582-7784

Merrel
P.O. Box 4249
South Burlington, VT, 05406

Metolius
63255 Lyman Place
Bend, OR, 97701
(503) 382-7585

Misty Mountain Threadworks
Rt. 6, Box 919
Boone, NC, 28607
(704) 264-5413

Mountain Hardwear
2190 W. Drake #103
Fort Collins, CO, 80526
(303) 493-2849

New England Ropes
Pope's Island
New Bedford, MA, 02740
(617) 999-2351

North American Mountaineering
P.O. Box 7404
Boulder, CO, 80306
(303) 443-5546

Omega Pacific, Inc.
217 10th St. South
Kirkland, WA, 98033
(206) 822-9020

One Sport/Cocida
7877 S. 180th St.
Kent, WA, 98032
(206) 251-5020

Petzl S.A.
Z.I. Crolles
38190 Brignoud
France
(33) 76 08 10 53

Pigeon Mountain Industries, Inc.
P.O. Box 803
Lafayette, GA, 30728
(404) 764-1437

Recreational Equipment, Inc.
1525 11th Ave.
P.O. Box 88125
Seattle, WA, 98138-0125
(206) 323-8333

Rivory-Joanny
BP 81 rue du Pont-Fournas
42402 St-Chamond
France

Rock Exotica, Inc.
530 South 4th East
Centerville, UT, 84014
(801) 295-9241

Salewa
8000 Munchen 15
Munchen, Bavaria
West Germany

SMC
12880 Northrup Way
Bellevue, WA, 98005
(206) 883-0334

Sole Survivor Corporation
4183 Southbank Rd.
Oxnard, CA, 93030
(805) 983-6245

Sport Climbing Systems, Inc.
P.O. Box 8417
Berkeley, CA, 94707-8417
(415) 499-7657

Stubai
P.O. Box 31
A 6-166 Fulpmes, Tirol
Austria

Troll Safety Equipment, Ltd.
Spring Mill
Uppermill, Oldham, OL3 6AA
United Kingdom

Vertical Concepts
3225 A N.W. Shevlin Park Rd.
Bend, OR, 97701
(503) 389-5198

Wild Country UK, Ltd.
Townhead
Eyam, Derbyshire, S30 1RE
United Kingdom
(0433) 31673

Wired Bliss Corporation
555 Blackbird Roost, #9
Flagstaff, AZ, 86001

Yates Gear, Inc.
1600 Cypress Avenue, Suite #8
Redding, CA, 96002
(916) 222-4606

Mail Order Companies

Climbing gear mail order companies usually provide a wide variety of gear at reasonable prices. I recommend that as soon as you buy this book, you order the catalogs from the companies listed below. These are by no means all the mail order companies around, but they are enough to expose you to the gear: you will see who actually makes the gear and how much it costs. Once you have this basic information, you can be more selective when you actually buy gear, whether you do it through the mail or from your local climbing store. (For more information, see Where To Buy Your Gear, pg. 29). And these catalogs will be a resource throughout your climbing career.

Some Mail Order Company Addresses

A5 Adventures
1109 S. Plaza Way, #286
Flagstaff, AZ, 86001
(602) 779-5084

Backcountry Trading Post, Inc.
Murray Hill Rd.
Candia, NH, 03034
(603) 483-2224

Climb High
1861 Shelburne Rd.
Shelburne, VT, Vermont, 05482
(802) 985-5056

Colorado Mountain Equipment
29007 Richmond Hill Rd.
Conifer, CO, 80433
(800) 635-6483 and (303) 697-0539

Mountain High Ltd.
123 Diamond Peak Ave.
Ridgecrest, CA, 93555
1-800-255-3182 and (619) 375-2612

Mountain Tools
PO Box 22788
Carmel, CA, 93922
(408) 625-6222
(This catalog costs $1)

PMI
PO Box 803
Lafayette, GA, 30728
(404) 764-1437

REI
PO Box 88125
Seattle, WA, 98138-0125
(800) 426-4840

Magazines

Domestic Climbing Magazines

Climbing
editor: Michael Kennedy.
P.O. Box 339, 502 Main St.
Carbondale, Colorado, 81623
(303) 963-9449

Rock & Ice
editor: George Bracksieck
P.O. Box 3595
Boulder, Colorado, 80307
(303) 499-8410

American Alpine Journal
113 East 90th St.
New York, N.Y., 10128-1589
(212) 722-1628

International Climbing Magazines

Australia

Wild
P.O. Box 415
Prahran, Victoria 3181

Rock
P.O. Box 415
Prahran, Victoria 3181

Canada

Canadian Alpine Journal
P.O. Box 1026
Banff, Alberta, Toloco

France

Alpirando
7 Rue de Lille
75007, Paris

La Montagne
9 rue la Boetie
75008, Paris

Montagnes
1 rue de la Prevachere
38400 St. Martin D'Heres

Vertical
8, Rue Paccard, B.P. 125
74403 Chamonix

Japan

The Iwa To Yuki
Yamakei Co. Ltd. (publishers)
1-1-33 Shiba Daimon
Minato Ku, Tokyo

India

Indian Mountaineer
Official journal of the Indian Mountaineering
  Foundation.
Benito Juarez Road
New Delhi-110021

Himalayan Journal
Published by The Himalayan Club
contact Oxford University Press
P.O. Box 31 Oxford House
Appollo Bunder, Bombay 400001

Italy

Alp
Corso Vittorio Emanuele 11, 167, 10139
Torino

Rivista Della Montagna
Via della Rocca
29-10123 Torino

Norway

Norklatt
Postboks 8292 Hammersborg
0129 Oslo 1

Poland

Taternik
ul Stanow Zjednoczonych 53 p.
227,04-028 Warsaw

Spain

Desnivel
Diego de Leon, 27
1 isda. 48006 Madrid

Extem
Travesera de Dalt 82
08024 Barcelona

Pyrenaica
Alameda de San Mames
29-1 izda. 48010 Bilbao, Euskadi

Sweden

Bergsport
c/o Niklas Bjornerstedt
Bergstigen 7
S-138 00 Alta

United Kingdom

The Alpine Journal
74 South Audley Street
London, W1Y 5FF

Mountain
P.O. Box 184
Sheffield, S11 9DL
(0742) 586553

West Germany

Rotpunkt
Stuttgarter Strasse 45
7064 Remshalden-Grunbach

Der Bergsteiger
Postfach 27
D-8000 Munchen 20

Alpin
Ortlerstrasse 8
8000 Munchen 70

Bibliography

Books

Aleith, R.C. *Basic Rock Climbing*. Revised ed. NY: Charles Scribner's Sons, 1975.

Bridge, Raymond. *Climbing, A Guide to Mountaineering*. NY: Charles Scribner's Sons, 1977.

Foster, Lynne. *Mountaineering Basics*. San Diego Chapter of the Sierra Club, 1983.

Gregory, John F. *Rock Sport*. Harrisburg, PA: Stackpole Books, 1989.

Larson, Lane and Peggy. *Caving, The Sierra Club Guide to Spelunking*. San Francisco, CA: Sierra Club Books, 1982.

Long, John. *How To Rock Climb!*. Evergreen, CO: Chockstone Press, 1989.

Lovelock, James. *Climbing*. London, UK: B.T. Batsford, Ltd., 1971.

Lyman, Tom, and Bill Riviere. *The Field Book of Mountaineering and Rock Climbing*. NY: Winchester Press, 1975.

Lyon, Ben. *Venturing Underground*. East Ardsley, UK: EP Publishing Limited, 1983.

March, Bill. *Modern Rope Techniques*. 3d ed., reprinted. Milnthorpe, UK: Cicerone Press, 1988.

May, W.G. *Mountain Search and Rescue Techniques*. Boulder: Rocky Mountain Rescue Group, Inc., 1972.

Meredith, Mike, and Dan Martinez. *Vertical Caving*. 2nd ed., revised. Dent, Sedbergh, Cumbria, UK: Lyon Equipment, 1986.

Meyer, Kathleen. *How To Shit In The Woods*. Berkeley: Ten Speed Press, 1989.

Middendorf, John. *Big Wall Tech Manual*. Flagstaff, AZ: A5 Adventures, 1988.

Padgett, Allen, and Bruce Smith. *On Rope*. Huntsville, AL: National Speleoloogical Society, 1987.

Peters, Ed, ed. *Mountaineering, The Freedom of the Hills*. 4th ed. Seattle, WA: The Mountaineers, 1982.

Scott, Doug. *Big Wall Climbing*. NY: Oxford University Press, London, UK: Daye & Ward Ltd, 1974.

Traister, Robert. *Cave Exploring*. Blue Ridge Summit: TAB Books, Inc., 1983.

Whymper, Edward. *Scrambles Amongst The Alps*. Berkeley: Ten Speed Press, 1981.

Periodicals

Climbing, volumes 80-117.

Rock & Ice, volumes 25-31.

Mountain, volumes 115-129.

Glossary/Index

The terms included in this combined glossary/index describe climbing gear, climbing techniques, rope work, and rock features. The page numbers listed after each entry refer only to the first use of the term in any chapter.

Knifeblade Piton: A thin-bladed horizontal piton. Similar to a Bugaboo, but with a slightly thinner blade. 47

Laid Construction: A type of rope construction. Common laid ropes have three twisted strands made up of hundreds of fibers. Laid ropes are not suitable for rock climbing. 272

Large Pear Locking Carabiner: A type of carabiner. It has a large, pear-like shape, and a locking gate. 24, 129

Lead: To be the first member of your climbing party up the rock. 11, 18, 103, 133, 255, 340

Leader: Someone who climbs a route from the ground up, placing protection as he climbs, and connecting his rope to this protection. 13, 49, 77

Leader Fall: The act of a leader falling. A leader fall is the most severe type of fall (it can have a fall factor of two). When the leader falls, he plummets twice the distance to his protection. For example, a leader connects his rope to a piece of protection, then climbs up 10 feet. If he falls, he will drop 20 feet (plus a few more feet due to rope stretch) before the rope stops his fall. 13

Leeper Z: A type of piton. It has a "Z" cross section. 27, 47

Lieback: A climbing technique. Hanging off to one side while your arms pull and your legs push. 46

Load Capacity: The maximum load that a piece of gear can withstand.

Load Limiter: A type of runner. It has two sleeves that are sewn together with many bartack stitches; when the load it is supporting becomes too high, the stitches rip out. This gradually reduces the load, until the load limiter is fully opened, at which point the load is very small. 26, 154

Locking Carabiner: A carabiner whose gate has a metal sleeve which, when in the closed position, prevents the gate from opening. 26, 53, 88, 153, 158, 199, 256, 262, 296

Locking Sleeve: The sleeve which slides along a locking carabiner's gate. 132

Lost Arrow Piton: A type of Horizontal piton. 47

Major Axis: A carabiner's strong axis. It runs lengthwise, from one end of the carabiner to the other. 128

Mantling: A climbing technique; involves lifting and supporting yourself with your hands, which lie palms-down on the rock.

Minor Axis: A carabiner's weak axis. It runs from one side of the carabiner to the other side (the gate). 128

Multi-day Climb: A climb so long and difficult that it takes more than one day to complete. 12

Multi-directional Anchor: An anchor that will remain secure no matter what direction a load comes from. Bolts, some fixed pitons, and some chock configurations are multi-directional anchors. 54, 99

Multi-Pitch Route: A climb consisting of more than one pitch. 47, 338

Munter Hitch: A belaying knot. Use in conjunction with a carabiner. Also called the Italian Hitch. 132

Nailed Boots: A boot whose sole is nailed in place. 6

Natural Anchor: A tree, boulder, or other natural feature that is strong enough to make a good anchor. 25

Off-Finger Crack: A crack that is too wide to finger jam, but too thin to hand jam.

Off-Hand Crack: A crack that is too wide to hand jam, but too thin to fist jam. 10

Offwidth: A crack that is wider than a fist crack. 9

Offwidth Protection: Chocks that are large enough to anchor in an offwidth.

On-Sight: To climb a route without previous knowledge of its moves. This is good style. Previous knowledge of a route might come from another climber providing the beta, or from studying the route. Note: a climber who "on-sights" a route may have fallen while climbing it. If he "on-sight flashes" the route, however, he didn't fall, which is the best style. 11

Opposing Chock: A chock that is anchored in the opposite direction of another chock. Together, the two chocks protect against a multi-directional load.

Oval Carabiner: A type of carabiner that has an oval shape. 25, 129, 168

Oval Screw Link: A screw link that has an oval shape. 261

Overhand Knot: A simple knot that is useful for many utility jobs. 245, 293, 313

Parallel Crack: A crack whose sides run parallel. 10, 235

Passive Camming Chock: A type of chock. It anchors by rotating slightly (not as much as an active camming chock) into the sides of a crack. 25, 31, 40, 49, 65, 182, 188, 248, 291, 325

Pear Carabiner: A type of carabiner. See Small Pear and Large Locking Pear.

Piece Of Aid: An item of gear used for aid. This may be a piton, chock, copperhead, bolt, or hook, among others. 153, 173, 248

Piggyback Hauling System: A type of hauling system. It offers a 4:1 mechanical advantage.

Pin: Another name for a piton.

Pinkpoint: To lead a climb, without falling or resting on aid, while clipping your rope to pre-placed protection. The leader may have previously attempted the route. See also Redpoint.

Pitch: The distance between belay stations. 11, 50, 77, 177, 207, 248, 255, 262, 273, 303, 346

Piton: A metal wedge-like device that aid climbers hammer into thin seams and cracks. 26, 29, 39, 50, 102, 148, 153, 189, 191, 228, 256, 295

Piton Scar: A groove in the rock formed by the placement and removal of a piton. 148

Place Your Protection: To insert and anchor a chock in a crack.

Placing Gear On The Lead: To place your protection, or to connect a quickdraw to a bolt, while you are leading a climb.

Pocket: A shallow hole in the rock. 8

Portaledge: A portable cot that climbers haul up the rock on multi-day climbs. At the end of the day they anchor the portaledge and sleep on it. 27, 30, 207, 259

Protecting A Climb: Placing protection while climbing a route. 7

Protection: The anchors (such as chocks, bolts, and pitons) that a climber connects his rope to as he climbs. 39, 49, 89, 99, 167, 199, 256, 269, 331

Protection Placement: The position of one's protection.

Protection-Clipping Carabiner: The carabiner on one end of a quickdraw that you clip to your protection. This carabiner may be different from the rope-clipping carabiner (which might have a bent gate). 26

Protection System: A configuration of anchors, runners, carabiners, rope, harness, and belayer (also his belay device) that combine to stop a falling climber. 87, 127, 270, 329

Prusik Knot: An ascending knot. You need a loop of accessory cord to make this knot. 46, 76, 89, 159, 262

Prusik Loop: The loop of accessory cord that you use to rig Prusik Knots. 26, 291

Pulley: Climbers use pulleys to haul their haulbags up the cliff.
Note: climbers only bring haulbags on long, multi-day climbs where they will need a lot of gear. 27, 50

Pushing A Lead: A term climbers occasionally use to describe a difficult lead.

Put Up: To make the first ascent of a route. 16

Quickdraw: A runner that is rigged with a carabiner on either end. 25, 39, 66, 95, 133, 199, 291, 331

Rack: A climber's gear sling and all the chocks, carabiners, and runners that he is going to carry up the cliff. 20, 39, 50, 69, 127, 181, 185, 192, 197, 262

Racking: To set up your rack (by connecting various chocks, carabiners, and runners to your gear sling).

Racking Loops: The loops encircling the swami belts of some harnesses. They are designed to hold gear. 43, 186

Rand: The rubber strip which encircles rock climbing boots above the sole.

Rappel: Noun: a controlled descent of a rope.
Verb: using a technique and device to descend a rope. 16, 46, 49, 76, 89, 108, 132, 157, 189, 199, 270, 309

Rappel Device: Any device which you can use to rappel. Rappel devices include figure-eights, bobbins, rappel racks, Bankl Plates, and Seilbremses.

Rappel Loop: The loop of webbing that connects the anchors of a belay station. Climbers loop their ropes through the webbing and rappel down the cliff. They are then able to pull their ropes down, leaving the rappel loop behind. 291

Rappel Rack: A type of descender that is often used by cavers, rarely by climbers. 157

Rating System: A term or number describing the difficulty of a climb. There are seven major rating systems, including the Yosemite Decimal System, the NCCS (old but occasionally used), the British system, the French system, the East German system, the UIAA's system, and the Australian system. 16, 57

Redpoint: To lead a climb without falling or resting on aid. You must place your protection as you progress up the rock. The redpoint may occur after the climber has practiced the route. See also Pinkpoint. 16

Resole: Resoling your rock climbing boots means to replace the rubber soles. You can buy a kit and do this yourself or take your boots to a cobbler.

Rerand: To rerand is to replace the rubber rands of your rock climbing boots. Have a cobbler do this for you.

Reversed Gate Notch: A unique carabiner gate design where the gate notch is on the gate instead of the carabiner's body. This design is patented by Camp.

Rig: Noun: a configuration of gear.
Verb: to set up gear in a certain way.

Ring Bend Knot: A knot climbers use to tie webbing into loops, which makes them runners. 245, 293

Rivet: A grade 5 (coarse) 5/16 by 3/4 of an inch steel hardware bolt hammered into an approximately 1/4-inch diameter hole (the #14 Rawl drill makes a perfect rivet hole). 27, 47, 100

Rivet Hanger: A cable loop that climbers hang on rivets, allowing them to connect a carabiner to the rivet. 27, 46, 101, 248

Rock Climbing Boots: A boot worn by rock climbers whose flat rubber sole is designed to securely grip rock. 8, 29, 39, 340

Rope: A climbing rope is dynamic and has a kernmantle construction. It is often very colorful. 29, 39, 49, 75, 87, 99, 113, 129, 157, 176, 195, 215, 233, 256, 259, 291, 325, 340

Rope Drag: The force that occurs when a rope has many bends or runs along another surface, creating friction. A rope under severe rope drag is impossible to move: it is essentially anchored. Avoid rope drag (by keeping your rope straight and free of the rock) when you lead a climb! 271

Roped Solo Climbing: Free or aid climbing a route alone, but protected by a rope. This is an advanced technique, and requires a lot of gear. 52, 81

Route: A course up a cliff - the route's holds make it apparent. A given cliff may have hundreds of routes, each having a name and rating. 8, 42, 50, 99, 116, 129, 148, 166, 269, 309, 337, 345

Route Information: The beta of a particular route. It may be nothing more than "there's a fixed pin on the third pitch," but it may also be a detailed map of a route, describing every rock feature and the location of every bolt. 17

Runner: A loop of webbing tied with a ring bend knot. Climbers use runners for rigging anchors, placing protection, as hero loops, gear slings, and for many other, more mundane jobs. 7, 29, 39, 50, 66, 76, 96, 99, 129, 146, 151, 153, 166, 174, 181, 185, 202, 209, 234, 244, 256, 262, 270, 341

Runner-strength: As strong as a runner - approximately 4000 pounds.

Runout: A section of a climb that is unprotectable (unless you drill a bolt - which is not encouraged in many places). A runout can be very scary, for if you fall, you will drop a long way, and maybe even hit the ground before your protection can stop you (it depends on the situation). 26, 278

RURP: A small piton with an almost-razor-thin blade. 27, 47

Safety Margin: The amount of over-kill built into something, particularly gear. For example, a carabiner may have a strength of 6000 pounds, but it must rarely support more than 3000 pounds. Thus, it has a safety margin of 3000 pounds. Climbing gear always has a high safety margin. 18, 137

Sandbagging: To mis-represent the difficulty of a climb, stating that it is easier than it actually is. 347

Screw Link: A strong steel connector that has a gate which screws open and closed. There are three types of screw links, based on their shape: oval, triangular, and half-circle.

Seam: A very thin crack; far too thin for fingers, but which will accept some small chocks, pitons, and copperheads. 10, 148, 227

Second: The climber who climbs the route his partner just lead. His partner belays him from above. The second usually cleans the pitch. 25

Seilbremse: A type of belay device. 89, 158

Self-Belay: The technique for protecting yourself while roped solo climbing. There are also self-belay devices, such as Rock Exotica's Soloist. 52, 81

Sewn Runner: A runner which is sewn into a loop. Bartacks are the most common stitches used for sewing a runner. The sewn connection is usually stronger than a knot. 25

Sharp End: The leader ties into the sharp end, or dangerous end, of the climbing rope. 49

Sherpa: A native of NE Nepal (the Nepalese Himalayas), of Mongolian origin. Mountaineers often recruit sherpas to carry their gear part-way up a mountain, and as guides. 27

Shoes: A climbing shoe is a low-cut type climbing boot. It is cut like a tennis shoe.

Shunt: A safety device for rappelling. It has a metal body which encircles a cam that will grip the rope when you pull the handle. A shunt can also be used as an ascender.

Single Gear Sling: A single loop of webbing or cord that is worn like a bandolier. Climbers use carabiners to connect their chocks and runners to gear slings. This enables them to carry the gear up a cliff. 185

Sit Bag: A cloth seat which climbers connect to the rock and sit in to make hanging from the cliff more comfortable. 30

Sling: A loop of accessory cord, usually tied with a double fisherman's knot. 31, 76, 88, 168, 181, 227, 244, 325

Slot: A short crack that looks like a small piton scar. 238

Small Pear Carabiner: A type of carabiner. It has an asymmetrical shape, meaning that one end is larger than the other. 26, 129

Smear: To use your climbing boots so that friction holds them to the rock. 8, 114

Solo: See Free Solo.

Solo Roped Climbing: See Roped Solo Climbing.

Spectra: A high-tech fiber that is very strong. It is used in accessory cord and sewn runners. 76, 230, 234, 292, 328

Spelean Shunt: A Gibbs ascender modified to make it a shunt. 168

Sport Climbing: A type of climbing where the emphasis is on gymnastic-like moves and good protection. 16

Sport Rappelling: Rappelling in a fast and bouncy manner. Speed is the goal. Although fun, sport rappelling abuses ropes and gear. 89, 160, 189

Square Knot: A good utility knot. The Square Knot isn't very strong, and shouldn't be used at any critical connection! 146

Squeeze Chimney: A chimney that is just wide enough to fit a body. 231

Stance: The position that a climber is in at any given time while climbing a rock. 10, 108

Static Belay: A method of belaying in which the belayer does not allow the rope to slide through his hands or belay device when he is stopping a climber's fall. This technique produces a sudden stop. 87

Static Load: A stationary load, such as a rock that you are trying to lift off the ground. 269

Stemming: A climbing technique; the climber pushes out, to the sides, with either, or both, his hands or legs. Also called Bridging.

Style: Style is very important in rock climbing. A climber has good style when he climbs a route in a certain way - the exact method depends on the game he is playing. See Games.

Sub-Aider: A sub-etrier.

Sub-Etrier: A smaller version of an etrier. Usually has two steps, and is used in conjunction with an etrier.

Superglue: A common glue that climbers put over their fingertips. It protects the skin from sharp rock. 26, 31

Supertape: A tightly-woven webbing. It is stronger than standard webbing. 187, 296

Swami Belt: The webbing on a waist harness that encircles the waist. 52, 107, 195

Technical Rock Climbing: Rock climbing with a protection system and other climbing gear. 204, 346

Thin Crack: A crack, such as a seam, that is very thin. 26

Three Camming Chock: An active camming chock that has three cams. 27

Three-Way Loading: Loading a carabiner from three directions. This means that the carabiner is loaded along its minor axis, which weakens the connection!

Tiered Gear Sling: A large gear sling designed for big wall climbing. It has four straps to which you can connect your carabiners. 46, 185

Tincture Of Benzoin: A solution of water, alcohol, and Benzoin (resin from a tree in Java). Climbers pour it on their hands; it provides a protective coating against rock abrasion. 26, 31, 303

Toe-Hooking: A climbing technique for supporting or balancing yourself; you hook a toe around a rock edge. See also Heel-Hooking. 117

Toprope: Noun: a rope anchored above a climber. As the climber scales the rock the belayer takes in rope. Climbers sometimes refer to a toprope as a "TR."
Verb: the act of rigging a climb so that a climber is protected from above. 11, 51, 123, 129, 269

TR: See Toprope.

Traditionalist: A term referring to a climber who practices a certain code in regards to the way he climbs. A traditionalist always climbs a route, and places protection, from the ground up. North American climbers are the only practicing traditionalists in the world. 16

Traditional Climbing: Climbing with the rules of a traditionalist. 108

Travelling Pulley: A hauling system that provides a 2:1 mechanical advantage.

Traverse: Noun: a section of a route that travels sideways. Verb: to climb to the side. 76

Triangular Screw Link: A screw link that has a triangular shape.

Tri-Cam: A type of passive camming chock made by Lowe. 26

Triple Fisherman's Knot: A knot for joining two rope ends. Climbers sometimes use it to tie slings made of Spectra and Gemini cord. 292

Tuber: A type of belay device. A tuber may also be used to Rappel. 89, 158

Tubular Webbing: A type of webbing. It is woven into a tube, so that one length has two sides (top and bottom). Tubular webbing is much stronger than flat webbing (the other type), and climbers use it almost exclusively. 70, 174, 187, 202, 227, 296

Tunnel Vision: Seeing only the smallest area in front of you. This often happens to beginning climbers who are apprehensive and tense. For example, the climber can't see a good hold which lies only a foot to one side. Deep breathing and consciously scanning the rock will prevent tunnel vision.

Twin Rope: A thin (8 to 8.5 millimeter) rope that climbers use in pairs.

Twin Rope Technique: The method of using twin ropes. It involves clipping both ropes to every piece of protection. This is compared with double rope technique. 273

Tyrolean Traverse: A rope "bridge" connecting two points. It involves only one rope (plus a backup safety rope to the climber crossing the Tyrolean), and is a very technical rig. 289

UIAA: The Union International des Associations d'Alpinisme. An international climbing organization, whose primary task is to conduct independent climbing gear tests. 11, 195

Uni-Directional Anchor: An anchor that will hold securely if loaded from one direction, but will pull free if loaded from any other direction.

Vertical Piton: A piton whose eye is on the same plane as its blade.

Visualization: Using mental imagery to improve one's climbing ability.

Waist Belay: A belay technique that requires no belay device. 87, 189

Waist Harness: A climbing harness that fits around the climber's waist. 81, 153, 228, 289

Water Knot: See Ring Bend Knot.

Webbing: Also called "flat rope." It is a flat weave of either nylon or Spectra which climbers loop and use as runners. See also Flat Webbing and Tubular Webbing. 7, 30, 39, 53, 145, 153, 159, 173, 186, 189, 193, 195, 209, 215, 235, 245, 257, 291, 310

Wedging Chock: A chock shaped like a wedge that jams securely in a crack. 25, 31, 40, 49, 65, 101, 148, 188, 233, 243, 291

Well-Protected: A climb that offers many points of protection. On such a climb you can anchor your rope to the rock every few feet, if you want. 18

Yosemite Lift: A hauling system that provides a 1:1 mechanical advantage.

Z Rig Pulley System: A hauling system that provides a 3:1 mechanical advantage.